INFORMATION
SECURITY

Advances in Management Information Systems

Advisory Board

INFORMATION SECURITY

POLICY, PROCESSES, AND PRACTICES

DETMAR W. STRAUB
SEYMOUR GOODMAN
RICHARD L. BASKERVILLE
EDITORS

ADVANCES IN MANAGEMENT
INFORMATION SYSTEMS
VLADIMIR ZWASS SERIES EDITOR

M.E.Sharpe
Armonk, New York
London, England

Library of Congress Cataloging-in-Publication Data

References to the AMIS papers should be as follows:

Mattord, H. J., and Wiant, T. Information System Risk Assessment and Documentation. D. W. Straub, S. Goodman, and R. L. Baskerville, eds., *Information Security: Policy, Processes, and Practices. Advances in Management Information Systems.* Volume 11 (Armonk, NY: M.E. Sharpe, 2008), 69–111.

ISBN 978–0-7656–1718–7
ISSN 1554–6152

Printed in the United States of America

The paper in this publication meets the minimum requirements of
American National Standards for Information Sciences
Permanence of Paper for Printed Library Materials,
ANSI Z 39.48-1984.

IBT (c) 10 9 8 7 6 5 4 3 2 1

ADVANCES IN MANAGEMENT INFORMATION SYSTEMS

AMIS Vol. 1: Richard Y. Wang, Elizabeth M. Pierce,
 Stuart E. Madnick, and Craig W. Fisher
Information Quality
ISBN 978–0-7656–1133–8

AMIS Vol. 2: Sergio deCesare, Mark Lycett, and
 Robert D. Macredie
Development of Component-Based Information Systems
ISBN 978–0-7656–1248–9

AMIS Vol. 3: Jerry Fjermestad and Nicholas
 C. Romano, Jr.
Electronic Customer Relationship Management
ISBN 978–0-7656–1327–1

AMIS Vol. 4: Michael J. Shaw
E-Commerce and the Digital Economy
ISBN 978–0-7656–1150-5

AMIS Vol. 5: Ping Zhang and Dennis Galletta
*Human-Computer Interaction and Management
 Information Systems: Foundations*
ISBN 978–0-7656–1486–5

AMIS Vol. 6: Dennis Galletta and Ping Zhang
*Human-Computer Interaction and Management
 Information Systems: Applications*
ISBN 978–0-7656–1487–2

AMIS Vol. 7: Murugan Anandarajan, Thompson S.H.
 Teo, and Claire A. Simmers
The Internet and Workplace Transformation
ISBN 978–0-7656–1445–2

AMIS Vol. 8: Suzanne Rivard and Benoit Aubert
Information Systems Sourcing
ISBN 978–0-7656–1685–2

AMIS Vol. 9: Varun Grover and M. Lynne Markus
Business Process Transformation
ISBN 978–0-7656–1191–8

AMIS Vol. 10: Panos E. Kourouthanassis and George
 M. Giaglis
Pervasive Information Systems
ISBN 978–0-7656–1689–0

AMIS Vol. 11: Detmar W. Straub, Seymour Goodman,
 and Richard Baskerville
Information Security: Policy, Processes, and Practices
ISBN 978–0-7656–1718–7

AMIS Vol. 12: Irma Becerra-Fernandez and Dorothy
 Leidner
Knowledge Management: An Evolutionary View
ISBN 978–0-7656–1637–1

Forthcoming volumes of this series can be found on the series homepage.
www.mesharpe.com/amis.htm

Editor in Chief, Vladimir Zwass (zwass@fdu.edu)

CONTENTS

SERIES EDITOR'S INTRODUCTION

VLADIMIR ZWASS

Information security is now everyone's business. The way we live is underwritten by information system (IS) infrastructures, with the Internet-Web compound the most foundational of them. In our information society, information courses as the lifeblood of our daily lives (as in online travel planning and e-ticket acquisition) and of our business relationships (in a wiki-based collaboration on a project by a virtual team, for example). The functioning of our business organizations (as in the sense-and-respond reaction to the real-time variances from projections on a new product line), the management of our multiorganizational supply chains (with more timely information substituting for inventories), and the operation of our governments (where a timely report on social services helps to serve better a population segment) depend on the secure flows of information. Consequently, our societies have been subject to a great variety of information-related risks for decades (Neumann, 1995). These have compounded manifold since the Internet has opened personal computers, organizational information systems, and national infrastructures to the world. The global network of networks is expanding rapidly and its contours are changing with the progress of the mobile Internet. All of this makes our societies, our organizations, and our own selves vulnerable to myriad of compounding threats. In an organizational environment, information security is a never-ending process of protecting information and information systems that produce it. Considering the potential effects of a failure in this protection, information security protects major financial and other assets of the organization. Nonfinancial assets, such as the brand, reputation, and relationships with customers, partners, and suppliers, can suffer grievously in a case of such a failure. Spoken plainly, information security today protects the ability of an organization to function.

The importance of its subject makes the present volume in the *Advances in Management Information Systems (AMIS)* the first of several to address the issues of information security. The volume is properly the first in this series, as it deals with the matters of policy, strategy, and processes that are necessary to establish the overall security posture of an organization. The range of technological and organizational measures needed to support this posture will be covered by the subsequent volumes of the serial. Designed as it is both to present and to serve to expand the state of our knowledge about IS, *AMIS* aims to make its contribution to this vital subdomain of our field.

As the way of life in the developed world is, and in the many rapidly developing parts of the world is becoming, dependent on multiple, complex, and interrelated information technologies, we need to design organizational processes and build information systems encapsulating and securing these technologies in a trustworthy manner. The editors of the present *AMIS* volume, Detmar W. Straub, Seymour Goodman, and Richard L. Baskerville, address the key issues that serve to build organizational information security on a firm foundation. In such environments, people, information technologies, and procedures combine to deliver information, provide collaborative environments, offer information-based products, and furnish other information-society benefits in a relatively secure fashion. The three editors of this volume have contributed over the years at the forefront of our knowledge about the managerial means of protecting information systems.

Information security protects the availability, integrity, confidentiality, and authenticity of information and underpins such societal goods as privacy, the protection of digital identity, and the protection of intellectual property. Information security comprises a dynamic system of measures taken to protect data, information, and information systems from unauthorized use or a disruption due to a human agency or a natural threat. There are multiple systematic technological and organizational categories of such measures. This *AMIS* volume concentrates on the latter. Assuring information security is inextricably intertwined with the process of risk management: there is no total security, and security policies and processes need to prioritize and control the risks depending on their likelihood and on the potential impacts of adverse events.

As the chapters of the volume make clear, information security is a continual managerial process that evolves policies, strategy, and organizational and IS architectures to build resistance to disruptions into the way the organization operates. Information security policy needs to be aligned with the strategic IS plan of a firm in numerous respects (Doherty and Fulford, 2006). Preemptive measures are the first, and preferred, line of defense. Contingency plans for the disruptions that nevertheless do take place need to include incident response plans, disaster recovery plans, and business continuity plans. Security measures are undertaken and must be adhered to through governance within this fundamental framework. These measures must work in harmony with the mission of the organizations, be it a government agency or a business firm (Sheffi, 2005). Regrettably, the largest global survey of the state of information security in the private- and public-sector organizations of fifty countries indicates that only 28 percent of the surveyed ones report aligning security policies with business objectives (Holmes, 2006). Most notably, only 37 percent have an information security strategy. The "strategy gap" has been noted: a focus on technologies, rather than on the strategies that have to drive the effort. This is precisely why this volume is important as the opening to the *AMIS* security sequence.

There is a degree of resistance in organizations to spending on information security: assessing the value of this security is difficult (while the value is manifest in a breach). Research studies allow to impute this value. Announcing a breach of Internet security has been associated with the loss of 2.1 percent of the stock-market value of a firm within two days of the announcement—a huge loss to the stockholders and an indicator of a damage to the confidence in the firm's management (Cavusoglu et al., 2004). In particular, in the firms deploying information systems strategically, the board of directors should exercise oversight over IS governance (Nolan and McFarlan, 2005).

Research on the organizational aspects of information security takes many directions. New, theory-based methods of risk assessment are being developed to include the relevant risk factors, as well as the countermeasures, and to facilitate cost-benefit analysis in risk management (Sun et al., 2006). Economic analysis is deployed to evaluate the comparative benefits and drawbacks of reactive and proactive approaches to intrusion prevention (Yue and Çakanyildirim, 2007). Technological solutions to mitigating risks, such as real-time threat assessment of an incipient security breach, are being proposed (Blyth and Thomas, 2006). Comprehensive emergency-response systems, encompassing multifaceted organizational and technological measures, are being modeled to improve their effectiveness in a crisis (Jennex, 2007).

Technological developments raise ever new concerns to be contended with. The emerging ubiquitous computing raises a new set of challenges to securing information (Müller, 2006). A major initiative, Service Oriented Architecture, aiming to construct large parts of organizational information systems of Web services, components drawn from the Web, further opens the organization's systems to the world at large and exposes firms to new vulnerabilities that need new sets of controls. A number of multilateral initiatives aim to enhance the trust in the security of this environment (Baresi et al., 2006).

As the spreading ubiquity of information technology ever more densely permeates our societies, and as technological change keeps changing the rules of the game, it is precisely the policies, processes, and practices of information security that the editors and the authors of this *AMIS* volume bring to your attention that are necessary to secure the way we live.

REFERENCES

Baresi, L.; Di Nitto, E.; and Ghezzi, C. 2005. Toward open-world software: issues and challenges. *IEEE Computer,* 39, 10 (October), 36–43.

Blyth, A., and Thomas, P. 2006. Performing real-time threat assessment of security incidents using data fusion of IDS logs. *Journal of Computer Security,* 14, 6, 513–534.

Cavusoglu, H.; Mishra, B.; and Raghunathan, S. 2004. The effect of Internet security breach announcements on market value: capital market reactions for breached firms and Internet security developers. *International Journal of Electronic Commerce,* 9, 1 (Fall), 69–104.

Doherty, N. F., and Fulford, H. 2006. Aligning the information security policy with the strategic information systems plan. *Computers & Security,* 25, 1 (February), 55–63.

Holmes, A. 2006. The global state of information security. *CIO* (September 15), 82–94.

Jennex, M. 2007. Modeling emergency response system. *Proceedings of the 40th Hawaii International Conference on System Sciences,* R. H. Sprague, Jr. (ed.). Waikoloa, Big Island, Hawaii (January 3–6), CD-ROM.

Müller, G. (ed.). 2006. Privacy and security in highly dynamic systems. Special Section, *Communications of the ACM,* 49, 9 (September), 28–62.

Neumann, P. G. 1995. *Computer-Related Risks.* New York: ACM Press.

Nolan, R., and McFarlan, F. W. 2005. Information technology and the board of directors. *Harvard Business Review,* 83, 10 (October), 96–106.

Sheffi, Y. 2005. *The Resilient Enterprise: Overcoming Vulnerability for Competitive Advantage.* Cambridge, MA: MIT Press.

Sun, L.; Srivastava, R.; and Mock, T. J. 2006. An information security risk assessment model under the Dempster-Shafer theory of belief functions. *Journal of Management Information Systems,* 22, 4 (Spring), 109–142.

Yue, W., and Çakanyildirim, M. 2007. Intrusion prevention in information systems: reactive and proactive response. *Journal of Management Information Systems,* 24, 1 (Summer), 329–353.

INFORMATION SECURITY

PART I

THE TERRAIN OF
INFORMATION SECURITY

Chapter 1

FRAMING THE INFORMATION SECURITY PROCESS IN MODERN SOCIETY

Detmar W. Straub, Seymour Goodman, and
Richard L. Baskerville

Abstract: *Describing the layout of the entire volume, this chapter explains how its parts emerged from an organic conception of organizations struggling to determine what their information security needs were and how to create viable security policies. Organizational issues exist within the context of both national and international developments in InfoSec and the final part deals with these critical arenas. Technological trends will dictate responses to the possibilities of security violations, and there are clear directions for such circumstances in the case of ubiquitous computing. The final chapter summarizes and reformulates the new directions that researchers should take in InfoSec.*

Keywords: *Information Security Processes, Policies, Practices, Guidelines, Technical Versus Managerial InfoSec Research, Key Research Questions, Future Research Directions, Landscape of Information Security*

The volume covers the managerial landscape of information security. It deals with how organizations and nations organize their information security policies and efforts. It covers how to strategize and implement security, with a special focus late in the volume on emerging technologies.

It shows wherein lie our strengths. It also shows where there are weaknesses. It points out our wealth of security technologies, particularly since the dawn of the Internet and 9/11. It likewise indicates as clearly as possible that the likely problem today is not the lack of technology, but its intelligent application. The management of information security is in its infancy, whereas the development of security technologies has reached a much more advanced state of maturity.

In attempting to cover the terrain of a broad subject that already has had a long history (however checkered), it is inevitable that much will be left out. So the subject matter selected for this volume calls for a rationale since there must be reasons why some topics were chosen and others were not, and the tale of the choosing says something about what should be valued most highly.

Before engaging in this exercise, though, it is useful to define and elaborate the term "information security" (InfoSec). The term "information" receives the initial stress since we feel strongly that the rendering of data into meaningful statements and comparisons, which we take to be information, has received light attention in both the academic and trade presses. Most of the work on security has been at the technological level, the level of protecting data bits and bytes from unauthorized interception and misuse while little work has focused on protecting these binary digits once they have been manipulated, formatted, and stored for managerial use. There are volumes of work on encryption algorithms and how to make these unbreakable, for example.[1] Hence the prevalence of terms in this technical literature on technologies described under rubrics like "data/database security," "computer security," "cyber/Internet security," and "network security."

In short, information is a managerial and organizational tool, and the protection of information from the managers' (and organizations') point of view has not been subject to the same intense scrutiny as have security technologies. Not only are the policies that protect this information much less frequently discussed, but the processes that lead to effective policies are even less favored by scientists and practitioners. Broad social issues, such as international laws, standards, and agreements that affect security of information, are part of a wide range of environmental issues that also receive scant attention. There are numerous technical working papers dealing with such matters, but assessments of this scattered work have not been forthcoming. Many of these papers have direct organizational impacts, but even those with indirect effects bear watching and understanding.

Focusing on organizational needs, therefore, is the first way in which we scoped the topics covered. What we know at this time and where research should be moving in the future to address lightly examined areas represent the basic goals of the volume.

The term "security" cries out for some definition as well. By security, we most often mean the protection of assets from unauthorized use, but the term is often extended to cover situations where mechanisms to protect assets are similar whether the damage that is inflicted comes from either a malicious, accidental, or a natural source. Organizations need to protect themselves from information losses whether these are caused by a terrorist or a tornado. Either will physically wipe out a firm's data center. The recovery procedures are only distinctive in terms of whether insurance or criminal investigations require a forensic analysis. In both cases, there would be loss of life of mission-critical employees as well as loss of information and the ability to produce information. As tragic as such events are, it would be a further loss if stakeholders who depend on the firm—employees and their families, shareholders, suppliers, customers, and the surrounding communities—were to continue to suffer from organizational unpreparedness.

Thus security as we define it includes business continuity planning, especially regarding information. Malicious elements need to be considered in scenarios in this planning effort, but equal attention must be placed on accidental and natural causes.

PARTS AND CHAPTERS

The perspective taken in this book is at an organizational level. Whether governmental, commercial, not-for-profit, or other, decision makers in organizations confront the need to specify organizational policies, define organizational processes, and manage organizational practices that assure the organization's information security. Table 1.1 lists an inventory of the various influences that drive these decisions.

Perhaps at the most global level are the regulations that emerge from non-governmental organizations. These include the recommended standards and practices of professional organizations (such as the Information Systems Audit and Control Association, which promotes an InfoSec framework called COBIT), industry standards and practices (such as the MasterCard and Visa collaboration that mandated a payment card industry data security framework), standards set by international agencies such as the International Standards Organization, and international agreements on issues such as personal data privacy through agencies like OECD and the UN.

Governments, aside from being organizations that must set their own internal policies, processes, and practices, are organizations that drive laws and regulations requiring conformity within their territorial borders. These laws and regulations define computer crimes, including insufficient protection of private personal data and insufficient transparency of information necessary for informed public decisions about organizations (such as disclosure of investment risks). With their

Table 1.1

Drivers Influencing Organizational Information Security Policies, Processes, and Practices

Non-governmental regulation
    International treaties
    International standards
    Industry standards and practices
    Professional standards and practices
Government regulation
    Computer crime
        Privacy protection
        Public disclosure requirements
    National security
    National information infrastructures
    Government internal policy
Organization
    Economics of security
        Costs and benefits
Functionality—Security tension (guns or butter)
Ethics of security
        Mandated or optional (due care)
Technological
    Computer security
    Network security
    Cryptology
Vicious circle

mandate for national security, governments may regulate advanced information technologies with military applications (such as cryptography) and set national policies to establish sufficient information security in key industry groups like finance, transportation, and energy. Such government regulation drives processes, policies, and practices in a very widespread range of commercial and private organizations (the effects of which may even be extraterritorial). Even the setting of internal government organizational processes, policies, and practices may have a widespread effect, as these may drive conforming requirements of government contracting organizations, or become regarded as emblematic standards of "due care" in InfoSec.

There are also internal drivers that determine organizational policies, processes, and practices. For example, improvements to organizational InfoSec usually require resources; an investment in InfoSec is therefore an economic decision. Costs and benefits are managed through risk analysis, and like any investment decision, improvements in InfoSec move forward under the shadow of their opportunity costs. Should the organization invest in improved information systems performance or instead invest in improved security for its existing systems? The "guns or butter" nature of the decision often pits systems performance advances against systems security advances. These conflicting goals bring forward the ethical dimensions of decisions about organizational InfoSec policies, processes, and practices. Where InfoSec features are mandated by regulations, the ethical aspects are clear. But in organizational systems where InfoSec is not required by regulation, organizations are left to follow their own ethical lights: instituting InfoSec policies, processes, and practices because these represent the measure of due care that a wide range of stakeholders would regard as responsible management of information.

Information technology is itself a driver of InfoSec management processes. Not only do newer

Table 1.2

Situating the Parts of Our Volume Among the Drivers Influencing Organizational Information Security Policies, Processes, and Practices

Part I. The Terrain of Information Security

Part II. Security Processes for Organizational Information Systems
Organization
    Economics of security
        Costs and benefits
Functionality—Security tension (guns or butter)
Ethics of Security
        Mandated or optional (due care)

Part III. Processes for Securing the Extra-Organizational Setting
Non-Government Regulation
    International treaties
    International standards
    Industry standards and practices
    Professional standards and practices
Government Regulation
    Computer crime
        Privacy protection
        Public disclosure requirements
    National security
    National information infrastructures
    Government internal policy

Part IV. Forces and Research Leading to Future Information Security Processes
Technological
    Computer security
    Network security
    Cryptology
Vicious Circle

technologies bring challenging new problems for security, but security for existing technologies is a vicious circle of technical developments. New InfoSec technologies lead adversaries to develop new techniques to defeat the new security technologies, forcing the need for even newer and even better InfoSec technologies. This is a constant race for effective technical solutions in areas like computer security, network security, and cryptology.

Indeed, the vicious circle involves more than just technology. The causal directions of the entire set of drivers are not straightforward. Various InfoSec events, like compromises and massive losses, occur within their contemporary frameworks, including the drivers noted in Table 1.1 and the various organizational InfoSec policies, processes, and practices. Such events lead to revisions in regulations and organizational values, as well as technologies. As a result, these drivers also set the stage for their own revisions, a form of self-remaking or autopoisis.

How does the work at hand fit into this landscape? We can situate the various parts of the book into the context shown in Table 1.2. The book begins with an overview and rationale and concludes with a review of the topics discussed in the book and a highlighting of what additional knowledge is critical for progress in the field on information security. Each of these composes a section to itself.

Given that our perspective is that of the organizational drivers, organizational processes that create security policies and execute them lie at the heart of what is covered and assessed. The first substantive part, entitled "Security Processes for Organizational Information Systems," deals with this broad subject. It is divided into chapters for strategy, risk assessment, governance, design, and implementation. The rationale for each of the chapters in Part I follows an explanation of the modular categorization.

Because organizational security must be responsive to policies, regulations, and activities occurring at supra-organizational levels like government and non-government regulation, the work at hand proceeds deeper than just the organizational drivers. Our second substantive part, "Processes for Securing the Extra-Organizational Setting," considers international legal conventions and other forms of international cooperation against unauthorized access to organizational systems that have been harmonized with national laws and given teeth, and have permitted prosecution across borders. Of interest are the possibilities for a dramatic impact on cyber criminal behavior and on the extent to which organizations can look for redress of wrongs. These influences take place at the national level, certainly, and increasingly at the international level. The problem of cyber crime is finally getting the worldwide attention it deserves. Many of these efforts are nascent, but at least the spotlight is now focused on the problem.

Above and beyond the issue of structures and internal organizational is the question of marketplace forces. The most important of these with respect to InfoSec are technological changes.

Our third substantive part, "Forces and Research Leading to Future Information Security Processes," places organizational and regulatory drivers in the context of the vicious circle, the never-ending race between the drivers and events. Here we situate and examine the issues arising from the bursting of new technologies on the scene. We have moved into a world that is vastly more complicated than the simple point-to-point telecommunications that characterized security in the old world. Not only has the Internet changed the nature of connectivity, but wireless and ubiquitous computing has opened up the floodgates for potential abuse.

In each of these parts we learn that there is a far too limited range of current research in InfoSec policies, processes, and practices. Much work remains to be done. In the final chapter of the volume, "Promising Future Research in InfoSec," we review the lessons learned and map out directions for new research. This represents both a summary and prioritization of the calls for research in the earlier chapters.

THE LOGIC OF THE CHAPTERS

Chapter 2, on security strategy, begins the volume since the goals of the organization with respect to security drive all other processes. This chapter wrestles with the serious questions of how security functions can create effective strategies and return more business value to the organization than they cost. The authors base their work on the straightforward assumption that it is more valuable to delineate how security strategy is made rather than articulate a set of cookie-cutter strategies that would, with contingencies, be applicable across many organizations. The latter is probably an unreachable objective in any case, but the point is that the authors focus on process and advocate a set of practices that should lead to robust strategy. In developing this theme, they show how critical is the alignment of security strategy with corporate goals and with goals of outsourcing partners. They extend this argument by suggesting that comparable organizational structures may also be necessary to coordinate inter-organizational information exchanges. Finally, the authors show how products, such as vision statements, and competencies, such as the competency to determine internal threats, are essential components of an overall security process.

In Chapter 3, on governance and the design of organizational structure, the process of determining useful structures is developed further. What are "structures"? The authors define them as what "determines who does what and how individuals collaborate to get the work completed." The key structural issue addressed in this chapter is centralization versus decentralization. This is placed within the context of alignment, as in the preceding chapter. Even though governance has to do with decision rights, it is clear that the concepts overlap since an issue about whether the security function should be centralized or decentralized involves both the creation of organizational roles and departments as well as who makes which decisions. The authors use a detailed case study to illustrate the pros and cons of centralizing versus decentralizing with regard to security.

One of the first activities that spring from a good strategy and an organizational design that aligns well with the organization is a risk assessment of security needs, which is elaborated upon in Chapter 4. The authors start with a catalog and critical assessment of existing risk assessment techniques. The most promising of these is threat-vulnerability-asset (TVA) analysis, which is introduced and then extended by the authors. The logical extension of the TVA model is through "control," which consists of ways to reduce the losses incurred by specific causes. To evaluate risks in a larger framework, the chapter goes on to discuss the value of benchmarking the organization's security against that of others. Establishing a baseline of current abuse is the first step in the metrics that are needed to assess progress.

Chapter 5 steps back and considers the process of risk assessment covered in Chapter 4 from a strategic point of view. Once the reader is clear on the process of analyzing risks, the strategic nature of the investment that follows this assessment can be raised and discussed. Whereas risk assessment at a tactical level, as in Chapter 4, is a useful and significant research area, there are questions as to what a firm should secure and what it should, for example, insure. Either is a perfectly acceptable means of handling risk, as individuals know when they insure their houses, cars, health, and so on.[2] Some systems need to be strengthened. Others may be insured at a more modest and less expensive level of security.

Chapter 6 covers policies that deal with security design, implementation, and maintenance issues, which is the natural consequence of a thorough risk assessment. The first step in creating and implementing countermeasures is policy making at a detailed level. Among the elements of such policies are statements of needs and methods to reduce risk, tying this chapter effectively to the previous chapters. Different types of policies and how to handle them is an important differentiator for managerial deployment in the chapter. Security awareness programs and education of organizational stakeholders are described next as these form the front line of approaches for implementing these policies.

Whereas Chapter 6 deals with security against individual attacks and threats, Chapter 7 on takes on the theme of protecting information assets at the macro-level. The risk from catastrophic failure can doom an enterprise, and the inadequate provision of bounce-back for systems is one of the central elements in a formula for success. The chapter stresses the need to think broadly about disaster planning, to the point where it may be possible to recover the data, systems, and networks through a series of strategies. However, without a plan that includes replacement of key personnel, all such plans will lead to failure.

Organizations operate within a sociopolitical context; Chapter 8 places this in the larger context of the national policy making of the United States. This chapter may be of interest beyond multinationals headquartered in the United States because of the international ramifications of any change in U.S. policy. The approach the author takes is historical and analogical. The basic argument is that large-impact innovations require time for society to adjust to their implications.

The automobile is an interesting parallel to computers in that both require an infrastructure, at least in the computer-to-computer, networking form of computing. Infrastructure for the provision of gasoline was originally at pharmacies, for example. It took a while before a national infrastructure of gasoline provision was in place. Licensing of drivers was similar in this regard. The bottom line for the history of the development of U.S. policy is that it has been patchy and responsive only to specific industry needs. There are currently proposals that would identify individual computers on the Internet, which may be a necessary development in the control of cyberspace. But the inadequacy of U.S. national policy is argued very convincingly in the chapter.

Chapter 9 surveys efforts to deal with security issues at the regional and international level. A large number and great variety of organizations have been created or expanded at the national, regional, and global levels in recent years to help address InfoSec problems in their various dimensions. Are they doing it well? Are they coming up with enforceable, scalable, and readily usable solutions that reduce vulnerabilities, deter malicious activity, and make cyberspace a safer and more secure infrastructure globally, or at least slow the rate at which things are getting worse?

So far, there is little information that would help us to provide convincing positive answers to these questions. Whereas international efforts are often embryonic and not necessarily converging, some regional efforts are beginning to make strides, especially in Europe. An example is the convention covering criminal and procedural law, information collection, and forms of cooperation regarding cybercrime across members of the Council of Europe and others. Much of this is unevenly distributed around the world, with the most extensive efforts in Europe, and not much in Africa at the other end of the spectrum. More multilateral legal and cooperative undertakings to provide early warning, standards and best practices, law enforcement assistance, training, and so on, and otherwise help deal with cybercrime are clearly needed to address the massive challenges that already exist and are worsening.

Chapter 10 analyzes ubicomp or ubiquitous computing, which poses an additional challenge to a world that already has a plethora of technologies that are inherently insecure and difficult to change. Assumptions about the skills of personnel to deal with new ubicomp technologies, about laws and regulations specific to them, and interfaces that can monitor their use are nearly all erroneous. Although the range of ubicomp technologies is fairly large, the authors illustrate their main points by focusing our attention on two case studies, which reveal different aspects about the generic ubicomp problem. Personal Audio Loop captures audio and cell phone messages whereas CareLog captures video and notes as well as audio. Privacy issues are the most obvious concern with unrestricted use of this technology, but the authors highlight many other conceivable problems.

Chapter 11 wraps up the volume by considering the various research questions and directions for future scientific work that are discussed in the preceding chapters. It is critical that we have at least one road map for where we might take discoveries about InfoSec and what this portends for organizations, nations, and the international community. The number of research questions covered in this chapter is voluminous, but a simple example will show what is in store for readers. Do businesses have plans for major InfoSec disasters? And if they do, have they tested these? What is the approach to developing such plans and is it effective? Among the many failure points in modern InfoSec is business continuity planning, and the need for much, much more research in this area is paramount.

CONCLUSION

This volume takes a uniquely process-oriented view of the management of information security. This viewpoint helps us to understand not only how management practices are evolving today, but why such an evolution is unfolding. In particular, this orientation helps reveal areas where we need better development of information security management practice. No volume can cover all the key issues that could be identified in InfoSec. Even after scoping our topic to the managerial and behavioral aspects of organizational security, the ground covered is still a relatively small part of the terrain. We offer tantalizing directions for new, intensive, and ground-breaking research. Will the scientific communities that have an interest in InfoSec take us up on this challenge? We obviously cannot know the answer to this challenge in advance. Nevertheless, our desire is to sketch out the state-of-the-art knowledge in each of these areas and to lay out research directions that could be profitable for MIS and other researchers. We hope that this book helps promote a new era of work in this critical arena.

ACKNOWLEDGMENTS

Some of the chapters/material in this volume is based upon work supported by Seymour Goodman's National Science Foundation Grant #0210644. Any opinions, findings, and conclusions or recommendations expressed in this material are those of the author(s) and do not necessarily reflect the views of the National Science Foundation.

Seymour Goodman, Neal Donaghy, Delphine Nain, and Giovanni Iachello would like to thank the John D. and Catherine T. MacArthur Foundation for generously providing funding in support of this work. However, all errors and omissions remain those of the authors.

NOTES

1. The comparable managerial-level work in this domain would examine such issues as whether new algorithms work in practice, how their implementation can be handled by busy managers, whether supplemental forms of protection such as point-to-point connections are needed or just an added cost without value, how managers learn about and decide to adopt new algorithms, and so on.

2. Of course, there is always the consideration of safety to human life in the case of health insurance, so the analogy is not perfect. One would presumably conduct oneself to ensure health—by eating well, for example—before insuring one's body.

PART II

SECURITY PROCESSES
FOR ORGANIZATIONAL
INFORMATION SYSTEMS

CHAPTER 2

INFORMATION SYSTEMS SECURITY STRATEGY

A Process View

RICHARD L. BASKERVILLE AND GURPREET DHILLON

Abstract: This chapter adopts a process view of information security strategy. That is, it is centrally concerned with how to "make" strategy; this extends the concern about what strategy "is." From a process viewpoint, information security strategy involves one or more strategy-setting processes. Such processes require an assessment of the goals for organizational information security. Examples include compliance with regulatory requirements, national and international standards, and professional practices. The strategy-setting process may be organized using a product criterion or a process criterion. A product criterion would organize the strategy-setting process by grouping activities according to the end products of the process. The products of strategy setting include statements of vision, core values, rationale, and strategic plans such as the security organization structure, security operations, and security budgeting strategy. A process criterion would organize the strategy-setting process by grouping activities according to major components, such as the alignment of security with organizational strategy, the planning of operational strategies, and the planning of security organizations. This chapter elaborates not just security goals, but the goal-assessment process; not just the security criteria, but the criterion organizing processes; and not just the products of the strategic processes, but the strategy-setting processes themselves.

Keywords: Information Security Strategy, Information Security Planning, Information Security Functions, Information Security Risk Management, Information Security Organization, Information Security Competence, IT Risk Management

INTRODUCTION

As commercial and government organizations have become more dependent on computer-based information systems (IS), they have become better at managing their information security. Downtime due to computer attacks, for example, has been driven down. Companies reporting downtime from computer attacks dropped from 26 percent in 2002 to 16 percent in 2003, while lengthy downtime dropped from 39 percent to 26 percent (Swartz, 2004). Such improvements in information security are not due to technology alone but improvements in the management of the technology. Good management is often founded on sound strategy.

Strategy, however, is a term used quite freely in the management literature. Indeed, just defining and explaining the meaning of the term would require a book unto itself. For example, Mintzberg, Ahlstrand, and Lampel (1998) detail five distinct views of strategic planning in the management

15

Figure 2.1 **Layers of Strategy**

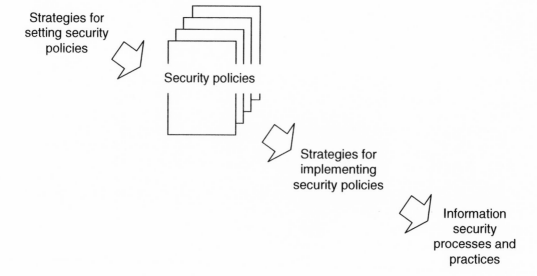

Strategies for setting security policies

Security policies

Strategies for implementing security policies

Information security processes and practices

literature: a plan or guide for action that leads the firm from a current state to a more desirable state; a pattern of consistent behavior; a positioning of products; a perspective or philosophy; a ploy that outmaneuvers or outwits a competitor. Such views unfold in at least ten different "schools" of strategy, including prescriptive schools like designing, planning, or positioning; and descriptive schools like entrepreneurial, cognitive, learning, power, cultural, environmental, and configuration. Individually, none of these views or schools seems to capture a complete understanding of strategy, but collectively, even given the standing contradictions, we grow closer to such an understanding.

Given the encompassing nature of the strategy concept among managers, little wonder that the terms strategy and policy are sometimes conflated. This interchangeability even inhabits dictionary definitions of the terms. Strategy is defined by Webster's as a careful plan or method: the art of devising or employing plans or schemes toward a goal (Merriam-Webster, 2001). The definition of policy is similar: a high-level overall plan embracing the general goals and acceptable procedures. Even in common parlance, it should not be surprising that the terms become entangled. However, policy is further defined as a definite course of action selected from among alternatives and in light of given conditions to guide and determine decisions. For our purposes, we must follow some terminological rule, and will use "strategy" in at least two ways: we can have a strategy for creating organizational security policies, and we can have a strategy for implementing security policies. This means that organizational strategy will help determine the security policies (see Figure 2.1), and these policies may in turn embody a determination for the strategy for carrying out the security policies. In this way, organizational processes and practices are determined by layers of security strategy. In this chapter, we are mainly concerned with the formulation processes for higher-level information security strategies, that is, those organizational-level strategies that drive security policy creation.

While usually thought to refer to the plans for attaining organizational missions and goals, intended strategies are rarely achieved as real strategies. Consequently, strategy theorists differ as to whether a strategy is a deliberate plan carried forward from an intended strategy to a realized strategy, or whether it is an emergent pattern that forms and reforms continuously as an organization adapts to its environment through a learning process (Mintzberg, Ahlstrand, and Lampel, 1998).

In formulating the strategy process, however, these differing views on strategy often result in remarkably similar processes in practice. Those who see strategy as a prescriptive design and planning process will view this process as a project with an ultimate goal of producing organizational strategic plans. Those who see strategy as a descriptive learning process will view this process as a changing experience with an ultimate goal of nurturing and growing the organization. The first group essentially focuses on a one-shot strategy formulation process. For them, a strategy framework such as the one in this chapter provides a guide for strategy setting. The second group expects to repeat this process continuously and that the process will change with each cycle. For them, the strategy framework such as the one in this chapter provides one example that might be used to formulate or adapt a living strategy-setting process.

For example, the Canadian Security Establishment was once tasked with recommending overall information security risk management for the government of Canada. The CSE examined standards in place in the U.S., British, and other governments as reference points in their decision. The unique problem in Canada was the need to adopt a standard risk assessment process that would apply equally well to organizational components of widely varying size and culture. The process had to work as well for a commander of a large air force base as for two police officers in a remote outpost. Accordingly, the CSE developed a strategy of defining criteria for the risk assessment process, and deferring the exact definition of the risk assessment process to the local organizational chief (Baskerville, 1995). This is the meaning of strategy in our context: an overall plan for managing and developing an organization's information security.

The remainder of this chapter explores information security strategy in seven sections. We will begin by exploring three views of information security strategic processes. Then we review the process of goals assessment as applied in developing security strategies. We then examine the products of the strategy-setting process, for example, documentation produced for strategic plans. Next, we discuss the organization of the strategy-setting process, organizing our approach by both product and process criteria. We also discuss the necessary organizational competencies for information security as a concern for pragmatics: where security competencies are unavailable, security strategy must be adjusted for the organizational realities. This means that choices like top-down versus federal strategy-setting processes should be shaped by an understanding of the competencies required for each of the different ways of organizing the strategy-setting processes.

THREE VIEWS OF STRATEGY PROCESSES FOR INFORMATION SECURITY

Strategy processes will usually entail examination of organizational values and purpose, along with baseline studies of both the external environment and internal characteristics of the organization. Ultimately the process should drive changes in organizational activities, and this may involve intermediate products such as documents about plans and goals.

The development of ideas in strategy with a particular emphasis on information security operates along three general lines of development. The first line of development results in ideas that evolve as more or less completely formulated strategies that provide whole exemplars or frameworks. Such frameworks fit nicely with the view of strategy as a prescriptive design or planning process and provide a cookie-cutter strategy for universal implementation in almost any organization. The second line of development results in ideas about fragments of security strategies. Often these fragments are recommendations for elements of an information security strategy that might

Figure 2.2   **Balancing as Information Security Strategy**

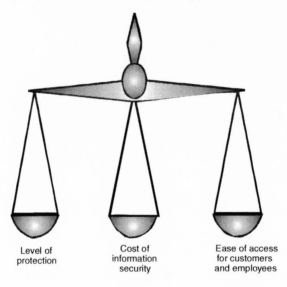

Level of
protection

Cost of
information
security

Ease of access
for customers
and employees

be advantageous if adapted or adopted into an organizational security setting. The third line of development results in ideas about how to formulate a process for information security strategy and aligns with the view of strategy as a descriptive learning process.

Universal Cookie-Cutter Strategy

The first line of development reaches for cookie-cutter strategies for adoption or adaptation as an information security strategy. These strategies are paradigms for the prescriptive design or project view of strategy formulation. Examples of such strategies include Gaston's successful information security management strategy, and Hong's integrated systems theory of information security management.

Gaston (1996) premised a goal of integrating technological security throughout the business with intermediate goals for protecting organizational assets, assuring quality, fostering competition, eliminating unnecessary expense, and customer service. This is a balancing strategy that operates with trade-offs between the level of protection, the cost of information security, and ease of access for customers and employees. In other words, security strategy fundamentally depends on where the organization places its priorities. Improvements in the level of protection will worsen customer access and/or security costs. Improvements in customer access will worsen the level of protection and/or security costs, and so on (see Figure 2.2). This balance is the fundamental strategic decision. The strategic plan consisted of (1) formulating the goals of information security, (2) positioning information security in relation to management and governance, (3) mobilizing the organization for its security, (4) creating an information security policy, (5) tailoring security measures such that policy becomes implemented.

Hong et al. (2003) premised their goals on five discrete theories that permeate information security thought. These include security policy theory, risk management theory, control and auditing theory, management system theory, and contingency theory. Many overall information

Table 2.1

Summary of Information Security Management Theories and Characteristics

Theory	Activities	Characteristics
Security policy theory	Policy establishment	• Policy is the main focus
	Policy implementation	• Emphasize sequential, structured procedures
	Policy maintenance	
Risk management theory	Risk assessment	• Understand and cope with insecure environments
	Risk control	• Ignore security policy and information audit mechanisms
	Review and modification	• Overemphasize structures
Control and auditing theory	Establish control systems	• Internal control and information audit is the main focus; ignore security policy and risk management
	Implement control systems	• Lack of requirements planning and contingency for the unexpected
	Information auditing	
Management system theory	Establish security policy	• Information auditing is ignored and the implementation is affected
	Define security scope	• Lack of periodic check
	Risk management Implementation	• Lack of feedback
Contingency theory	Policy strategy	• Consider environments both outside and inside of an organization, and choose appropriate security strategies
	Risk management strategy Control and audit strategy Management system strategy	• Lack of integration and structures

Source: Adapted from Hong et al., 2003, p. 246.

security strategies seem to be based on only one of these five theories. However, each of the five theories brings its own unique characteristics into the security strategy framework (see Table 2.1). By merging the theories into a cohesive security management process, we achieve an integrated strategy for information security (see Figure 2.3). The result is an overall strategic framework for organizing information security. This framework is called contingency management. Contingency management responds to its environment with four information management activities: security policy setting, risk management, internal control management, and information auditing.

Fragments of Security Strategies

Examples of security strategy fragments that have arisen in the second line of development include susceptibility audits and the information security chain. Susceptibility audits (Hale, Landry, and Wood, 2004) involve a process of producing a susceptibility map, which locates assets and risk in a two-dimensional plane against measures of the likelihood of successful attack and the impact or cost of successful attack on the organization (see Figure 2.4). There is a three-step process for developing a susceptibility map consisting of (1) valuing the information assets, (2) assessing threats, and (3) evaluating the cost of securing assets. The results of each step are used to develop

Figure 2.3   **An Integrated Strategy for Information Security Management**

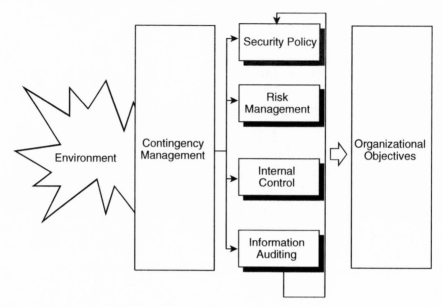

Source: Adapted from Hong et al., 2003, p. 247.

Figure 2.4   **Susceptibility Map**

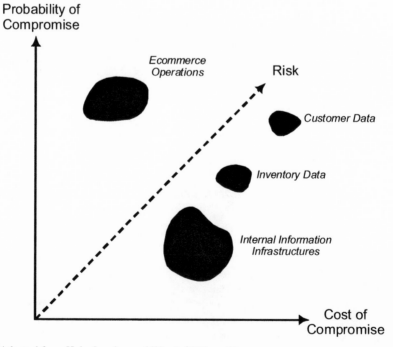

Source: Adapted from Hale, Landry, and Wood, 2004, p. 62.

Figure 2.5 **Adapting Susceptibility Mapping into the Integrated Strategy**

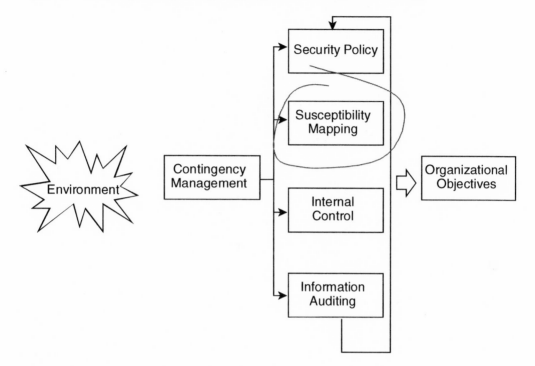

the map, which can then be used in formulating strategies for reducing the likelihood of successful attacks. In this example, a susceptibility audit is a fragment of strategy that can be integrated into a larger strategic framework for a complete information security strategy.

We can better understand the relationship between strategy fragments, such as susceptibility maps, and overall frameworks by illustrating how the fragments such as susceptibility mapping might be integrated into an overall framework. Suppose, for example, that the organizational managers are keen on the use of susceptibility maps as a means of risk assessment. This strategic fragment could be adapted to an overall framework such as the balanced security strategy or the integrated security strategy. In Figure 2.5, we illustrate how susceptibility mapping can be adapted to the integrated strategy by using it as the chosen risk management element in the strategy.

The information security chain (Finne, 1996) is a concept that involves isolating and compartmentalizing security safeguard elements into modules and submodules. Each module forms a link in the chain that should completely encompass information vulnerabilities and protect the organization from the surrounding world. For example, in Figure 2.6 the modules are numbered 1 through 13, forming links in the chain around information security. Each link/module contains many submodules (as illustrated in module 1). For example, module 1 could contain intrusion protection. Within each module or submodule are safeguards like biometric access control, passwords, virus detection, and the like. In this example, the security chain concept provides a fragment of information security strategy that can be adopted into a larger framework similar to susceptibility maps.

For example, suppose the organization managers believe that the information security chain is very appropriate for their organization. The security chain concept could be adapted into the

Figure 2.6   **The Information Security Chain**

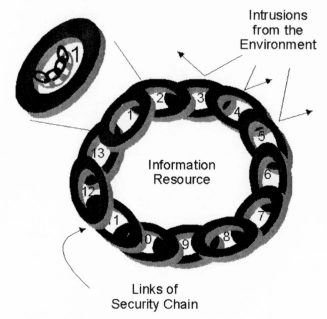

Source: Adapted from Finne, 1996, p. 298.

Figure 2.7   **Adapting the Security Chain Concept into the Integrated Security Framework**

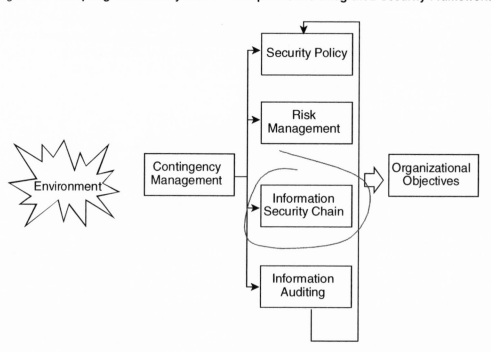

Figure 2.8 **PFIRES: Policy Framework for Information Security**

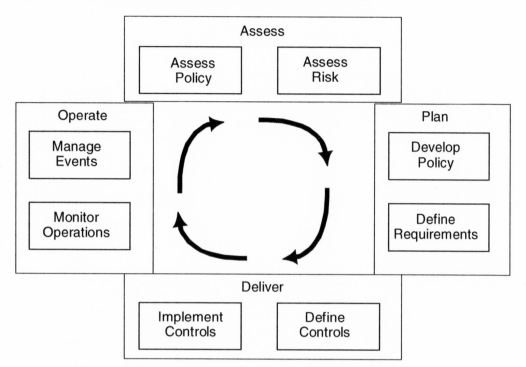

Source: Adapted from Rees, Bandyopadhyay, and Spafford, 2003, p. 102.

integrated strategy framework as a model for internal controls. This adaptation is shown in Figure 2.7. Various strategy fragments can be integrated together within an overall framework, whether the framework is a cookie-cutter universal framework or one specifically designed for a particular organization.

Formulated Processes for Security Strategy

The final line of development aims to help in the creation of processes for setting organizational strategy. Such developments adopt the view that strategy setting is a continuous emergent process. An example is found in PFIRES (Policy Framework for Information Security) (Rees, Bandyopadhyay, and Spafford, 2003). This framework aims to provide a means by which a usable security strategy can be developed and kept aligned with the overall information technology lifecycle. It defines a continuing cycle of four phases consisting of (1) assess phase, (2) plan phase, (3) deliver phase, and (4) operate phase. This cycle is shown in Figure 2.8. Each phase consists of two major activities. The assessment phase includes policy assessment and risk assessment. The planning phase includes policy development and requirements definition. The deliver phase includes controls definition and controls implementation. The operation phase includes monitoring operations, reviewing trends, and managing events. Adopting or adapting this framework will lead the organization to continuously redevelop its information security strategies. While the framework is broader than just a cookie-cutter strategy, it does incorporate a somewhat complete organizational security strategy as a starting framework from which various organizational learning activities in the assessment phase can begin to enable the overall strategic framework and process to adapt and emerge.

GOALS ASSESSMENT

The information security strategy process starts with an assessment of the goals for organizational information security. These goals are likely to include compliance with regulatory requirements, national and international standards, and professional practices. The goals assessment process must take into account the type of organization and include activities to align the security strategy with the strategic goals of the organization as a whole. Goals assessment processes must also take into account the type of security environment. In particular, high-risk organizational environments like electronic commerce or industries operating in areas of national critical infrastructures will need more care and rigor in security strategy processes.

Compliance

A major focus of the development of information security strategic goals will be the compliance requirements dictated by the environment. The organization's situation may require compliance by law or by industry standards. In some cases, the organizational situation may not impose legal requirements, but the organization may choose to comply in keeping with standards of due care or prudent practice. Ultimately, any comprehensive process for defining strategic goals for information security must review potential regulatory requirements, national and international standards, and professional practices. We will briefly review each of these categories of compliance.

The most prevalent regulatory requirements are privacy requirements for personal information recorded and processed in computer systems. Because these requirements are established in international treaties, countries respond by establishing these requirements in law. Examples of such laws in the United States include the Privacy Act of 1974, the Privacy Protection Act of 1980, Right to Financial Privacy Act of 1978, the Family Educational Rights and Privacy Act of 1974, the Children's Online Privacy Protection Act of 1998, the Electronic Communications Privacy Act of 1986, the Cable Communication Policy Act of 1984, and Department of Health and Human Services regulations effective in 2001 protecting the privacy of medical records.

Privacy is not the only area in which laws have been enacted that may determine the goals to be set by a strategy-setting process. For example, the Sarbanes-Oxley Act of 2002 defines requirements for external auditors to assess the testing of security controls on computer-based accounting systems. Compliance with this act means that security controls for accounting systems must not only be designed and operated, but also must be routinely tested for effectiveness. The strategy-setting process would need to evaluate such compliance. For example, compliance is required by law for publicly held companies. While the law does not require compliance by privately held companies, the existence of the law suggests that any standard of prudent accounting will mean such testing will become a goal even in privately held companies.

Compliance with national and international standards must also be reviewed in setting security goals during the strategy process. The most prevalent such standard is ISO/IEC 17799 and ISO 27002, Information Technology–Code of Practice for Information Security Management (ISO/IEC, 2000). The standard suggests best practices for security policies, infrastructure, asset classification, physical security, communications security, access control, systems development, and business continuity. The information security strategy process must evaluate such standards and determine the degree to which the organization should comply. Some parts of this extensive standard may not be relevant to a particular organization. Other parts may be relevant, but in the careful opinion of the security strategists the alternative security activities may be more prudent. Indeed there may be conflicting standards. Consequently, compliance is not a straightforward goal, but requires a careful process for reviewing standards and determining which standards apply and the degree to which such standards should be implemented.

Professional practices may also be codified in a form for easy review in a manner similar to compliance with national and international standards. Such practices are sometimes provided as frameworks or guidelines and may be specific to certain industries or certain kinds of systems. In some cases such frameworks may become a de facto requirement in a related law. For example, the Sarbanes-Oxley Act references responsible frameworks for practice. An effective reference for this purpose is a specific framework developed by the Committee of Sponsoring Organizations of the Treadway Commission (COSO). This framework provides details of recommended internal controls, and has become a reference tool for efforts to comply with the law. The COBIT framework (Control Objectives for Information and related Technology) framework is another detailed framework of particular interest in setting information security goals (COBIT, 2005). It was developed by the Information Systems Audit and Control Foundation and can have a similar impact to COSO as a reference framework for prudent practice.

Organization Structure and Processes

An important step in goals assessment is the clarification of organizational structures and processes and the assessment of the integrity of the communication channels. There is also a further need to align disparate activities to each other to provide adequate assurance. When responsibility and authority structures are not defined well, there is a risk of breakdown in internal organizational controls. The notion of establishing responsibility and authority structures is not necessarily limited to the drawing up of an organization chart. It has more to do with understanding the existing social norms and designing structures and processes that align with the dominant normative structures.

There are two further aspects of structures and processes that need to be considered. First is the alignment of structures and processes with the technical infrastructure. Second is the communication among established roles and key stakeholders. It is a documented fact that a majority of security vulnerabilities are a consequence of lack of integrity between organizational structures and access control mechanisms (Backhouse and Dhillon, 1996). This is essentially because there usually is a lack of alignment between the manner in which organizational structures and processes are created and the design of the information technology infrastructure. The lack of alignment gets manifested at two levels. First, when security controls are instituted in the systems, they are generally an afterthought, thus leading to development duality problems (White and Dhillon, 2005). Second, there is usually little communication between those designing security controls and the rest of the organization. This results in problems with the manner in which roles are created, how they are manifested in the organization, and the nature of responsibility structures mandated by the technical system. In terms of establishing information system security goals, understanding the nature and scope of organizational structures, processes, and their relationship with security control structures is important.

The second issue that needs careful understanding is the nature and scope of communication between key stakeholders and organizational security roles. Proper communication is essential across organizational hierarchies. There is a reciprocal relationship between assessing security goals and ensuring proper implementation. Communication is fundamental in ensuring good implementation of the goals, largely through coordination. And a lack of predictability as to how coordination will manifest itself is a barrier to communication, which could be a cause of security and integrity problems.

Table 2.2

Security Strategy Alignment with Organizational Strategy

Corporate goal	Security contribution (alignment)
Quality assurance	Medium
Completeness	Low
Accuracy	Low
Timeliness	None to low
Authorization	High
Privacy and confidentiality	Depends
Authentication	High
Continuity and availability	High
Logicality	Medium

Source: Adapted from Gaston, 1996, p. 19.

In summary, both the responsibility structures and communication among key stakeholders are important issues that need to be carefully understood. The formal means by which authority is identified and subsequently delegated should have a visible relation to an organization's purpose. Responsibility of different roles should be fixed such that teamwork is encouraged and solutions to security problems are provided close to the point of action. There are opportunities to share objectives whenever organizational structures and processes have been well designed and communication channels well formed. Shared objectives lead to a setting where responsibility will exceed authority.

Alignment Activities

An information security strategy should also be aligned with the overall organizational strategy. The security strategy should support organization-wide strategy and positively help in reaching an organization's goals. For example, Table 2.2 illustrates the degree to which organizational strategic goals for information can be supported by information security strategy. A corporate goal of high quality would align with typical information security policies, while it may not be necessary to align security strategies closely with an organizational goal of accuracy in its information. Gaston (1996) characterizes the relationship of security with accuracy and completeness as one in which information is allowed to be created or altered only by those with the knowledge to do so correctly and only by using authorized application programs. Other organizational goals, such as privacy and confidentiality of information, may be heavily related to information security strategy depending on the kind of information that the organization is processing and the laws, practices, and standards with which the organization must comply. Activities to align the security strategy with the strategic goals of the organization as a whole should be typical, and most strategy-setting processes for information security should aspire to maintain that integrity.

Security Environment

An appreciation of the organizational context is important for setting security strategy goals. This is more so the case especially when companies are outsourcing a significant proportion of their information technology operations.

Kalfan (2004) notes that one of the most important issues to consider is the service level agreement (SLA) between the client and the vendor. Such an agreement needs to include legal clauses of non-disclosure and penalties for violations. Such SLAs may, however, not dissuade some information technology workers from subverting the controls and selling confidential information for personal gain. On June 23, 2005, British Broadcasting Service reported claims by the tabloid newspaper *The Sun* that its journalists bought personal details including passwords, addresses, and passport data from a Delhi IT worker for £4.25 each.

Occurrences of this kind call for increased vigilance for ensuring security. Preventive mechanisms need to be instituted. Sherwood (1997) suggests four classes of principles that should guide a security strategy, particularly in the context of outsourcing:

1. Proper definition of responsibilities and liabilities of both parties
2. Definition of business processes linking the client and the vendor
   a. security policy mandated authorizations
   b. outsourcing service provider to act as "custodian," with implementation privileges
   c. adequate audit processes
3. Documents describing primary security requirements
4. Supporting documents on "security target" implementation

In implementing the principles, Sherwood proposes a security-outsourcing model (see Figure 2.9), where a liaison is maintained between the customer organization and the service provider through some sort of an outsourced services security forum. Desirable as these might be, such arrangements are only beginning to evolve. For instance, following the theft of personal details from a service provider in the Delhi IT worker case, the apex body in India (NASSOCOM) stepped up to provide assurances and a discussion forum for preventing such occurrences in the future.

Sherwood proposes some essential steps that need to be considered if a proper security environment is to be maintained:

- *Legally binding responsibilities.* Any outsourcing arrangement should identify and implement legally binding responsibilities.
- *Organizational structure.* There should be a mutually agreed organizational structure for ensuring proper allocation of responsibilities, liabilities, and subsequently attribution of blame.
- *Process clarity.* There should be clarity and agreement about the manner in which actions will be taken, both to proactively secure the facility and after an event has been discovered.
- *Performance measurement.* Both parties should establish measures that will be the basis for evaluating performance, especially with respect to risk management.
- *Proactive management.* Outsourcing security cannot be assured after a contract has been signed. All aspects of security, including penalties, need to be elaborated at a pre-contract stage.

An important aspect of maintaining a good security environment is the proper balance between various competing forces. Clearly, the security strategy has to balance with the current organizational capabilities and the future organizational opportunities. If this is not done and an environment to sustain it is not created, it might result in a lack of alignment between the goals and the means of achieving them. Two other important aspects for setting a security strategy include consideration of the level and extent of resources available and the corporate objectives.

Figure 2.9   **Organizational model for outsourcing security**

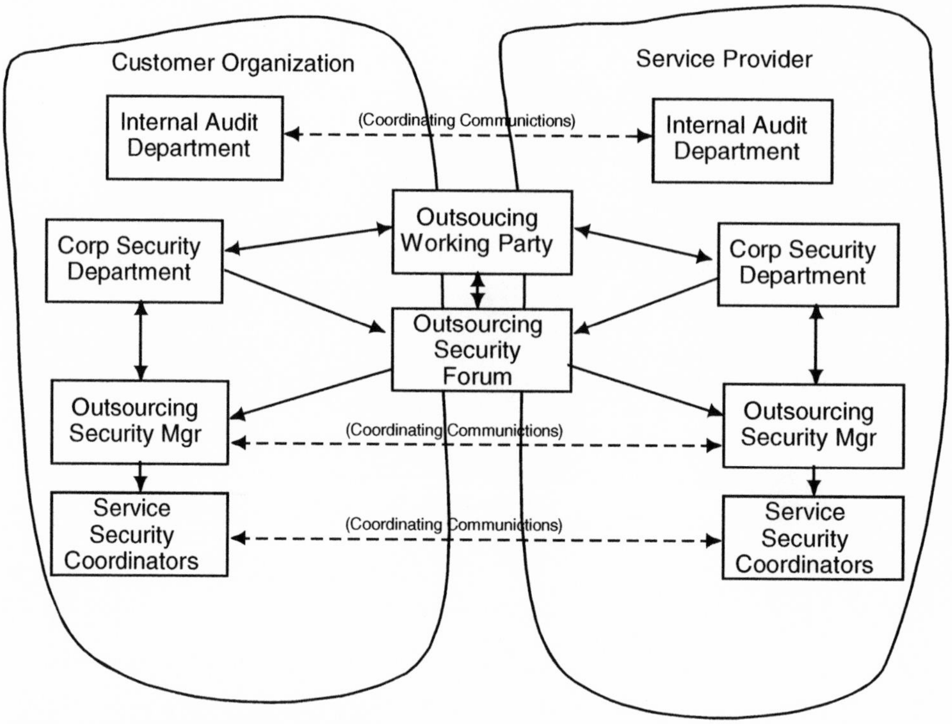

Source: Adapted from Sherwood, 1997.

SECURITY STRATEGY-SETTING PRODUCTS

Once the goals of the information security strategy process are set, the products of strategy setting must be delineated. These products can include statements of vision, core values, rationale, and strategic plans. In addition, the major components of organizational strategy should also be delineated. These components include the process for security strategy, its security operations strategy, and its security budgeting strategy. The operational strategy concerns whether the organization's information security operation will be centralized or distributed. This operational strategy will form the context for the budgeting strategy. For example, it should define whether information security is going to be a cost center or management overhead. An organizing strategy must also be defined for information security operations. This organizing strategy will be related closely to the operational strategy. Organizing strategies include hierarchical organizational designs that respond to strategic needs to centralize control over security, and network organizational designs that respond to needs for organizational agility with regard to information security. Matrix organizational strategies respond to needs for information security portfolios such as settings involving projects.

Statements

The central product of any strategy-setting process will be a set of statements that define the organization's information security strategic plan and instruct organizational members how this

Exhibit 2.1

Example of an Information Security Vision

All organizational information will at all times be responsibly insulated against all threats to information integrity, availability, and confidentiality.

Exhibit 2.2

Rochester Institute of Technology's Information Security Vision Statement

RIT is committed to making available appropriate information in the support of its mission to prepare students for successful lifetime career development. RIT is also committed to its stewardship role to protect the confidentiality, integrity, and availability of information entrusted to RIT by students, faculty, staff, alumni and partners from the public or private sectors, as deemed necessary by educational needs, privacy obligations, regulatory compliance or contractual obligation.

Source: RIT, 2004.

plan is to be implemented. Examples of such statements include vision statements, statements of core values, rationales for strategies, strategic maps, and strategic plans.

A vision statement is what the organization would ideally like to become. Such statements are often far on the horizon and are meant to provide an overall sense of the direction of the organization and its growth and development. A well-formed process for developing an information security strategy should encompass the stage in which the vision for the organization's information security is pronounced. For example, such a vision might enjoy the prospect of complete information security for all assets, for all time, against all threats (see Exhibit 2.1).

A statement of core values is another somewhat idealistic component of strategy setting in which the three or four key organizational values become pronounced in such a way as to distinguish the organization from its peers. A well-formed process for developing security strategies may be improved when such values have been explicated. An example of such a core value for a security strategy could be "We highly respect the right to privacy of our customers and our employees." Exhibit 2.2 is an example of a vision statement that includes core values.

Statements of strategic rationale form concrete explanations for the selection of strategic directions and activities. The statements are a record of the thinking by which strategic plans were designed. The statements are important for explaining how the strategists translated information security goals into information security strategic plans. For example, the rationale for the strategic plan that includes an improvement program for organizational passwords might show that password compromise has been a recurring problem that has led to violation of privacy of customer data.

Strategy maps can be used as a means for developing and documenting strategic plans and their rationale. Such maps are sometimes developed in stages that begin with cognitive maps developed by groups, which are later compiled into overall strategy maps (Eden and Ackermann, 2002). Such maps can be part of the process of determining strategic goals, programs, and actions for information security purposes. For example, a rationale that explains why a password awareness program must be continuous, could be mapped as in Figure 2.10.

Strategic plans are generally text documents that detail the vision, values, goals, and rationale. In addition, these plans include details for activities that will lead to the achievement of the goals and move the organization closer toward its vision. Descriptions of such activities are often ex-

Figure 2.10 **Strategy Map Fragment for Passwords**

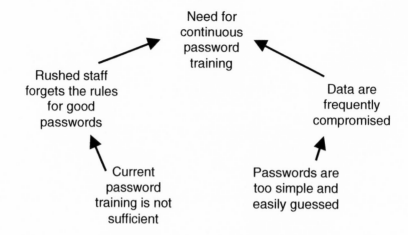

pressed in a form that is as measurable as possible. In this way, managers can determine whether or not the activity has been carried out. Not only is the organization planning to measure the achievement of its goals, but it is also planning to measure the activities developed as a means of achieving such goals. In circumstances where a goal is unmet, managers can determine whether the activities meant to achieve that goal have been successfully completed.

Major Components of Organizational Security Strategy

There are a number of activities that come together to form an organization's security strategy. The major activities are identified and described below (Backhouse and Dhillon, 1996).

Activity 1: Acknowledge possible security vulnerability. Oftentimes there is little consensus that a possible security vulnerability exists. This is usually a consequence of different perceptions of individuals. Therefore it is important to interview different stakeholders and develop some understanding of what their opinions on security vulnerability might be. This is an important step, particularly with respect to laying a foundation for further consensus building.

Activity 2: Identify risks and the current security situation. With particular attention to existing structures and processes, a detailed picture of the current situation is considered. The structure relates to the manner in which the formal reporting structures, responsibilities, authority structures, and formal and informal communication channels exist. Softer power issues are also mapped. Past research has shown that organizational power relationships play an important role in the management of information security. Process is looked at in terms of a typical input, processing, output, and feedback mechanisms. This involves considering basic activities related to deciding to do something, doing it, monitoring the activities as progress is made and the impact of external factors, and evaluating outcomes.

Activity 3: Identify the ideal security situation. Identification of the ideal situation involves understanding the nature and scope of improvements that are to be developed. The details of the ideal situation are then discussed with the concerned stakeholders to identify both "feasible" and "desirable" options. This involves a high-level definition of both technical and procedural aspects. Activity 3 is rooted in the ideal world. Here we detach ourselves from the real world and think of ideal types and conceptualize about ideal practices.

Table 2.3

Example of Measures of Performance

Assessment measure	Basic goal	Intrusion detection example
Efficacy	Safeguard produces an effect	Intrusions are detected
Efficiency	The cost of the safeguard compares positively with the value of its product	The losses due to intrusions are reduced to a level that justifies the cost of the detector
Effectiveness	Safeguard produces a decided, decisive, and desired effect	All important intrusions are detected

Activity 4: Model ideal information security. This stage represents the conceptual modeling step in the process. All activities necessary to achieve the agreed upon transformation are considered and a model of the ideal security situation is developed. In a perfect situation, the security features should match the ideal types defined in Activity 3. An important consideration at this stage is monitoring the operational system. The following three aspects are considered:

1. Definition of measures of performance. This generally relates to assessing efficacy, efficiency, and effectiveness (see Table 2.3 for an example). Other metrics besides efficacy, efficiency, and effectiveness may also be used.
2. Monitoring of activities according to defined metrics.
3. Control actions taken, where outcomes of the metrics are assessed in order to determine and execute actions.

Activity 5: Compare ideal with current. This stage involves comparison of conceptual models with real-world expression. The comparisons may result in multiple reiterations of Activities 3 and 4. Although there may be a tendency to engage in conceptual model building, it is prudent to move on to Activity 5 and return to Activity 4 later. This helps in undertaking an exhaustive comparison of the activities, particularly targeting:

1. Conceptual model as a base for structured questioning. This is usually done when the real-world situation is significantly different from the one depicted in the conceptual model.
2. Comparing history with model prediction. In this method the sequence of events in the past are reconstructed with possible predictions.
3. General overall comparison. This helps in defining features that might be different from present reality.
4. Model overlay. The real and conceptual models are compared and differences discussed.

Activity 6: Identify and analyze measures to fill gaps. The desired solutions are reviewed, particularly in the context of the problem domain. At this stage it is important to define the intent. Solutions are identified to address the intent. For instance, if procedures are to be defined, the possible solution would be to hire internal control design consultants who may have knowledge of the Sarbanes-Oxley Act.

Activity 7: Establish and implement security plan. Recommendations developed in Activity 6 are considered and solutions formulated. An implementation plan is devised. At this stage, integration of security into overall systems and information flows is also considered. Activity 7 also ensures that the solutions afforded do not conflict with the overall strategy or other procedures that might be in place.

ORGANIZING THE STRATEGY-SETTING PROCESS

As previously stated, the strategy-setting process may be organized using a product criterion or a process criterion. A product criterion would organize the strategy-setting process by grouping activities according to the end products of the process. For example, activities would include vision setting, core value determination, and planning. A process criterion would organize the strategy-setting process by grouping activities according to major components. For example, activities would include aligning security with organizational strategy, planning operational strategy, and planning security organization. The strategy-setting process can be top down or federal. A top-down strategy-setting process would begin with a high-level committee delegating elements of the strategy to lower-level committees. A federal process would begin with lower-level committees channeling draft strategy components up to higher-level committees where strategy would be assembled by rationalizing the collection of federated components.

Product Criterion

The product criterion is probably the most straightforward and intuitive principle for organizing the strategy-setting process. Under this principle, the goals of strategy setting are usually focused on the products. If, for example, the products are a vision statement, a core values statement, and a strategic plan, then the strategic planning process would be organized in three stages. The three stages would align with the three products. Stage one would be the creation of a vision statement. Stage two would be the creation of a values statement. Stage three would be the creation of a strategic plan.

Vision statements are usually pronounced from the upper echelons of the information security management function. This process may be simple, such as an autonomous statement crafted by the organization's chief information security officer and submitted for approval. The process may also entail a widespread effort by various stakeholders in information security. The organization's chief information officer, chief information security officer, chief privacy officer, and other senior management officials with responsibility related to information security may form a vision statement development committee. The vision statement may be set after a lengthy and in-depth discussion that may include reviews of organizational strategy, peer organization vision statements, and a retreat-style meeting. In a participative organization, the vision statements may be reviewed for comment by the entire information security organization.

The core values statement is usually developed in a bottom-up and participative process. Members of the organization are invited to propose statements of values they feel are of common importance across the entire organization. The information security management function collates these statements and collapses them into three to five common values that stretch across the information security organization.

Using these product criteria, the process for developing an information security strategic plan then focuses on ends and means. The vision statement becomes a guide for declaring the ends, while the core values statements become guides for selecting the means. In this fashion the elements of the vision become the organizing principle for the strategy-setting process. For example, if the vision declares that the organization will achieve customer data privacy, then the strategic planning process will include a development committee for setting a strategic plan for achieving customer data privacy. The strategic planning organization will be a rollup of the working parties necessary to achieve all elements of the vision statement and the values statements.

For example, an organizational security vision might state that "organizational information will be insulated against all threats to diminish information accuracy, availability, and confidentiality." Using a product criterion for organizing the information security strategy-setting process would lead to three working groups for setting the components of an information security: an accuracy working group, an availability working group, and a confidentiality working group.

Finally, an overview working group would compile the strategic components developed by the individual working parties. For instance, strategies developed independently for achieving accuracy, availability, and confidentiality would be compiled into a single strategic document with any overlaps removed. Most information security strategy documents developed with a product criterion will contain at least six components:

1. Acknowledgment of possible security vulnerability. This declaration is necessary to motivate any reasonable risk management strategy. Without this declaration, the motivation to protect important stakeholders, like the shareholders, is muted.
2. Risk identification and current security analysis plan. This component provides a baseline analysis and definition from which the information security strategy aims to move forward.
3. Plan for designing an ideal security situation. This component provides the strategy for defining the desired future information security state for the organization.
4. Plan for comparative analysis of ideal and current. This component provides the strategy for maintaining continuous information about future information security states of the organization.
5. Plan for analysis of measures to fill gaps. This component provides the strategy for defining continuous improvement in the information security state of the organization.
6. Plan for implementing measures. This component provides the strategy for financing and deploying future information security improvements.

Process Criterion

An integral part of the strategy-setting process is the competencies that may be necessary for identifying and grouping activities together. The way that managers conceive of information security holds enormous implications for the way they then manage the technological controls. In general, the early literature on information security reflected a "mechanistic" conceptualization of information technology. That is, resources were considered an asset that could be purchased and managed much like any tool to enable a task, something akin to purchasing an especially fine hammer for carpentry. Initial difficulties with integrating security were thus consistently interpreted to mean that a deficient hammer was purchased, or even more often, that the organization's nails and wood were somehow just not of the proper quality to handle the fine hammer. Thus energy was exerted at "fixing" security, or alternatively, properly training personnel and restructuring the organization to accommodate new security tools and techniques.

Before very long, a second school, sometimes referred to as the "Vitalist" school (see Lewin, 1993), reconceptualized the explanation for the often tremendous difficulties associated with information security implementation. Using a social construction lens, information security was considered an embodiment of the subjective views of the many organizational actors (e.g., see Armstrong, 1999) and thus issues of context, situation, and the related task of integrating different interest groups became paramount in addressing information security. In extending our above metaphor, the real problem that organizations faced, then, was that actors viewed their new tool as a wrench, screwdriver, or saw, while designers created their version of a hammer. Integration success became dependent on the extent that the tool produced actually could accommodate the uses and conflicts inherent in the organizational system. Both of these views provide very different models of managing information security, and they offer useful prescriptions in many cases.

These two viewpoints may be bridged by accepting that technical controls are both a physical artifact and social construction, and that the interaction of humans with their technical controls leads to a duality of cause and effect in understanding how security controls work in organizations (Dobson, 1991). In this model, the creation of meaning, norms, and power helps predict how technological controls are formed, shaped, and used over time, as well as how they interact to form and shape the behaviors and processes of the environment (Segev, Porra, and Roldan, 1998). This model directly implies that the cause-effect relationships between technical controls and organization is nonlinear; that is, there exists at the very least a closed loop that maintains that organizations shape the technical controls and the controls shape the organization. To return to our metaphor, information security systems represent the materials and machines for tool making, and thus their role is to produce hammers or saws according to the organization's requirements; at the same time, the organization must constantly structure itself to use and implement these materials and machines. In this sense, then, information security is not an asset, but an integral part of the process and dynamic capabilities of the organization, both shaping and being shaped by the organization.

MARSHALLING THE COMPETENCIES

In order to deliver performance on either the process or the product criteria, management must ensure the organization has assembled the necessary information security competencies. Without the necessary competencies, implementation of any strategy must fail. Where the competencies are unavailable, the strategies must be modified to compensate for the reality of the organizational situation.

What then are the competencies for identifying and managing information security in such an environment? Clearly there has been a lot of research undertaken in the mainstream organizational strategy arena. McGrath et al. (1995) argue that competencies necessary are an idiosyncratic combination of individual skills and the understanding of the business processes. The process criteria for managing information security, therefore is intricately linked with the notion of competencies that may be necessary. The rest of this section identifies and describes key competencies for managing information security in organizations.

Competency to Create Adequate Business Processes

An understanding of business processes and how these relate to ensuring integrity of information flows is a key competence that is necessary for strategizing about security. The business processes are an indication of how a company's vision and goals are identified and communicated. Properly designed and defined business processes are universally thought to be the foundation for effective information security. Organizations must be able to realize their strategic objectives and create effective business processes in accordance with those objectives. It is on these clear and cohesive business processes that all security strategies should be built.

Competency to Clearly Define Roles

An important step toward securing information lies in the organization's ability to clearly define the roles and responsibilities of all its members. Definition of functions is critical for the health of any organization's structure (see Schlenker et al., 1994).

All employees need to fully understand the purpose and the scope of their distinctive roles within the organization. It is in every organization's interest not only to assign roles in accordance with business processes, but also to explain the purpose of each role and to clarify individual responsibilities. Information security design should take into account roles distributed throughout the organization, and always support, rather than limit, the execution of duties related to these roles. In particular, information security design must carefully consider each role's required access to information. In organizations where roles are clearly and precisely defined and employees understand their position's contribution to the company's overall strategy, security issues are much easier to manage.

Competency to Recognize Importance and Scope of Security Concerns

As discussed previously, security processes must be designed in accordance with an organization's strategic and business goals. No security system will be effective unless it follows business processes. For successful and effective information protection to be developed, top management must acknowledge how crucial information security is to business success and understand how severe the outcome of a security breach could be. Once this is realized, it is much easier for the company to commence its journey toward design, development, and implementation of an effective information security plan.

Over-standardization of protection tools can be an impediment to developing a secure environment. All security procedures and tools should follow specific business processes and must be adjusted to fit specific business settings and operations. Thus, for a company to properly develop its security policies, controls, and procedures, top management needs to be able to identify major threats every organizational system faces. It is crucial that those in charge of developing a structure to protect the information, be qualified for the task. They must possess the knowledge of security issues, current trends, and solutions. However, security managers' knowledge cannot be limited to technological issues; they need to keep in mind the company's core business and understand the company's business processes.

Competency to Identify Internal Threats to Information Security

There is a necessity of distinguishing between employees committing unintentional breaches of information security, and the malicious, conscious acts that aim to steal, tamper with, or destroy information possessed by an organization. In many cases employees are genuinely unaware that they are breaching security. Yet, both of these threats are real and both can result in severe consequences. However, each demands a slightly different approach when developing security controls and protection tools. When designing information security systems, every company must be cognizant of the need to prevent both malicious acts and unintentional giving away or destroying information, and each must be able to protect its information from both types of security breaches.

Accidental acts that result in security breaches can be avoided only if the organization acknowledges the possibility of the occurrence of such acts. Therefore, organizational competencies that are critical, in this context, consist of the company's ability to anticipate and prevent situations in which information can be endangered by unintentional announcement of sensitive and confidential information or unintentional deletion of data. To be able to predict all possible, undesirable scenarios, the organization needs to possess in-depth knowledge of the reality in which its business processes are performed. Only by possessing this knowledge can companies create security systems that will protect against unintentional abuse or deletion of information.

Intentional acts or deliberate sabotage of information is another threat every company must be aware of when designing its information security system. Here, the ability to conduct accurate risk analysis is one of the most important competencies an organization may possess. Ignorance of the need to, or negligence in implementing necessary precautions to protect data theft and information sabotage, may seriously jeopardize both the financial stability of a company and its competitive position in the industry. The ability to foresee all possible situations in which information security could be breached is certainly a base for proper design of protection systems.

Competency to Implement Information Security Policies

Undeniably, organizations need to possess the competency to design functional and effective information security policies. However, this competency is not sufficient; it must be complemented by the organization's ability to execute these policies. Organizations need to be able to actively enforce their procedures. An organization may expend great effort and resources to design security regulations and policies, yet afterward fail to execute these policies properly and scrupulously. Policies and controls are useful only if an organization is able to devote the time and resources necessary to utilize them properly. Enforcement of security procedures is equally vital in the context of technological security and managerial controls. In addition, even if business processes and information security controls are compatible, the end user must be kept in mind. If processes are cumbersome, employees are likely to skip them or bypass them to make their jobs easier, unaware of the potential for damage. For example, bank tellers may avoid logging off the computer every time they step away from the terminal because customers are waiting, they are very busy, it takes too long to log back on, and/or a supervisor's key is required.

Similarly, from a managerial standpoint, competent individuals should diligently and actively perform managerial controls and monitoring. In addition, the entire organization must have a clear understanding of the lines of command and know who should perform which control procedures and to whom suspicious behaviors should be reported. Furthermore, every employee should be able to report suspicious behaviors to an individual outside of his or her department who does not report to the same supervisors.

Competency to Maintain Policy Flexibility

Despite the obvious necessity to design effective and strong protection systems, flexibility of established security systems, controls, and procedures also seems essential. Flexibility in this context is understood as the ability of the rule makers in the organization to revise established rules and procedures. Information security managers need to be able to accept suggestions/criticisms from the members of the organization. Organizations do not operate in a perfect world. Unanticipated problems are likely to arise. Therefore, the organization should have a method of evaluating and, if necessary, revising its security system to adapt to and meet the changing needs of the organization. If too many times employees demand more access to information, it can mean that the current rules are inhibiting them from executing their roles efficiently and effectively. In such situations, reevaluation and redesign of the security processes may be necessary.

Competency to Regulate the Flow of Information

Limiting access to sensitive information is one of the most frequently mentioned issues in information security. This issue is directly related to the role definition aspects discussed earlier. Access to information should be assigned according to roles or tasks. Employees should have access only to that information that is required for them to fulfill their duties. Therefore, organizations need to develop the competence to regulate and control the information flows, both within the organization and throughout the business network.

Competency to Communicate the Necessity for Information Security Procedures

Information security is not only the domain of the top management. It is true that those responsible for core business tasks need to understand the importance and the scope of information protection. However, employees must understand the organizational processes and business goals of their organizations, and provide protection along the entire course of the information flow. Therefore, an organization must have the ability to convey the criticality of maintaining information security throughout the whole organization. Top management has to be willing to provide the resources necessary to develop effective security systems, while employees need to be convinced of the usefulness and importance of these systems.

Insider threats to information security are a serious category of risk. It is also important to acknowledge that this threat can be as much a result of a conscious act as of unintended acts due to unawareness, lack of knowledge, or ignorance. One of the most important barriers to creating an effective information security plan is the lack of awareness of the consequences uncontrolled information exchange can cause. Prevention is far more important than crisis management. Therefore, managers need to be able to conduct accurate and relevant risk analysis. A "big picture" approach is critical for effective risk analysis, as what may seem to be an insignificant mistake or innocent information exchange can, in reality, have much more far-reaching effects than the organization could anticipate. Any information handled, processed, or passed over should always be handled with the understanding that it could potentially be misused or stolen.

General awareness of the company's business processes and goals is critical to ensure information security. It is also important for the employees to understand both the purpose and the scope of information security policies, controls, and protections. Organizations should have the ability to convince their employees that access to information goes hand in hand with a corresponding level of liability. The ability to communicate this level of personal accountability, and the willingness to continually remind employees of this rule, will make them less likely to demand unlimited access to data.

Competency to Facilitate Informal Communication about Information Security

Competency to facilitate communication between management and employees should be present at both the formal and informal levels of the organizational environment. Written policies are the most formal form of communication across the organization. Training is an integral part of formal communication, although organizations must also encourage interaction and opinion exchange on the informal level. In many organizations, formal levels of communication are in place. However, they are rarely supported by management's ability to develop informal settings that would facilitate interaction between management and employees, leading to effective understanding of the security issues (see Trompeter and Eloff, 2001). An informal level of communication—an equally important link in communication competency—is often lacking.

Communication is one of the most important means of increasing employee awareness of information security issues. Issues of information security involve more than just the manner and channels an organization chooses to use to communicate with their employees. It is also important to understand what kind of information should be communicated. The ability to provide employees with proper content, through effective channels, as often as necessary is a combination of skills and processes that constitutes what we define as a competency in internal communication.

In terms of what to communicate, employees need to know why it is important to limit access, why it is important to protect data, and what can happen when security is breached. However, one more issue requires clear and strict announcement. In addition to communicating to employees the importance of information security, it is important to inform them that they can be monitored. It is also necessary that they understand why they can be monitored.

The Competency to Monitor Adequately

The ability to track and monitor business role execution is critical to the security of systems. The process of monitoring should always be intentional and thorough. It should be unconditionally performed by competent employees able to verify the accuracy and correctness of all the procedures conducted by the monitored employee. At times it is enough for the employee to know that he/she can be monitored to minimize the risk of security breach. Proper reporting systems and transparency of the monitoring process and mechanisms for reporting suspicious activities are critical factors for achieving good security.

Monitoring should be a multilevel process. Employees who, due to their roles or external liaisons, could have interest in breaching security rules and norms (e.g., those in direct contact with clients or competition) should be monitored more closely than those who are detached from external temptations. Advantages of a good monitoring system go beyond the prevention of a security breach. Recognizing employees' behavioral patterns, understanding of problems with business processes, and potential technological flaws are some of the aspects that good monitoring can reveal (D'Antoni, 2002; O'Rourke, 2005).

These competencies affect the organization's ability to operate any particular strategy. As a result, a strategy may be infeasible if the competencies are unavailable. In such a case, the organization may choose to acquire the necessary competencies by contracting, hiring, or training. It may also compensate for missing competencies by adjusting its strategies.

For example, we will delineate two fundamentally different approaches to setting strategy: top-down, and federal. Organizational security competencies have a great deal to do with the ability to operate either strategy-setting process. For a top-down approach, centralized competencies may be sufficient for generating strategy because strategy setting at lower levels of the organization can be reviewed competently at the higher levels. Federal strategy setting, however, requires widespread competencies throughout the organization's management structures. Strategies set at lower levels of the organization may not be subject to review centrally.

TOP-DOWN STRATEGY-SETTING PROCESS

As stated previously, any security strategy process needs to be aligned with organizational challenges. It is also imperative to identify short- and long-term business goals since the security strategy needs to be in sync with the business objectives. Ultimately, good security strategy depends upon good policies and procedures. Adequacy of a good policy is determined through a complete internal analysis. The steps involved in the top-down security setting process include:

- Internal analysis and self-assessment
- Security procedure development and review
- Policy development and format
- Administration

Internal Analysis and Self-Assessment

Different names have been attached to internal analysis and self-assessment. The process is called security audits or sometimes risk assessment (Parker, 1981). The terminology has evolved to more precision. Risk assessment usually means the determination of the needs or suitability of controls, while audits are part of an assurance process to assess whether the selected controls (or the controls mandated by standards) are in place and functioning (Whitman and Mattord, 2004). At a strategic level, however, the purpose is the same—to understand the range of activities coming together to form business processes and vulnerabilities if any. A formal internal analysis and self-assessment exercise helps in reviewing the security challenges an organization might face and coordinating existing security procedures.

Internal analysis and self-assessment are usually a committee/team effort. Particular attention needs to be placed on creating a cross-functional team. This is particularly helpful in ensuring that all operating units are brought into the fold. Furthermore, it ensures that security procedures and the policy is well received by key stakeholders. The stakeholders need to be drawn from beyond the IT department. This helps in moving the emphasis from being more technocentric to organizational.

Security Procedure Development and Review

Sometimes security procedures get developed in isolation of the nature of work an organization might be involved in. This can result in misapplication of rules. This is usually a consequence of an inability to map, for instance, access to system rules with organizational hierarchies. Clearly, there is a need to have a good balance between structures, processes, and technological means of controlling. A complete assessment to this effect allows for the development and improvement of procedures.

The team working on developing procedures needs to come up with a range of alternatives. All alternatives should be circulated to stakeholder groups for evaluation and proper buy in. Based on the input, the final set of procedures should be developed. Constant interaction with stakeholder groups is essential in order to ensure integrity of the procedures.

Policy Development

In top-down strategy setting, policies are enacted by an aggregation of procedures that have been codified in a certain manner to comply with the policy. Many critical or highly sensitive security procedures are at times not included in the policy, essentially because of the public nature of the document. One of the main purposes of security policy is to act as a communication link between different members of the organization. There may not be any mandatory compliance with the policy, but it certainly acts as a guiding document for compliance.

There are different ways in which a security policy may be organized. In certain cases it may just be useful to create a separate policy for every technology or system. In other cases it may be useful to have a single comprehensive security policy covering all technologies employed and providing guidance for a range of systems. In some other cases a more modular policy may be useful. Choice of organizing various elements in a security policy is a function of the nature of the enterprise and the business need (Whitman, 2003). At a minimum, the security policy should have at least seven sections covering the following topic areas (Whitman and Mattord, 2004):

1. Statement of policy
2. Authorized access and usage of equipment
3. Prohibited usage of equipment
4. Systems management
5. Penalties for policy violations
6. Review and modifications
7. Limitations of liability

Administration

The security policy only becomes worthwhile if proper training and user awareness are undertaken. This means that organizations need to establish an education and awareness program to fulfill the purposes set out in the policy. An issue related to training is that of ongoing review of the policy. Clearly a policy is good insofar as it is up to date and remains acceptable to organizational members. For this reason, it is essential that a review and evaluation mechanism be set in place. Finally, enforcement and compliance issues need to be set in place.

Primarily, this means that the information security organization must establish owners for each element in the information security policy. Regarding authorized access and usage of equipment (item 2 in the list above), it must be very clear in the policy exactly which organizational element is responsible for providing authorized access to equipment. It must be clear what documents and records are to be maintained, and who within the organization is responsible for this maintenance. The attachment of ownership to each element of the security policy will help to ensure that the policy is properly administered and not deposited in organizational records without enforcement.

FEDERAL STRATEGY-SETTING PROCESS

A federal strategy-setting process may not be that dissimilar in organization from a top-down strategy-setting process. However, the initiation and power configuration of the process will be quite different. In general, a federal strategy-setting process will begin with lower-level committees that produce strategy components and channel all of these components as fixed strategy documents to higher-level committees in which the organization-wide strategy is assembled from these components by rationalizing the collection of federated components.

A federal organization is one in which power is disseminated across organizational units. An example would be an organization divided into divisions in which each division operates with a certain degree of autonomy. In such an organization the information security responsibilities for each division would fall under the supervision of a division information security officer.

Even in organizations with centralized control, it may be desirable to set up a federal information security organization. Such a federal organization may be desirable in a case where the security budget is inadequate to support proper organization-wide information security. The security organization can be layered over the real organization using co-opted members to whom responsibility has been assigned for information security.

In addition, it is necessary for federated organizations to maintain clear security standards within which each division and security manager will operate. These overall organizational security standards constrain the individual unit security components in such a way that these will conform with each other in order to ensure organization-wide information security. As a result, federated security strategy setting begins with establishment of organization-wide security standards.

Once the standards are established, the process for developing the security strategy within each unit is delegated to the division security managers, or the co-opted security representatives within the federal organization. Within each unit, the processes may be similar to the top-down approach in organization. In other words, the unit process would still involve at least four major elements (viz., internal analysis and self-assessment, security procedure development and review, policy development and format, and administration).

Organization-wide Security Strategy Standards

The central information security authority initiates the security strategy-setting process by developing the organizational security strategy standard. This device may be as simple as declaring that each unit in the organization must complete a strategy-setting process that includes the four major elements described in the top-down strategy approach. In such a case, the standards must provide a sufficient level of detail about the product of each of these processes such that the security across the organization meets the minimum goals.

Internal Analysis and Self-Assessment

In a federated approach, the internal analysis and self-assessment may still be a team effort. However, there will be multiple teams, each located within one of the federal units. The teams will need to be cross-functional in the sense that they must be developed from members of each function within the federal unit. The federal standard should define the minimum requirements for such an analysis, including suggested outlines and assessment documents.

Security Procedure Development and Review

Similarly, multiple teams will develop and review security procedures within each federal unit. Alternatives will be evaluated by the stakeholder groups within each unit. Each unit will also develop its final set of procedures and maintain constant interaction with its stakeholder groups. The federal standard should provide recommendations for the kinds of procedures that might emerge from this process and define the minimum set of stakeholders required to properly complete the development and review.

Policy Development

Each federal unit will develop its policies from its aggregation of procedures. The federal standard may permit each unit to develop an organization for its security policies, or it may define a required outline of sections such as that described above as the minimum seven sections and topic areas.

Administration

The administration of the information security policy within a federated organization will occur at multiple levels. Within each federated unit, the managers tasked with responsibility for security will be responsible for administering the strategy in a manner similar to that described in the top-down strategy-setting approach. However, administration of the security strategy will also occur at the central level. In addition to its responsibility for setting the information security strategy standards, the central authority will be responsible for collecting the strategy documents and reviewing them to ensure that they conform to the standard. The central authority will be responsible for reporting deviations from the standard to both the central organization and to the managers tasked with responsibility for the federated units. The central authority is also responsible for maintaining and extending the federal standard for security strategy setting.

SUMMARY AND OPEN QUESTIONS

The information security strategy process starts with an assessment of the goals for organizational information security. These goals are likely to include compliance with regulatory requirements, national and international standards, and professional practices. The goals assessment process must take into account the type of organization and include activities to align the security strategy with the strategic goals of the organization as a whole. The security goals assessment process must also take into account the type of security environment in which the organization exists. In particular, high-risk organizational environments like electronic commerce or industries operating in areas of national critical infrastructures will need more care and rigor in security strategy processes.

Once the goals of the information security strategy process are set, the products of strategy setting must be delineated. These products can include statements of vision, core values, rationale, and strategic plans. In addition, the major components of the organizational strategy should also be delineated. These components include the organization's security organizing strategy, its security operations strategy, and its security budgeting strategy. The operational strategy involves whether the organization's information security operation will be either centralized or federated and whether it is a cost center or management overhead. An organizing strategy must also be defined for information security operations. This organizing strategy will be related closely to the operational strategy. Organizing strategies include hierarchical organizational designs that respond to strategic needs to centralize control over security, and network organizational designs that respond to needs for organizational agility with regard to information security. Matrix organizational strategies respond to needs for information security portfolios such as settings involving projects.

The strategy-setting process may be organized using a product criterion or a process criterion. A product criterion would organize the strategy-setting process by grouping activities according to the end products of the process. For example, activities would include vision setting, core value determination, and planning. A process criterion would organize the strategy-setting process by grouping activities according to major components. For example, activities would include aligning security with organizational strategy, planning operational strategy, and planning security organization. The strategy-setting process can be top-down or federal. A top-down strategy-setting process would begin with a high-level committee delegating elements of the strategy to lower-level committees. A federal process would begin with lower-level committees channeling draft strategy components up to higher-level committees where strategy would be assembled by rationalizing the collection of federated components.

These strategy-setting processes are not unique to information security. Indeed most of the strategy-setting processes described above for information security follow reasonably common models that can be used for any organizational strategy setting task. This aspect of current information security strategy practice leaves many openings for new studies to improve security strategy-setting practices by developing better practices that are unique to security (see Table 2.4).

Table 2.4

Openings for New Studies in the Security Setting Process

Area	Issue	Impact
1. Security strategy and security policy	1.1 How do we distinguish the two concepts when these operate at different levels?	There are situations in which security strategy determines security policy and others where security policy determines security strategy.
	1.2 How does the security strategy-setting process differ in settings where strategies must be defined according to a set policy?	A deterministic process for creating security strategy may be applied when creativity and innovation is needed instead.
2. Quality measures for security strategy	2.1 How do we know if a newly defined security strategy is the right one for the setting?	Both good and bad security strategies, like other "best" practices, can be mindlessly replicated across organizations without critical regard.
	2.2 What strategy-setting processes are most effective in known organizational settings or conditions?	Standard processes for creating security strategies are adopted without regard for the nature of the particular organization.

Area 1. A primary issue is the distinction between security strategy and security policy. While we operated with definitions and recognized multiple levels of strategy (for example, strategies for setting policies and strategies for implementing policies), this is a source of much confusion in the literature and the principles and practice. Because security policies are so central to most organizational security operations, we need new studies that better develop the relationship between strategies and policies. We see two major issues in this area:

Issue 1.1—How do we distinguish the two concepts when these operate at different levels? Writers about security policy intertwine the two concepts, making it appear across the literature as if they were synonymous. The impact of this confusion is that it is difficult to recognize that there are situations in which security strategy determines security policy and other situations where security policy determines security strategy.

Issue 1.2—How does the security strategy-setting process differ in settings where strategies must be defined according to a set policy? If security must fit a preset framework, a deterministic process for creating security strategy may be applied. The security strategy may almost be the result of a formula in such situations. However, where there is no set policy, then security strategy may need to be determined in a way that is highly creative and innovative.

Area 2. There is very little empirical research that regards information security strategy as either a process or a product. Most information in this area is found in the practical literature as case descriptions. We need new studies that compare the information security strategy-setting processes of similar kinds of organizations in order to gain some sense of what the ideal strategy-setting processes would be for such organizations. Such studies would suggest the most successful strategy-setting processes for specific organizational situations. Similarly, we need studies of the ideal strategy products for different organizational settings. Linking such studies of security strategy-setting processes and products with organizational security compromises would help illuminate those processes and products that proved most successful in meeting organizational information security goals.

Issue 2.1—How do we know if a newly defined security strategy is the right one for the setting? There is too little research that reveals which strategies have worked and which have failed. As a result, both good and bad security strategies may be viewed and promoted as "best" practices. In the absence of better strategy-setting processes, such practices can be mindlessly replicated across organizations without critical regard.

Issue 2.2—What strategy-setting processes are most effective in known organizational settings or conditions? Following closely on the issue of our poor understanding of which strategies have succeeded and which have failed, we similarly lack research into what security strategy-setting processes have good records for determining effective security strategies. At the moment, standard processes for creating security strategies have unknown effectiveness histories, yet still must be adopted without regard for the nature of the particular organization.

While there are many open questions and issues, there is much that we do know about the processes of information security strategy. It clearly involves an assessment of the goals for organizational information security. The processes may be organized using a product criterion or a process criterion, grouping activities by the ends or the means. The goal assessment process is also important, registering the strategic goals with the reality of the organizational conditions, such as the available security competencies.

REFERENCES

Armstrong, H. 1999. A soft approach to management of information security. Ph.D. dissertation, Curtin University, Perth, Australia.

Backhouse, J., and Dhillon, G. 1996. Structures of responsibility and security of information systems. *European Journal of Information Systems,* 5, 1, 2–9.

Baskerville, R. 1995. The second order security dilemma. In W. Orlikowski, G. Walsham, M. Jones, and J. DeGross (eds.), *Information Technology and Changes in Organizational Work.* London: Chapman & Hall, pp. 239–249.

Cherry, S. 2000. DoubleClick recants on privacy issue. *IEEE Spectrum,* 37, 4, 63.

COBIT. 2005. *COBIT Overview* (available at www.isaca.org/cobit.htm, accessed on January 23, 2005).

D'Antoni, H. 2002. Defenses mount against internal threats. *InformationWeek,* 896, 86.

DeLoughry, T.J. 2000. DoubleClick takes its licks for changing privacy policy. *Internet World,* 6, 5, 20.

Dobson, J. 1991. A methodology for analyzing human and computer-related issues in secure systems. In K. Dittrich, S. Rautakivi, and J. Saari (eds.), *Computer Security and Information Integrity.* Amsterdam: Elsevier Science Publishers, pp. 151–170.

Eden, C., and Ackermann, F. 2002. A mapping framework for strategy making. In A.S. Huff and M. Jenkins (eds.), *Mapping Strategic Knowledge.* London: Sage, pp. 173–195.

Finne, T. 1996. The information security chain in a company. *Computers & Security,* 15, 4, 297–316.

Gaston, S.J. 1996. *Information Security: Strategies for Successful Management.* Toronto: Canadian Institute of Chartered Accountants.

Hale, J.C.; Landry, T.D.; and Wood, C.M. 2004. Susceptibility audits: a tool for safeguarding information assets. *Business Horizons,* 47, 3, 59–66.

Hong, K.-S.; Chi, Y.-P.; Chao, L.R.; and Tang, J.-H. 2003. An integrated system theory of information security management. *Information Management & Computer Security,* 11, 5, 243–248.

ISO/IEC 2000. *ISO/IEC 17799: Information Technology—Code of Practice for Information Security Management.* International Standard No. ISO/IEC 17799:2000(E). Geneva: International Standards Organization.

Kalfan, A.M. 2004. Information security considerations in IS/IT outsourcing projects: a descriptive case study of two sectors. *International Journal of Information Management,* 24, 1, 29–42.

Lewin, R. 1993. *Complexity: Life on the Edge of Chaos.* London: Phoenix.

McGrath, R.G.; MacMillan, I.C.; and Venkataraman, S. 1995. Defining and developing competence: a strategic process paradigm. *Strategic Management Journal,* 16, 4, 251–275.

Merriam-Webster 2001. *Collegiate Dictionary and Thesaurus.*

Mintzberg, H.; Ahlstrand, B.; and Lampel, J. 1998. *Strategy Safari: A Guided Tour through the Wilds of Strategic Management.* New York: Simon & Schuster.

O'Rourke, M. 2005. Data secured? Taking on cyber-thievery. *Risk Management,* 52, 10, 18–22.

Parker, D. 1981. *Computer Security Management.* Reston, VA: Reston Publishing.

Petersen, A. 2000. DoubleClick reverses course after privacy outcry. *Wall Street Journal,* March 3, p. B.1.

Rees, J.; Bandyopadhyay, S.; and Spafford, E.H. 2003. PFIRES: a policy framework for information security. *Communications of the ACM,* 46, 7, 101–106.

RIT [Rochester Institute of Technology]. 2004. *RIT Information Security Vision Statement,* June 2 (available at http://security.rit.edu/procedures/00_InfoSec_vision.pdf, accessed on Nov. 24, 2005).

Schlenker, B.R.; Britt, T.W.; Pennington, J.; Murphy, R.; and Doherty, K. 1994. The triangle model of responsibility. *Psychol Review,* 101, 4, 632–652.

Segev, A.; Porra, J.; and Roldan, M. 1998. Internet security and the case of Bank of America. *Communications of the ACM,* 41, 10, 81–87.

Sherwood, J. 1997. Managing security for outsourcing contracts. *Computers & Security,* 16, 7, 603–609.

Swartz, N. 2004. Survey assesses the state of information security worldwide. *Information Management Journal,* 38, 1, 16.

Thibodeau, P. 2002. DoubleClick settlement may affect corporate IT policies. *Computerworld,* 36, 15, 7.

Trompeter, C.M., and Eloff, J.H.P. 2001. A framework for implementation of socio-ethical controls in information security. *Computers & Security,* 20, 5, 384–391.

White, E.F.R., and Dhillon, G. 2005. Synthesizing information system design ideals to overcome developmental duality in securing information systems. In R.H. Sprague (ed.), *Proceedings of the 38th Annual Hawaii International Conference on System Sciences.* Los Alamitos, CA: IEEE Computer Society, pp. 186–195.

Whitman, M.E. 2003. Enemy at the gate: threats to information security. *Communications of the ACM,* 46, 8, 91–95.

Whitman, M.E., and Mattord, H.J. 2004. *Management of Information Security.* Boston: Thomsom.

CHAPTER 3

IT GOVERNANCE AND ORGANIZATIONAL DESIGN FOR SECURITY MANAGEMENT

MERRILL WARKENTIN AND ALLEN C. JOHNSTON

Abstract: *In order to achieve the goals of IS security management, each organization must establish and maintain organizational structures and governance procedures that will ensure the execution of the firm's security policies and procedures. This chapter presents the problem and the framework for ensuring that the organization's policies are implemented over time. Since many of these policies require human involvement (employee and customer actions, for example), the goals are met only if such human activities can be influenced and monitored and if positive outcomes are rewarded while negative actions are sanctioned. This is the challenge of corporate governance and IT governance. A central issue in the context of IT security governance is the degree to which IT security controls should be centralized or decentralized. This chapter utilizes a comparative case study in which IT security controls are considered within both a centralized and a decentralized IT governance environment.*

Keywords: *Centralization, Decentralization, Governance, IT Governance, Security Policy, Procedures, IT Architecture, Case Study*

The goals of information security management are obtainable only if the policies and procedures are complete, accurate, available, and eventually implemented. Organizations must be cognizant of the pitfalls that impede technology diffusion within the firm and must demonstrate this through the purposeful creation of policy. It is also critical that firms employ measures to ensure that policy is translated into effective security management practices. This is obtainable only if effective organizational designs are present and if proper information assurance procedures are followed. Additionally, stakeholder compliance requires stringent enforcement of internal controls to ensure organizational policy and procedure execution.

IT security management goals are to maintain the confidentiality, integrity, and availability of data within a system. The data should be accurate and available to the appropriate people, when they need it and in the appropriate condition. While perfect security is desirable, it is unfortunately unattainable. With this in mind, security professionals seek to provide a level of security equivalent to the value of the information they are asked to protect.

Individuals (including entrepreneurs who own small firms) are presumed to act in their own best interests, and are expected to manage and direct their personal and business affairs in ways that support their own objectives. Larger organizations are often managed by professional managers who may not share the same intrinsic motivations as the owners of those organizations. All managers should direct and control the activities of the enterprise in order to achieve the objectives of the stakeholders. For governmental organizations (agencies, etc.), the key stakeholders are citizens. For "public companies" (firms owned by those who hold publicly traded shares of

Figure 3.1 **Security Policy, Procedure, and Practice**

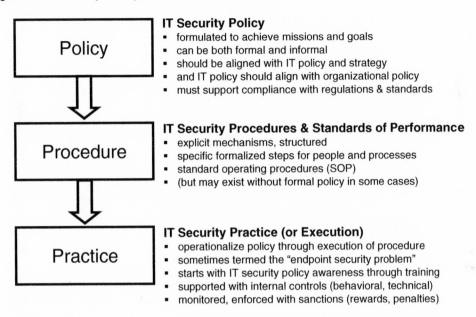

IT Security Policy
- formulated to achieve missions and goals
- can be both formal and informal
- should be aligned with IT policy and strategy
- and IT policy should align with organizational policy
- must support compliance with regulations & standards

IT Security Procedures & Standards of Performance
- explicit mechanisms, structured
- specific formalized steps for people and processes
- standard operating procedures (SOP)
- (but may exist without formal policy in some cases)

IT Security Practice (or Execution)
- operationalize policy through execution of procedure
- sometimes termed the "endpoint security problem"
- starts with IT security policy awareness through training
- supported with internal controls (behavioral, technical)
- monitored, enforced with sanctions (rewards, penalties)

stock), the primary stakeholders are the shareholders. Smaller ("closely held") companies may also have a separation between the owners of the firm and its managers.

An organization's structure and governance procedures enable it to address the issues of responsibility, accountability, and coordination toward the achievement of its purpose and goals. Organizations are continually evolving to enhance their position within their business domain. These evolutions typically involve changes in governance and organizational design, and are reflected in the IT component of the organization. However, one objective is constant: to protect the information assets of the organization. In this context, the roles of IT governance and organization design toward the fulfillment of the security management commitment are presented and discussed.

POLICIES–PROCEDURES–PRACTICE

The policies and procedures of a firm dictate the posture the firm will take in protecting its information assets. However, success in this quest is the direct result of how well these policies and procedures are translated into actions. Ultimately, if managers, developers, and users are not aware of existing policy and procedures, they will not execute them. Therefore, an emphasis should be placed on the establishment of an enterprise training program with verifiable training protocols so that personnel are made fully aware of such policies and procedures in order that they can be put into practice on a daily basis (see Figure 3.1).

ORGANIZATIONAL STRUCTURE AND DESIGN

A sole proprietor "does it all," but as organizations grow, it becomes necessary to formulate and implement a structure capable of coordinating the activities of the units so that they act in concert toward achieving the organization's mission. The organization design comprises several key principles, including (1) division of labor (departmentalization and specialization), (2) command structure (line of command, unitary command), (3) authority and responsibility relationships (line, staff, power), and (4) spans of control (levels of control, degree of centralization).

It is imperative that the organizational structure formalize the roles and reporting relationships between employees at different positions in the organization. The design process must be dynamic as the organization continually redefines its goals and strategies, as the organization's environment changes, and as changes in technology facilitate modifications in the organizational structure. Indeed, one of the most monumental impacts of technology over the past two decades is the "flattening" of most large organizations and the elimination of several layers of middle management. IT has been attributed as an enabler of this lean organizational form by increasing span of control and communications provided by modern networked computer systems.

Some of the key questions to be answered include the following. Who makes the decisions and how many decision makers are there (for each unit and at each level)? How should the command structure be partitioned, and how should tasks be assigned? What are the formal communications structures between decision-making individuals and groups?

The process of organizational design often involves making determinations between competing design forms where there may be trade-offs between efficiency, flexibility, accountability, and other factors (Straub, 1988). Most employees are more motivated (and therefore more effective) if they have more control ("responsibility with authority") over their work. If they are able to react to changes in their environment without seeking approval or waiting for oversight, they can quickly satisfy customer demand or respond to competitive pressures. However, the lack of control may open the organization to certain risks. For example, unencumbered employees, motivated by localized priorities, may make decisions that have a positive short-term benefit on the departmental level, but a negative long-term impact on the organization. Organizations must seek a balance between these extremes of "span of control" and find that "sweet spot" with maximum benefits for the enterprise.

In addition, the organization should be structured so that duplication of effort is eliminated. All special or scarce skills should be effectively utilized and shared; sometimes this entails distributing these resources across the organization. Employees must also be given the opportunity to develop their skills and advance in their positions. To this end, employees must be provided with the necessary information to maintain a global perspective. Most employees want to feel they have an opportunity to "work their way up the ladder." Motivation and morale are crucial to the organization's success, and are highly influenced by the structure of the enterprise. Who evaluates their work? How is their work activity connected to that of other individuals? How much control do they have over their work product? Is cooperation and coordination supported by the organization's structure?

Accountability is an important consideration for all organizational members (as it is in the IS security arena). Each member's assigned responsibilities must not conflict with or duplicate the duties of any other position. Each member must have sufficient decision-making authority and control to affect the parameters for which he or she will be measured. Supervisory structure is one of the most crucial elements of an organizational design. Managers must have a sufficiently large span of control to enable them to coordinate the "big picture" within their departments, rather than isolated silos independent of other units. But the span of control can also easily be too large, leading to a lack of responsiveness.

Organizational structure encompasses the formal structure embodied in the organizational chart (reporting hierarchy, etc.) as well as the informal organization. Furthermore, the structure includes the *processes* that combine people into workgroups and teams, teams into departments, and departments into divisions as work flows within the organization and between the organization and its external constituents (customers, suppliers, regulators, competitors, partners, etc.). The structure determines who does what and how individuals collaborate to get the work completed. Within the context of IT security, the organizational structure takes on added importance as additional layers of hierarchical complexity are embedded within the organization in the form of user access privileges. Often the hierarchical reporting structure breaks down when translated into the rights assigned to users in support of their roles. This is especially true for information systems that maintain sensitive information at various levels of confidentiality throughout the system. It is not uncommon in these situations for members of the same team to have different user privileges in terms of the information they are able to access within the system. Simply stated, a digital user hierarchy does not necessarily match a human management hierarchy.

The two primary structures for large modern organizations are often termed "functional" and "product" structures. Functional structures have departments oriented by function—finance, accounting, marketing, production, human resources, IT, and so on. They have the advantage of efficiency (less duplication of activities) and professionalism (technical specialization and expertise), but the members of each functional area have a narrow perspective with less attention to the needs of each product area and its customers and markets. It is also difficult to coordinate the activities of such individuals.

On the other hand, the "product" structure, also known as "divisional organization," is divided by output or product lines. A conglomerate may have a division for its aerospace products, another for its consumer electronics, and another for its financing (lending) operations. (This is how GE and many other organizations are essentially organized.) This improves decision making and forces greater accountability for specific performance objectives. It also increases the coordination of functions, because the managers of the functions report to a divisional manager (e.g., director of Industrial Soaps Division). On the other hand, this structure is less efficient (duplicated activities) and may foster rivalry among divisions that is not always healthy.

A third organizational form is the matrix organizational structure, in which the managers of functions within each division also have a "dotted line" reporting relationship with their functional managers—essentially they have at least two bosses, the functional manager and a project manager, and spend a generous portion of time negotiating their responsibilities. Assuming a grid-like formation, the matrix organizational structure can provide superior performance compared with traditional hierarchical structures if its members can leverage the natural conflict of interests between the functional manager's desire for quality and the project manager's interest in time and service. The focus of this structural form is to distribute expertise to the parts of the organization that need them most (project teams) at the right time. A matrix structure can facilitate innovation and efficiency, but can also create conflict because of its reduced clarity of authority.

GOVERNANCE

Governance encompasses activities that ensure that the organization's plans are executed and its policies are implemented. *Planning* leads to *strategies* that are embodied in *policies* that are translated into *procedures,* which are executed and enforced through the *governance* process. One might say that governance is the method of ensuring that policies and procedures are put into practice.

Enterprise governance is the overall framework, which can be decomposed into corporate governance (or "conformance") and business governance (or "performance"). The International Federation of Accountants (IFAC) defines enterprise governance as "the set of responsibilities and practices exercised by the board and executive management with the goal of providing strategic direction, ensuring that objectives are achieved, ascertaining that risks are managed appropriately and verifying that the organization's resources are used responsibly" (CIMA/IFAC, 2004).

The *corporate governance structure* is the organizational design that assigns rights and responsibilities to various players, such as the board of directors, managers, and shareholders. It provides guidance for developing reporting relationships, internal controls, checks and balances, and other means to ensure that the corporation's missions are ultimately fulfilled. The fundamental concerns of corporate governance are to (1) ensure that conditions apply whereby a firm's directors and managers act in the interests of the firm and its shareholders, and (2) ensure the means are in place whereby managers are held accountable to investors for the use of assets. The aim of corporate governance is to (1) describe the rules and procedures for making decisions on corporate affairs, (2) provide the structure through which the corporate objectives are set, (3) provide a means of achieving the set objectives, (4) monitor the corporate performance against the set objectives, and (5) establish procedures to reduce or eliminate deviations from the path toward the set objectives, including sanctions for employees who do not support the process.

Corporate governance consists of any laws that may apply to the formulation of corporate bodies, the official bylaws established by the corporate body, its organizational structure or design, and even its standard operating procedures (SOP) and corporate culture, to the extent that they support the purposes of corporate governance.

Organizations also implement internal controls and procedures to ensure that risk (business risk, legal risk, market risk, security risk, etc.) is managed and that resources are utilized efficiently and effectively in the pursuit of the organization's mission and strategies. This process is sometimes termed *business governance* and refers to "performance" rather than "conformance." By supporting the process of value creation, IT systems typically contribute to performance, though recent attention has shifted toward IT's role in conformance. IT can become a central guarantor of accountability. Recent legislation (discussed below) is aimed at ensuring that electronic record-keeping supports the goals of conformance and reduces the chances that recent business scandals (Brand and Boonen, 2004) will be repeated.

IT Governance

To support the goals of corporate governance, there must be a formalized process to guide the acquisition, management, and utilization of all strategic corporate assets, including information resources. *IT governance describes the distribution of IT decision-making responsibilities within the firm and focuses on the procedures and practices necessary to create and support strategic IT decisions* (see Table 3.1).

The IT Governance Institute (2003) states that the purpose of IT governance is to direct IT endeavors and to ensure that IT's performance meets the following objectives: strategic alignment, value delivery, risk management, and performance measurement. Risk management ensures the appropriate management of IT-related risks, including the identification and implementation of appropriate IT security measures. Activity and performance monitoring and measurement are critical to ensure that objectives are realized, but require feedback loops and positive measures to proactively address deviation from goals.

The IT Governance Institute (www.itgi.org) has established the Control Objectives for Information and related Technology (COBIT) to facilitate conducting all audits. This methodology is especially helpful in establishing the scope and plan for IT audits, and can guide managers in identifying appropriate controls and selecting effective infrastructure processes. This methodology of IT governance and control can also aid in maintaining compliance with the Sarbanes-Oxley Act and other applicable

Table 3.1

IT Governance and Corporate Governance Resources

1.	IT Governance Institute	www.itgi.org
2.	Encyclopedia about Corporate Governance	www.encycogov.com
3.	Corporate Governance Network	www.corpgov.net
4.	International Corporate Governance Network	www.icgn.org
5.	European Corporate Governance Institute	www.ecgi.org
6.	World Bank Group	www.worldbank.org/wbi/governance

legislation. It can help a firm "obtain benchmarks for assessing automated controls embedded in key business processes and assess the control activities performed by the company's application support team." Furthermore, it is designed to help ensure alignment between technology investments and business strategies. (For an expanded discussion of COBIT, see Dhillon and Mishra [2006].)

IT Architecture

IT governance can be effective only if the enterprise organizes its information technology (hardware, software, procedures) in a manner consistent with its organizational and technical requirements. There are numerous formalized approaches to establishing an appropriate configuration for the organization's information resources. Such configurations are termed "IT architecture" and are intended to efficiently and effectively support IT governance mandates as articulated in policy and procedure and enacted in practice.

Important considerations for IT managers in contemplating the appropriate IT architecture for their organization are the characteristics of the user component of the system. It is critical that IT managers possess a familiarity with the experience levels, technical proficiencies, or any other traits of the users within their organization that may predicate their potential for success. For example, highly decentralized systems require a more substantial commitment to and proficiency of system operations by the user community. By understanding their users' limitations, effective managers will be able to align talent and technology in a manner conducive to success.

Within the U.S. federal government, the Clinger-Cohen Act of 1996 (40 USC 1401[3]), also known as the Information Technology Management Reform Act (ITMRA), was intended, among its many other purposes, to "reform . . . information technology management of the Federal Government." The ITMRA defines information technology as "computers, ancillary equipment, software, firmware and similar procedures, services (including support services), and related resources." The act defines information technology architecture (ITA) as "an integrated framework for evolving or maintaining existing information technology and acquiring new information technology to achieve the agency's strategic goals and information resources management goals."

Section 5125(b) of the act further assigns each agency's chief information officer (CIO) the responsibility of "developing, maintaining, and facilitating the implementation of a sound and integrated information technology architecture." Furthermore, the U.S. White House Office of Management and Budget (OMB) has issued a memorandum (OMB-M-97–16) stating that

> for the purpose of conforming to the requirements of ITMRA, a complete ITA is the documentation of the relationships among business and management processes and information technology that ensure:

Exhibit 3.1

Enterprise Architect Role

The role of the enterprise architect is much like that of a city planner. Too often, in a city, buildings are constructed using completely independent designs, infrastructure is slapped together over time, and attempts to build comprehensive plans for coherent growth are stymied by competing goals and unmanageable egos. In the same way, business units in organizations of any size often pursue their own individual business and technology goals, creating separate infrastructures that defy attempts to "federate" the organization's business and computing resources.

Without a clear understanding of critical business requirements, any attempt to articulate strategic IT plans is doomed. That's why, first and foremost, an enterprise architecture provides a structure for defining business goals and processes. Once that "business architecture" is explicitly stated and widely agreed on, IT can then begin the task of defining the information needed to support business requirements, and the IT infrastructure needed to support the creation and management of that information.

Source: Bolles, 2004.

- alignment of the requirements for information systems . . . with the processes that support the agency's missions;
- adequate interoperability, redundancy, and security of information systems; and
- the application and maintenance of a collection of standards (including technical standards) by which the agency evaluates and acquires new systems.

Within this framework, the OMB guides each agency to identify and specify the organizational level to which each "sub-architecture" will be addressed (business processes, information flows, applications, data descriptions, and technology infrastructure).

To develop an effective enterprise architecture, the CIO must have a clear picture of the current state, a vision for the future, and a road map for getting there. The enterprise architecture creates a blueprint that includes a set of standards toward which the organization migrates, and it introduces processes and controls to ensure that all new technologies are linked to a specific business requirement (see Exhibit 3.1).

The Institute of Electrical and Electronic Engineers (IEEE) defines an architecture as "the structure of the components, their relationships, and the principles and guidelines governing their design and evolution over time." In building construction, the blueprint establishes the design, and the building is the actual embodiment of that design. In IT, the architecture establishes the design of the infrastructure, whereas the actual hardware and software installation is the embodiment of that design.

INFORMATION SYSTEMS CENTRALIZATION AND DECENTRALIZATION

Regardless of specific organizational function, there are trade-offs in terms of the degree of centralized managerial control. For instance, functions such as supply chain management and purchasing are heavily tied to economies of scale, and as such are generally more efficiently operated if highly centralized. Functions such as customer support, on the other hand, may operate more effectively and efficiently if decentralized. However, most functions exhibit some level of trade-offs between

Table 3.2

Features of Governance Structures

Feature	Centralized governance	Decentralized governance
Acquisition/control decisions	Single business unit	All business units
Primary concerns	Control, efficiency, and economy	Response times
Chief advantage	Leveraging established technology and vendors	Flexibility and empowerment
Chief disadvantage	Slower to respond	Conflicts and policy clashes
Values	Uniformity and interoperability	Reliability and ownership
Initial costs	Higher	Lower

highly centralized and highly decentralized control. Information systems or IT functions are also subject to this continuum.

A firm's information systems (IS) will include hardware (such as storage servers), software components (application servers, etc.), data resources (often maintained in data servers), telecommunications, and personnel that build and maintain the system. These resources may be highly centralized in one IT department, highly decentralized (in the control of all the organization's departments), or somewhere along the continuum between the two extremes. One of the most fundamental characteristics of a firm's IT architecture or structure is the degree to which its IS is centralized or decentralized. A key role of IT managers is determining the IT architecture for the organization's information system, and one of the most important aspects of the architecture is the degree of centralization. The focus of this chapter is primarily on control and decision-making centralization, rather than on the physical location of IT assets. Table 3.2 provides a summary of the comparison of the features in centralized and decentralized governance discussed below.

Centralized Information Systems

Within centralized information systems, information resources and decisions concerning their acquisition and control are the responsibility of one particular business unit that provides IT services to the whole firm. The primary concerns of a centralized approach are of control, efficiency, and economy. While some centralized IS have historically been centralized, others have evolved for various reasons, such as cost savings resulting from the consolidation of an organization's IS, to one particular location.

The chief advantage of centralized systems is centralized control through the leveraging of established technology and vendors (Kroenke and Hatch, 1994). Hardware and software standards facilitate economies of time and money in purchasing, installation, and support, and enable greater interoperability of systems and sharing of data between divisions and departments. ERP and other enterprise-class applications require seamless intraorganizational data exchange. This uniformity is built on a formal assessment of technology requirements and a professional evaluation of various technology choices, resulting in lower technical risks. Approved system components will typically function together more easily, with few surprising system compatibility issues. Centralized IT departments are typically staffed by highly trained and qualified IT professionals who employ structured systems design and maintenance procedures, leading to highly reliable systems. Professional IT managers often excel at selecting superior IT staff members.

Centralization also enables efficiency gains, which include reduced duplication of effort, resources, and expertise. Savings are realized through joint purchasing procedures and sharing of system resources (such as storage solutions, output devices, etc.). Further efficiencies are realized from the enterprise-wide administration of contracts and service agreements, licenses, and asset management. Training costs can be minimized when the IT staff can specialize in a small set of hardware and software components. Planning is easier and IT alignment can be more easily accomplished when all IT resources are under one group's control. An organization can more easily afford key niche IT professionals with specialized skills within a large IT division than if IT staff is dispersed throughout the enterprise and has smaller budgets.

It should be noted, however, that centralized systems may entail an initial cost disadvantage (Kroenke and Hatch, 1994). Considering the high salaries of systems professionals, the added bureaucracy, and the inflexibility of such systems, it is not difficult to foresee initial costs escalation (Robson, 1997). Because of their propensity to command large budgets, centralized centers may be perceived within the organization as cost centers (rather than profit centers). Centralized operations, unlike decentralized systems where each business unit has its own autonomous system for local tasks, may also slow various tasks (Robson, 1997). Autonomy to perform IT-related functions is synonymous with decision-making authority and can provide expedited responses to pressing matters. Reliance on single central components (servers, etc.) may increase the vulnerability of the entire system, should any of those central components fail. Furthermore, central systems are isolated from customers and real business concerns, leading to a lack of responsiveness and personal attention to individual groups. Relationships between the centralized support unit and other business units within the same organization become more formalized and less flexible. Any time decision-making authority is taken away from the departments and given to the organization, disparities between the goals of decision-making activities and their resultant outcomes may occur. This is because the knowledge of the unique requirements of the departmental or individual elements is either absent or undervalued.

Decentralized Information Systems

At the opposite end of the continuum, decentralized systems allow individual units the autonomy to manage their own IT resources without regard to other units. The primary advantages of the decentralized approach are the added flexibility and empowerment of individual business units. As a result, response times to business demands are often faster. Additionally, the proximity to the users and their actual information requirements can lead to closer fit, and the added involvement of end users with system development can lead to superior systems designs.

For decentralized information systems, the initials costs are relatively minimal (Kroenke and Hatch, 1994), as is the ease at which the system components can be customized and scaled to fit the needs of the individual departments. Furthermore, there is increased autonomy (Hodgkinson, 1996), leading to increased flexibility and responsiveness. This enables far greater motivation and involvement of users as they perceive a sense of ownership (Robson, 1997). The redundancy of multiple computer systems may increase the reliability of the entire system—if one component fails, others may fill the gap. Finally, a decentralized approach reduces the conflicts that may arise when departments must compete for centralized IT resources.

For organizations consisting of highly diverse business units that operate in very different marketplaces with very different business requirements, decentralized IT management is clearly more appropriate. If each unit is subject to different regulations, competitive pressures, and technology environments, then a centralized system may severely limit each unit's effectiveness. But a decentralized approach (which can still achieve information sharing through networking) will allow each unit to react to its unique environment.

Decentralized systems typically have increased accountability, motivation, and management responsiveness (Hodgkinson, 1996) over centralized systems because the locus of control is closer to the point of impact. However, increased understanding and customer focus is not without its costs. A lack of centralized control can lead to conflicts and policy clashes. Sourcing from multiple vendors can certainly create incompatible systems, and inefficiencies can result from a high degree of duplication of resources, effort, and expertise. Additionally, the autonomous actions of the individual units (and perhaps the users within the units) can have disastrous results if the motivation or efficacy for compliance with the policies and procedures of the organization is missing. In other words, the facilitation of autonomy through decentralized managerial control may present a scenario in which increased decision-making authority and IT support activities are necessitated, but the desire or expertise necessary to adequately fulfill the requirements is lacking.

IT Security Management Centralization

For most information assurance mechanisms, the manner in which they are deployed and managed is consistent with the preferred level of centralization. For example, firewall protection may be administered at an enterprise level by a single administrator or unit within the firm. It may also be administered in a decentralized manner through the use of individually operated personal firewall solutions. The latter may be appropriate for environments characterized by a highly autonomous end-user community. Anti-virus protection software is another example of a security technology that can be deployed and managed in either a centralized or decentralized manner. While most organizations would probably choose to integrate anti-virus protection into their enterprise-level protection strategies, it is possible to deploy anti-virus protection at the end-user level. In fact, for many organizations that allow mobile computing or remote connectivity, reliance on end users to appropriately manage an anti-virus solution is commonplace. Many other end point security solutions, such as anti-spyware protection, have yet to mature to the status of an enterprise level solution and share a similar fate.

At this time, it is difficult to argue against the use of a centralized IT security management strategy for providing the most effective protection for an organization. When considered from the standpoint of prevention, detection, and remediation, it could be argued that each of these lines of defense could be addressed more immediately and precisely at the individual level. Unfortunately, there are no definitive answers to this problem because of the element of the human condition and its associated complexities. While many solutions may appear on the surface to be best suited for enterprise-level management, issues of culture, competency, and/or politics may force individual-level management.

The following case study provides insight into the outcomes associated with malware attacks on two distinct IT security management strategies. Within this analysis is evidence of the human condition's impact on the rationale for IT security management strategies.

THE CASE OF "TECHUNIT" VERSUS "MEDUNIT"

In an analysis of two organizational units with very different organizational structures, the authors have assessed the impact of centralization on the units' ability to prevent and address the threat posed by two specific malware incidents.[1] This case (Johnston et al., 2004) will help elucidate the trade-offs between highly centralized and highly decentralized information system management functions.

Released on August 11, 2003, W32.Blaster.Worm (Blaster) quickly infiltrated hundreds of thousands of unprotected networks and infected unpatched systems running the Windows 2000 and Windows XP versions of Microsoft's operating system. Only eight days later the mass-mailing worm W32.Sobig.F@mm (Sobig.F) was launched. As the worms propagated on the Internet, many networks experienced extreme latency and inoperable e-mail systems (Jaikumar, 2003). The nature of the worms, as well as the close proximity of the release dates, required timely and careful attention by individuals responsible for information technology (IT) security. On a global scale, these proliferations of malicious code caused significant damage to information systems environments. Damage estimates were in the billions of U.S. dollars only days after the initial release of the worms (Bekker, 2003).

In the aftermath of any security crisis, steps are taken to guard against repeated aggression of a similar form. By taking a broad perspective of the general threat malicious codes pose to IT, patterns of security management strategy emerge that have roots in organizational design. This study explores the impact of malicious code on two distinct IT security management cultures. Specifically, we examine the security threat created by Blaster and Sobig.F within a functional business unit (FBU) with a centralized approach to IT security management and an FBU with a decentralized approach. These particular worms were selected due to their large impact, national exposure, and timeliness to the study. Following a detailed presentation of the cases, comparisons are made that articulate the successes and failures of these FBUs in the prevention, detection, and remediation of the worm activity. Additionally, this study provides insight into the unique challenges imposed by a particular management philosophy on IT security practices. By examining instances of extremes, we can observe the environments and identify relevant variables in order to understand of the impact of Blaster and Sobig.F on IT security management practices.

Background

Advances in IT technologies allow managers to remain flexible in tailoring their organizational design to fit the needs of the business (Walker, 1993). While dealing with complex and dynamic business environments is a primary activity for organizational management (Milliken, 1987), effectively organizing the IT component within an organization is also a major concern (Brown and Magill, 1994; Sambamurthy and Zmud, 2000; Watson and Brancheau, 1991). Sambamurthy and Zmud (2000) describe enterprise-wide economies and efficiencies, localized business needs, and opportunities and challenges as the typical forces that drive the selection of an IT support design. The prevailing corporate governance architecture, the capabilities of the central IT unit in serving its clients, and the ability and willingness of the clients to participate in self-supported IT activities are also factors that influence the selection of an IT support design (Brown and Bostrom, 1994; Sambamurthy and Zmud, 1999; Sambamurthy and Zmud, 2000).

Prior research efforts point to a trend in which firms are centralizing technology management efforts while simultaneously decentralizing technology usage management (Allen and Boynton, 1991; Brown and Bostrom, 1994; Sambamurthy and Zmud, 2000; Zmud, 1984). Referred to as a "federal governance architecture," this form of IT design is a compromise between a completely centralized design and a completely decentralized structure. A centralized IT environment is one in which the locus of responsibility rests on a central IT unit, while a completely decentralized IT environment is one in which the locus of responsibility is with a business unit (Brown and Bostrom,

1994). Clearly, the federal governance architecture can be characterized as an IT environment that requires a more technically active end-user community.

As trends in organizational design have evolved from centralized to more decentralized environments, such as the federal governance design, the changes have been reflected in IT (Mukherji, 2002). Benefits of decentralization include improving response time, increasing effectiveness, and flattening of the organization in an effort to accommodate employee empowerment initiatives (Walker, 1993). Furthermore, such management structures have been found to be more conducive to successfully dealing with rapidly changing environments (Mukherji, 2002). However, with an increasing emphasis on IT security management in response to the prospect of a rapidly changing threat milieu, the ultimate success of a decentralized IT structure is unclear.

It could be expected that a centralized approach to IT security management is more effective. However, given the argument for adequate security practices, a more decentralized approach may fulfill the requirements for security as deemed necessary. A primary goal of any IT security manager is to establish a computing environment that has an adequate level of confidentiality, integrity, and availability of resources (Pfleeger and Pfleeger, 2002). Because complete security is unobtainable, the concept of adequacy is significant. Conventional security practice dictates that security professionals must allocate only the resources required for protection consistent with the value of the systems and data to be protected (Pfleeger and Pfleeger, 2002). IT managers must assess current and potential vulnerabilities, threats, countermeasures, and acceptable risk in order to promote an acceptable level of security for their computing environment. In a decentralized security management environment, such responsibility rests more heavily on the shoulders of the end user. Unfortunately, user attitudes toward self-managed computer security are typically not consistent across an entire user community (Delio, 2003; Monds and Wang, 2003). This inconsistency will ultimately impair efforts to thwart an instance of malicious activity, as some users are unaware or misinformed of or disinterested in fulfilling their IT obligations.

As threats evolve, security management practices must evolve as well. This is complicated in that IT professionals, while frequently aware of the intrinsic quality of IT security, are often oblivious of the threats posed to their computer resources (Loch et al., 1992; Whitman, 2003). Users are even less cognizant than IT professionals (Delio, 2003). The difficulty of threat assessment is amplified by an ever-changing threat landscape (Landwehr and Goldschlag, 1997). Whitman (2003) identifies deliberate software attacks, of which malicious code is included, as the most significant threat, with technical software failures or errors ranked second. These findings are significant in the study of Blaster and Sobig.F worm security management because of the nature by which the worms propagate.

Also known as W32/Lovesan.worm.a or simply Lovesan, Blaster exploits the DCOM RPC vulnerability in Windows 2000 and XP machines via TCP port 135. Blaster affects those systems by downloading and executing msblast.exe. The worm causes severe instability that is difficult to trace because of the nature of the alert message (Delio, 2003). Primarily, the Blaster worm allows the malicious hacker remote access to the infected system. The worm also makes it difficult for the system administrator to patch the operating system by performing denial of service (DoS) attacks against the Microsoft Windows Update web server. Sobig.F is a mass-mailing worm that propagates itself through e-mail message delivery to all addresses found in files with certain extensions, such as .htm, .txt, .dbx, and .eml. Sobig.F's primary purpose is to overwhelm networks and e-mail systems with massive amounts of spam message traffic.

The identification of threats such as Blaster and Sobig.F is only one part of a holistic IT security management practice. Another aspect of IT security management involves the timely evaluation of vulnerabilities in relation to the threats (Landwehr and Goldschlag, 1997). This assessment should involve both known and potential vulnerabilities based on information obtained from trusted security response organizations (Landwehr and Goldschlag, 1997). If a vulnerability is discovered, the associated risk must be evaluated. For each environment, risk assessment takes on a unique significance. Risk is directly proportional to the value of the exposed resource. Any response to the threat should reflect a commensurate level of risk. Unfortunately, reactions to risks associated with malicious code are generally reactive rather than proactive (Loch et al., 1992), thereby creating urgencies that IT departments struggle to overcome.

Design and Methodology

The researchers chose a qualitative approach to the study given the need to explore and describe the complexities of organizational responses to the worms. Marshall and Rossman (1989) laud the applicability of such an approach since it "stresses the importance of context, setting, and subjects' frame of reference" (p. 46). This study delves into the details of a particular situation facing contrasting organizational environments.

Specifically, interviews with key informants were used as the data collection technique within the case study strategy. Both case study subjects are functional business units at a large, public university located in the southeastern United States. One of the functional business units employs a centralized approach to IT security management. For the purposes of this study, we will refer to this entity as "TechUnit" or FBU #1. The other functional business unit, referred to as "MedUnit" or FBU #2, utilizes a decentralized approach to IT security management.

Within each FBU, three IT security management personnel were interviewed. Each interviewee represents a different level of management. In both cases, hour-long interview sessions were held with the director of IT, a network manager, and a systems analyst.

TechUnit can be characterized as a centralized organization both in terms of its human resource structure as well as its IT environment (see Figure 3.2). Described as having a single point of control for decision making, centralized organizations such as the TechUnit often pattern their IT support after their management hierarchy. The TechUnit is governed by an executive board that consists of senior officials of the university as well as influential members of the research community. This board is ultimately responsible for the direction and success of the TechUnit as an entirety. Within the TechUnit, there are five independent research units that have unique research agendas and funding sources. In support of the research units is an administrative office that fulfills any business and accounting requirements. IT support is provided by a group of seven systems analysts under the direction of a senior systems analyst who also oversees the administrative office.

IT support for the organization is reflective of the centralized organizational management support structure in that IT personnel maintain decision-making responsibilities with minimal input from the end-user community. This responsibility includes anything from decisions related to new technology implementations to the creation of computing resource usage policies.

From a purely technical standpoint, the computing resources at TechUnit are maintained in such a manner as to minimize reliance on behavioral controls. Even though their policies and procedures are carefully crafted and frequently articulated to the users, the majority of the controls are technical. For example, policy dictates that a user must follow a prescribed formula for password creation and maintenance. The policy restricts the use of dictionary words and character or numerical sequential strings as well as passwords of less than eight characters. However, instead of relying on users to comply with the written policy, technical controls in the form of scripts are in place to force compliance. These technical controls are reflective of the written policies and indicative of the centralized nature of the IT environment in that the goal is to minimize end-user autonomy.

Figure 3.2   **Tech Unit Organizational Structure**

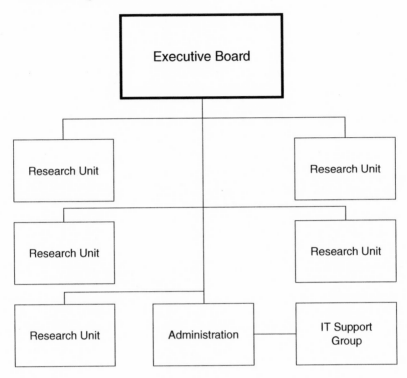

Findings of Case Study

After evaluating the interview data, the following findings were identified. Within FBU #1 (TechUnit), all new employees are asked to read IT orientation (policies) and to participate in specific IT training programs. A committee collectively formulates strict policies with regard to many aspects of IT management and use. There is a culture of IT control in which new employees are expected to work within a structure, which is consistent with their background and experience. (They generally understand advantages of centralized control.) Users understand and expect a formalized approach to IT management. Most are career professionals (faculty or full-time research staff) with a long-term relationship with the organizational unit, leading to greater loyalty and commitment. The IT manager (who is well compensated) reports to (and is evaluated by) a committee of tech-savvy individuals with engineering and science backgrounds. Functionally, aside from Internet connectivity, TechUnit does not use the organization-wide IT services for any features—they even operate their own DNS server and e-mail server.

An interesting event provides an example of the occasional breakdown in the unit's internal controls and of the redundancy that prevents threats from causing serious damage. An important guest was allowed to bring in a laptop without the inconvenience of the traditional virus screening. But that laptop contained a worm, which spread to other resources in the network. However, the external perimeter controls are backed up by additional server controls and protections, which prevented the worm from causing further damage. Additionally, the infected laptop was identified through network monitoring and appropriately patched. Had this incident occurred within

MedUnit's environment, there would have been no possibility for determining the source of the infection.

Ideally, behavioral controls will work in harmony with technical controls. Traditionally articulated in policy and detailed in procedure, behavioral controls are the first line of defense against inappropriate activity. They define the boundaries for practice and are reinforced by technical controls when possible. However, behavioral controls may not be supported by technical controls due to resource constraints, governing dynamics, inadequate technologies, and the like. Organizational security is ultimately ensured through a combination of behavioral and technical controls.

Within FBU #2 (MedUnit), there is a system of *ad hoc* IT administration. Individual users primarily address their own technical issues, if possible. Larger issues are addressed as they arise; IT support staff "put out fires" as they occur. There are few proactive processes to deflect and block various security threats. The unit has no official policies regarding security procedures; new employees are not required to undergo IT-related training and orientation. The unit uses the organization-wide IT services for e-mail and various other IT functions, but is not influenced heavily by organizational-level IT planning, standards, or policy. The IT manager at MedUnit reports to single administrator with no tech background, rather than to a tech-savvy committee, as in TechUnit.

MedUnit does not have a culture of IT control. Users have no expectation that they must conform to strict usage policies. New members of the unit enter with expectations that they can control their own systems, and are also responsible for their own IT security, including software installation and management, virus scanning, spam and spyware control, data backup, and so forth.

MedUnit's user base is diverse and includes hundreds of individuals who bring their own computers into the organization during their four-year involvement. These computers are supported by the unit's IT staff. Because of the high turnover, the unit is more dynamic and less consistent, so there is less organizational commitment and loyalty.

Regardless of whether IT security management practices are centralized or decentralized, the mechanisms by which assurance is gained are similar. However, the manner in which each protection mechanism is implemented is dependent upon the particular IT security management philosophy. Whitman's study (2003) includes a discussion and ranking of protection mechanisms employed by IT executive respondents. Adapting this ranking of protection mechanisms, we can present a tabular representation (Table 3.3) of the manner in which various protection mechanisms are deployed within the two functional business units.

TechUnit epitomizes the concept of centralized IT security management. As described in Table 3.3, TechUnit maintains a centralized approach to the deployment of the various protection mechanisms. From the provision of services in support of end-user computing to the physical infrastructure and security controls, TechUnit promotes a centralized IT security management design.

From the interviews with TechUnit's IT personnel, it is clear that they maintain a consistent opinion as to the role of IT within their organization. All three interviewees described the role of IT as an instrument for enabling research through the support of facilities, computing resources, and publishing. As stated by TechUnit's IT director, "The staff provides a wide variety of services to the user community. [The support] could be as simple as a user not knowing how to log on to a system to change their password, to something much more complex such as trying to debug a parallel FORTRAN application or trying to run an application on one of our computational servers, or to evaluate new software that might enable [the user] to perform their research mission."

TechUnit's IT personnel are physically located in the same facility as the user community. This deployment strategy is a requirement for the desired end-user computing support efforts. As dictated in policy and strictly adhered to in procedure, TechUnit's end users are completely

Table 3.3

Categories of Threats to Information Systems

Protection mechanism	"TechUnit" (centralized)	"MedUnit" (decentralized)
Password	The centralized password management policy requires end users to maintain a single user ID and password for access to all systems. Additionally, end users are required to adhere to specific password standards.	The decentralized password management approach allows users to establish their own unique password schemes. There are no specific requirements.
Media backup	IT management personnel are solely responsible for initiating and monitoring all data redundancy procedures.	IT personnel, as well as end users, actively participate in media backup efforts.
Virus protection software	Anti-virus activities are initiated and supported for all end user and computational systems by IT personnel only.	IT personnel, as well as end users, actively participate in anti-virus efforts.
Employee education	Formal training programs such as workshops and Intranet support webs are developed and implemented by IT personnel only.	End users are responsible for handling their specific training requirements.
Audit procedures	IT personnel monitor all relevant system and network logs.	End users are asked to monitor their respective systems for inappropriate activity.
Consistent security policy	IT personnel establish security policy for the entire TechUnit.	End users are instrumental in the establishment of security policy. Each unit within MedUnit may have its own security policy.
Firewall	IT personnel maintain a single firewall for the entire TechUnit.	End users are asked to maintain personal firewalls for their respective systems.
Monitor computer usage	IT personnel are solely responsible for monitoring computer usage and resource allocation.	End users may monitor computer usage for their respective systems.
Control of workstations	Only IT personnel have administrative rights to computing resources. End user access is restricted.	End users have either power-user or administrator accounts on their respective workstations depending on their requirements.
Host intrusion detection	IT personnel are solely responsible for host intrusion detection.	End users are asked to maintain their own host intrusion detection mechanisms, such as ZoneAlarm®.

Source: Adapted from Whitman, 2003.

reliant on IT personnel for the long-term and immediate support of their computing needs. From software acquisitions and deployment to system maintenance procedures, IT personnel are solely responsible. Specifically, end-user computing resources are initiated and maintained only by IT personnel. While this support structure involves a consistent element of interaction among users and IT personnel and allows for input from users regarding operating procedures and policies, end users have absolutely no autonomy in dealing with issues regarding the support of their respective computing environments. The IT director for TechUnit explains, "Sometimes the researcher may propose a solution that works for them, but it may not work for the rest of the community or it may not integrate well into our system. In such cases, our staff would evaluate the request and make a determination as to whether the solution can be implemented, would require tweaking prior to implementation, or should not be implemented. As an example, we have a firewall configuration that is preventing certain users from being able to access our network. We're still determining the exact cause . . . but, in this particular case, one of our admin (IT personnel) would perhaps open the firewall to allow ftp access as long as we are not compromising the remaining part of our system."

The practice of centralized IT security management provided TechUnit with a highly effective framework from which to address issues specific to the Blaster and Sobig.F worms. As the director of IT stated, "All of our PCs have anti-virus software and multiple layers of protection and, in terms of the worms (Sobig.F and Blaster), it was all hands-off to the users." This is a consistent theme among the other IT personnel. The only actions taken by TechUnit IT personnel to deal with the worms were slight modifications to their firewall and e-mail server filter. There were only a few observations of Blaster or Sobig.F worm activity in TechUnit's computing environment. These instances were identified and resolved solely by IT personnel with no impact in terms of cost, time, philosophy, or credibility (user confidence). The IT director noted, "If we have done our job properly, the impact is minimal, if at all felt, to the user community." Perhaps the minimal amount of end-user interaction required by TechUnit's IT personnel to deal with the worms could help explain the notable absence of specific knowledge of the worms' functionality. Notably, the level of specific knowledge of the Blaster and Sobig.F worms increased as the level of management decreased and the degree of user interaction increased.

A consistent thread among TechUnit's IT personnel is their perception of the significance of external threats relative to internal threats. All interviewed personnel perceived the external security threat to be much greater than the internal security threat. The TechUnit network manager summarizes the situation: "We spend more time and effort securing the perimeter than we do the inside." Blaster and Sobig.F are representative of an external threat; however, because the worms can be introduced to a network by an unsuspecting end user, the internal threat is real. According to a survey conducted by the security firm TruSecure, 22.6 percent of 1,504 corporate respondents acquired the Blaster infection from the inside (Varghese, 2003). In addressing the issue of internal threat, every one of TechUnit's IT personnel who was interviewed evaluated his or her extent of preparedness in terms of the knowledge level of the end users. As the IT director explained, "Our user base here tends to be more computer savvy than the typical user base." Because accidental or unknowledgeable user error is considered to be a top-five threat to an organization (Whitman 2003), this rationale for a de-emphasis on the internal threat potential seems justified; however, deliberate acts of sabotage or vandalism also rank highly as a threat to an organization. A more knowledgeable user base has a greater potential to inflict deliberate malicious acts; so, it is unclear as to whether a technically savvy user base justifies a reduced level of internal security.

A decentralized approach to IT security management is one in which there is a high level of autonomy for end users in dealing with the security of their respective computing resources. The

IT environment of MedUnit is highly reflective of such an approach. Although certain protection mechanisms are deployed in a manner consistent with centralized IT security management, such as the use of virus protection software, the majority of IT security management practices are decentralized, as described in Table 3.4.

Like their counterparts at TechUnit, MedUnit's IT personnel sustain a high level of interaction with end users. In this decentralized environment, however, the type of support that is provided varies significantly from one client to the next. As stated by the systems analyst for MedUnit, "We're here to not only support the end users in the use of technology, but we're also responsible for helping them to incorporate technology into their area of expertise. This basically means that as new technologies become available, our end users want to experience them. We're here to facilitate that." From the provision of pricing information for the purchase of software and hardware to the maintenance of computing resources, MedUnit IT personnel act as a source of information and resources. Their end users are empowered to initiate and maintain any computing and network services that they warrant necessary for the successful competition of their respective tasks. The degree to which an end user acts autonomously varies relative to the person's technical interests and abilities.

MedUnit end users are expected to assess and act on any instances of malicious activity that they view as threats to their personal computing environment. As the IT director states, "We pretty much let them do what they want to do." From the use of personal firewalls to the deployment of personal wireless access points, end users have a high degree of autonomy. The source of this freedom is found in the culture of the FBU. "Over the years, certain end users have determined that they are above [policy], and if they really don't like something they take action to have it reversed in their favor," states the IT director. This political orientation to IT management not only creates a strain on IT personnel and end-user relationships, it also lays a foundation for future IT security disasters.

MedUnit's users dictate IT security management policy and procedures. As explained by the MedUnit systems analyst, "While we have some end users that are technically savvy, it makes supporting those that aren't, very difficult. [End users] dictate what is going to happen. If several [end users] want something to happen, it's going to happen." When faced with a malicious epidemic such as Blaster and Sobig.F, this approach to security management is not effective in the discovery or eradication of the worms. "We were hit pretty hard. It just hit us all of a sudden. For about two weeks, we could expect to come to work every morning and patch systems."

Among the end-user population there exist various assessments of the risks posed by the worms; therefore, a consistent and comprehensive eradication of Blaster and Sobig.F is difficult. As expressed by the MedUnit IT director, "We can't always guarantee that our end users have anti-virus software on their machine." The success of a decentralized form of IT security management is dependent on the knowledge and abilities of the end-user community. Unfortunately for the unit, these end-user qualities are not consistent. The IT director explained, "Security is not a concern for very many of our end users. Unfortunately for us, most of our end users don't know enough about what is going on, security wise, to even have a clue as to how to fix their computer."

The level of coordination among end user and IT personnel was necessarily high. MedUnit's method of remediation for Blaster and Sobig.F involved a systematic evaluation of nearly two hundred general purpose computers for which IT personnel have a direct support role. Additionally, a notice was distributed to end users stating the significance of the worms with instructions outlining the steps required to avoid and remove the worms and patch the operating systems. The network manager stated, "We've become much more aggressive on the attention we give

Table 3.4

Characteristics of IT Environment as Described by IT Personnel

Characteristic	"TechUnit" (centralized)	"MedUnit" (decentralized)
Role of IT	Role of IT was clearly and consistently articulated by all interviewed IT personnel	Role of IT was less clearly articulated by each interviewee as we progressed down the management chain
End-user interaction	IT personnel frequent interact with end users and encounter a wide variety of issues	IT personnel frequently interact with end users and encounter a wide variety of issues
End-user autonomy	End users have no autonomy	End users have a high degree of autonomy
End-user input into policy	End users can make recommendations and requests, but ultimately do not have policy-editing authority	End users ultimately dictate or ignore policy where policy exists
External vs. internal threat perception	IT personnel describe 80 percent of threats to be of external origin; 20 percent of threats are of internal origin	IT personnel believe 90 percent of threats are of external origin; 10 percent of threats are of internal origin
Internal threat perception	IT personnel believe highly skilled and knowledgeable end users present less of a threat to security	IT personnel believe minimally skilled and unknowledgeable end users present less of a threat to security

to Windows' updates." However, the effectiveness of the enhanced policy for Windows patching will be dictated, in part, by how well the IT personnel articulate this policy to end users responsible for their own computing resources. The specific knowledge of the worms was greater for MedUnit's IT personnel than for TechUnit's IT personnel. The amount and type of interaction with end users by MedUnit IT personnel in dealing with instances of Blaster and Sobig. F infections may explain this difference. For eradication attempts to be successful, MedUnit's IT personnel were required to be more active in terms of remediation attempts and interaction with end users. By contrast, TechUnit's IT personnel were not required to interact with end users and were able to perform a minimal amount of modifications to firewall and e-mail filters to remedy the threat.

As with TechUnit, MedUnit's IT personnel perceive the significance of external security threats to be high relative to internal threats. A significant difference exists in the rationale behind this perception. While TechUnit IT personnel point to an elevated knowledge and skill level possessed by their end users as a reason for a low internal security threat, MedUnit IT personnel point to a low end-user knowledge and skill level as the rational for a low internal security threat.

The successes and failures experienced by the IT personnel in both units in addressing the Blaster and Sobig.F worms were guided by their respective IT security management strategies. While TechUnit's centralized approach was clearly more successful in terms of minimizing the impact of the worms on their environment, we can look to a number of characteristics that predicated this outcome. Table 3.4 provides a summary look at some of the consistencies and contrasts that between the two IT environments.

Table 3.5

Scientific Questions in Need of Further Study

Area	Issue	Impact
1. Governance	1.1 Must IT security governance be entirely consistent with general IT governance, or can the two approaches differ?	If the trade-offs are different, a firm might choose different strategies for IT governance and security governance, unless they must be the same.
	1.2 Are there differences in IT governance and security governance strategies from one industry to the next?	To generate and support effective governance strategies, industry-specific nuances must be identified and addressed.
2. Degree of information systems centralization	2.1 Does a centralized IT security management strategy provide the most assurance?	Understanding the most effective IT security management practices would allow firms to consider their strategy alternatives.
	2.2 Are there differences from one action to another in terms of user discretion?	Effective end-point security depends on a consistent approach to information assurance actions.

CONCLUSIONS AND DIRECTIONS FOR FUTURE RESEARCH

In the current climate, the security of information systems needs to be properly managed in order to ensure availability of resources. Organizations planning their IT security management strategies can benefit from the findings of this research. While the decentralized approach and federal governance architecture facilitate meeting end-user requirements, security may need to be increasingly centrally managed. This is not necessarily contradictory to improving functionality for end users, since under the decentralized approach, end users are expected to take an active role in activities such as auditing and intrusion detection. This takes time and effort, and end-user failure to practice these functions can potentially compromise the whole network for all users. Users may consider high IT activity in security breach remediation as a positive sign of service, but this may not last with repetitive loss of network availability. If MedUnit is indicative of security management under a decentralized approach, and considering the increasing external security threats, we expect a shift toward more centrally managed security in the future. Further research is necessary to examine how to combine adequate security with realistic expectations regarding end-user involvement in security practices. This study examines two polar opposites of centralization and decentralization in IT security management. Future research endeavors can include varying levels of centralization across a larger number of FBUs.

Table 3.5 provides a list of research questions in areas in need of further investigation. If advances in security governance are to be made, more knowledge is needed in the areas of governance, organizational structure and design, and IS centralization. Perhaps these questions could shape the progress toward filling this void. Each item described in the table is addressed in greater detail below.

Details on Issue 1.1

Managerial decisions, including strategic decisions about how to structure the organization transcend IT, transcend issues of security and information assurance. Is it possible to successfully deploy an IT governance system that is highly decentralized (in order to capture the benefits of flexibility, for example), while maintaining a highly centralized IT security environment (in order to maintain tight perimeter controls, for example)? Must the two decisions be linked, or can a firm implement greater centralization for IT security than it may for broader IT issues? This question might be investigated through in-depth investigation of firms that employ consistent designs versus those that do not. Firms that have explicitly chosen to deploy different postures may be particularly interesting to explore. What prompted this design and what are the outcomes?

Details on Issue 1.2

Many industries, such as banking, are subject to significant regulation affecting information asset management. Privacy laws and other legislation impose compliance requirements that impact firms differentially. A framework of compliance guidelines that is industry- and nation-specific would provide a normative model for secure IT governance. Further, comparative case studies across numerous industries may illuminate important market-driven differences that could enable other firms to alter their posture to benefit from knowledge gained in other industries that experience similar environmental conditions.

Details on Issue 2.1

IT management strategies are often a reflection of a firm's business strategy. Along the IT management continuum from decentralized to centralized, IT efficiencies are found that work well for certain organizational models and not for others. However, for security management purposes, can we assume that a centralized management model provides the highest level of assurance? How do firms with decentralized IT management structures achieve high levels of assurance without reshaping their management strategy? Future insights based on empirical evidence would greatly enhance our understanding of these issues.

Details on Issue 2.2

To ensure against end point security vulnerabilities, IT security policies and procedures should promote a consistent approach among users tasked with following assurance procedures. However, are there circumstances whereby certain individuals or roles within a firm may be required to perform a different set of actions for the good of their unit? In highly centralized environments, are there situations that may require users to protect their assets at their discretion? Further research is required to better understand the benefits and detriments of a user empowered IT security management approach.

Aside from these open issues, we can see that information systems security managers should establish and maintain organizational structures and governance procedures with security goals in mind. Otherwise, security policies and procedures may not be properly executed. Fundamental governance frameworks develop over time, and require the involvement of employees, customers, and others. To meet their security goals, organizations must influence and monitor these human activities in order to reward positive outcomes while imposing sanctions in response to negative outcomes. Such monitoring and influencing is a complex process. For example, fundamental decisions about IT governance, such as the degree to which IT security controls should be centralized or decentralized, have deep impacts on the degree and the manner in which IT security controls are developed and enacted.

ACKNOWLEDGMENTS

This research has been supported by the Center for Computer Security Research at Mississippi State University and funded provided by NSA Grant H982300510101 05080782 and NSF Grant DUE-0513057. Elements of this chapter are inspired by Warkentin and Johnston (2006).

NOTE

1. This case was previously presented at a conference (Johnston et al., 2004).

REFERENCES

Allen, B.R., and Boynton, A.C. 1991. Information architecture: in search of efficient flexibility. *MIS Quarterly,* 15, 4, 435–445.

Beath, C.M., and Straub, D.W. 1991. Department level information resource management: a theoretical argument for a decentralized approach. *Journal of the American Society for Information Science,* 42, 2, 124–127.

Bekker, S. 2003. Sobig damage estimate increased. *ENT* (available at www.entmag.com/news/article. asp?EditorialsID=5936, accessed on May 1, 2005).

Bolles, G.A. 2004. Whiteboard: business by design. *CIO Insight* (available at www.cioinsight.com/ article2/0,1397,1457058,00.asp, accessed on May 1, 2005).

Brand, K., and Boonen, H. 2004. *IT Governance: A Pocket Guide Based on COBIT,* 3rd ed. The Netherlands: van Haren.

Brown, C.V., and Bostrom, R.P. 1994. Organization design for the management of end-user computing: reexamining the contingencies. *Journal of Management Information Systems,* 10, 4, 183–211.

Brown, C.V., and Magill, S.L. 1994. Alignment of the IS functions with the enterprise: toward a model of antecedents. *MIS Quarterly,* 18, 4, 371–404.

CIMA/IFAC. 2004. *Enterprise Governance: Getting the Balance Right* (available at www.cimaglobal.com/ downloads/enterprise_governance.pdf, accessed on Jan. 1, 2005).

Delio, M. 2003. Worm exploits weak link: PC users. *Wired News* (available at www.wired.com/news/ infostructure/0,1377,59994,00.html, accessed on May 1, 2005).

Dhillon, G., and Mishra, S. 2006. The impact of the Sarbanes Oxley (SOX) act on information security governance. In M. Warkentin and R. Vaughn (eds.), *Enterprise Information Security Assurance and System Security: Managerial and Technical Issues.* Hershey, PA: Idea Group Publishing, pp. 62–79.

Hodgkinson, S. 1996. The role of the corporate IT function in the federal IT organization. In M. Earl (ed.), *Information Management: The Organizational Dimension.* New York: Oxford University Press, pp. 247–269.

IT Governance Institute. 2003. *Board Briefing on IT Governance* (available at www.ITgovernance.org/ resources.htm, accessed on Sept. 6, 2004).

Jaikumar, V. 2003. IT managers say they are being worn down by wave of attacks. *ComputerWorld,* 37, 34, 1–2.

Johnston, A.C.; Schmidt, M.B.; and Bekkering, E. 2004. IT security management practices: successes and failures in coping with Blaster and Sobig. F. *Proceedings of the 2004 ISOneWorld International Conference.* Las Vegas, NV.

Kroenke, D., and Hatch, R. 1994. *Management Information Systems.* Watsonville, CA: McGraw-Hill.

Landwehr, C.E., and Goldschlag, D.M. 1997. Security issues in networks with internet access. *Proceedings of the IEEE,* 85, 12, 2034–2051.

Loch, K.D.; Carr, H.H.; and Warkentin, M.E. 1992. Threats to information systems: today's reality, yesterday's understanding. *MIS Quarterly,* 16, 2, 173–186.

Marshall, C., and Rossman, G.B. 1989. *Designing Qualitative Research.* Beverly Hills, CA: Sage.

Milliken, F.J. 1987. Three types of perceived uncertainty about the environment, state, effect, and response uncertainty. *Academy of Management Review,* 12, 1, 133–143.

Monds, K.E., and Wang, C.P. 2003. CDC's new epidemic: an investigation into awareness, attitudes, actions, and knowledge of computer viruses among students utilizing campus computer labs. *Journal of Computer Information Systems,* 43, 3, 118–126.

Mukherji, A. 2002. The evolution of information systems: their impact on organizations and structures. *Management Decisions,* 40, 5, 497–507.

Pfleeger, C.P., and Pfleeger, S.L. 2002. *Security in Computing,* 3rd ed. Upper Saddle River, NJ: Prentice Hall.

Robson, W. 1997. *Strategic Management and Information Systems: An Integrated Approach.* London: Pitman.

Sambamurthy, V., and Zmud, R.W. 1999. Arrangements for information technology governance: a theory of multiple contingencies. *MIS Quarterly,* 23, 2, 261–288.

Sambamurthy, V., and Zmud, R.W. 2000. Research commentary: the organizing logic for an enterprise's IT activities in the digital era—a prognosis of practice and a call for research. *Information Systems Research,* 11, 2, 105–114.

Straub, D.W. 1988. Organizational structuring of the computer security function. *Computers and Security,* 7, Summer, 185–195.

Varghese, S. 2003. Blaster worm took heavy toll: survey. *Sydney Morning Herald Online* (available at www.smh.com.au/articles/2003/09/23/1064082983214.html, accessed on May 1, 2005).

Walker, K.B. 1993. Centralized information systems services: managing the transition to decentralization. *Industrial Management & Data Systems,* 93, 8, 8–12.

Warkentin, M., and Johnston, A.C. 2006. IT security governance and security centralization vs. decentralization. In M. Warkentin and R. Vaughn (eds.), *Enterprise Information Security Assurance and System Security: Managerial and Technical Issues.* Hershey, PA: Idea Group Publishing, pp. 16–24.

Watson, R.T., and Brancheau, J.C. 1991. Key issues in information systems management. *Information & Management,* 20, 3, 213–223.

Whitman, M.E. 2003. Enemy at the gate: threats to information security. *Communications of the ACM,* 46, 8, 91–95.

Zmud, R.W. 1984. Design alternatives for organizing information systems activities. *MIS Quarterly,* 8, 2, 79–93.

CHAPTER 4

INFORMATION SYSTEM RISK ASSESSMENT AND DOCUMENTATION

HERBERT J. MATTORD AND TERRY WIANT

Abstract: Risk assessment is the process of discovering and documenting the risks present in an environment. Within a broader context, known as risk management, risk assessment is considered part of the due care an organization applies to the operation of a computerized information system. Using an organized and systematic approach to risk assessment is essential. There are many models proposed and in use to structure the risk assessment effort. This chapter identifies some of the more widely known models and explores a widely used approach.

An approach that has been widely adopted in the information assurance industry is known as the Threat-Vulnerability-Asset (TVA) matrix. In the middle part of this chapter, this model is explored by explaining the processes used to enumerate and characterize assets, discern and evaluate threats against those assets, and identify the active and latent vulnerabilities that are present or likely. Once the three primary dimensions of the TVA model are explained, the chapter continues with an exploration of some of the more salient details regarding asset valuation and threat and vulnerability estimation.

In order to extend the TVA model, the chapter adds the dimension of controls (or counter-measures) to the model; this includes the process of identifying and explaining existing controls, exploring the need for possible additional or enhanced controls, and planning for moving the information security program forward as these possible controls are deployed.

A final section about documenting the results of the risk assessment processl concludes the coverage of the TVA model.

The conclusion of the chapter is a review of literature on the topic of risk assessment and some observations on the directions future research may take.

Keywords: Information Risk Assessment, Information Threat Vulnerability Asset Analysis, Information Control, Information Loss, Information Security Benchmark, Information Abuse, Information Security Baseline, Information Security Metrics

INTRODUCTION

Many models have been proposed to assess the risk of operating information systems. The absolute perfection of a specific methodology chosen by any given organization is not as important as the existence of a functional methodology that is carefully implemented to become an integral part of the organizational culture. The first section of this chapter explores some of the more widely known models.

The discussion of risk assessment then continues by describing what will be called the common body of knowledge for risk assessment. The core of this collection of practices is represented in the widely used Threat-Vulnerability-Asset (TVA) matrix. The chapter will explain the processes used to enumerate and characterize assets, discern and evaluate threats against those assets, and identify the active and latent vulnerabilities that are present or likely to be present. Once the three primary dimensions of the TVA model are explained, the chapter will continue with an exploration of some of the more salient details regarding asset valuation and threat and vulnerability estimation.

In order to extend the TVA model, the chapter will add the dimension of controls (or counter-measures); this will include the process of identifying and explaining existing controls, exploring the need for possible additional or enhanced controls and the process of planning for moving the information security program forward as these possible controls are implemented.

The final element in the coverage of the TVA model will be a short description of methods used to document the results of the risk assessment effort.

To conclude the discussion of risk assessment, the chapter will end with a review of literature on the topic and present some observations on the direction future research may take.

CURRENT PRACTICES IN RISK ASSESSMENT

Risk Management Methodologies

Chinese general Sun Tzu remarked, "If you know the enemy and know yourself, you need not fear the result of a hundred battles. If you know yourself but not the enemy, for every victory gained you will also suffer a defeat. If you know neither the enemy nor yourself, you will succumb in every battle." This observation, made over 2,500 years ago, continues to have direct relevance to the practice of risk assessment today. The practice of risk assessment is strategic in nature and is a reason why it is a key function of management. Assessing defenses is the foundation of any successful risk assessment program. Hence, as Sun Tzu recommends, in order to assess the risks it faces, an organization must know itself completely and know the dangers faced by its assets. In other words, managers of any organization must take care to identify the weaknesses of their organization's operations, how its information is processed, stored and transmitted, and what control mechanisms are available, before developing any strategic plan of defense.

Survey of Methodologies

Risk assessment is a process of discovering, documenting, and evaluating the risks present in an environment. Operating in a broader context, known as risk management, risk assessment is con-sidered part of the due care an organization applies to its operation of a computerized information system. Using an organized and systematic approach to risk assessment is essential and many models have been proposed and in use to structure the risk assessment effort.

Today, many organizations use the risk management methodologies documented by the U.S. National Institute of Standards and Technology (NIST). Another approach to risk assessment is encompassed in the Operationally Critical Threat, Asset, and Vulnerability Evaluation (OCTAVE) approach, which is being adopted by some organizations. The more recent adoption of the ISO/IEC 17799, Information Technology–Code of Practice for Information Security Management, is challenging organizations within its purview to adopt its far-reaching information security model that includes risk assessment components. Another practical approach to risk assessment is well defined in the Facilitated Risk Analysis and Assessment Process (FRAAP) (Peltier, 2005). Another approach that has been promoted as guidance for undertaking risk assessment by the IT Governance

Institute (ITGI) and Information Systems Audit and Control Association (ISACA) is the Control Objectives for Information and related Technology (COBIT) (COBIT, 2005).

Many organizations use a set of common industry practices, very much like those listed above and promoted by professional organizations such as the International Information Systems Security Certification Consortium (ISC^2) in its Common Body of Knowledge (CBK). The various models listed above are described briefly in the next few paragraphs, while the explanation of the TVA model that is at the heart of the CBK, occupies much of the balance of this chapter.

Models from the National Institute of Standards and Technology

Risk management and the necessary steps for assessing risk are at the center of the information security methodologies promulgated by NIST. These broad information security management methodologies are described in the many documents available from NIST's Computer Security Resource Center of the National Institute for Standards and Technology (csrc.nist.gov).

These documents have two notable advantages over many other sources of security information: (1) they are publicly available at no charge, and (2) they have been available for some time and thus have been broadly reviewed by government and industry professionals.

The first of these that should be considered for its impact to the process of risk assessment is *Risk Management for Information Technology Systems* (NIST SP 800–30) (Stoneburner et al., 2002). This document provides:

> a foundation for the development of an effective risk management program, containing both the definitions and the practical guidance necessary for assessing and mitigating risks identified within IT systems. The ultimate goal is to help organizations to better manage IT-related mission risks. (p. 1)

This 55-page guide can help one develop or evaluate the risk management process.

Another valuable resource for the risk assessment program is NIST SP 800–26, *Security Self-Assessment Guide for Information Technology Systems*. This checklist encompasses seventeen areas that span managerial, operational, and technical controls. The areas are the core of the NIST security management structure and can be used to ensure that all information assets and methods of control are considered.

Other NIST publications that refer to the practices of risk assessment are:

- NIST SP 800–12, Computer Security Handbook
- NIST SP 800–14, Generally Accepted Security Principles & Practices
- NIST SP 800–18, Guide for Developing Security Plans
- NIST SP 800–37, Guidelines for the Security Certification and Accreditation of Federal Information Technology Systems

An additional resource that can be very useful for risk assessment is the federal government website for government agencies. While not every organization is a federal agency, most organizations will be able to find useful examples that can be converted to their environment. Since this website was established for government agencies to share best security practices (see http://fasp.nist.gov), it is known as the Federal Agency Security Project (FASP). It was the result of an effort to identify, evaluate, and disseminate best practices for computer information protection and security from many U.S. federal agencies.

The OCTAVE[SM] Model

A comprehensive approach to risk management provided from a single source is the Operationally Critical Threat, Asset, and Vulnerability Evaluation[SM] (OCTAVE[SM]) (Alberts and Dorofee, 2003). OCTAVE is a risk assessment and evaluation methodology that allows organizations to balance the protection of critical information assets against the costs of providing protection and detection controls. It can assist the organization by enabling it to measure against known or accepted good security practices to establish an organization-wide protection strategy and information security risk mitigation plan.

As noted by Alberts and Dorofee (2003):

> The Operationally Critical Threat, Asset, and Vulnerability Evaluation[SM] (OCTAVE[SM]) Method defines the essential components of a comprehensive, systematic, context-driven, self-directed information security risk evaluation. By following the OCTAVE Method, an organization can make information-protection decisions based on risks to the confidentiality, integrity, and availability of critical information technology assets. The operational or business units and the IT department work together to address the information security needs of the organization.

Using a three-phase approach, the OCTAVE method examines organizational and technology issues to assemble a comprehensive picture of the information security needs of an organization. The phases are:

- Phase 1: Build asset-based threat profiles
- Phase 2: Identify infrastructure vulnerabilities
- Phase 3: Develop security strategy and plans

For more information, the OCTAVE method implementation guide is available at www.cert.org/octave/omig.html.

The ISO/IEC 17799 Model

The stated purpose of ISO/IEC 17799 is to "give recommendations for information security management for use by those who are responsible for initiating, implementing or maintaining security in their organization. It is intended to provide a common basis for developing organizational security standards and effective security management practice and to provide confidence in inter-organizational dealings" (National Institute of Standards and Technology, 2001). The International Standards component is actually the first volume of the two-volume British standard BS 7799. The first of these volumes is an overview of the various areas of security. Volume 1 provides information on 127 controls over ten broad areas and contains a section devoted to risk management and risk assessment. Volume 2 provides information on how to implement Volume 1 (17799) and how to set up an information security management structure (ISMS), including structures specific to risk assessment activities.

In the United Kingdom these standards are used to evaluate organizations as they comply with government mandates to obtain ISMS certification and accreditation, as determined by a BS 7799 certified evaluator. The standard was originally developed to be used between private entities, but has evolved into a legislated requirement. Many countries, including the United States,

Germany, and Japan, have not formally adopted 17799 as national policy, although the concepts represented by the standard are gaining increasing acceptance. This is demonstrated by the fact that the standards are being integrated into common practices including the NIST and CBK approaches discussed elsewhere in this chapter.

As this is written in early 2006, a new standard, ISO 27001, has been released in its final draft version. When the final version is published it will directly replace BS7799–2:2002 in the UK.

This new standard defines an information security management system, creating a framework for the design, implementation, management, and maintenance of information systems processes throughout an organization. Just as ISA 17799 was an extension of BS7799–1, ISO 27001 is planned as an interpretation of BS7799–2. Note that ISO 17799 is a code of practice, providing details of individual controls for potential implementation, and ISO 27001 defines the information management system itself.

FRAAP

Information Security Risk Analysis, Second Edition, a book by Thomas Peltier, proposes a process known as the Facilitated Risk Analysis and Assessment process, or FRAAP. In his book, Peltier notes:

> [FRAAP] has been developed as an efficient and disciplined process for ensuring that information security-related risks to business operations are considered and documented. The process involves analyzing one system, application, platform, business process, or segment of business operation at a time. (p. 69)

The process is described in a comprehensive methodology and is provisioned with supporting guidance and useful techniques in the book.

COBIT

Promoted by the Information Systems Audit and Control Association (ISACA) and the IT Governance Institute (ITGI), the Control Objectives for Information and related Technology (COBIT®) provides a widely applicable and accepted standard for good information technology security and control practices. COBIT presents itself as a reference framework for IT managers, IT consumers, and IT practitioners who audit, create, or secure information systems.

As noted by ISACA:

> COBIT, issued by the IT Governance Institute and now in its third edition, is increasingly internationally accepted as good practice for control over information, IT, and related risks. Its guidance enables an enterprise to implement effective governance over the IT that is pervasive and intrinsic throughout the enterprise. In particular, COBIT's Management Guidelines component contains a framework responding to management's need for control and measurability of IT by providing tools to assess and measure the enterprise's IT capability for the 34 COBIT IT processes. (COBIT, 2005)

COBIT continues to grow in its number of adopters and in its influence as noted in its wide acceptance as a reference and as a source of best practices among companies engaged in online commercial activities.

Table 4.1

Summary and Comparison of Risk Assessment Models

Model	Perceived strengths	Perceived weaknesses	Comments
NIST SP-800–30	Publicly available; broadly reviewed by government and industry	Issued June 2002, which may make it somewhat outdated with the changes in technology and threats to information security	Can help develop or evaluate the risk management process
OCTAVE	Focuses on organizational risk and strategic, practice-related issues, balancing operational risk, security practices, and technology	Requires a team of 3–5 personnel with a broad understanding of the organization plus problem-solving ability, analytical ability, ability to work in a team; possess leadership, and time to invest in the process	Examines organizational and technology issues to assemble a comprehensive picture of the information security needs of an organization
ISO/IEC 17799 and ISO 27001	Provides a common basis for developing organizational security standards, practices, and coordination	The standard is a comprehensive and reasonably complex, therefore guidance, acquired at high cost, and is often necessary to help organizations decide where to start and what priorities should be applied to the implementation process	These standards are being integrated into common practices, including the NIST
FRAAP	Ensures information security related risks to business operations are considered and documented	No documented weaknesses with this model	Systems, applications, platforms, business processes, and business operations are examined one at a time
COBIT	Provides a widely applicable and accepted standard for good information technology security and control practices	A review of 31 client assessments of COBIT reveals no weaknesses	A source of best practices among companies engaged in E-commerce.

Summary and Comparison of Risk Assessment Models

Table 4.1 summarizes the risk assessment models discussed above and provides a synopsis of some of the perceived strengths and weaknesses of each model.

So far, this chapter has looked at a cross-section of the dominant methodologies in the field of risk assessment, save one. There exists a consensus approach, perhaps best referred to as an industry common body of knowledge. This is known as the TVA model for risk assessment.

Figure 4.1   **The TVA Model Matrix**

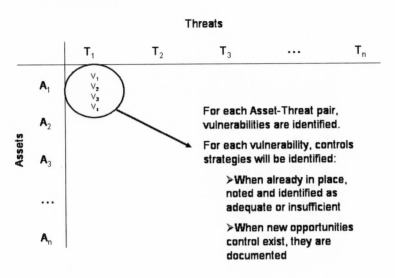

THE TVA MODEL FOR RISK ASSESSMENT

The TVA model begins the risk assessment process with the creation of an ordered inventory of the organization's information assets. Next, a comprehensive list of the perceived threats against those assets is developed. The information assets and threats are organized into a matrix with the asset list arranged individually in columnar form on the left side of the matrix and the threat list organized individually in a row across the top of the matrix. At the intersection of each of the asset-threat pairs, the vulnerabilities that are known or suspected to exist are enumerated. This approach is shown in Figure 4.1. Further use of the model examines each vulnerability for its current state of control and assesses the costs and benefits of additional required controls.

The preceding paragraph used several terms that need definition to gain a complete understanding of how they are used in the context of risk assessment. The following section defines the terms "asset," "threat," "vulnerability," and "control."

Assets (or information assets in this context) are the information or data possessed and used by the organization as well as the systems that process, store, and transmit that information or data. In order to protect these assets it is important to identify the assets, to understand the value of the assets to the organization, and to understand the impact to the organization if the assets are lost or compromised. Some organizations discover that their most valuable assets are their information assets (Whitman, 2005).

In this context, a *threat* is an object, person, or other entity that represents a constant danger to an asset. To understand the wide range of threats that pervade the interconnected world, researchers have interviewed practicing information security personnel and examined information security literature on threats. While the categorizations may vary, threats are relatively well researched and, consequently, fairly well understood.

The 2004 Computer Security Institute/Federal Bureau of Investigation (CSI/FBI) Computer Crime and Security Survey is a representative study that spans many industries and organizations. The CSI/FBI study found that 79 percent of the organizations responding (primarily large corpora-

Table 4.2

Threats to Information Security

Categories of threat	Examples
Acts of human error or failure	Accidents, employee mistakes
Compromises to intellectual property	Piracy, copyright infringement
Deliberate acts of espionage or trespass	Unauthorized access and/or data collection
Deliberate acts of information extortion	Blackmail or information disclosure
Deliberate acts of sabotage or vandalism	Destruction of systems or information
Deliberate acts of theft	Illegal confiscation of equipment or information
Deliberate software attacks	Viruses, worms, macros, denial-of-service
Forces of nature	Fire, flood, earthquake, lightning
Deviations in quality of service	ISP, power, or WAN service issues from service providers
Technical hardware failures or errors	Equipment failure
Technical software failures or errors	Bugs, code problems, unknown loopholes
Technological obsolescence	Antiquated or outdated technologies

tions and government agencies) identified cybersecurity breaches within the last twelve months, a number that is on the decline. The study also found that 54 percent of these organizations reported financial losses, totaling over $141,496,560, due to computer security breaches. The number of respondents identifying unauthorized computer use was 53 percent, down from 56 percent in 2003 (Gordon et al., 2004). It should be noted that this study is drawn from self-selected respondents, many of whom may be reluctant to divulge the type of information the study collects.

The categorization scheme shown in Table 4.2 consists of twelve general categories that represent a clear and present danger to an organization's people, information, and systems (Whitman, 2003). Each organization must prioritize the dangers its personnel, information, and systems face based on three criteria: the particular security situation in which the organization operates, the organization's strategy regarding risk, and the organization's exposure to risk based on its operational environment. Upon reviewing the right-hand column of Table 4.2, one may observe that many of the examples of threats (i.e., acts or failures) could be listed in more than one category. For example, an act of theft performed by a hacker falls into the category of deliberate acts of theft, but is also often accompanied by defacement actions to delay discovery and thus may also be placed within the category of deliberate acts of sabotage or vandalism.

A *vulnerability* is a known, suspected, or anticipated weakness in a system, where controls are not present or are no longer effective. Unlike threats, which are always in existence, vulnerabilities exist when a specific act or action can occur that may cause a potential loss.

A *control* (or safeguard or countermeasure) is a mechanism by which an organization seeks to reduce the loss of value to an information asset when a vulnerability is exploited. Controls might consist of a policy statement, a training program, or an implemented technology that will avoid, mitigate, or transfer the negative outcome of the loss event.

ASSET IDENTIFICATION

The TVA model-building process begins with the identification of information assets, including people, procedures, data and information, software, hardware, and networking elements. This should be done without prejudging the value of each asset. Values are assessed later in the process.

Table 4.3

Information Assets Used in Systems

IT system components	Risk assessment components	
People	People inside an organization	Trusted employees Other staff
	People outside an organization	People at organizations we trust Strangers
Procedures	Procedures	IT and business standard procedures IT and business sensitive procedures
Data	Data/Information	Transmission Processing Storage
Software	Software	Applications Operating systems Security components
Hardware	Hardware	Systems and peripherals Security devices
Networking	Networking components	Intranet components Internet or DMZ components

Table 4.3 suggests an outline of the assets usually found in an IT system and the associated risk assessment components. Note that this is meant as a means to generate a nomenclature and classification system and not to imply that these categories are fixed within industry usage.

Table 4.3 proposes a classification model based on one possible approach; the standard IT system components (people, procedures, data and information, software, hardware, and network elements). This could be used to organize an extended model for examining systems components from a risk assessment perspective. When information assets are classified in this manner, the result will be a detailed breakdown of the components that comprise a system. The following section describes this breakdown more fully.

People are divided into insiders (employees) and outsiders (non-employees). Insiders either hold trusted roles and have correspondingly great authority and accountability, or they are regular staff, without special privileges. Outsiders are other users who have access to the organization's information assets.

Procedures are split into two categories: IT and business standard procedures and IT and business sensitive procedures. Sensitive procedures have the potential to enable an attack, or to otherwise introduce risk to the organization. For example, the procedures used by a telecommunications company to activate new circuits pose special risks because they reveal aspects of an internal critical process that can be subverted by outsiders for the purpose of obtaining unbilled, illicit services.

Data components account for information in all of its states of transmission, processing, and storage. These states expand the conventional use of the term data from its usual association with databases to include the full range of information used by modern organizations.

Software elements can be grouped into one of three categories: application, operating systems, or security components. Software components that provide security controls may fall into operating systems or applications categories, but are differentiated by the fact that they are part of the information security control environment and must be protected more thoroughly than other systems components.

Hardware is split into two categories: the usual systems devices with their peripheral items, and the devices that are part of information security control systems. The latter must be protected more thoroughly than the former.

Networking components are extracted from software and hardware because networking subsystems are often the focal point of attacks against a system. Therefore, networking components should be considered separately, rather than combined with general hardware and software components.

Identifying People, Procedures, and Data Assets

Human resources, documentation, and data information assets must also be identified and documented. Responsibility for identifying, describing, and evaluating these information assets should be assigned to managers who possess the necessary knowledge, experience, and judgment. As these assets are identified, they should be recorded into a reliable data handling process such as the one used for hardware and software.

The record keeping system should be flexible, allowing the linking of assets to attributes based on the nature of the information asset being tracked. The following sections identify some basic processes used to classify assets.

Identifying Hardware, Software, and Network Assets

Many organizations use purchased asset inventory systems to keep track of their hardware, network, and perhaps software components. There are a myriad of these packages on the market today and it is up to the CISO or CIO to determine which package best serves the needs of the organization. Organizations that do not use an automated inventory system must create an equivalent manual process.

Whether automated or manual, the information inventory system requires a certain amount of planning. It is very important to determine which of the attributes of each information asset should be tracked. This will depend on the needs of the organization and its risk management efforts, as well as the preferences and needs of the information security and information technology communities.

When deciding which attributes to track for each information asset, consider the asset attributes shown in Table 4.4.

Classifying and Categorizing Assets

Once the initial inventory is assembled, one must determine if the asset categories it produces are meaningful to the organization's risk management program. Such a review may cause managers to further subdivide the categories or create new categories that more adequately meet the needs of the risk management program.

The next step in the risk assessment process will add information to reflect the sensitivity and security priority to be given to each information asset to the inventory.

Assessing Values for Information Assets

As each information asset is identified, categorized, and classified, a relative value must also be assigned. Relative values are comparative judgments made to ensure that the most valuable information assets are given priority when managing risk. It may be impossible to know in advance—in

Table 4.4

Asset Attributes

Name	List all names commonly used for the device or program
Function	Identify the primary and all secondary purposes of the asset
IP address	Useful for network and server devices in static addressing settings—does not usually apply to software
MAC address	Also called an electronic serial number or hardware address since all network interface hardware devices have a unique assigned number
Asset type	Describes the function of each asset
Serial number	Uniquely identifies a specific device. Some software vendors also assign a software serial number to each instance of the program licensed by the organization
Manufacturer's name	Can be useful when analyzing threat outbreaks when certain manufacturers announce specific vulnerabilities
Manufacturer's model or part number	Identifies exactly what the asset is, which can be very useful in later analysis of vulnerabilities, since some only apply to specific models of certain devices and/or software components
Version or FCO number	Keeps current information about software and firmware versions and, for hardware devices, the current field change order (FCO) number
Physical location	May not apply to software elements, but some organizations may have license terms that indicate where software can be used
Logical location	Specifies where an asset can be found on the organization's network
Controlling entity	Identifies which organizational unit controls the asset
Dependencies	Identifies which other information assets are interdependent with this asset

economic terms—what losses will be incurred if an asset is compromised; however, a relative assessment helps to assure that higher-value assets are protected first.

As each information asset is assigned to its proper category, posing the following questions can help develop the weighting criteria needed for information asset valuation or impact evaluation. One can use a worksheet, such as the one shown in Figure 4.2, to collect the answers for later analysis. The impact evaluation questions are:

- Which information asset is the most critical to the success of the organization?
- Which information asset generates the most revenue?
- Which information asset generates the most profitability?
- Which information asset is the most expensive to replace?
- Which information asset is the most expensive to protect?
- Which information asset's loss or compromise would be the most embarrassing or cause the greatest liability?

There are other organization-specific questions uniquely applicable to your organization that you may need to identify and add to the evaluation process.

Figure 4.2 **Sample Asset Classification Worksheet**

AnyCompany, Inc. Information Asset Data Collection Worksheet				
System Name: _____ Date Evaluated: _____ Name of Evaluator: _____				
Information Asset Type	Description	Data Classification	Impact to Profitability
Hardware	Application Server #AS489	Confidential	Medium
Network	Router #R67	Confidential	High
Data	Application Support Downloads via FTP server	Public	Low
Software	Navaho Web Server on #AS489	Conficential	Medium
Data	Customer Service Requests via Email	Private	Medium
Data	EDI Orders from trading partners for AnyCo. Fulfillment	Confidential	High

Listing Assets in Order of Importance

The final step in the preparation of the asset dimension of the TVA model is to list the assets in order of importance. This can be achieved by using a weighted factor analysis worksheet similar to the one shown in Table 4.5. In this process, each information asset is assigned a score for each critical factor. Table 4.5 uses the NIST SP800–30 recommended values of 0.1 to 1.0. (Your organization may choose to use another weighting system.) Each criterion has an assigned weight, showing its relative importance in the organization.

It is not expected that any individual will be capable of providing the assessment of relative weight for all of an organization's assets. This process is best accomplished by well-structured groups, working in a collaborative environment with adequate feedback between and among the groups and individuals involved in the process.

A quick review of Table 4.5 shows that the customer order via SSL (inbound) data flow is the most important asset on this worksheet, and that the EDI Document Set 2—Supplier fulfillment advice (inbound) is the least critical.

Threat Identification

To continue the development of the TVA model, the second dimension, that of threats, will be added to the first dimension, the information assets of the organization. The ultimate goal of risk identification is to assess the circumstances and setting of each information asset to reveal any potential for loss. With a properly classified inventory, one can assess potential weaknesses in each information asset. This process is known as *threat identification.*

Any organization typically faces a wide variety of threats. If one assumes every threat can and will attack every information asset, the project scope becomes too complex. To make the process manageable, each step in the threat identification and vulnerability identification processes is managed separately and then coordinated at the end. At every step the manager is called upon to exercise good judgment and draw on experience to make the process function smoothly.

Table 4.5

Example Weighted Factor Analysis Worksheet

Information asset	Criteria 1: Impact to revenue	Criteria 2: Impact to profitability	Criteria 3: Public image impact	Weighted score
Criterion weight (1–100)—must total 100	30	40	30	
EDI Document set 1—logistics BOL to outsourcer (outbound)	0.8	0.9	0.5	75
EDI Document set 2—supplier orders (outbound)	0.8	0.9	0.6	78
EDI Document set 2—supplier fulfillment advice (inbound)	0.4	0.5	0.3	41
Customer order via SSL (inbound)	1.0	1.0	1.0	100
Customer service request via e-mail (inbound)	0.4	0.4	0.9	55

Notes:
EDI = Electronic Data Interchange
SSL = Secure Sockets Layer

Identify and Prioritize Threats

Twelve categories of threats to information security have been identified (Whitman, 2003), as shown earlier in Table 4.2. Each of these threats presents a unique challenge to information security and must be handled with specific controls that directly address each threat and the threat agent's attack strategy. But before threats can be assessed in the risk identification process, each threat must be further examined as to its potential to impact on the targeted information asset. In general, this is referred to as a threat assessment. Posing the following questions can clarify the threat and its potential impact on an information asset:

- Which threats present a danger to the organization's information assets in its current environment?
- Which threats represent the most danger to the organization's information assets?
- How much would it cost to recover from a successful attack?
- Which threats would require the greatest expenditure to prevent?

This list of questions may not cover everything that affects risk identification. An organization's specific guidelines or policies should influence the process and require the posing of additional questions.

Vulnerability Identification

As the TVA model's matrix begins to take shape, now having the two dimensions of Assets and Threats, the third dimension is added. This dimension is created by identifying the vulnerabilities posed to each asset-threat pair. Having identified the information assets of the organization and documented the threats posed to the organization, one can begin to review each information asset for the vulnerabilities that may exist for each pair. Each pair will be determined to have zero,

Table 4.6

Example of a Vulnerability Assessment for a DMZ Router

Threat	Possible vulnerabilities
Deliberate software attacks	Internet protocol is vulnerable to denial-of-service attack
	Outsider IP fingerprinting activities can reveal sensitive information unless suitable controls are implemented
Act of human error or failure	Employees or contractors may cause outage if configuration errors are made
Technical software failures or errors	Vendor-supplied routing software could fail and cause an outage
Technical hardware failures or errors	Hardware can fail and cause an outage
	Power system failures are always possible
Quality of service deviations from service providers	Unless suitable electrical power conditioning is provided, failure is probable over time
Deliberate acts of espionage or trespass	Router has little intrinsic value, but other assets protected by this device could be attacked if it is compromised
Deliberate acts of theft	Router has little intrinsic value, but other assets protected by this device could be attacked if it is compromised
Deliberate acts of sabotage or vandalism	Internet protocol is vulnerable to denial-of-service attacks
	Device may be subject to defacement or cache poisoning
Technological obsolescence	If not reviewed and periodically updated, the device may fall too far behind its vendor support model to be kept in service
Forces of nature	All information assets in the organization are subject to forces of nature unless suitable controls are provided
Compromises to intellectual property	Router has little intrinsic value, but other assets protected by it could be attacked if it is compromised
Deliberate acts of information extortion	Router has little intrinsic value, but other assets protected by it could be attacked if it is compromised

one, or more vulnerabilities. The cell formed by the intersection of each asset for each threat will contain this list of identified vulnerabilities for each pair.

As noted above, vulnerabilities are specific faults in a system that any specific threat can exploit to cause a loss for an information asset. They are chinks in the armor—a flaw or weakness related to an information asset, security procedure, design, or control that can be exploited intentionally or unintentionally to breach security. Table 4.6 presents an example analysis of the threats to, and possible vulnerabilities of, a DMZ router.

A list like the one presented in Table 4.6 must be created for each information asset to document how each of possible or likely threat could be perpetrated. This list is usually long and shows *all* of the many vulnerabilities of the information asset from across all of the threat categories. Some

Figure 4.3   **Risk Identification Estimate Factors**

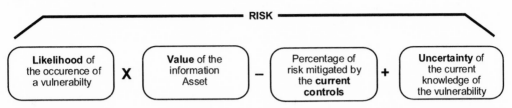

threats manifest themselves in multiple ways, yielding multiple vulnerabilities for that asset-threat pair. The process of listing vulnerabilities is somewhat subjective and is based on the experience and knowledge of the people creating the list. Therefore, the process works best when groups of people with diverse backgrounds work together in a series of brainstorming sessions. For instance, the team that reviews the vulnerabilities for networking equipment should include the networking specialists, the systems management team that operates the network, the information security risk specialist, and even technically proficient users of the system.

At the end of the process, a list of assets and their vulnerabilities has been developed. This list is the starting point (with its supporting documentation from the identification process) for the next step, risk assessment.

Assessing the relative risk for each vulnerability is accomplished in a process called risk assessment. Risk assessment assigns a risk rating or score to each specific vulnerability. While this number does not mean anything in absolute terms, it enables one to gauge the relative risk posed by each vulnerable information asset and facilitates the creation of comparative ratings later in the risk control process.

Assessing Risk

The four factors that go into the risk-rating estimate for each of the vulnerabilities are (1) the likelihood of the occurrence of a vulnerability, *multiplied by* (2) the value of the information asset, *minus* (3) the percentage of risk mitigated by the current controls, *plus* (4) the uncertainty of current knowledge of the vulnerability (see Figure 4.3.)

The goal is to create a method to evaluate the relative risk of each of the listed vulnerabilities. The next section describes the factors that are used to calculate the relative risk for each vulnerability.

Likelihood

Likelihood is the overall rating—a numeric value on a defined scale—of the probability that a specific vulnerability will be exploited. NIST recommends in Special Publication 800–30 (Stoneburner et al., 2002) that vulnerabilities be assigned a likelihood rating between 0.001 (low) and 1.0 (high). For example, the likelihood of an employee or system being struck by a meteorite while indoors would be rated 0.001, while the likelihood of receiving at least one e-mail containing a virus or worm in the next year would be rated 1.0. One could also choose to use a number between 1 and 100, but not zero, since vulnerabilities with zero likelihood have already been removed from the asset/vulnerability list.

A number of rating mechanisms have been noted in the industry. One method for assessing likelihood comes from Bruce Schneier, who proposes a mechanism he refers to as attack trees, which involve layered defenses and the sequence of dependencies between information assets. As described by Schneier "attack trees provide a formal, methodical way of describing the security of systems, based on varying attacks. Basically, you represent attacks against a system in a tree structure, with the goal as the root node and different ways of achieving that goal as leaf nodes" (Schneier, 2005).

Whatever rating system one chooses for assigning likelihood, use professionalism, experience, and judgment and use them consistently. Whenever possible, use external references for likelihood values, after reviewing and adjusting them for your specific circumstances. Many asset/vulnerability combinations have sources for likelihood, for example:

- The likelihood of a fire has been estimated actuarially for each type of structure.
- The likelihood that any given e-mail will contain a virus or worm has been researched.
- The number of network attacks can be forecast depending on how many network addresses the organization has assigned.

Asset Valuation

Earlier, weighted scores for the value of each information asset were assessed. If the values that were assigned to the assets are still meaningful and perceived to be accurate, they are a component in the risk estimation procedure. If the values need to be revised, revisit the process used in their initial creation and update the valuations.

Percentage of Risk Mitigated by Current Controls

If a vulnerability is fully managed by an existing control, it can be set aside. If it is partially controlled, estimate what percentage of the vulnerability has been controlled.

Uncertainty

It is not possible to know everything about every vulnerability, such as how likely it is to occur or how great an impact a successful attack would have on the organization. The degree that a current control can reduce risk is also subject to estimation error. A factor to allow for uncertainty must be added to the equation. This factor is an estimate made by the manager using good judgment and experience.

Risk Determination

The objective of this part of the TVA model process is to determine a relative risk rating score for each identified vulnerability. While the numbers used may appear arbitrary and should not be used in any way to generate absolute loss estimates, they can be used to compare the best estimates of the relative impact of a vulnerability when it comes into play against a specific information asset.

For example:

- Information asset A has a value score of 50 and has one vulnerability: Vulnerability 1 has a likelihood of 1.0 with no current controls; one estimates that assumptions and data are 90 percent accurate.
- Information asset B has a value score of 100 and has two vulnerabilities: Vulnerability 2 has

a likelihood of 0.5 with a current control that addresses 50 percent of its risk; Vulnerability 3 has a likelihood of 0.1 with no current controls. One estimates that assumptions and data are 80 percent accurate.

The resulting ranked list of risk ratings for the three vulnerabilities is:

- Asset A: Vulnerability 1 rated as 55 = (50 × 1.0)—0% + 10%
- Asset B: Vulnerability 2 rated as 35 = (100 × 0.5)—50% + 20%
- Asset B: Vulnerability 3 rated as 12 = (100 × 0.1)—0% + 20%

Identify Possible Additional Controls

For each threat and its associated vulnerabilities that have residual risk, create a preliminary list of control ideas. Residual risk is the risk that remains even after the existing control has been applied.

Controls, safeguards, and countermeasures are terms for security mechanisms, policies, and procedures. These mechanisms, policies, and procedures counter attacks, reduce risk, resolve vulnerabilities, and otherwise improve the general state of security within an organization. In general, controls are considered preventive or detective. Controls that seek to keep risk from loss from affecting the environment are *preventative controls*. Controls that seek to determine if and when losses are occurring are *detective controls*.

There are three general categories of controls: policies, programs, and technical controls. Programs are clusters of activities performed within the organization to improve security. These include security education, training, and awareness programs as well as various enforcement and compliance programs that may be undertaken. Security technologies are manifested in the implementations of technology systems that are integral to, or overlay, the information systems of the organization and are used to implement the policies defined by the organization.

Risk Control Strategies

When an organization's general management determines that risks from information security threats are creating a competitive disadvantage, it empowers the information technology and information security communities of interest to control the risks. Once the project team for information security development has created the ranked vulnerability worksheet, the team must choose one of four basic strategies to control the remaining, uncontrolled risks that result from these vulnerabilities:

- *Avoidance/Prevention:* applying safeguards that eliminate or reduce the remaining uncontrolled risks for the vulnerability
- *Transference:* shifting the risk to other areas or to outside entities
- *Mitigation:* reducing the impact should the vulnerability be exploited
- *Acceptance:* understanding the consequences and accepting the risk without control or mitigation

Avoidance/Prevention

Avoidance is the risk control strategy that attempts to prevent the exploitation of the vulnerability. This is the preferred approach, as it seeks to avoid risk rather than dealing with it after it has been realized. Avoidance is accomplished through:

- Application of policy
- Application of training and education
- Countering threats
- Implementation of technical security controls and safeguards

Application of Policy. As discussed elsewhere, the application of policy allows all levels of management to mandate that certain procedures are always to be followed. For example, if the organization needs to control password use more tightly, it can implement a policy requiring passwords on all IT systems. Note that policy alone may not be enough, and effective management always couples changes in policy with the training and education of employees, or an application of technology, or both.

Application of Training and Education. Communicating a new or revised policy to employees may not be adequate to assure compliance. Awareness, training, and education are essential to creating a safer and more controlled organizational environment and achieving the necessary changes in end-user behavior.

Countering Threats. Risks can be avoided by countering the threats facing an asset and by eliminating its exposure to threats. Eliminating a threat is difficult but possible. For example, when an organization becomes susceptible to cyberactivism or hacktivism (the use of computer-related technologies to advance a political agenda), it must take steps to avoid potential attacks. Recently McDonald's Corporation sought to reduce risks to its image by imposing stricter conditions on egg suppliers regarding the health and welfare of chickens (Greenberg, 2002). This had been a source of contention between animal rights activists and the corporation for many years. This strategy, along with other changes made by McDonald's, has led to improved relationships with animal rights activists, which has reduced the company's exposure to the risk from cyberactivism.

Implementation of Technical Security Controls and Safeguards. In the everyday world of information security, technical solutions are often required to assure that risk is reduced. For example, systems administrators can configure systems to use passwords where policy requires them and where the administrators are both aware of the requirement and trained to implement it.

Transference

Transference is the control approach that attempts to shift the risk to other assets, other processes, or other organizations. This may be accomplished by rethinking how services are offered, revising deployment models, outsourcing to other organizations, purchasing insurance, or by implementing service contracts with providers. One of the most visible outcomes of a transference strategy is to transform the variable nature of the costs for these risks to a more stable, fixed cost.

In the popular book *In Search of Excellence* management consultants Tom Peters and Robert Waterman present a series of case studies of high-performing corporations, and assert that one of the eight characteristics of excellent organizations is that they "stick to their knitting. They stay reasonably close to the business they know" (Peters and Waterman, 1982). What does this mean? It means that Kodak focuses on the manufacture of photographic equipment and chemicals, while General Motors focuses on the design and construction of cars and trucks. Neither company spends strategic energies on the technology of developing of websites. They focus energy and resources on what they do best while relying on consultants or contractors for other types of expertise.

These lessons should be taken to heart whenever an organization begins to expand its operations, including information and systems management, and even information security. If an organization does not have quality security management and administration expertise, it should hire individuals or firms that provide such capabilities. For example, many organizations want Web services, including Web presences, domain name registration, and domain and Web hosting. Rather than implementing their own servers, and hiring their own Webmasters, Web systems administrators, and even specialized security experts, savvy organizations hire an ISP or a Web consulting organization. This allows the organization to transfer the risk associated with the management of these complex systems to another organization that has experience in dealing with those risks. A side benefit of specific contract arrangements is that the provider is responsible for disaster recovery and, through service level agreements, for guaranteeing server and website availability. As noted by Boyce and Jennings, "As some organizations realize the difficulty of keeping trained and qualified IA staff, the demand for outsourcing managed security services has grown" (Boyce and Jennings, 2002).

Outsourcing, however, it not without its own risks. It is up to the owner of the information asset, IT management, and the information security team to ensure that the disaster recovery requirements of the outsourcing contract are sufficient and have been met *before* they are needed for recovery efforts. If the outsourcer has failed to meet the contract terms, the consequences may be far worse than expected.

Mitigation

Mitigation is the controlled approach that attempts to reduce, by means of planning and preparation, the damage caused by the exploitation of a vulnerability. It is most often accomplished in conjunction with other strategies to prepare for the residual risks that remain after other control mechanisms are implemented. It is possible for mitigation to be the exclusive strategy undertaken for some risks, but that is not viewed as a good practice unless very special circumstances apply.

The mitigation strategy involves three types of plans: the disaster recovery plan (DRP), incident response plan (IRP), and business continuity plan (BCP). Mitigation depends upon the ability to detect and respond to an attack as quickly as possible.

Table 4.7 summarizes each of the three types of mitigation plans, including characteristics and examples.

Acceptance

As described above, mitigation is a control approach that attempts to reduce the impact of an exploited vulnerability. In contrast, acceptance of risk is the choice to do nothing to protect an information asset and to accept the outcome from any resulting exploitation. This may or may not be a conscious business decision. The only use of the acceptance strategy that industry practices recognize as valid occurs when the organization has done the following:

- Determined the level of risk posed to the information asset
- Assessed the probability of attack and the likelihood of a successful exploitation of a vulnerability
- Approximated the annual rate of occurrence of the exploit

Table 4.7

Mitigation Plan Summaries

Plan	Description	Example	When deployed	Timeframe
Incident response planning (IRP)	Actions an organization takes during incidents (attacks)	List of steps to be taken during disaster; intelligence gathering; information analysis	As incident or disaster unfolds	Immediate and real-time reaction
Disaster recovery plan (DRP)	Preparations for recovery should a disaster occur; strategies to limit losses before and during disaster; step-by-step instructions to regain normalcy	Procedures for the recovery of lost data; procedures for the reestablishment of lost services; shut-down procedures to protect systems and data	Immediately after the incident is labeled a disaster	Short-term recovery
Business continuity planning (BCP)	Steps to ensure continuation of the overall business when the scale of a disaster exceeds the DRP's ability to restore operations	Preparation steps for activation of secondary data centers; establishment of a hot-site in a remote location	Immediately after the disaster is determined to affect the continued operations of the organization	Long-term

- Estimated the potential loss that could result from attacks
- Performed a thorough cost-benefit analysis
- Evaluated controls using each appropriate type of feasibility
- Decided that the particular function, service, information, or asset did not justify the cost of protection

This control, or rather lack of control, assumes that it may be a prudent business decision to examine the alternatives and conclude that the cost of protecting an asset does not justify the security expenditure. For example, say it would cost an organization $100,000 per year to protect a server. The security assessment determined that for $10,000 it could replace the information contained in the server, replace the server itself, and cover associated recovery costs. Therefore, management may be satisfied with taking its chances and saving the money that would be spent on protecting this particular asset.

Note that if every risk of loss an organization identifies is handled through acceptance, it may reflect an inability to conduct proactive security activities and an apathetic approach to security in general. It is not acceptable for an organization to assume the policy that ignorance is bliss and hope to avoid litigation by pleading ignorance of the requirements of protecting employees' and customers' information. It is also unacceptable for management to hope that if it does not try to protect information, the opposition will imagine that there is little to be gained by an attack. The risks far outweigh the benefits of this approach, which usually ends in regret, as the exploitation of the vulnerabilities causes a seemingly unending series of information security lapses.

Figure 4.4   **Risk Handling Action Points**

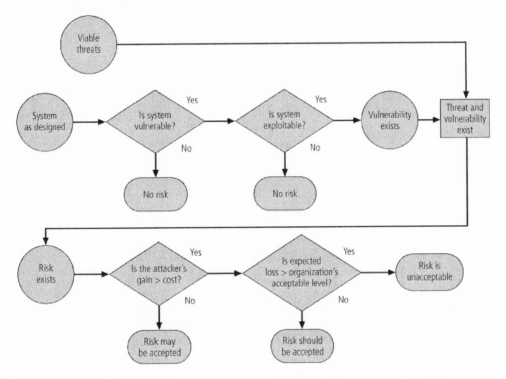

Now that the four strategies that are used to control risk are explained, the next step in the process is the selection of the proper strategy to defend the specific vulnerability of a specific information asset.

Risk Control Strategy Selection

Risk control involves selecting one of the four risk control strategies for the vulnerabilities present within the organization informed by the risk assessment that has been prepared for information assets in question. Figure 4.4 illustrates the process of deciding among the four strategies. As shown in this flowchart, after the information system is designed, one must ask whether the system has vulnerabilities that can be exploited. If the answer is yes, and a viable threat exists, examine what an attacker would gain from a successful attack. Then, estimate the expected loss the organization will incur if the vulnerability is successfully exploited. If this loss is within the range of losses the organization can absorb, or if the attacker's gain is less than the expected costs of the attack, the organization may choose to accept the risk. Otherwise, one of the other control strategies will have to be selected.

For further guidance, some rules of thumb on strategy selection are presented below.

- When weighing the benefits of these different strategies: Keep in mind that the level of threat and the value of the asset should play a major role in strategy selection.
- When a vulnerability (flaw or weakness) exists: Implement security controls to reduce the likelihood of a vulnerability being exploited.

Figure 4.5 **Risk Control Cycle**

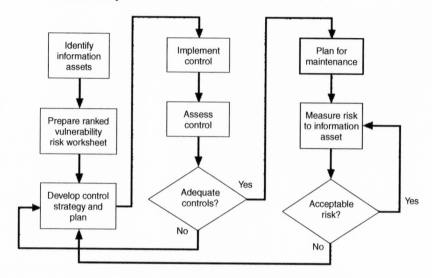

- When a vulnerability can be exploited: Apply layered protections, architectural designs, and administrative controls to minimize the risk or prevent occurrence.
- When the attacker's perceived gain is greater than the costs of attack: Apply protections to increase the attacker's perception of cost, or reduce the attacker's perception of gain, using technical or managerial controls.
- When potential loss is substantial: Apply design principles, architectural designs, and technical and nontechnical protections to limit the extent of the attack, thereby reducing the potential for loss (Stoneburner et al., 2002).

Evaluation, Assessment, and Maintenance of Risk Controls

Once a control strategy has been selected and implemented, the effectiveness of controls should be monitored and measured on an ongoing basis to determine its effectiveness and the accuracy of the estimate of the risk that will remain after all planned controls are in place. Figure 4.5 shows how this cyclical process is continuously used to assure risks are controlled.

EXTENDING THE TVA MATRIX

At this point in the description of the TVA model you have developed its matrix in three dimensions (see Figure 4.2). The first dimension is that of the organization's information assets (A_1, A_2, A_3, . . . A_n). The second dimension is that of the threats facing the organization (T_1, T_2, T_3, . . . T_n). The third dimension is that of the vulnerabilities that exist for each threat-asset pair (V_1, V_2, V_3, . . . V_n).

Planning for Future Controls

The next step in the TVA model approach to risk assessment is to develop the controls that exist or are identified as possible improvements for each of the vulnerabilities identified in the matrix.

This process consists of identifying current or anticipated deficiencies, researching possible controls to address those deficiencies, and planning the steps used to select and then justify the additional controls.

Identifying Current or Anticipated Deficiencies in Controls

It is necessary to have a process for identifying gaps in the control of vulnerabilities. Any such process should identify the current or anticipated deficiencies in controls, including situations that have no existing controls. At the end of this process a list of all deficiencies in the control environment that pose a risk of loss to the organization should be identified, and initial options for remedying the deficiencies should be identified,.

Developing the Possible Controls List

The deficiency list, including vulnerabilities where no controls currently exist, now needs to be used to develop a list of candidate controls. This list of control improvements will serve as the basis for the steps that follow to estimate control cost, benefits from implementing the control concept, and the correlation of the effect of various controls across multiple vulnerabilities. It is important to recognize that the process described here isolates the threat-asset pairs and yields lists of vulnerabilities that may be controllable by common control policies, strategies, or technologies. This cross-vulnerability synergy of controls will become an important part of the justification process as one moves forward.

Selecting and Justifying Possible Controls

There are several ways to determine the advantage of a specific control or group of controls. The primary means is to determine the value of the information assets that it is designed to protect and assign that asset a dollar amount of benefit for its being protected. This can then be compared with the costs of providing the control. This is, however, not the only method of justification. It is true that the business community often favors the use of *quantitative assessment* techniques even when there is a high degree of uncertainty in the estimates that go into the calculations. There is also an extensive field of *qualitative assessment* techniques for justifying various control strategies and technologies. Both methods are discussed in the sections that follow.

There are also many ways to determine the disadvantages associated with specific risk controls. The following sections discuss some of the more commonly used techniques for making these choices. Some of these discussions involve dollar expenses and savings implied from economic cost avoidance, and other discussions deal with noneconomic feasibility criteria. *Cost avoidance* is the money saved by avoiding, via the implementation of a control, the financial impact of an incident.

Cost-Benefit Analysis (CBA)

The criterion most commonly used when evaluating a project that implements information security controls and safeguards is economic feasibility. While there may be a number of alternatives that solve a particular problem, they may not all have the same economic feasibility. Most organizations can spend only a reasonable amount of time and money on information security, and the definition of reasonable varies from organization to organization, and even from manager to manager. Organizations are urged to begin a cost-benefit analysis by evaluating the worth of the information assets to be protected and the loss in value if those information assets are compromised by the exploitation of a specific vulnerability. It is only common sense that an organization should not spend more to protect an asset than it is worth. This decision-making process is called a *cost-benefit analysis* or an *economic feasibility study.*

Just as it is difficult to determine the value of information, it is difficult to determine the cost of safeguarding it. Some of the items that affect the cost of a control or safeguard include:

- Cost of development or acquisition of hardware, software, and services
- Training fees (cost to train personnel)
- Cost of implementation (installing, configuring, and testing hardware, software, and services)
- Service costs (vendor fees for maintenance and upgrades)
- Cost of maintenance (labor expense to verify and continually test, maintain, and update)

Benefit is the value to the organization of using controls to prevent losses associated with a specific vulnerability. The benefit is usually determined by valuing the information asset or assets exposed by the vulnerability and then determining how much of that value is at risk and how much risk there is for the asset. This is expressed as the annualized loss expectancy, which is defined below.

It is often necessary to assess the value of an information asset to determine how much benefit can be achieved by implementing a control. As discussed earlier, asset valuation is the process of assigning value or worth to each information asset. In this context, the value or worth must be expressed in financial terms. Some argue that it is virtually impossible to accurately determine the true financial value of information and information-bearing assets. Perhaps this is one reason why insurance underwriters currently have no definitive valuation tables for assigning worth to information assets.

Assessing the value of information assets is among the most challenging activities in the information security program. The valuation process involves estimation of the real and perceived costs associated with the information asset being assessed. This may include the design, development, installation, maintenance, protection, recovery, and defense against loss and litigation incurred in placing the asset into service. The measured costs or estimates for these factors are computed for every set of information-bearing systems or information assets. Some component costs are simple to determine, such as the cost to replace a network switch or the hardware needed for a specific class of server. Other costs are almost impossible to accurately determine, such as the dollar value of the loss in market share if information on new product offerings were released prematurely and a company lost its competitive advantage. A further complication is the value that some information assets acquire over time that is beyond the *intrinsic value*—the essential worth—of the asset under consideration. This higher *acquired value* is the more appropriate value in most cases.

Some of the components of asset valuation may include these factors to determine the financial value attributable to a specific information asset:

- Value retained from the cost of creating the information asset
- Value retained from past maintenance of the information asset
- Value implied by the cost of replacing the information
- Value from providing the information
- Value acquired from the cost of protecting the information
- Value to owners
- Value of intellectual property

- Value to adversaries
- Loss of productivity while the information assets are unavailable
- Loss of revenue while information assets are unavailable

Once an organization has estimated the financial value of its various information assets, it can begin to examine the potential loss that could occur from the exploitation of a vulnerability. This process results in the estimate of potential loss. The questions that must be asked here include:

- What damage could occur and what financial impact would it have?
- What would it cost to recover from the attack, in addition to the financial impact of damage?
- What is the single loss expectancy for each risk?

A *single loss expectancy*, or SLE, is the calculation of the value associated with the most likely loss from an attack. It is a calculation based on the value of the asset and the expected percentage of loss that would occur from a particular attack, as shown below.

$$SLE = asset\ value\ (AV)\ multiplied\ by\ the\ exposure\ factor\ (EF)$$

where EF = the percentage loss that would occur from a given vulnerability being exploited.

As difficult as it is to estimate the value of information, the estimation of the probability of a threat occurrence or attack is even more difficult. There are not always tables, books, or records that indicate the frequency or probability of any given attack. However, there are sources available for some asset-threat pairs. For instance, the likelihood of a tornado or thunderstorm destroying a building of a specific type of construction within a specified region of the country is available to insurance underwriters. In most cases, however, an organization can rely only on its internal information to calculate the security of its information assets. Even if the network, systems, and security administrators have been actively and accurately tracking these occurrences, the organization's information is sketchy at best. As a result, this information is usually estimated. In most cases, the probability of a threat occurring is usually a loosely derived table indicating the probability of an attack from each threat type within a given time frame (for example, once every ten years). This value is commonly referred to as the ARO, or *annualized rate of occurrence*. ARO is simply how often one expects a specific type of attack to occur. For example, if a successful act of sabotage or vandalism occurs about once every two years, then the ARO would be 50 percent (.50), whereas some kinds of network attacks can occur multiple times per second. In order to standardize calculations, one converts the rate to a yearly (annualized) value. This is expressed as the probability of a threat occurrence.

Once the values for the loss from a single event (SLE) and the likely number of occurrences per year (ARO) values are determined, the equation can be completed to determine the overall potential loss per risk. This is usually determined via an *annualized loss expectancy*, or ALE, using the values for the ARO and SLE.

$$ALE = SLE \times ARO$$

With an example of an SLE of $100,000 and an ARO of .50, then:

$$ALE = \$100,000 \times 0.50$$
$$ALE = \$50,000$$

This indicates that unless one increases the level of security on one's website, the organization can expect to lose $50,000 per year, every year. This figure is used along with the anticipated expenses for control improvements for planning and justification purposes. Sometimes noneconomic factors are considered in this process, so that in some cases even when ALE amounts are not huge, control budgets can be justified.

The Cost-Benefit Analysis (CBA) Formula

Put simply, CBA (or economic feasibility) determines whether or not a control alternative is worth its associated cost. CBAs may be calculated before a control or safeguard is implemented, to determine if the control is worth implementing. Or, they can be calculated after controls have been implemented and have been functioning for a time. Observation over time adds precision to the evaluation of the benefits of the safeguard and the determination of whether the safeguard is functioning as intended. While many CBA techniques exist, the CBA is most easily calculated using the ALE from earlier assessments.

$$CBA = ALE(prior\ to\ control) - ALE(post\ control) - ACS$$

- ALE(prior to control) is the annualized loss expectancy of the risk before the implementation of the control.
- ALE(post control) is the ALE examined after the control has been in place for a time.
- ACS is the annual cost of the safeguard.
- CBA must be zero or larger.

Once the controls are implemented, it is crucial to continue to examine their benefits, to determine when the controls must be upgraded, supplemented, or replaced. As Frederick Avolio states in his article "Best Practices in Network Security": "Security is an investment, not an expense. Investing in computer and network security measures that meet changing business requirements and risks makes it possible to satisfy changing business requirements without hurting the business' viability" (Avolio, 2000).

Decision Making Using Risk Assessment

The various methods of decision making regarding risk management in general can be discussed in two broad categories: quantitative methods and qualitative methods. While some of the methods discussed below are categorized as qualitative, others may have considered them quantitative in other discussions. The critical factor used in this categorization is that in order to be considered quantitative, an approach must use objective, mutually agreed upon, and repeatable processes that will arrive at the same conclusion without regard to who prepares the analysis. Any method subject to an analyst's subjective assessment will then necessarily be considered in this chapter as qualitative.

Quantitative Approaches

The previous discussion of the TVA model concluded with a self-styled quantitative and econometric calculation to use anticipated annual losses for the operation of unprotected or under-protected information assets as a basis for justification. Quantitative approaches used in this manner are often perceived as inaccurate or simply wrong. When used improperly, some of the quantitative processes discussed may not operate as expected. In general, risk assessment techniques that use loss expectancies, annualized rates of occurrence, and estimate annual losses should not be construed as a forecast of planned economic loss or benefit; rather they should be relied upon to produce numbers that can be used for assessing relative probabilities.

Therefore, if a given vulnerability is forecast to have an ALE of $20,000 and another is estimated to have an ALE of $40,000, rather than budget $60,000 for planned losses, the prudent business manger will use the numbers to make decisions when allocating resources to reduce the total risk of loss to the organization's information assets.

While the approach of using quantitative assessment has a long track record in the business community, there are always variations in application that often make the procedure, as put into practice, a qualitative exercise. A shortfall is the frequent failure to include all aspects of expenses in the estimates for loss and estimates of costs for control. When all aspects of the acquisition and operation of a control strategy or technology are included in the estimate, it is known as using the *total cost of ownership* (TCO) approach. The use of TCO-derived values is a prerequisite for any quantitative approach.

Another consideration that is brought to bear on control strategy and technology implementation estimates is the concept of the *time value of money*. It is often the case that control implementation projects span many months or years in large organizations. Occasionally, organizational procedures require that the time value of expenses and investment costs be factored against the anticipated schedule of benefits from the planned project.

Limitations of Quantitative Approaches

At the present, there are no truly quantitative risk assessment approaches available. As opposed to the insurance underwriting of commercial or residential buildings against loss, where there is a significant ability to empirically derive loss estimates for most situations, information system risk assessment has almost no reliable empirical estimate infrastructure and is almost always done in a qualitative fashion.

Qualitative Approaches

When justifications that use factors other than purely financial or statistical models are implemented, it is qualitative models that are being utilized.

Standards of Due Care/Due Diligence

For legal reasons, an organization often adopts a certain minimum level of security. When organizations adopt minimum levels of security for a legal defense, they may need to show that they have done what any prudent organization would do in similar circumstances; this is known as a standard of due care. Implementing and maintaining controls at this minimum standard demonstrates that an organization has performed due diligence. Due diligence requires that an organization ensure that the implemented standards continue to provide the required level of protection. Failure to support a standard of due care or due diligence can open an organization to legal liability, provided it can be shown that the organization was negligent in its application or lack of application of information protection. This is especially important when the organization maintains information about customers, including medical, legal, or other personal data.

The information security protection environment an organization must maintain can be large and complex. It may, therefore, be impossible to implement best practices in all categories. Based on the budget assigned to the protection of information, it may also be financially impossible to provide security levels on a level with organizations that can spend more money on information security.

Information security practices are often viewed relatively, as noted by Avolio: "Good security now is better than perfect security never" (Avolio, 2000). Some organizations might wish to implement the best, most technologically advanced controls available, but for financial or other reasons, cannot. It is counterproductive to establish costly, state-of-the-art security in one area, only to leave other areas exposed. Organizations must make sure they have met a reasonable level of security in all areas, and have adequately protected all information assets, before improving individual areas to the highest standards.

Benchmarking

Instead of determining the financial value of information and then implementing security as an acceptable percentage of that value, an organization could take a different approach to risk management, and look to peer organizations for benchmarks. *Benchmarking* is the process of seeking out and studying the practices used in other organizations that produce results one would like to duplicate in one's organization. An organization typically benchmarks by selecting a measure with which it may compare itself to the other organizations in its market. The organization then measures the difference between the way it conducts business and the way the other organizations conduct business. The industry website *Best Practices Online* puts it this way:

> Benchmarking can yield great benefits in the education of executives and the realized performance improvements of operations. In addition, benchmarking can be used to determine strategic areas of opportunity. In general, it is the application of what is learned in benchmarking that delivers the marked and impressive results so often noted. The determination of benchmarks allows one to make a direct comparison. Any identified gaps are improvement areas. Benchmarking can take several forms. Internal benchmarking studies the practices and performance within the client organization. External benchmarking determines the performance of other, preferably world-class, companies. (Best Practices, LLC, 2004)

When benchmarking, an organization typically uses one of two types of measures to compare practices: metrics-based measures or process-based measures.

Metrics-based measures are comparisons based on numerical standards, such as:

- Numbers of successful attacks
- Staff-hours spent on systems protection
- Dollars spent on protection
- Numbers of security personnel
- Estimated value in dollars of the information lost in successful attacks
- Loss in productivity hours associated with successful attacks

An organization uses numerical standards like these to rank competing organizations that are similar to it in size or market to determine how it compares to its competitors. The difference between an organization's measures and those of others is often referred to as a performance gap. Performance gaps provide insight into the areas that an organization should work on to improve its security postures and defenses.

The other measures commonly used in benchmarking are process-based measures. Process-based measures are generally less focused on numbers and metrics-based measures and more on strategic measures. For each of the areas the organization is interested in benchmarking, process-based measures enable it to examine the activities it performs in pursuit of its goal, rather than the specifics of how goals are attained. The primary focus is the method the organization uses to accomplish a particular process, rather than the outcome.

Best Security Practices

Security efforts that seek to provide a superior level of performance in the protection of information are referred to as best business practices or simply *best practices*. Some organizations refer to these as recommended practices. Security efforts that are among the best in the industry are referred to as best security practices (BSPs). These practices balance the need for information access with the need for adequate protection. Best practices seek to provide as much security as possible for information and information systems while demonstrating fiscal responsibility and ensuring information access. Companies with best practices may not be the best in every area; they may only have established an extremely high quality or successful security effort in one area. As was noted previously, U.S. federal agencies have access to a website providing them with the opportunity to share best security practices with other agencies (see fasp.nist.gov). This project is known as the Federal Agency Security Project. It was the result of:

> the Federal Chief Information Officer Council's Federal Best Security Practices (BSP) pilot effort to identify, evaluate, and disseminate best practices for computer information protection and security. . . . The FASP site contains agency policies, procedures and practices; the CIO pilot BSPs; and, a Frequently-Asked-Questions (FAQ) section.

While few commercial equivalents exist at this time, many of the BSPs used in the FASP program are applicable to the area of information security in both the public and private sector.

The Gold Standard

Best business practices are not sufficient for organizations that prefer to set the standard by implementing the most protective, supportive, and yet fiscally responsible standards possible. They strive toward the gold standard. The gold standard is a model level of performance that demonstrates industrial leadership, quality, and concern for the protection of information. The implementation of gold standard security requires a great deal of support, both in financial and personnel resources. While there is some public information on best practices, there are no published criteria for the gold standard. The gold standard is a level of security out of reach for most organizations. Many vendors claim to offer a gold standard in one product or service, but this is predominantly marketing propaganda.

Selecting Best Practices

Choosing which recommended practices to implement can pose a challenge for some organizations. In industries that are regulated by governmental agencies, government guidelines are often requirements. For other organizations, government guidelines are excellent sources for identifying best practices to control information security risks that are most suitable to the organization. When considering best practices for your organization, consider the following:

- Does your organization resemble the identified target organization of the best practice?
- Are you in a similar industry as the target? A strategy that works well in manufacturing organizations might have little relevance to a nonprofit organization.
- Do you face similar challenges as the target? If you have no functioning information security program, a best practice target that assumes you do will not be of great value.
- Is your organizational structure similar to that of the target? A best practice proposed for a small office is not applicable to a multinational company.
- Are the resources you can expend similar to those called for by the best practice? A best practice proposal that assumes unlimited funding is of limited value if your program has budget constraints.
- Are you in a similar threat environment as the one assumed by the best practice? Best practices of months or even weeks ago may not answer the current threat environment. Consider the best practice for Internet connectivity required in the modern organization at the opening of the twenty-first century compared to best practices of five years ago.

Another source for best practices information is the CERT website (www.cert.org/security-improvement/), which presents a number of security improvement modules and practices in HTML and PDF format. Similarly, Microsoft has published a set of best practices in security at its website (www.microsoft.com/mscorp/twc/). Microsoft focuses on four key areas:

- Security
- Privacy
- Reliability
- Business integrity

Another consideration is to join professional societies that provide information on best practices for their members. The Technology Manager's Forum (www.techforum.com) has an annual best practice award in a number of areas including information security. The Information Security Forum (www.isfsecuritystandard.com) has a free publication titled "Standard of Good Practice" that outlines information security best practices.

Many organizations have seminars and classes on best practices for implementing security. For example, the Information Systems Audit and Control Association (www.isaca.com) hosts seminars on a regular basis. Similarly, the International Association of Professional Security Consultants (www.iapsc.org) has a list of best practices, as does the Global Grid Forum (www.gridforum.org). One can also peruse Web portals for posted security best practices. There are several free portals dedicated to security that have collections of practices, such as SearchSecurity.com and NIST's Computer Resources Center.

These are but a few of the many public and private organizations that promote solid best security practices. Investing a few hours searching the Web reveals dozens of locations for additional information. Finding information on security design is the easy part. Sorting through the collected mass of information, documents, and publications can require a substantial investment in time and human resources. The result of this effort should be a framework to develop and implement a security system that addresses policy, education and training, and technology.

Baselining

Related to the concept of benchmarking is the process of *baselining*. A baseline is a level of performance against which changes can be usefully compared. An example is a baseline for the number of attacks per week an organization experiences. In the future, this baseline can serve as a reference point to determine if the average number of attacks is increasing or decreasing. Baselining is the process of measuring against established standards. In information security, baselining is the comparison of security activities and events against the organization's future performance. Thus baselining can provide the foundation for internal benchmarking. The information gathered for an organization's first risk assessment becomes the baseline for future comparisons.

When baselining, it is useful to have a guide to the overall process. The National Institute of Standards and Technology has two publications specifically written to support these activities:

- SP 800–27 Engineering Principles for Information Technology Security (A Baseline for Achieving Security), June 2001.
- SP 800–26 Security Self-Assessment Guide for Information Technology Systems, November 2001 (discussed elsewhere in this chapter).

Both of these documents are available at http://csrc.nist.gov/publications/nistpubs/index.html.

Baselining and researching best practices provide less detail for the design and implementation of a security program than does a complete methodology. However, by baselining and using best practices, one can piece together the desired outcome of the security process, and thus work backwards to an effective design.

Limitations of Qualitative Approaches

The biggest problem with benchmarking in information security is that organizations do not talk to each other; a successful attack is viewed as an organizational failure, and is kept secret, insofar as possible. As a result, the entire industry suffers as valuable lessons are not recorded, disseminated, and evaluated. However, more and more security administrators are joining professional associations and societies like the Information Systems Security Organization (ISSO) and sharing their stories and lessons learned. An alternative to this direct dialogue is the publication of lessons learned. Individual security administrators are beginning to publish in security journals sanitized versions of the attacks on their organizations and information in an effort to share what they have learned.

Another problem with benchmarking is that no two organizations are identical. Even if two organizations are producing products or services in the same market, their size, composition, management philosophies, organizational culture, technological infrastructure, and budgets for security may differ dramatically. Even if organizations do exchange information, they may not be able to apply the strategies of the other. What organizations seek most are lessons that can help them strategically, rather than information about specific technologies they should adopt. Remember that security is a managerial problem, not a technical one. If it were a technical problem, then implementing the same technology would solve the problem regardless of industry or organizational composition. As a managerial and people problem, the number and types of variables that impact the security of the organization differ radically in any two businesses.

A third problem is that best practices are a moving target. What worked well two years ago may be completely worthless against today's threats. Security programs must keep abreast of new threats as well as methods, techniques, policies, guidelines, educational and training approaches, and, yes, technologies to combat them.

One last issue to consider is that knowing what was happening a few years ago, as in benchmarking, does not necessarily tell one what to do next. While it is true that, in security, those who do not prepare for the attacks of the past will see them again, it is also true that preparing for past threats does not prepare one for what lies ahead. It is important to be as prepared as possible to contain the threats one knows about, and then focus efforts on monitoring the communications and new listings directed toward systems and security administrators to determine what is coming and how to prepare for it.

Blended Approaches

The reality of the current state of the practice in risk assessment is the use of a blended approach. This combination of qualitative and quantitative methods can be seen in most dominant practices today, but is especially obvious in the TVA and FRAAP models, as discussed earlier in this chapter.

DOCUMENTING RESULTS OF RISK ASSESSMENT

The goal of the risk assessment process is to identify information assets and their vulnerabilities, rank them according to the need for protection, and then identify control strategies and technologies that may help in controlling the exposure to loss that all organizations face. In preparing this list a wealth of factual information about the assets and the threats they face is collected. Also, information about vulnerabilities and controls is collected. A final, summarized document providing a ranked vulnerability risk worksheet should be prepared, similar to the example shown in Table 4.8. A review of this worksheet shows similarities to the weighted factor analysis worksheet shown in Table 4.5.

Table 4.8 is used as follows:

- *Asset:* List each vulnerable asset.
- *Asset impact:* Show the results for this asset from the Weighted Factor Analysis Worksheet. In the example, this is a number from 1 to 100.
- *Vulnerability:* List each uncontrolled vulnerability.
- *Vulnerability likelihood:* State the likelihood of the realization of the vulnerability by a threat agent as indicated in the vulnerability analysis step. In the example, the number is from 0.1 to 1.0.
- *Risk-rating factor:* Enter the figure calculated from the asset impact multiplied by the likelihood. In the example, the calculation yields a number from 0.1 to 100.

Looking at the sample results shown in Table 4.8, it may be surprising that the most pressing risk requires making the mail server or servers more robust. Even though the impact rating of the information asset represented by the customer service e-mail is only 55, the relatively high likelihood of a hardware failure makes it the most pressing problem.

Now that the risk identification process is complete, what should the documentation package look like? In other words, what are the deliverables from this stage of the risk management project? The risk identification process should include designating what function the reports serve, who is responsible for preparing the reports, and who reviews them. The ranked vulnerability risk worksheet is the initial working document for the next step in the risk management process: assessing and controlling risk. Table 4.9 shows a sample list of the worksheets that have been prepared by an information asset risk management team.

Table 4.8

Example Ranked Vulnerability Risk Worksheet

Asset	Vulnerability	Asset impact	Vulnerability likelihood	Risk-rating factor
Customer service request via e-mail (inbound)	E-mail disruption due to hardware failure	55	0.2	11
Customer service request via e-mail (inbound)	E-mail disruption due to software failure	55	0.2	11
Customer order via secure sockets layer (SSL) (inbound)	Lost orders due to Web server hardware failure	100	0.1	10
Customer order via SSL (inbound)	Lost orders due to Web server ISP service failure	100	0.1	10
Customer service request via mail (inbound)	E-mail disruption due to SMTP mail relay attack	55	0.1	5.5
Customer service request via e-mail (inbound)	E-mail disruption due to ISP service failure	55	0.1	5.5
Customer service request via e-mail (inbound)	E-mail disruption due to power failure	55	0.1	5.5
Customer order via SSL (inbound)	Lost orders due to Web server denial-of-service attack	100	0.025	2.5
Customer order via SSL (inbound)	Lost orders due to Web server software failure	100	0.01	1
Customer order via SSL (inbound)	Lost orders due to Web server buffer overrun attack	100	0.01	1

Table 4.9

Risk Identification and Assessment Deliverables

Deliverable	Purpose
TVA matrix	Document assets, threats, vulnerabilities, control strategies and technologies and the associated values and costs
Information set classification worksheet	Assembles information about information assets and what impact or value they have to the organization
Weighted criteria analysis worksheet	Assigns ranked value or impact weight to each information asset
Ranked vulnerability risk worksheet	Assigns risk rating ranked value for each uncontrolled asset-vulnerability pair

Comprehensive Information Security Operational Risk Assessment

A key component used to document the results of risk assessment (and later used in ongoing activities for risk management) is the *comprehensive information security operational risk assessment* (RA for short). The RA is a method of identifying and documenting the risk that a project, process, or action introduces to the organization and may also involve offering suggestions for controls to reduce that risk. The information security group is in the business of coordinating the preparation of many different types of RA documents, including:

- *Network connectivity RA:* Used to respond to network change requests and network architectural design proposals. May be part of or support a business partner's RA.
- *Dialed modem RA:* Used when a dial-up connection is requested for a system.
- *Business partner RA:* Used when a proposal for connectivity with business partners is being evaluated.
- *Application RA:* Used at various stages in the life cycle of a business application. Content depends on the project's position in the life cycle when the RA is prepared. Usually, multiple RA documents are prepared at different stages. The definitive version is prepared as the application is readied for conversion to production.
- *Vulnerability RA:* Used to assist in communicating the background, details, and proposed remediation as vulnerabilities emerge or change over time.
- *Privacy RA:* Used to document applications or systems that contain protected personal information that needs to be evaluated for compliance with privacy policies of the organization and relevant laws.
- *Acquisition or divesture RA:* Used when planning for reorganization as units of the organization are acquired, divested, or moved.
- *Other RA:* Used when a statement about risk is needed for any project, proposal, or fault that is not contained in the preceding list.

The RA process identifies risks and proposes controls. Most RA documents are structured to include the components shown in Table 4.10.

A risk assessment's identification of the systemic or latent vulnerabilities that introduce risk to the organization can provide the opportunity to create a proposal for an information security project. When used as part of a complete risk management maintenance process, the RA can support the

Table 4.10

Risk Assessment Documentation Components

Component	Description	When and how used
Introduction	A standard opening description to explain the RA to readers who are unfamiliar with the format. The exact text varies for each RA template.	Found in all RA document templates
Scope	A statement of the boundaries of the RA.	Found in all RA document templates
Disclaimer	A statement that includes language that identifies limits in the risk assessment based on where in the project life cycle the report was developed. The information available at different times in the life of the project will affect how comprehensive and accurate the report is. Often, risk assessments are the most imprecise at the earliest stages of a project, and it is important that decision makers are made aware of the lack of precision in the risk assessment when it is based on incomplete information. This statement is sometimes removed in the final RA when all information about the project is available, but it may be left in order to provide awareness that some imprecision in the assessment of risk is inherent in the process.	Found in all draft RA document templates; some issues may remain in the disclaimer in some final RA templates
Information security resources	A list of the names of the information security team members who collected information, analyzed risk, and documented the findings.	Found in all RA document templates
Other resources	A list of the names of the other organization members who provided information, assisted in analyzing risk, and documented the findings.	Found in all RA document templates
Background	A documenting of the proposed project, including network changes, application changes, and other issues or faults.	Found in all RA document templates
Planned controls	A documenting of all controls that are planned in the proposed project, including network changes, application changes, and other issues or faults.	Found in all RA document templates
IRP and DRP planning elements	A documenting of the incident response and disaster planning elements that have been or will be prepared for this proposed project, including network changes, application changes, and other issues or faults.	Recommended in all document templates
Opinion of risk	A summary statement of the risk to the organization introduced by the proposed project, network change, application, or other issue or fault.	Found in all RA document templates
Recommendations	A statement of what needs to be done to implement controls within the project to limit risk from the proposed project.	Found in all RA document templates
Information security controls recommendations summary	A summary of the controls that are planned or needed, using the security architecture elements of the system as an organizing method.	Recommended in all document templates

information security program as a powerful and flexible tool that helps identify and document risk and remediate the underlying vulnerabilities that expose the organization to risks of loss.

PREVIOUS RESEARCH IN THE FIELD OF RISK ASSESSMENT

Exploring Past Research in Risk Assessment

Current research in risk assessment appears to be divided into six distinct areas. These are: analysis techniques, software security, security investment, documentation, motivation, and audits. The topics are presented in the following paragraphs.

Analysis Techniques

Reliable risk assessment involves data collection of all facets influencing system risk (Fung et al., 2003). A notable difficulty when performing a risk analysis is to determine the input parameters to the analysis, which may include facts and opinions concerning threats, vulnerabilities, and costs (Josang et al., 2004). There may or may not be statistical information on each of these three areas which in turn may cause decision makers to rely more heavily on subjective opinions when performing their risk analysis (Josang et al., 2004).

It then must be noted that in the current research of risk assessment, a topic of interest is risk analysis techniques in which there appear to be two distinct schools of thought. On the one hand there are those who believe that the computational complexity of risk analysis is so difficult that it requires appropriate software to eliminate the ineffectiveness of current simplified methods of risk assessment (Hamdi and Boudriga, 2003). Hamdi and Boudriga propose an algebraic methodology that states that attacks are irreversible and that security decisions can be regarded as pseudo-inverses for those attacks.

Josang, Bradley, and Knapskog (2004) propose that risk analysis should use subjective beliefs about threats and vulnerabilities as input parameters and then use the belief calculus of subjective logic to combine those parameters. They further contend that belief calculus considers the uncertainty about threat and vulnerability estimates and reflects more realistically the nature of each estimate. The intent of this subjective approach to risk analysis is to allow for the consideration of ignorance in the analysis process. The results of such an analysis reveal the degree of ignorance the analysis contains.

Farahmand, Navathe, Sharp, and Enslow (2003) reviewed the existing taxonomy of threats to information systems and discussed subjective analysis for a probability assessment of threats to information systems. Their work provided a five-stage risk management model designed to help managers identify business assets, recognize threats, assess the level of business impact if a threat materialized, analyze vulnerabilities, suggest countermeasures, and recommend an implementation plan.

Software Security

Wang and Wang (2003) note software security as another area of interest in risk assessment. They stated that there are three categories of software risks and threats based on the target of attack: application layer, platform layer, and network layer. They presented an evaluation of current individual security technologies for these three layers and an effectiveness evaluation for each technology. Risk must be systematically assessed to effectively manage it and must also include the software development phase (Cavusoglu et al., 2004).

Another aspect of software security is Web application security as explored by Huang, Huang, Lin, and Tsai (2003). They describe a number of software testing techniques to include dynamic analysis, black-box testing, and behavior monitoring and then present their tool they named the Web Application Vulnerability and Error Scanner (WAVES). Their study determined that WAVES is a viable tool to assess Web application security.

Security Investment

Little study has been attempted that addresses the economic aspects of information security (Gordon and Loeb, 2002). This may be because the costs associated with computer security are hard to assess due to the lack of accurate metrics. Exacerbating the problem of cost analysis is the fact that traditionally industry has appeared willing to write off a degree of computer service downtime and loss of access to, or misuse of, information and equipment as a standard business practice. This practice may soon change due to the increased reliance on computation services and the fact that information has become increasingly critical to business daily operations (Mercuri, 2003).

Tools such as cost-benefit analysis, comprehensive analytical models, and economic models have been considered to assist in the investment analysis decision. Three such tools are described briefly in the following paragraphs.

Recently, cost-benefit analysis (CBA) techniques have become the most popular metrics applied to the assessment of computer related risks. Mercuri (2003) points out that CBA models may be more effective as they incorporate the use of risk-adjusted cash flows in order to examine internal rate of return (IRR) and the maximum net present value (NPV) computed as a percentage of information security expenditures.

The cost-benefit analysis and security audit information should be included in a formal report to provide management with the information it needs to select appropriate countermeasures. A sample cost-benefit analysis is available in the NIST Risk Management Guide (Dark and Poftak, 2004).

Cavusoglu, Mishra, and Raghunathan (2004) proposed a comprehensive analytical model to evaluate security investment decisions. Their goal was to create a model to analyze IT security investment problems that incorporates specific features of IT security technologies to assist in decision making at all levels of an IT security setting.

Gordon and Loeb (2002) sought to derive an economic model to determine the optimal amount to invest in information security. The researchers constructed a model to specifically consider how the vulnerability of information and the potential loss from such vulnerability affect the optimal amount of resources that should be devoted to securing that information. Gordon and Loeb contend that managers should normally focus on information that falls into the mid range of vulnerability to security breaches. This action would also require organizations to group their information into various levels of security breach vulnerability.

Documentation

In addition to CBA and audit information, it is recommended that organizations maintain a running, annotated, and current documentation file that supports their decision making relative to all security implementation specifications (Johnson and Schulte, 2004) as comprehensive and current, information security documentation is a keystone of good information security management. Documentation, along with associated risk assessment strategies is evidence that security officers have acted with a high level of professional competence (Fung et al., 2003).

Lund, den Braber, and Stølen (2003) note the time and cost required for security audits and propose a methodology to address the maintenance of security assessment results and a component-oriented approach to security assessment in general. The methodology is presented within the context of model-based security assessment as developed by the EU-project CORAS, with a primary focus on maintenance. CORAS addresses security critical systems in general but places an emphasis on IT security. An IT system to CORAS includes technology, the interaction of humans and technology, plus all relevant organizational and societal factors that surround technology and human interaction.

Motivation

The question of what motivates any individual to engage in information security breaches is a topic of ongoing discussion. To gain a better understanding of motivational factors, research has been conduced using attacker intent, objectives, and strategies (AIOS) and social identity theory to aid in the explanation of motivational factors.

The ability to model and infer AIOS may advance the literature of risk assessment, harm prediction, and predictive or proactive cyber defense. However, according to Liu and Zang (2003), existing AIOS inference techniques are ad hoc and system or application specific. They present a general incentive-based method to model AIOS and a game theoretic AIOS formalization that can capture the inherent inter-dependency between AIOS and defender objectives and strategies in such a way that AIOS can be automatically inferred. The results of their work found that the concept of incentives can unify a large variety of attacker intents; the concept of utilities can integrate incentives and cost in such a way that attacker objectives can be practically modeled.

In a study of Web defacements by Woo, Kim, and Dominick (2004), social identity theory was used to try to determine the motivational factors behind Web defacement. The theory suggests that individuals have an innate and powerful tendency to organize themselves into groups. The extent to which people associate themselves with groups establishes their social identities. The groups may be founded upon political, religious, ethnic, or social concerns. Their findings suggest that hackers are members of an extensive social networks that are eager to demonstrate their reasons for hacking and often leave calling cards, greetings, and taunts on Web pages. While, approximately 30 percent of Web defacements had some political motive with the remaining 70 percent being classified as a prank, the concern is that what begins as a prank may become politically motivated and escalate into cyber terrorism.

Audits

A security audit should be treated as an essential management function (Dark and Poftak, 2004). Supporting this argument, in 2004 Hale, Landry, and Wood proposed a three-step susceptibility audit designed to assist executive management develop a comprehensive information security strategy. The steps of the audit are: valuing information assets, assessing threats, and evaluating the cost of securing assets. The susceptibility audit is the point of departure for evaluating an organization's vulnerability to cyber attack. The end result is a picture that allows managers to visualize their firm's overall information security status, the nature of its vulnerability, the costs of preventing losses, and the potential financial impact of threats to the firm.

DIRECTIONS FOR FUTURE RESEARCH IN RISK ASSESSMENT

To gain an understanding of the present state of information security risk assessment and to glean future research topics, the results of five information security surveys were reviewed (CIO Magazine, 2003; Gordon et al., 2004; Ernst & Young, 2003; KPMG, 2002; PriceWaterhouseCoopers, 2004). In general, there are five possible research areas presented in Table 4.11 and in the following sections: education and training; information security culture; reporting; aligning information security and business strategy; and perceptions.

Organizations are influenced by a broad spectrum of factors that include opportunities, threats, and benefits when addressing information security. The very high level of importance survey respondents assigned to information security is not supported by the relatively low self-assessment among responding organizations. Viruses and worms are the leading information security concerns and continue to generate the most media and public attention. However, CIOs and other IT executives are increasingly recognizing the significance of internal threats such as employee misconduct involving information systems (Ernst & Young, 2003).

The threat to information security is seen as being external in that viruses and worms are the leading information security concerns (Ernst & Young, 2003; PriceWaterhouseCoopers, 2004), while internal threats are being neglected. For example, wireless networks are not being controlled (PriceWaterhouseCoopers, 2004). Also, organizational control of e-mail and Web browsing has decreased due to the number of new users (PriceWaterhouseCoopers, 2004). The net result of this apparent inattention to all information security threats is that organizations suffered downtime of 8+ hours over information security incidents (CIO Magazine, 2003).

Education and Training

The general finding of one study indicates that companies responded to new and emerging threats in the year prior to the survey with education and communication campaigns, tightened policies and procedures for overall security, and disaster recovery plans (CIO Magazine, 2003). The vast majority of the organizations view security awareness training as important; although (on average) respondents from all sectors do not believe their organization invests enough in this area (Gordon et al., 2004).

Q: What is the significance of an organization's information security education and training program, to include time allocated, funds allocated, and personnel required to attend, in reducing the number and seriousness of information security abuse incidents?

Information Security Culture

The culture of information security was noted to be one-dimensional and reactive in nature. Security initiatives are still driven in large part by external factors like regulations and industry practices and not from a risk assessment perspective (CIO Magazine, 2003; Ernst & Young, 2003). Senior management and boards of directors are under greater scrutiny for risk management oversight. Yet, the overall responses gathered in this survey seem to suggest that many organizations are continuing to take a piecemeal approach to information security (Ernst & Young, 2003). Despite the widely held views about how critically important risk assessment is, only 27 percent of survey respondents placed "addressing information security assessment findings" among the top three influential factors when their organizations consider adopting new information security solutions (Ernst & Young, 2003).

Large companies suffer the greatest number of security incidents, but many organizations wait until an incident has occurred before putting countermeasures in place (PriceWaterhouseCoopers, 2004). Most respondents were pessimistic about the future for information security incidents

Table 4.11

Research Areas in Risk Assessment

Area	Issue	Impact
Education and training	What is the significance of an organization's information security education and training program?	Determine the degree of influence from an organization's information security education and training program, to include time allocated, funds allocated, and personnel required to attend in reducing the number and seriousness of information security abuse incidents.
Information security culture	Does the approach to information security affect information security abuse incidents?	Determine the degree of influence a holistic and proactive approach to information security has in an organization's ability to reduce the number and seriousness of information security abuse incidents.
	Does security assessment reduce the number and seriousness of information security abuse incidents?	Determine the degree of influence of security assessment findings when adopting effective information security solutions in reducing the number and seriousness of information security abuse incidents.
	Does self-assessment reduce information security abuse incidents?	Determine the degree of influence an organization's engaging in an information security self-assessment plays in reducing the number and seriousness of information security abuse incidents.
	Does alignment of information security spending with its key business objectives reduce the number and seriousness of information security abuse incidents?	Determine the degree of influence that an organization's alignment of its information security spending with its key business objectives has in reducing the number and seriousness of information security abuse incidents.
Reporting	Does having formalized information security abuse incident reporting affect information security abuse incidents?	Determine the degree of influence that an organization having formalized information security abuse incident reporting procedures in place is able to reduce the number and seriousness of information security abuse incidents?
	Does having formalized procedures to measure and report information security performance affect information security abuse incidents?	Determine the degree of influence that an organization achieves from having formalized procedures to measure and report information security performance on the number and seriousness of information security abuse incidents.
	How can reporting of intrusions to law enforcement be increased?	Identify mechanisms that organizations can implement and incentives that may be adopted to encourage reporting intrusions to law enforcement without incurring negative publicity over the incident.
Aligning information security and business strategy	Does manager articulation regarding information security affect information security abuse incidents?	To what degree does an information security manager being able to articulate the relevance of information security and information security spending to the broad, overall business strategy reduce the number and seriousness of information security abuse incidents?
Perceptions	Do individual and group perceptions affect the implementation of information security programs?	To what degree do individual and group perceptions concerning the number and seriousness of information security abuse incidents affect the implementation of an effective information security program?

(PriceWaterhouseCoopers, 2004). However, barely half say they align their spending well with their key business objectives (Ernst & Young, 2003).

Q: What significance does a holistic and proactive approach to information security have in an organization's ability to reduce the number and seriousness of information security abuse incidents?

Q: What is the significance of addressing information security assessment findings when adopting effective information security solutions in reducing the number and seriousness of information security abuse incidents?

Q: What is the significance of an organization's engaging in an information security self-assessment in reducing the number and seriousness of information security abuse incidents?

Q: What is the significance of an organization aligning its information security spending with its key business objectives in reducing the number and seriousness of information security abuse incidents?

Reporting

The percentage of organizations reporting computer intrusions to law enforcement is on the decline due to concerns over negative publicity (KPMG, 2002). Only 60 percent of respondents to the same survey have any form of security violation reporting (KPMG, 2002). When asked whether their organization measures and reports on security performance, only 35 percent of respondents said that they did so now, and only a further 17 percent said they planned to in the future (KPMG, 2002).

Q: What is the significance of an organization having formalized information security abuse incident reporting procedures in place in reducing the number and seriousness of information security abuse incidents?

Q: What is the significance of an organization having formalized procedures to measure and report information security performance on the number and seriousness of information security abuse incidents?

Q: How can organizations be encouraged to report intrusions to law enforcement without reaping negative publicity over the incident?

Aligning Information Security and Business Strategy

Information security managers are harder pressed than ever to formulate and present a good business case because of their inability to explain the relevance of information security to the broad, overall business strategy (Ernst & Young, 2003).

Q: What is the significance of an information security manager being able to articulate the relevance of information security and information security spending to the broad, overall business strategy in reducing the number and seriousness of information security abuse incidents?

Perceptions

Many organizations are overconfident in the measures they use to protect themselves, with the most successful organizations adopting a layered security approach using a series of overlapping controls (KPMG, 2002). Of those organizations that said that they strongly agreed that they were reasonably protected the following facts are presented (KPMG, 2002):

- 10 percent do not test their security measures and therefore cannot know if these measures are effective in practice.
- 52 percent have no form of intrusion detection system.
- 87 percent have suffered some form of security breach this year, including:
  - 61% from virus incidents,
  - 28% form unwanted e-mail intrusions,
  - 15% from denial of service attacks,
  - 13% from loss of software, and
  - 12% from website intrusion/hacking.

In addition, most organizations continue to have major gaps in risk coverage, while the impact of information security failures on market value has grown exponentially (Ernst & Young, 2003).

Q: What is the significance of individual and group perceptions concerning the number and seriousness of information security abuse incidents on implementing an effective information security program?

CONCLUSION

While there is much work remaining to be done in the area of risk assessment, the current processes of discovering and documenting the risks present in an environment are widely known and practiced. Part of the due care in operating modern information systems requires a systematic approach to risk assessment. Organizations can choose from a wide variety of models for structuring their efforts; we have summarized above the most widely known of these models. Prominent among these is Threat-Vulnerability-Asset (TVA) matrix that we have featured above. By adding the dimension of controls (or countermeasures) to the model, a more complete risk management process becomes more available. But this process still does not provide a complete management solution. Organizations need complete risk management *programs* that include for example, careful documentation of the risk management processes.

REFERENCES

Alberts, C., and Dorofee, A. 2003. *Managing Information Security Risks: The OCTAVE Approach.* Boston: Addison-Wesley.

Avolio, F. 2000. Best practices in network security. *Network Computing*, 5 (April), 60–66.

Best Practices, LLC. 2004. *What Is Benchmarking?* (available at www.best-in-class.com/site_tools/faq.htm, accessed on March 20, 2004).

Boyce, J., and Jennings, D. 2002. *Information Assurance: Managing Organizations IT Security Risks.* Amsterdam: Butterworth & Hineman.

Cavusoglu, H.; Mishra, B.; and Raghunathan, S. 2004. A model for evaluating IT security investments. *Communications of the ACM*, 47, 7, 87–92.

CIO Magazine & PricewaterhouseCoopers. 2003. *Worldwide Information Security Study. Security without the Hype: It's Hard Work* (available at www.cio.com/article/29841/The_State_of_Information_Security, accessed October 27, 2007).

COBIT. 2005. *Control Objectives for Information and Related Technology* (available at www.isaca.org/cobit. htm, accessed on July 17, 2005).

Dark, M., and Poftak, A. 2004. How to perform a security audit. *Technology & Learning*, 24, 7, 20–22.

Ernst & Young. 2003. *Global Information Security Survey* (available at www.ey.com/global/download. nsf/UK%20/Survey_-_Global_Information_Security_03/$file/EY_GISS_%202004_EYG.pdf, accessed on July 15, 2005).

Farahmand, F.; Navathe, S.B.; Sharp, G.P.; and Enslow, P.H. 2003. Managing vulnerabilities of information systems to security incidents. *ACM ICEC 2003*. Pittsburgh.

Fung, P.; Kwok, L.; and Longley, D. 2003. Electronic information security documentation. *Australasian Information Security Workshop 2004* (AISW 2004). Dunedin, New Zealand.

Gordon, L., and Loeb, M. 2002. The economics of information security investment. *ACM Transactions on Information and System Security*, 5, 4, 438–457.

Gordon, L.; Loeb, M.; Lucyshyn, W.; and Richardson, R. 2004. 2004 CSI/FBI Computer Crime and Security Survey.

Greenberg, J. 2002. Corporate press release: McDonald's Corporation—First Worldwide Social Responsibility Report (available at www.mcdonalds.com/corporate/press/corporate/2002/04152002/index.html, accessed on April 15, 2002).

Hale, J.; Landry, T.; and Wood, C. 2004. Susceptibility audits: a tool for safeguarding information assets. *Business Horizons*, 47, 3 (May–June), 59–66.

Hamdi, M., and Boudriga, N. 2003. Algebraic specification of network security risk management. *FMSE '03*. Washington, D.C.

Huang, Y.; Huang, S.; Lin, T.; and Tsai, C. (2003). Web application security assessment by fault injection and behavior monitoring. *WWW 2003*. Budapest.

Johnson, L., and Schulte, J. 2004. Job security: 7 steps for HIPAA compliance. *Healthcare Financial Management*, 58, 10 (October), 46.

Josang, A.; Bradley, D.; and Knapskog, S. 2004. Belief-based risk analysis. *Australasian Information Security Workshop 2004* (AISW 2004). Dunedin, New Zealand.

KPMG 2002. *Global Information Security Survey* (available at www.kpmg.com/microsite/informationsecurity/isssurvey.html, accessed July 15, 2005).

Liu, P., and Zang, W. 2003. Incentive-based modeling and inference of attacker intent, objectives, and strategies. *Proc. of the 10th ACM Computer and Communications Security Conference* (CCS'03). Washington, D.C., October, pp. 179–189.

Lund, M.; den Braber, F.; and Stølen, K. 2003. Maintaining results from security assessments. *Seventh European Conference on Software Maintenance and Reengineering* (CSMR03). Benevento, Italy.

Mercuri, R. 2003. Analyzing security costs. *Communications of the ACM*, 46, 6 (June), 15–18.

National Institute of Standards and Technology. 2001. *Information Security Management, Code of Practice for Information Security Management*. ISO/IEC 17799.

Peltier, T. 2005. *Information Security Risk Analysis*, 2nd ed. Boca Raton, FL: CRC Press.

Peters, T., and Waterman, R. 1982. *In Search of Excellence: Lessons from America's Best Run Companies*. New York: Harper & Row.

PriceWaterhouseCoopers Ltd. 2004. *Information Security Breaches Survey* (available at www.pwc.com/extweb/pwcpublications.nsf/docid/C18B9A7D47B764ED802570BA0044D7C5, accessed July 15, 2005).

Schneier, B. 2005. *Attack Trees* (available atwww.schneier.com/paper-attacktrees-ddj-ft.html, accessed July 17, 2005).

Stoneburner, G.; Goguen, A.; and Feringa, A. 2002. *Risk Management Guide for Information Technology Systems*. SP 800–30. National Institute of Standards and Technology.

Wang, H., and Wang, C. 2003. Taxonomy of security considerations and software quality. *Communications of the ACM*, 46, 6 (June), 75–78.

Whitman, M. 2003. Enemy at the gates: threats to information security. *Communications of the ACM*, 46, 8, 91–96.

Whitman, M., and Mattord, H. 2005. *Principles of Information Security*. Boston: Course Technology.

Woo, H.; Kim, Y.; and Dominick, J. 2004. Hackers: militants or merry pranksters? A content analysis of defaced web pages. *Media Psychology*, 6, 63–82.

CHAPTER 5

STRATEGIC INFORMATION SECURITY RISK MANAGEMENT

RICHARD L. BASKERVILLE

Abstract: *Risk management entails more than traditional risk analysis or risk assessment. These traditional tools are limited in fundamental ways, such as the lack of reliable frequency data about past risk events and the relative rarity of many kinds of risks that must still be managed. Risk management involves four types of risk treatments: self-protection, risk transfer, self-insurance, and risk avoidance. This chapter introduces an approach to risk management in which the risks and risk treatments are strategically managed using a portfolio approach. With a portfolio approach, different risk portfolios are managed through a portfolio of risk treatments.*

Keywords: *Information Security, Computer Security, Risk Analysis, Risk Assessment, Risk Treatment, Insurance, Security Control*

INTRODUCTION

Risk analysis is one of the central techniques used in managing information systems risks. As part of a risk assessment process, risk analysis provides the basic cost-benefit justification for the acquisition of security safeguards. It is a well-established technique with a long history.

The limitations of risk analysis have been widely recognized for many years. For example, its best characteristic is certainly not its accuracy in predicting probabilities and losses from recognized threats. Indeed, attempts to improve the sophistication of the technique, for example with Bayesian statistical operations, can even capsize its validity (Baskerville, 1991a). Perhaps its best characteristic is its ability to communicate to general management the expert opinions about an organization's information risk profile in terms of threats and safeguards (Baskerville, 1991b).

There are at least two intractable problems that limit the effectiveness of common risk analysis practices: (1) the lack of reliable empirical data about the frequency and amount of losses attributable to information security compromises, and (2) the relative rarity of many kinds of information security compromises.

Reliable empirical data that would be necessary for proper calculation of risk analysis profiles are very difficult to find in practice. There are two basic reasons why these data seem so unavailable. The first is because most organizations do not collect or retain such data. When losses due to security compromise arise, there often follows a period of rather chaotic activity necessary to recover from the compromise. During this period, it is difficult to justify the resources necessary to maintain a database of exactly what the compromise is costing. The resources of the organization are often totally dedicated to the rapid restoration of full business processing capability. Where such data are collected, it is often done after the fact with questionable completeness and accuracy.

The second basic reason why these data are unavailable is because of the extreme sensitivity and confidentiality attached to the data. Management is often concerned that disclosure of a large loss due to inadequate computer security practices will not only be embarrassing to the organization, but also undermine the public confidence in the organization. The loss of such public confidence can impact the value of organizational shares on the market, creating potentially greater losses for the organization's owners than were directly attributable to the security compromise. There is very little motive for any organization to disclose data about the costs and frequency of information security compromises.

A second intractable problem in information security risk analysis is related to both the fundamental arithmetic assumptions being made in probability calculations and the relative rarity of events that are being measured. Many security compromise events are, by their very nature, intended to be unusual and very nearly unique. An example is insider fraud. People very often realized that the perpetration of a commonplace fraud is more easily detected by organizational authorities than one that is invented to be unique and unexpected. This means that an important section of the data being used in risk analysis comprises data about nonrandom events.

Probability calculations represent a branch of the arithmetic theory of evidence that depends upon random events that exhibit a randomly distributed statistical curve (Klir, St. Clair, and Yuan, 1997). As a result, all probability arithmetic is appropriate only for security compromise events that can be construed to be randomly distributed. Current examples of such events include attacks by viruses and worms, website defacements, and other relatively high frequency, randomly targeted kinds of attacks. Where the attacks are uniquely targeted, and of a relatively low frequency, probability arithmetic is altogether invalid.

These two intractable problems mean that most risk analysis techniques in common use today have little relevance as a fact-based prediction of the benefits of security safeguards. The underlying data do not provide any real measures of actual events. The calculations applied to these data are not altogether legitimate. The results of these calculations are trustworthy only to the extent that the data usually represent the informed estimates of experts in information security, and the results of the calculations are usually reviewed by these experts in a holistic way for reasonableness. From this perspective, risk analysis provides a useful technique for formulating and communicating the opinions of experts.

Anyway, it is not altogether clear just how widespread is the use of risk analysis for information security management. The serious usage of risk analysis techniques requires compound calculations on a fairly large database of threats, frequency data, and loss data. There are a number of software-based tools available to help manage the calculations and the complex database. It appears that only about 25 percent of organizations are using the seven most common of these risk analysis tools (Baskerville, 2005). This evidence suggests that most organizations are not using risk analysis for information security decisions in any rigorous way.

In this chapter we will review a comprehensive framework that provides a more expansive approach to risk management than through the stand-alone use of risk analysis. Like risk analysis, this framework also recognizes that the two essential features of the risk landscape are the frequency and the impact of loss. However, these features are used to construct a risk treatment framework rather than directly used in the calculation of loss expectancies.

RISK MANAGEMENT: FOUR BASIC TYPES OF TREATMENTS

Figure 5.1 illustrates a common risk management framework constructed from the two major dimensions of organizational information risk. The vertical dimension is represented as the impact

Figure 5.1 **Risk Treatments Framework**

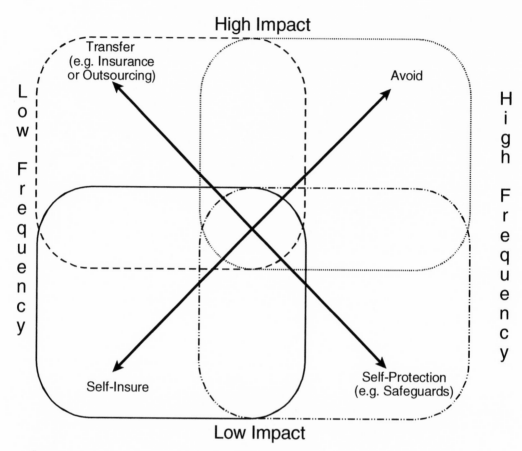

Source: Adapted from Jones and Ashenden, 2005.

of information security compromise in terms of the cost of loss, loss of reputation, loss of share-holder value, and so on. This impact is represented on a casual scale running from little impact (bottom) to high impact (top). The horizontal dimension is represented as the frequency with which information security compromises occur. At the left side of the diagram or low-frequency compromises in the scale runs casually from left to right, with high-frequency compromises represented on the right side of the diagram.

Each quadrant within the diagram represents one of the four combinations of impact and frequency. In the lower left-hand corner, we would locate information security compromises that occur with low frequency and low impact. For some organizations, an example might be the small, relatively rare, occurrences of outsider theft of service in which an outsider breaks into a consulting organization's organizational newsletter service in order to access the information without paying for the service. The quadrant is represented by a box drawn with a solid line. The edges of the box are rounded to indicate that edges of such categories are necessarily soft.

In the upper left-hand quadrant, we would locate information security compromises that occur with low frequency and high impact. These are relatively unusual occurrences of compromises that individually represent large losses to the organization. For some organizations, an example might be a large-scale denial of service attack on an essential processing system. Such an attack might interrupt business altogether, thereby causing large revenue losses. The box representing this quadrant is drawn with dashed lines.

In the upper-right-hand quadrant, we would locate information security compromises that occur with high frequency and high impact. These are relatively common occurrences of compromises that individually represent large losses to the organization. For some organizations, an example could be a compromise involving phishing spam intended to glean from the organization's customers their account login passwords in order to transfer funds. This quadrant is represented by a box of drawn with dotted lines.

In the lower-right-hand quadrant, we would locate information security compromises that occur with high frequency and low impact. These are relatively common occurrences of compromises that individually represent only small losses to the organization. For some organizations, an example might be common computer viruses that infect an individual workstation. The box representing this quadrant is drawn with lines that alternate between dotted and dashed lines.

The general categories of typical risk solution or treatments are represented by labels in each of the quadrants. For example, it is typical to treat low-impact low-frequency risks by self-insurance. Low-frequency, high-impact risks are often treated by techniques that transfer the risk to other organizations, for example through insurance or outsourcing. High-frequency, high-impact risks are those that are usually avoided if at all possible. Self-protection, for example, through the use of security controls on safeguards are the risk treatment usually applied for high-frequency, low-impact risks.

The four arrows in the diagram indicate the degree to which these categories of risk treatments inhabit each quadrant. For example, the more extreme the high-impact high-frequency risks, the more avoidance strategies are used to treat the risk. It is also a feature of this diagram that each of the quadrants overlaps each of the other quadrants. This overlapping is meant to represent that the risk treatments used in each quadrant are available and frequently used in combination with treatments from other quadrants. This illustrates how risks that occupy the middle of the diagram, that is, risks that are moderate in impact and moderate in frequency, will inevitably be treated with a combination of all four types of risk treatments. Similarly, high-frequency moderate-impact risks will be treated with a combination of self-protection and avoidance.

Self-Protection

The basic idea behind self-protection is that the organization implements practices that prevent risks in this category from having an impact on the organization. This category of risk treatment represents the approach to managing risk that most commonly comes to mind when managing information security. The safeguards employed in this category are commonly preventative in nature. It is in this category that information security safeguards and controls would be used to provide the self-protection. Technologies such as intrusion detection, firewalls, virus protection software, and VPNs, represent the implementation of risk treatments in this area.

Risk Transfer

As an alternative to self-protection, risk transfer involves distributing all or part of the impact of certain risks across multiple organizations. This is probably the second most common category of risk treatment that comes in to mind when managing information security. Mechanisms available to reduce risk in this category include the purchase of insurance on the market, such as business interruption insurance, or the use of outsourcing to transfer parts of the risky information systems to other organizations. Well-constructed outsourcing contracts will contain clauses that specify responsibilities for security performance and losses. Such specifics may include either risk sharing by both parties or straightforward risk assignment to the outsourcing vendor.

Self-Insurance

It is a mistake to regard this category of risk treatment as a "do-nothing" option. Although the risk treatment may not involve either self-protection (safeguards, controls, etc.) or risk transfer (insurance or outsourcing), it does involve various active forms of preparedness. The most common example is the maintenance of savings accounts to provide the funds necessary to restore proper operations after the occurrence of some information security compromise. Such savings accounts are a form of economic buffer on which the organization can draw in the event of a loss. There are other forms of buffer that might be categorized as self-insurance. Examples include maintaining excess capacity in information processing in order to permit the systems to operate effectively even when compromised and loaded with unauthorized processing. Many robust network configurations would be categorized as self-insurance. Self-insurance may also include some kinds of detective controls that enable the organization to discover compromises quickly enough to limit the damage to a minimum.

Avoidance

This category of risk treatment encompasses the basic business decision not to engage in certain forms of information processing because of the threat of compromise that might result frequently in high losses. For example, an organization may regard a Web-based business-to-consumer operation as entirely too risky because of the high frequency of intrusion attacks and high potential impact of such successful intrusions. It may choose to entirely avoid going into business in this area, thereby avoiding the risk entirely.

Other forms of avoidance involve risk treatments that effectively move the risk from the avoidance quadrant into one of the other quadrants. A common example is found in business-to-consumer e-commerce systems that confront the risk of having customer credit card data compromised through an intrusion into the customer database. Intrusion attacks on consumer websites are frequent and the losses that can follow disclosure of banking information can be very high. The most common risk treatment in this area is simply to avoid processing or retaining customer credit card data. This avoidance is accomplished by transferring the transaction interaction from the consumer site to a banking service for the final execution of credit card charges. The consumer site never has any processing retention of the credit card data. This risk resides entirely at the bank. In this way the risk is avoided entirely by not engaging in this form of customer data processing and transferring the risks to the bank. This treatment effectively moves the risk from the avoidance quadrant to the transfer quadrant.

ROLE OF RISK ANALYSIS AND SECURITY STANDARDS

The use of a risk transfer framework, such as that illustrated in Figure 5.1, does not necessarily eliminate economic risk analysis from the toolbox of information security managers. Cost and benefit valuation of risk treatment options within the framework may be sensible. For example, risk analysis might be used to determine values and parameters for insurance policies. Within the self-protection quadrant, risk analysis might be used to determine the economic value of certain

Figure 5.2   **The COBIT Framework**

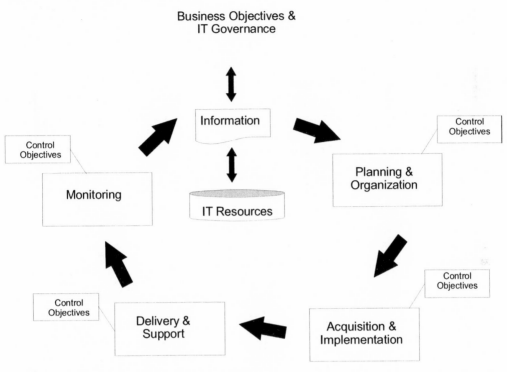

Business Objectives &
IT Governance

Information

Control
Objectives

Control
Objectives

Monitoring

IT Resources

Planning &
Organization

Control
Objectives

Control
Objectives

Delivery &
Support

Acquisition &
Implementation

Source: Adapted from "COBIT—Overview," 2005.

safeguards. In more complex decisions, risk analysis might be used to determine the optimum level of investments in safeguards versus investments in insurance.

Similarly, the use of a risk treatment framework does not necessarily eliminate the need for information security standards within the organization. Indeed, information security standards may be legislated by government or defined as necessary by industry or professional guidelines. In the United States for example, such legislation includes the Sarbanes-Oxley Act of 2002 and the Health Insurance Portability and Accountability Act of 1996. An example of an industry guideline would be the Payment Card Industry Data Security Standard (PCI).

Internal and external auditors involved in organizations that need to comply with such legislation or guidelines may adopt security standards such as ISO/IEC 17799 or COBIT (COBIT, 2005; ISO/IEC, 2005). As a result, decisions to adopt such external standards may be comprehensive. Standards such as these provide an encyclopedic inventory of safeguards and controls. This inventory is necessary in order for the security safeguards to be comprehensive and universal. This kind of universality requires the standards to have a solid architectural framework. The overall architecture of COBIT, for example, is illustrated in Figure 5.2.

Risk analysis or standards can be used within the risk treatment framework as decision aids helping to determine exactly which safeguards or controls will be used within the framework to treat various risks. However, these two vehicles represent diametrically opposed approaches to such a determination. Risk analysis, in a very essential way, operates with a default decision not to adopt any particular safeguard or control. In other words, the adoption of a safeguard must be justified through risk analysis.

Table 5.1

Risk and Treatment Portfolio Layout

Portfolio category	Portfolio of risks	Portfolio of treatments
Low frequency, low impact	Risk One	Self-insurance Treatment One
	Risk Two	Self-insurance Treatment Two
	Risk Three	Self-insurance Treatment Three
	. . .	. . .
Low frequency, high impact	Risk One	Risk Transfer Treatment One
	Risk Two	Risk Transfer Treatment Two
	Risk Three	Risk Transfer Treatment Three
	. . .	. . .
High frequency, low impact	Risk One	Self-Protection Treatment One
	Risk Two	Self-Protection Treatment Two
	Risk Three	Self-Protection Treatment Three
	. . .	. . .
High frequency, high impact	Risk One	Avoidance Treatment One
	Risk Two	Avoidance Treatment Two
	Risk Three	Avoidance Treatment Three
	. . .	. . .

Without a favorable risk analysis, or indeed without any risk analysis and all, the safeguard will not be adopted. However, when standards are used, the basis of the decision is the exact opposite. Most standards specify an encyclopedic inventory of safeguards and controls. The decision not to adopt one of the safeguards and controls must be justified in the face of the standard. The default decision is changed by standards: now the default is adoption of standard safeguards. Without some risk analysis basis for deciding not to follow the standard, every safeguard will be adopted.

PORTFOLIOS OF RISKS AND RISK TREATMENTS

The risk treatment framework, together with appropriate use of risk analysis and security standards, provides the basis on which information security managers can formulate sound risk strategies that include the most appropriate treatments for the various information security threats the organization confronts.

The basic risk and risk treatment portfolio can be organized according to the risk treatment framework in Figure 5.1. Various organizational risks can be characterized according to their general impact and frequency. The portfolio of risk treatments, including safeguards for self-protection, risk transfer, and self-insurance, can be equally organized. In this way, a portfolio arranges the different kinds of information security risks faced by the organization, and organizes an appropriate collection of treatments that balance the portfolio (see Table 5.1).

Five best practices have been identified as a process for developing the risk treatment portfolio (Baskerville, 2005):

1. *Define an overall organizational risk management strategy.* Such a strategy can be constructed from the risk treatment framework and incorporate processes for identifying risks in developing risk treatments. These processes can include security standards and risk analysis, as detailed below.
2. *Adhere to one of the prevalent IT security standards.* This practice is usually a good

Table 5.2

Octave Method

Phase 1: Build asset-based threat profiles
    Process 1: Identify senior management knowledge
    Process 2: Identify operational area knowledge
    Process 3: Identify staff knowledge
    Process 4: Create threat profiles
Phase 2: Identify infrastructure vulnerabilities
    Process 5: Identify key components
    Process 6: Evaluate selected components
Phase 3: Develop security strategy and plans
    Process 7: Conduct risk analysis
    Process 8: Develop protection strategy

substitute for the development of an overall IT security architecture because such an architecture is typically coded into the standard. However, adopting such a security standard should be done with critical consideration for the encyclopedic nature of the controls and safeguards inventory. Mechanisms, such as economic risk analysis, should be considered that promote the best possible decision making with regard to which safeguards and controls are not to be adopted. In this way, the standard and risk analysis become a dialectic in which safeguards and controls are adopted as a result of the interplay and the tension between the universal inventory of controls and the economic justification of each control through the cost-benefit operation of risk analysis.

3. *Develop and deploy safeguards and controls that provide the optimal combination of risk treatments.* These will include combinations of safeguards that collectively provide both preventative and recovery measures. Such measures will operate across the risk treatment quadrants, including self-insurance, self-protection, and transfer.

4. *Provide system risk review mechanisms.* These reviews should be formulated such that decisions can be taken to cancel development of risky systems, or risky parts of systems, or to otherwise opt out of risky information system components that are unnecessary to the organization's mission.

5. *Test all risk treatments.* The common testing mechanisms, such as penetration testing, are important. However, testing and assurance practices should include all risk treatment quadrants, including self-insurance, self-protection, and transfer.

These five practices provide an overall risk management framework within which risk analysis plays an appropriate function. In this framework, risk analysis is not the primary means for determining the appropriate safeguards, but rather it is a tool for fine tuning decisions about individual treatments appropriate for the categories of risks and treatments.

Basic risk management concepts are inadequate as a stand-alone approach to IT risk management, although many existing information security methodologies adopt just this approach. In order to become adequate, a strategic risk framework is needed that adopts a portfolio view of risk treatment strategies. Where these methodologies have a strategic orientation, their adoption is made easier. For example, the OCTAVE approach (described in Chapter 4) has three major phases in its method (see Table 5.2). In the OCTAVE approach, Process 7, in phase 3 is "Conduct risk analysis" (Alberts and Dorofee, 2001). Because the method does a great deal of research leading up to this analysis, the use of a strategic risk treatment portfolio as a component in OCTAVE fits quite well.

Figure 5.3   **The ITIL Security Management Process**

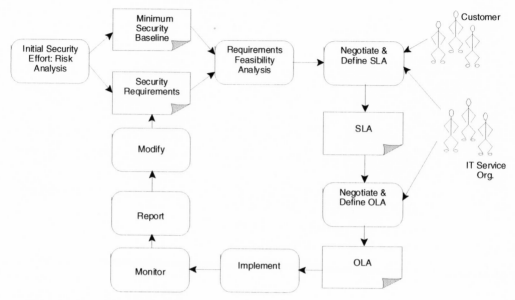

Source: Adapted from Weil, 2004.

Similarly, the strategic risk framework integrates well into the best practices defined by the security management volume of the IT Infrastructure Library (ITIL). This alignment is not surprising since ITIL, like the strategic risk framework, is developed with best practices as a guide and takes a business-strategy focus (although ITIL is oriented toward IT service delivery). The ITIL security management approach develops four kinds of products: policies, processes, procedures, and work Instructions (Weil, 2004). These correspond to processes at the strategic, tactical, and operational level. The method for developing these products is illustrated in Figure 5.3.

In the case of ITIL, unlike OCTAVE, the risk analysis is conducted as part of a baseline study of security requirements. These requirements must then be analyzed with a requirements feasibility study. Such feasibility studies are inherently economic in nature, and this means that the economics of risk treatment remains a key part of the decision making. The feasibility study then drives the negotiations for service-level agreements and operations-level agreements. After implementation of the security services, the quality and cost-effectiveness of the services are monitored and used in modifying further security requirements definitions. Again, the economics focus means that the risk treatment framework fits well into the ITIL approach.

FUTURE RESEARCH

Table 5.3 details possible future research areas.

Details on Table 5.3, Issues 1.1 and 1.2

There are no published inventories of security safeguards or controls that are categorized by the risk treatment type. Every IT risk manager must decide which controls fit within each risk category, and then determine whether or not each control should be included in a particular portfolio. Each

Table 5.3

Future Research

Area	Issue	Impact
1. Security safeguards and controls	1.1 No published inventories of security safeguards or controls classified by risk treatment type	Every designer must innovate controls that fit each category
	1.2 No clearinghouse for new kinds of safeguards and controls	Diffusion of security controls and safeguards is inhibited
2. Success of risk controls and safeguards	2.1 Fit between safeguards and risk settings	We do not know what organizational characteristics best define ideal settings for certain risk treatments
3. Poorly explored categories of treatments	3.1 What are the strategies for self-insurance?	Self-insurance needs to be elevated from its "do-nothing" assumptions

manager must "reinvent the wheel" in terms of deciding the character of the controls with the creation of each risk portfolio. In the process, managers may discover new kinds of safeguards or controls by thoughtful search of the solution space for different categories of risk treatments. Extensive research is needed to provide inventories of existing and new safeguards, both technical and managerial, that fit in the different risk treatment categories. Such inventories will make the job of constructing risk management portfolios much more straightforward.

Details on Table 5.3, Issue 2.1

The fit between the risk treatment inventories and the organization needs further study. What are the characteristics of different kinds of organizations that make them conducive to the effective use of different kinds of risk treatments? A better understanding of general relationships between organization characteristics (size, industry segment, leadership style, etc.) will help risk management strategists to be more effective in selecting IT risk management portfolios.

Details on Table 5.3, Issue 3.1

One of the most poorly understood categories of risk treatment is self-insurance. There are many different ways in which organizations can reduce the financial impact of a risk occurrence aside from depositing reserve money into a savings account. Further study is needed to expand our understanding of this category, and to explore and innovate new safeguards that enact this category of risk treatment for future strategic IT risk management portfolios.

This chapter has explored the ways in which IT risk management can move beyond the direct activities of risk analysis or risk assessment. While commonly discussed, these traditional risk management tools are limited in fundamental ways, making them difficult in practice. Beyond risk analysis, operational risk management can be seen to involve four types of risk treatments: (1) self-protection, (2) risk transfer, (3) self-insurance, and (4) risk avoidance. An example of an approach to risk management that goes beyond risk analysis and assessment involves more strategic management with a portfolio approach. Such a portfolio approach manages different risk portfolios with a matching portfolio of risk treatments.

REFERENCES

Alberts, C., and Dorofee, A. 2001. OCTAVE Criteria, version 2.0, December. Software Engineering Institute (available at www.sei.cmu.edu/publications/documents/01.reports/01tr016.html).

Baskerville, R. 1991a. Risk analysis as a source of professional knowledge. *Computers & Security*, 10, 8, 749–764.

Baskerville, R. 1991b. Risk analysis: an interpretive feasibility tool in justifying information systems security. *European Journal of Information Systems*, 1, 2, 121–130.

Baskerville, R. 2005. Best practices in IT risk management: buying safeguards, designing security architecture, or managing information risk? *Cutter Benchmark Review*, 5, 12, 5–12.

COBIT. 2005. *COBIT—Overview* (available at www.isaca.org/cobit.htm, accessed on January 23, 2005).

ISO/IEC. 2005. *ISO/IEC 17799: Information technology—Security techniques—Code of Practice for Information Security Management*. International Standard No. ISO/IEC 17799:2005(E). Geneva: International Standards Organization.

Jones, A., and Ashenden, D. 2005. *Risk Management for Computer Security: Protecting Your Network & Information Assets*. Oxford: Butterworth-Heinemann.

Klir, G.J.; St. Clair, U.H.; and Yuan, B. 1997. *Fuzzy Set Theory: Foundations and Applications*. Upper Saddle River, NJ: Prentice-Hall.

Weil, Steven. 2004. How ITIL can improve information security. *Security Focus* (available at www.securityfocus.com/infocus/1815).

CHAPTER 6

SECURITY POLICY

From Design to Maintenance

MICHAEL E. WHITMAN

Abstract: *The development of effective information security policy is essential to any information security program. The legal pitfalls associated with ineffective policy can undermine even the most well-intentioned process. This chapter overviews the development of information security policy: the investigation, analysis, design, implementation, and maintenance and change of the policy documents. It also examines the requirements of effective policy in ensuring that the developed policy is distributed, read, understood, and agreed to by employees, and uniformly applied by the organization in order to stand up to external scrutiny and potential legal challenge.*

Keywords: *Information Security Policy, Information Security Policy Development, Design, Implementation of Information Security*

INTRODUCTION

This chapter analyzes the complex process associated with designing, implementing, and supporting information security policy. It is a well-documented point that quality security programs begin and end with policy (Fulford and Doherty, 2003; Whitman and Mattord, 2005; Wood, 2000). Information security is a function that is the responsibility of an organization's management, supported by the technical staff of the organization. As information security is primarily a management problem, not a technical one, policy guides personnel to function in a manner that will assure the security of an organization's information assets, rather than to act as a threat to those same assets. Security policies are one of the least expensive controls to execute, but are among the most difficult to properly implement. They are the lowest cost in that they involve only the time and effort of the management team to create, approve, and communicate them. Even if the management team decides to hire an outside consultant to assist in the development of policy, the costs are minimal compared to almost any technical controls.

Shaping policy is difficult because it must: (1) never conflict with laws; (2) stand up in court, if challenged; and (3) be properly administered, including thorough dissemination and documentation by personnel showing they have read, understood, and agreed to the policies (Whitman and Mattord, 2005). This chapter introduces the concept of the policy development life cycle, demonstrating the stages of development from business need, through the implementation and maintenance of policy.

This chapter begins with a clear definition of policies and then overviews the challenges associated with creating them. The chapter then enumerates the various types of policies, documenting the best practices used in their creation and implementation. It continues with an overview of work published on the development of policy and concludes with a discussion of areas in which additional research is needed.

INFORMATION SECURITY POLICY

The term "security policy" will vary in meaning depending on the context of its usage. A policy is "a plan or course of action, as of a government, political party, or business, intended to influence and determine decisions, actions, and other matters" (Merriam-Webster, 2002). The concept of security policy within governmental agencies addresses the security of nations and their dealings with foreign states. In the context of this chapter, security policies are established rules that provide guidance in the protection of an organization's assets. Within the organization, policies specify acceptable and unacceptable behavior, in essence serving as organizational laws—dictating to the employees of the organization what they may and may not say, and how they may or may not act, within the scope of the professional association and within the context of the organizational culture. Similar in design and implementation to law, policy is formulated by an authorized entity, ratified into an enforceable code, made public knowledge, and enforced with clear penalties and procedures for violations. An information security policy provides rules for the protection of the information assets of the organization. The purpose of an information security program is to "protect the confidentiality, integrity, and availability of information and information systems, whether in transition, storage or processing through the application of policy, education and training programs, and technology" (Whitman and Mattord, 2005). Information has confidentiality when disclosure or exposure to unauthorized individuals or systems is prevented. Confidentiality ensures that only those with the rights and privileges to access information are able to do so. Information has integrity when it is whole, complete, and uncorrupted. The integrity of information is threatened when the information is exposed to corruption, damage, destruction, or other disruption of its authentic state. Availability enables authorized users—persons or computer systems—to access information without interference or obstruction, and to receive it in the required format.

Policy's role in this regard is the iteration of the intent of management in the protection and use of organizational information assets. Policies should be considered living documents, meaning that they will require constant modification and maintenance as the needs of the organization and the environment in which the organization operates evolve. Policies are written to support the mission, vision, and strategic planning of an organization. Policies should not be confused with standards, practices, procedures, or guidelines, although they are commonly combined in organizational documents. Standards are effectively the measurement criteria by which policy compliance is assessed, and carry the same requirement for compliance as policy. Practices provide examples of how to comply with policies, with procedures providing detailed step-by-step guidance. Guidelines provide practical advice on how to effectively comply with policy.

Exactly how the organization will be affected by a policy is in part dictated by the type of policy in question. In general, there are three types or levels of information security policy, each with a specific focus and audience and each with a clearly defined purpose. As illustrated in the National Institute of Standards and Technology (NIST) Special Publication 800–14 (1996) and Whitman and Mattord (2005), these types include the enterprise information security policy (EISP) or security program policy; the issue-specific security policy (ISSP), and the system-specific security policy (SysSP). This three-level delineation of policy is reflected in other studies, including Baskerville and Siponen (2002) and Abrams and Bailey (1995). Each of these types of policy is examined in greater detail.

Enterprise Information Security Policy

The EISP is also known as the security program policy, general security policy, IT security policy, or most simply, information security policy. This policy sets the strategic direction, scope, and tone for all security efforts within the organization. The EISP is an executive-level document, usually drafted by, or in cooperation with, the chief information officer of the organization. This policy is a brief document usually only two to five pages long. The EISP is designed to shape the philosophy of information security in the organization. The EISP is based on and directly supports the mission, vision, and ethics of the organization. The EISP serves to guide the development, implementation, and management of the security program, and the processes used to assure safe and secure operations of the organization's information assets. It contains the requirements to be met by the information security blueprint or framework, as well as defines the purpose, scope, constraints, and applicability of the security program in the organization. It also assigns responsibilities for the various areas of security, including systems administration, maintenance of the information security policies, and the practices and responsibilities of the users. Finally, it addresses legal compliance. The EISP typically addresses compliance in two areas:

1) General compliance to ensure meeting the requirements to establish a program and the responsibilities assigned therein to various organizational components and 2) the use of specified penalties and disciplinary action. (NIST, 1995)

When the EISP has been developed, the chief information security officer (CISO) begins forming the security team and initiates development or review of an institutional security program. The EISP is a relatively stable document and usually does not require continuous modification, unless there is a change in the strategic direction of the organization. A periodic updating of key personnel and contact information is usually all that is required.

A typical EISP will contain the sections shown in Table 6.1. This framework is similar in design to the model proposed by Forcht and Ayers (2000), which recommends the following sections:

A. Scope
B. Definitions
C. Responsibilities
D. Risk profile
E. Corporate requirements
F. Other security measures
G. Disaster recovery
H. Internet security
I. Enforcement
J. Policy coordinator

The relevant sections of this framework, based on an assessment of existing federal and industry recommendation for policy structure, share commonality with the previous framework, save for sections on risk profile, disaster recovery, and Internet security, which are deemed inappropriate for the strategic information security policy (EISP) as these topics are so detailed as to preclude their inclusion except in very general summation. These subjects are more appropriate in subordinate policies specifically crafted for their own purposes.

Table 6.1

Components of the EISP

Component	Description
Statement of purpose	Answers the question, "What is this policy for?" Provides a framework that helps the reader understand the intent of the document. Can include text such as the following:
	"This document will:
	Identify the elements of a good security policy
	Explain the need for information security
	Specify the various categories of information security
	Identify the information security responsibilities and roles
	Identify appropriate levels of security through standards and guidelines
	This document establishes an overarching security policy and direction for our company. Individual departments are expected to establish standards, guidelines, and operating procedures that adhere to and reference this policy while addressing their specific and individual needs." (WUSTL, n.d.)
Information technology security elements	Defines information security. For example:
	"Protecting the confidentiality, integrity, and availability of information while in processing, transmission, and storage, through the use of policy, education and training, and technology . . ."
	This section can also lay out security definitions or philosophies to clarify the policy.
Need for information technology security	Provides information on the importance of information security in the organization and the obligation (legal and ethical) to protect critical information whether regarding customers, employees, or markets.
Information technology security responsibilities and roles	Defines the organizational structure designed to support information security within the organization. Identifies categories of individuals with responsibility for information security (IT department, management, users) and their information security responsibilities, including maintenance of this document.
Reference to other information technology standards and guidelines	Lists other standards that influence and are influenced by this policy document, perhaps including relevant laws (federal and state) and other policies.

Source: From Whitman and Mattord, 2004. Reprinted with permission of Course Technology, a division of Cengage Learning: permissions.cengage.com. Fax (800) 730–2215.

Issue-Specific Security Policy (ISSP)

As the organization executes various technologies and processes to support routine operations, certain guidelines are needed to instruct employees to use these technologies and processes properly. In general, the ISSP (1) addresses specific areas of technology as listed below, and as a result, is

Table 6.2

Issue-Specific Policy Statement

1. Statement of policy
   Scope and applicability
   Definition of technology addressed
   Responsibilities
2. Authorized access and usage of equipment
   User access
   Fair and responsible use
   Protection of privacy
3. Prohibited usage of equipment
   Disruptive use or misuse
   Criminal use
   Offensive or harassing materials
   Copyrighted, licensed, or other intellectual property
   Other restrictions
4. Systems management
   Management of stored materials
   Employer monitoring
   Virus protection
   Physical security
   Encryption
5. Violations of policy
   Procedures for reporting violations
   Penalties for violations
6. Policy review and modification
   Scheduled review of policy
   Procedures for modification
7. Limitations of liability
   Statements of liability
   Other disclaimers

Source: Whitman, Townsend, and Alberts, 1999. Used with permission.

closely linked to that technology implementation within the organization, (2) requires frequent updates, and (3) contains a statement on the organization's position regarding appropriate use of the technology. Sometimes the ISSP may be referred to as an "appropriate use" or a "fair and responsible use" policy. An ISSP addresses one or more of the following topics:

- Electronic mail
- Use of the Internet and WWW
- Specific minimum configurations of computers to defend against worms and viruses
- Prohibitions against hacking or testing organization security controls
- Home use of company-owned computer equipment
- Use of personal equipment on company networks
- Use of telecommunications technologies (fax, phone)
- Use of photocopy equipment

Table 6.2 presents an outline of a sample ISSP, which can be used as a model. What must be added above and beyond this structure are the specific details dictating what the security procedures are for individual issues not covered beyond the general guidelines.

Each major category presented in the sample issue-specific policy above is explained below in order to elaborate the components involved in each section. While the details may vary from policy to policy, and some sections of a modular policy may be combined, it is essential for management to address each section in order to formulate a complete policy.

Statement of Policy

The ISSP should begin with a clear statement of purpose. The introductory section should outline the scope and applicability of the policy, specifically noting: What does this policy address? Who is responsible and accountable for policy implementation? What technologies and issues does the policy document address?

Authorized Access and Usage of Equipment

This section of the policy statement addresses who can use the technology governed by the policy, and what it can be used for. Remember, in most organizations, especially private companies, the organization's information systems are the exclusive property of an organization, and users have no particular rights of use. Each technology and process is provided for business operations. Use for any other purpose constitutes misuse of equipment. This section defines "fair and responsible use" of equipment and other organizational assets and should also address key legal issues, such as protection of personal information and privacy.

Prohibited Usage of Equipment

While the policy section described immediately above detailed what the issue or technology can be used for, this section outlines what it cannot be used for. Unless a particular use is clearly prohibited, the organization cannot penalize its employees. The following actions could be prohibited: personal use, disruptive use or misuse, criminal use, offensive or harassing materials, and infringement of copyrighted, licensed, or other intellectual property.

Appropriate Use

The ISSP documents noted above ("Authorize Access and Usage of Equipment" and "Prohibited Usage of Equipment") may be more efficiently presented under a single policy that could be titled "Appropriate Use Policy." Many organizations use an ISSP with that name to cover the policy needs and issues for both subject areas.

Systems Management

There may be some overlap between an ISSP and a systems-specific policy (SysSP), but this section of the policy statement focuses on the users' relationship to systems management. Specific rules from management about how to use e-mail and other electronic documents may be required to regulate the use of e-mail, the storage of materials, authorized employer monitoring, and the physical and electronic security of the contents of e-mail and other electronic documents. It is important that all responsibilities be delegated to either be the user's or the systems administrator's accountability, otherwise both parties may infer that the responsibility for taking an action belongs to the other party.

Violations of Policy

Once guidelines on equipment use have been outlined and responsibilities have been assigned, the individuals to whom the policy applies must understand the penalties and repercussions of violating the policy. Violations of policy should carry appropriate penalties: do not impose the death penalty for parking violations. Not only should this section of the policy statement contain the specifics of the penalties for each type or category of violation, it should also provide instructions on how individuals in the organization can report observed or suspected violations, either openly or anonymously. Many individuals feel that powerful individuals in the organization could discriminate against, single out, or otherwise get back at someone who reports violations. Anonymous submissions are often the only way to convince individual users, especially lower-level employees and lay staff, to report the unauthorized activities of other, more influential employees.

Policy Review and Modification

When policies are perceived as out-of-date, they are not taken seriously. Therefore, each policy should contain procedures and a timetable for periodic review to validate the timeliness of the document. As the needs and technologies change in an organization, so must the policies that govern their use. This section should contain a specific methodology for the review and modification of the policy, to ensure that users do not begin circumventing it as it grows obsolete.

Limitations of Liability

The final section is a general statement of liability or set of disclaimers. If an individual employee is caught conducting illegal activities with organizational equipment or assets, management does not want the organization held liable. So the policy should state that if employees violate a company policy or any law using company technologies, the company will not protect them and the company is not liable for their actions. It is inferred here that such a violation would be without the knowledge of or authorization by the organization (Whitman, Townsend, and Aalberts, 1999).

There are a number of approaches toward creating and managing ISSPs within an organization. Three of the most common are:

1. Create a number of independent ISSP documents, each tailored to a specific issue
2. Create a single comprehensive ISSP document attempting to cover all issues
3. Create a modular ISSP document that unifies policy creation and administration, while maintaining each specific issue's requirements

The individual policy approach to creating and managing ISSPs typically results in a shotgun effect. Each department responsible for a particular application of technology creates a policy governing its use, management, and control. This approach to creating ISSPs may fail to cover all of the necessary issues, and it can suffer from poor policy distribution, management, and enforcement. The comprehensive policy approach is centrally managed and controlled. With formal procedures for the management of ISSPs in place, the comprehensive policy approach establishes guidelines for overall coverage of necessary issues and clearly identifies processes for their dissemination, enforcement, and review. Usually, technology providers within the organization that centrally manage the information technology resources develop these policies. This approach may be sufficient for smaller organizations but can become unwieldy for medium-to-large organizations. The optimal balance between the individual ISSP and the comprehensive ISSP approaches is the modular approach. It is also centrally managed and controlled, but custom-tailored to the individual technology issues. The modular approach provides a balance between issue orientation and policy management. The policies created with this approach include individual modules, each created and updated by capable individuals each of whom is regarded as a subject-matter expert and is responsible for the issue addressed. These individuals report to a central policy administration group that incorporates issue specifics into an overall comprehensive policy.

Systems-Specific Policy (SysSP)

While issue-specific policies are formalized as written documents, distributed to users, and agreed to in writing, SysSP are frequently presented as hybrid documents that combine policy factors with the articulation of a system for standards and procedures used when configuring or maintaining systems. An example of a systems-specific policy is the access control list that defines which users may and may not access a particular system, complete with levels of access for each authorized user. Systems-specific policies can be organized into two general groups: managerial guidance SysSPs, and technical guidance SysSPs.

Managerial Guidance SysSPs

For a systems administrator to properly configure a piece of the organization's information security technology, as part of an active security posture, the administrator must first receive clear guidance outlining the organization's intent with regard to that implementation. For example, before a firewall administrator restricts access to the organization's intranet by filtering all external FTP connection requests, he or she must have been advised by management that such an action is needed and desired. If administrators are not provided with this specific guidance, then they may take it upon themselves to configure the technology according to their own personal beliefs and experiences rather than as a result of true managerial guidance. While the format and structure of this document will vary widely between implementations, the common components are as follows.

Overview of the Scope and Purpose of the SysSP. Similar to the previous sections, this section provides the tone and focus for this document.

Managerial and Organizational Intent of the Implementation of the Technology. Focusing on the specific technology for which the policy is issued, this section enforces the philosophical intent of the organization's leadership and addresses the logic and reasoning behind the policy. It is this additional justification that provides support to the systems administrator when challenged by other managers and users. Specific implementation requirements in the form of permits and denies:

1. Permit the following actions: . . .
2. Deny the following actions: . . .

This section specifically outlines the shoulds and should nots of the technology: what the technology should and should not allow. This section could be written in the context of specific technologies or protocols, as in "should allow SMTP or POP3 traffic," or it could be in terms of general usage, as in "should allow all e-mail based communications."

Guidance for Permitting Exceptions. With every rule there is inevitably cause for exceptions. In the event that a user requests an exception to a rule, there must be a procedure in place for processing, reviewing, and approving or denying such requests. This section specifies the what, what, when, and how of such a procedure.

Technical Guidance SysSPs

The second category of SysSPs address systems configurations by systems administrators. These guidances are frequently systems configuration, rather than printed policies. As a firewall administrator configures a firewall, the administrator creates this technical guidance SysSP, just as a systems administrator does when setting up user accounts. Technical guidance SysSPs commonly fall into two sub-categories: ACLs and configuration rules. Access control lists (ACLs) consist of the access control lists, matrices, and capability tables governing the rights and privileges of a particular user to a particular system. As indicated earlier, an ACL is a list of access rights used by file storage systems, object brokers, or other network communications devices to determine which individuals or groups may access an object that it controls. A similar list, referred to as a capability table, is associated with users and groups to specify which subjects and objects a user or group can access. These specifications are frequently complex matrices, rather than simple lists or tables. In general ACLs regulate the who, what, when, where, and how of access:

- *Who* can use the system
- *What* authorized users can access
- *When* authorized users can access the system
- *Where* authorized users can access the system from
- *How* authorized users can access the system

Configuration rules comprise the specific configuration codes entered into security systems to guide the execution of the system when information is passing through it. Rule policies are more specific to the operation of a system than ACLs, and may or may not deal with users directly. Many security systems require specific configuration scripts telling the systems what actions to perform on each set of information they process.

Other references to designing security policies can be found in the work of Charles Cresson Wood (2003), and the references available through NIST such as SP 800–12 (1995) and the Federal Agency Security Practices (FASP, n.d.).

Information Security Policy Development

Designing information security policy is frequently the work of a single security manager, CISO, or security administrator. This is unfortunate because the work of any individual is unlikely to be as comprehensive as it might be if the information security policies were developed by a team representing the disparate constituencies of the organization. It also may suffer if the single individual responsible for the design and maintenance of the policy leaves the organization. In fact, the development of an effective policy closely mirrors that of an information system, with clear investigation, analysis, design, implementation, and maintenance and change phases. These phases are summarized in Table 6.3 and discussed in additional detail in the following sections.

Policy development begins with an investigation of the problem facing the organization, con-

Table 6.3

Phases of the Policy Development Life Cycle

Phase	Action
Investigation	An examination of the event or plan that initiates the process. Includes the specification of the objectives, constraints and scope of the policy.
Analysis	An assessment of the organization, the status of current policies, and the anticipated perception of those to whom the policy will be applied.
Design	The selection of policy components that specifically address the needs of the users and of the organization, and creation, review, and approval of draft policy.
Implementation	The distribution, reading, understanding, agreement and uniform enforcement of policy.
Maintenance and change	The support, review, and modification of policy for the remainder of its useful life cycle.

tinues with an analysis of current organizational practices and extant policies, and then proceeds into the logical and physical design phases. In the design phases, drafts of the proposed policy are created and reviewed by the appropriate authorities. Next, in the implementation phase policies are published, individual users are briefed on the policy and are provided the appropriate security awareness and training to reinforce the policy. Finally, the policy moves into its maturity phase, where it is maintained and modified over the remainder of its operational life. Like the information systems implementation, the policy development life cycle may have multiple iterations, as over time the cycle is repeated. Only through constant examination and renewal can any system, especially a security policy, be expected to perform to standard in the constantly changing environment in which it is placed.

Investigation

The first step is the most important. What is the problem the policy is being developed to address? The investigation phase begins with an examination of the event or plan that initiates the process. During the investigation phase the objectives, constraints and scope of the policy are specified. Preliminary discussions with key management officials will help to ensure the policy is in fact being drafted to resolve the actual issue at hand, and not simply a symptom of an underlying problem. If an organization is experiencing a problem with employees downloading unauthorized software, will a policy prohibiting this resolve the problem, or could the underlying problem be the employees do not have the necessary software to accomplish their tasks? Investigations into this problem could prevent unnecessary effort in an unproductive direction. The investigation stage also involves the formulation of the policy team as mentioned earlier. Beginning with the champion—the executive level official who will sanction the work of the policy team, and mandate its enforcement—a team of representatives from across the organization at all levels is assembled. It is important that this team include users as well as managers, technical as well as administrative staff. This team will also include key representatives from the information security communities of interest—managerial representatives from the information security, information technology, and general management communities—who have been tasked with assisting in the development and implementation of

Table 6.4

Stages of Policy Implementation

Phase	Action
Dissemination (distribution)	Delivery of policy in hard copy or electronic format, ensuring the employee receives each policy document
Review (reading)	Ensuring the individual to whom the policy applies can and does read the document, including those literacy challenged
Comprehension (understanding)	Assessment of employee grasp of policy content and meaning
Compliance (agreement)	Documentation of policies agreement by act or affirmation, indicating willful compliance
Uniform enforcement	Organizational enforcement of policy equally and without prejudice

information security in general. At the end of the investigation phase, the project manager, most typically the CISO, or other information security manager tasked with the authoring of the policy document itself, should have gained a better understanding of the problem at hand, how the policy will fit into the organizational culture, and the scope and purpose of the policy.

Analysis

The analysis phase begins with a review of the information learned during the investigation phase. Analysis consists primarily of an assessment of the organization, the status of current policies, and the anticipated perception of those to whom the policy will be applied. The purpose of the policy is focused and refined and other policies are reviewed to ensure no unintentional overlap will occur. The policy team should also examine current legislation to ensure no conflict between policy and law is introduced. This phase ends with the documentation of the findings and a feasibility analysis update.

Design

In this phase, the information gained from the analysis phase is used to begin drafting the proposed policy. In any policy solution it is imperative that the first and driving factor is the business need. Then, based on the business need, the team selects policy components that specifically address the needs of the users and of the organization, and creates a draft policy. During the design phase, the draft policy is presented to various approval authorities for review and comment. Once management approves the policy, implementation can commence.

Information Security Policy Implementation and Maintenance

The details of the implementation of policy can either support or hinder the use of the policy in the organization. The implementation of a policy will involve multiple stages and will vary depending on policy type. In general, policy is only enforceable if it is properly implemented using a process that assures repeatable results and avoids legal challenges. One approach known to be effective is to use the following five stages: dissemination (distribution), review (reading), comprehension (understanding), compliance (agreement), and uniform enforcement. These phases are overviewed in Table 6.4, and discussed in subsequent sections.

Dissemination of Information Security Policy

The dissemination or distribution of an information security policy, while seemingly self-evident, can require a substantial investment by the organization in order to be done effectively. Some organizations prefer hard-copy distribution, in which a printed copy of the document must be delivered to the individual to whom the policy will apply. While the most common distribution of policy is by mail (external or internal), there is no guarantee that the individual will actually receive the document, unless it is physically delivered with proof of receipt. As many information security policies may contain information that the organization does not want publicly disclosed, it may be to the organization's advantage to label the document using a developed classification scheme, and control its dissemination. Document classification schemes vary depending on the organization and the relative sensitivity of the information in question. "A simple scheme can allow an organization to protect its sensitive information such as marketing or research data, personnel data, customer data, and general internal communications, such as:

- Public: For general public dissemination, such as an advertisement or press release.
- For official use only (FOUO): Not for public release but not particularly sensitive, such as internal communications.
- Sensitive: Important information that could embarrass the organization or cause loss of market share if compromised.
- Classified: Essential and confidential information, disclosure of which could severely damaged the well-being of the organization. (Whitman and Mattord, 2004)

For organizations preferring electronic document distribution, there are a number of options. Publication via secure intranet is a common example. Organizations with secure intranets can elect to store these documents on the intranet in HTML or PDF format. While this simplifies the distribution, it can cause difficulties in ensuring 100 percent distribution, with proof of receipt. An alternate method to ensure effective delivery with receipt and compliance is through electronic policy distribution software, as described in a later section. This software can be used to manage the entire implementation process, documenting each stage, along with approval, posting information, and user receipt, comprehension, and compliance. Once the organization has documented the distribution of the policy, the next stage is reading or review of the policy.

Review of Information Security Policy

As the user receives the policy, whether in hard-copy or electronically, the next stage the organization must implement to support enforcement is review or reading. In this stage the organization must ensure the individual to whom the policy applies can and does read the document. This reading requirement may be a function of literacy or technology. From a literacy standpoint, organizations may employ individuals without functional reading skills. Many jobs in the organization are open to those with poor literacy skills, from custodial to production line. Even if individuals have physical access to the policies, it is important to ensure that all members of the organization have the opportunity and ability to read policy documents, even if this means that some policies will have to be read to the individuals.

The second challenge in review also pertains to literacy, but from a language standpoint. As organizations increasingly become multinational in scope, language barriers may impact the ability of individuals to review the policy. Simple translations of policy may not resolve the problem, as the language barrier may extend beyond the simple grammar of the document. Language barriers in international communications (while beyond the scope of this chapter) have long created challenges in business. For example, a translation miscue occurred in 1989 when Nike Corporation ran an advertisement showing a Samburu tribesman speaking in his native language appearing to echo the company slogan—"Just do it." He really says "I don't want these. Give me big shoes" (Ricks, 1993). Thus it becomes important to enlist the assistance of appropriate language specialists when implementing policies that apply to individuals speaking languages other than the organization's native tongue.

Comprehension of Information Security Policy

As the Chinese proverb states, "Tell me, and I forget; show me, and I remember; let me do and I understand" (Confucius, n.d.). In the policy context, this means that simply distributing a document that an individual can read may or may not guarantee that the individual will understand the content. While the research and study of human comprehension is beyond the scope of this chapter, comprehension can be defined as "the ability to grasp the meaning of material. This may be shown by translating material from one form to another (words to numbers), by interpreting material (explaining or summarizing), and by estimating future trends (predicting consequences or effects). These learning outcomes go one step beyond the simple remembering of material, and represent the lowest level of understanding" (Bloom et al., 1964). In this context of Bloom's taxonomy of learning, comprehension is synonymous with understanding (ECSA, 2003). Thus it is necessary but not sufficient for the individuals to whom the policy applies to be able to grasp the language of the policy document. It is equally important to ensure they can grasp its meaning.

There are several ways to gauge comprehension. One of the simplest is assessment through testing. It would therefore be in the organization's best interest to evaluate the ability of an employee to fully comprehend the policy by quizzing the employee on the policy's key points. Next, the specifics of comprehension are determined by the identification of a target goal commensurate with commonly accepted practices—for example, scores of 70 percent or better indicate successful completion. Just as the policy document could be hard-copy or electronic, so could the quiz. The important point is that the policy is assessed.

Compliance with Information Security Policy

Policies must be agreed to by act or affirmation, indicating willful compliance. Agreement by act occurs when the employee performs an action that indicates acknowledgment and understanding of the policy prior to use of a technology or organizational resource. Network banners, end-user license agreements, and posted warnings can assist in meeting this burden of proof. However, these in and of themselves may not be sufficient. Agreement by affirmation occurs when the employee signs a document indicating that he or she has read, understood, and will comply with a specific policy. The direct collection of a signature or the equivalent digital alternative can assist the organization in proving that it has obtained an agreement to comply with policy. This can be accomplished by including a renewal of policy compliance during the signing of employee contracts. The policy documents can be issued to the employee when the contract is up for renewal, and employment can be made contingent on agreement. However, in an employment-at-will environment, where there are no formal contracts, or at least no annually renewed contracts, compulsory agreement can become an issue. The organization may be faced with the last resort option of threatening termination or denial of use for failure to agree to policy.

A key part of the information security program is new employee orientation on information security policies. During a new hire's in-briefings, security training and awareness programs also include indoctrination into the organization's information security culture. New employees should immediately receive copies of existing policies and complete any necessary comprehension and compliance measures, including needed nondisclosure agreements (Whitman and Mattord, 2004; Tursi, 2003). Once the organization begins formalizing the documentation of compliance agreement, it may be able to use these values to report these facts.

Compliance may also be assessed through the collection of data on the numbers of violations of policy or of data on the number of incidents detected or reported to the appropriate agency within the organization. If the number of problems associated with the use of a technology decline considerably after a policy has been implemented, this fact can assist the organization in determining the effectiveness of the policy.

Uniform Application of Information Security Policy

Enforceability of policy is similar to the enforceability of law in that it must withstand the rigor of external scrutiny. If an organization fails to enforce a policy equally and without prejudice, it may be opening itself to litigation. For instance, if an organization has a clear policy requiring name badges to be prominently displayed and upper management decides not to comply with this policy, other employees should not be sanctioned for their noncompliance. If they are and then are able to produce evidence that the policy was not uniformly applied, then the organization may not only be held liable for compensatory damages but punitive damages as well.

Enlisting all employees in the enforcement of policy can help assuage concern over uniform application of policy. In a real-world example, a manager issued a name badge policy, but within two weeks was seen violating the policy himself. An employee spied him walking around a restricted area without his name badge being clearly displayed. The colleague in jest, but with an undertone of sincerity, asked if the manager were a visitor, since all employees were required by policy to display their name badges. The manager reached into a jacket pocket and produced the name badge, along with a $20 bill, which he promptly gave the employee as a reward for his diligent enforcement of the policy. Within weeks the entire staff was energetically challenging any and all individuals in accordance with the newly implemented policy.

This concept is reiterated by Nosworthy (2000), who recommends senior management should "be seen to be doing"; that is, supporting the program and policy by overt compliance. This can provide direct motivation to the rest of the organization, increasing not only the compliance level but also the acceptance of and attitudes toward the security policy.

In 1990, Eloff and Badenhorst examined the role of senior management commitment in implementing information security (then referred to as computer security). Their findings identified management commitment as a key success factor in the implementation of security in general. They also found the inverse to be true, that the lack of senior managerial support to be a leading cause of failure in the implementation of security. Their findings also suggest that failures in the implementation of information security were directly linked to failures in the implementation of security policy, illustrating the plight of the "rudderless ship" analogy. Eloff and Badenhorst proposed a security methodology, very similar to the policy development life cycle illustrated here, with security policy constituting the second phase in the process (Eloff and Badenhorst, 1990).

Maintenance and Change

In the policy development life cycle, the maintenance and change phase is the longest and most expansive phase of the process. This phase consists of the tasks necessary to support and modify the policy for the remainder of its useful life cycle. Even though formal development and implementation may conclude prior to this phase, the life cycle of the project will continue indefinitely, until such time as it is determined that the process should begin again from the investigation phase. At periodic points, the policy is reexamined for compliance, and the feasibility of continuance versus discontinuance is evaluated; updates and changes are managed. As the needs of the organization change, the policies that support the organization must also adapt to the change. It is imperative that those who manage the policies, as well as those to whom they apply, continually monitor the effectiveness of the policies in relation to the organization's environment. When it is determined that a current policy can no longer support the changed mission of the organization, the policy is brought up for dramatic redevelopment and a new policy is implemented. Maintenance of policy involves four key functions:

- Support for policy-violations reporting
- Equitable adjudication of violations
- Periodic review and revision
- Destruction of policy documents

Each of these is discussed in the following sections.

Support for Policy-Violations Reporting. As indicated earlier, effective policy documents should contain provisions by which employees can report suspected violations of policy. Whether anonymous or not, it is important that every user be employed as the eyes and ears of the organization to serve as detection and early warning of policy violations. Once these employees have detected violations, they should have a means of reporting them. Some options to consider in violations reporting include:

- Anonymous e-mail forms,
- E-mail to abuse@organziation.com,
- Anonymous phone reporting,
- Paper form drop boxes,
- Reporting procedures through supervisory channels, among others.

The advantages of anonymous reporting include an increased willingness for employees to report violations without "being involved." Most employees do not want to be involved in conflict, and as such may not be willing to become involved in a dispute. However, anonymous venues, in whatever format desired, can increase the probability of violations being reported. Disadvantages include the increased probability of "false positives" where disgruntled employees could report false allegations or accusations in an attempt to "get even" with a peer or supervisor. Supervisory channels, while important, may result in some violations not getting reported to the proper authorities. Supervisors may feel that the reporting of one of their employees would reflect badly on their managerial competence, and thus may attempt to resolve the issues "in-house." This may or may not be in the organization's best interest. At a minimum it serves to compartmentalize information and prevents a better assessment of problems occurring across the organization.

Equitable Adjudication of Violations. As indicated earlier, policies must be applied uniformly. Policies, in addition to being uniformly applied, must be swift and fair. The organization must prepare for the inevitability of dealing with policy violators. Some organizations may choose to allow the immediate supervisor deal with the problems, while others may prefer the executive-level manager responsible for the division to handle the matter. Wherever the organization chooses to place the responsibility for dealing with policy violators, there must be clear-cut policies and methods for processing policy violators. Few organizations prefer trial scenarios, with witnesses, testimony, and reasonable doubt, opting instead for summary judgments by a single manager with a predefined set of discretionary penalties, who only has to meet a reasonable preponderance of evidence criteria. Organizations may opt to implement an appeal process, whether to the next higher level of management or to some central ombudsman. The reasoning behind such a complex process is to ensure fairness and equity in the process and reduce arbitrary behavior in the organization, so that if the accused employee decides to transfer the matter to civil court, the organization can demonstrate reasonable process and policy.

Periodic Review and Revision. Policy documents inevitably lose their relevance and applicability with time. Effective policy documents should contain provisions indicating the review and revision process. Policy documents should be reviewed at least annually, and at a minimum by an individual knowledgeable in the policy process as well as the information security environment, such as the CISO or other senior information security manager. During the review, the document should be scrutinized for passages and provisions that differ from the current operations of the organization. Technologies evolve, processes and markets change, and the policies that regulate employee behavior must change with them. As policy is revised, it must be reviewed by a central policy committee to determine if the revisions are acceptable to the organization, and finally approved by an appropriate authority.

Destruction of Policy Documents. Once a policy has outlived its usefulness, and has been superseded or retired, it is important to require proper destruction of these potentially compromising documents. As a classified document, even FOUO policies can negatively impact the organization if obtained by a compromising individual. As such the organization's management of classified documents policy should specify the proper destruction of these documents. The organization may choose to combine the distribution of the new policy with a collection process in which a security representative collects the outdated policy as that person distributes the new policy. Some organization may simply wish to advise the individual to properly destroy the old policies, through shredding or placement in a central collection point for outsourced document destruction.

Information Security Policy Reinforcement—SETA Program

One of the most widely recognized mechanisms for informing employees on policy, assessing comprehension, and gathering compliance agreement is the security education training and awareness program (SETA) (Nosworthy, 2000; Whitman and Mattord, 2004; Whitman and Mattord, 2005). The SETA program is designed to influence employee behavior as a control by better preparing employees to perform their duties in compliance with (rather than in ignorance of) security policy and controls. One of the top threats to information security comes from acts of human error or failure (Whitman, 2003), and represents the individual user's inability to (a) perform a task correctly, making mistakes and thus putting information at risk, or (b) follow policy and procedures, thus consciously and possibly intentionally risking the security of information. In either case, SETA programs can reinforce the organization's policies (and penalties) for the protection of information. SETA programs can provide two major benefits:

1. They can improve employee behavior through the provision of proper methods of using technology and complying with policies, and
2. They enable the organization to hold employees accountable for their actions by illustrating and documenting the instruction of proper procedures and organizational policies, thus negating the defense of ignorance by the employee (Whitman and Mattord, 2004).

Nosworthy (2000) iterates the need for information security education and training programs as a method of communicating the program "to the people" as well as to business and IT managers. She advocates the use of a SETA life cycle to manage the SETA process, using steps including (1) defining objectives; (2) identifying requirements; (3) identifying training sources; (4) defining the information security management education and training program; (5) implementing the program; and (6) monitoring and testing the effectives of the program. This approach is similar to the one discussed in later sections.

Accountability is a key facet of information security. It is important, however, that employees recognize the necessity of accountability, not as a punitive measure, but as a preventative one. Using accountability to protect the viability of the organization is essential to ensuring it will have sustainable operations, unimpeded by negligence or misconduct. A failure to maintain accountability can result in the organization suffering unrecoverable financial or operational losses, and thus a termination of function.

SETA program consist of three functions designed to increase security:

- By building in-depth knowledge, as needed, to design, implement, or operate security programs for organizations and systems
- By developing skills and knowledge so that computer users can perform their jobs while using IT systems more securely
- By improving awareness of the need to protect system resources (NIST, 1995).

INFORMATION SECURITY EDUCATION

Security education consists of those actions taken to provide formal education in information security for information security professionals, IT professionals, or others with formal information security responsibilities. As security education is best left to the educational institutions, the details of how to implement a security education program is not discussed in this chapter. For organizations seeking institutions qualified to provide security education, resources that describe information security training programs include the NIST training and education site at http://csrc.nist.gov/ATE/training_&_education.html, the Virginia Alliance for Security Computing and Networking (VA SCAN) at www.vascan.org/training.html, and the National Security Agency (NSA)–identified Centers of Academic Excellence in Information Assurance Education (CAEIAE) at www.nsa.gov/isso/programs/nietp/newspg1.htm.

Information Security Training

Security training involves providing members of the organization with detailed information and hands-on instruction to enable them to perform their duties securely. Management of information security can choose whether it will develop customized in-house training or outsource all or part of the training program. A number of training options are available, ranging from formal outsourced training through national organizations like ISC2 (www.isc2.org) and SANS (www.sans.org) and through local training agencies. Organization may also select to conduct training in-house using existing staff as trainers. These trainers may borrow from established documents like those found at the Computer Security Resource Center at NIST (csrc.nist.gov), or the Committee on National Security Systems' library (www.cnss.org). A useful document for information security practitioners and those developing training programs is NIST SP 800–16. This manual describes training with an emphasis "on training criteria or standards, rather than on specific curricula or content. The training criteria are established according to trainees' role(s) within their organizations, and are measured by their on-the-job performance. This emphasis on roles and results, rather than on fixed content, gives the Training Requirements flexibility, adaptability, and longevity" (Wilson et al., 1998).

For federal agencies, such training is mandatory. The Computer Security Act of 1987 requires federal agencies to provide mandatory periodic training in computer security awareness and accepted computer practices to all employees involved with the management, use, or operation of their computer systems. Other federal requirements for computer security training are contained in OMB Circular A-130, Appendix III, and OPM regulations. Training is most effective when it is designed for a specific category of users, that is, general, managerial, and technical. The more closely the training is designed to match the specific needs of the users, the more effective it is, as in customizing training based on technical background or levels of proficiency. Training includes teaching users not only what they should or should not do, but also how they should do it (Whitman and Mattord, 2004). According to Wood (2004), many organizations use a decentralized approach to information security training, receiving piecemeal training from constituent departments.

Information Security Awareness

Of extreme importance in the process of implementing information security policy is the need to keep the policies fresh in the employees' minds. While the employees may be mindful of the policies when they are first implemented, eventually the day-to-day operations of the organization will cause the employees to become less attentive to the policies unless they are constantly reinforced. This reinforcement comes in the form of information security awareness. Employee awareness is recognized as one of the greatest challenges in implementing security in general (Ernst & Young, 2001; Siponen, 2000).

As noted in the NIST document SP 800–12, security awareness programs: "(1) set the stage for training by changing organizational attitudes to realize the importance of security and the adverse consequences of its failure; and (2) remind users of the procedures to be followed" (NIST, 1995). The security awareness program serves to constantly remind the employees of their responsibilities in the area of information security. According to Whitman and Mattord (2005), "When developing an awareness program, there are certain important ideas to keep in mind:

- Focus on people both as part of the problem and as part of the solution.
- Refrain from using technical jargon; speak the language the users understand.
- Use every available venue to access all users.
- Define at least one key learning objective, state it clearly, and provide sufficient detail and coverage to reinforce the learning of it.
- Keep things light; refrain from "preaching" to users.
- Don't overload the users with too much detail or too great a volume of information.
- Help users understand their roles in information security and how a breach in that security can affect their jobs.
- Take advantage of in-house communications media to deliver messages.

- Make the awareness program formal; plan and document all actions.
- Provide good information early, rather than perfect information late."

As Susan Hansche (2001) indicated in her article "Designing a Security Awareness Program," good security awareness programs should be "supported and led by example from management, simple and straightforward, a continuous effort. They should repeat important messages to ensure they get delivered. They should be entertaining, holding the users' interest and humorous where appropriate in order to make slogans easy to remember. They should tell employees what the dangers are (threats) and how they can help protect the information vital to their jobs." Hansche also notes that awareness programs should focus on topics that the employees can relate to, including "threats to physical assets and stored information, threats to open network environments, [and] federal and state laws they are required to follow, including copyright violations or privacy act information. It can also include specific organization or department policies and information on how to identify and protect sensitive or classified information, as well as how to store, label, and transport information. This awareness information should also address who they should report security incidents to, whether real or suspect" (Hansche, 2001).

The purpose of security awareness and security training is to modify employee behavior so that the individual performs according to organizational standards. These standards are designed to ensure a harmonious and productive work environment. By preparing employees to properly handle information, use applications, and operate within the organization, the organization can minimize the risk of accidental compromise, damage, or destruction of information. By making employees aware of, and constantly reinforcing awareness of, threats to information security, the potential damage that can result from these threats, and ways that these threats can occur, the organization can reduce the chance that the individuals will not take such threats seriously. By making employees aware of policy, the penalties for failure to comply with policy, and the mechanism by which policy violations are discovered, the organization can reduce the probability that an employee will try to get away with intentional misuse and abuse of information.

Effective training and awareness programs also make employees accountable for their actions. Demonstrating due care and due diligence by warning employees that misconduct, abuse, and misuse of information resources will not be tolerated and that the organization will not defend employees who engage in this behavior, can help indemnify the institution against lawsuits. Under the legal concept of "deep pockets," lawyers tend to prefer legal action against organizations and employers who typically have greater assets than individual employees. They will attempt to prove that the alleged conduct was not clearly prohibited by organizational policy, thereby making the organization liable for it.

Awareness Techniques. The NIST SP 800–12 also describes the essentials of developing effective awareness techniques: "Awareness can take on different forms for particular audiences. Appropriate awareness for management officials might stress management's pivotal role in establishing organizational attitudes toward security. Appropriate awareness for other groups, such as system programmers or information analysts, should address the need for security as it relates to their job. In today's systems environment, almost everyone in an organization may have access to system resources and therefore may have the potential to cause harm" (NIST, 1995).

Information security awareness programs can use multiple techniques to deliver the information security message. These techniques include the use of newsletters, posters, bulletin boards, flyers, presentations, computer-based training videos, and a host of other options. Awareness programs can be integrated into training programs, where employees receive training on new applications or methods and are then reminded of the reasons the proper use of these are essential. Unless constantly reinforced, employees can "tune-out" the information security message, and for this reason posters and bulletin boards should be changed frequently, newsletters revised, and new methods to reinforce the security message constantly reviewed (NIST, 1995).

The costs of developing information security awareness programs is relatively negligible, save for the costs of acquiring trinkets. If purchased externally or outsourced, information security awareness programs can be quite expensive, with professionally developed newsletters costing thousands of dollars annually. However, with a minimal investment in time, a Web-based intranet information security newsletter, highlighting upcoming security events, describing current threats to the organization, and providing reminders of contact information in information security, can be developed and implemented effectively. Similarly, posters, bulletin boards (physical or electronic), and flyers can be developed and distributed at low cost, to serve as constant and changing reminders of the threats to information security and the methods employees can adopt to combat these threats.

Success of Information Security Training and Awareness

Fulford and Doherty (2003) examined the application of information security policies in large UK-based organizations, finding 76 percent of respondents indicating the presence of a documented information security policy, with 43 percent of respondents disseminating these policies through a staff handbook and 60 percent through an intranet (multiple responses possible). Employee awareness training was used to reinforce these policies in many other organizations.

The annual CSI/FBI study examined the use of security awareness in the organization: "First, respondents were asked to rate the degree to which they agreed with the statement, 'My organization invests the appropriate amount on security awareness.' . . . On average, respondents from all sectors do not believe that their organization invests enough in security awareness. Survey participants were also asked to rate the importance of security awareness training to their organizations in each of several areas. For five of the eight security areas listed, the average rating indicated that training for [security awareness] was very important" (Gordon et al., 2004). In this report awareness for information security policy ranked the highest at 70 percent (cryptography—28%, investigation and legal issues—43%, security systems architecture—48%, economic aspects of computer security—51%, security management—63%, access control forms—64%, network security—70%).

Information Security Policy Automation

Electronic policy distribution software provides a controlled mechanism to facilitate the distribution of and compliance with a policy. The software frequently allows an individual policy creator to draft policy, submit it to a management representative for review and approval, and then post the policy in a user area, where user access, comprehension, and compliance can be measured. A typical policy management tool would provide the using organization with the following support:

- Facilitate the creation of information security policy.
- Facilitate the review and approval of information security policy.
- Facilitate the publication of policy.
- Facilitate the creation of quizzes on policy content to gauge comprehension.
- Document user access to policy.
- Document user acceptance of policy (compliance).
- Document user performance on policy comprehension quizzes.
- Track policy revision dates and remind policy administrators when updates are scheduled.

There are a number of products available that can assist in this process, such as VigilEnt Policy Center (VPC) from NetIQ (www.netiq.com/products/vpc/default.asp#). VPC provides two key functions: a design facility to support the creation, review, and approval of policies and comprehension quizzes and a distribution center for the publication, evaluation, and compliance of policies and their supporting quizzes. The key benefits that can emerge from using automated policy software include the ability to:

- Develop best practices policies more quickly
- Centralize information
- Improve policy enforcement
- Streamline policy creation processes
- Improve policy distribution
- Provide a complete solution (NetIQ, 2005).

Previous Research in Information Security Policy

Information security policy is an underdeveloped field, with little research dedicated to the examination of policy (Fulford and Doherty, 2003). As noted by many authors, effective information security management is predicated on effective policy (Hone and Elof, 2002; Fulford and Doherty, 2003; Whitman, 2003; among others), which forms the basis for the entire security program. Many articles on information security call for security policy as a recognized means to provide safeguards to information assets (see Hoffer and Straub, 1989; Straub and Nance, 1990; Whitman, 2003).

The problem is that even in organizations with information security policies, the degree of success in effective design and the degree of compliance often make the mere presence of policy an ineffective control (Moule and Giavara, 1995). As stated earlier, however, without policy, security would be implemented at the will of the administrator and would lack clear objectives and responsibilities (Higgens, 1999; Fulford and Doherty, 2003).

In 1990, Bergeron and Bérubé studied the presence and perceptions of end-user policies, including microcomputer security policy. This study asked two questions: (1) What policies are in force in organization? and (2) Are end users satisfied with these policies? Their findings indicated that only 68 percent of organizations had formulated microcomputer security policies (which fall under the category of ISSPs). They also identified an inverse relationship between the number of policies in general and the overall satisfaction of the end users. As part of their findings, they make the following recommendations for the formulation of policies:

1. All policies must contribute to the growth of the organization;
2. Ensure the adequate sharing of responsibility; and
3. End users should be involved with the formulation of microcomputer policies.

They also found that there can be an inverse relationship between the number of policies implemented and the satisfaction of the users, with excessive policies perceived as an increased imposition upon the duties of the users. The authors do emphasize, however, that some policies are necessary for the effective protection of information (Bergeron and Bérubé, 1990). This study represents one of the earliest examinations of computer security policies in organizations.

The largest challenges in the design of security policy lie in the willingness of management to formally endorse information security policies, and in the organization's diligence in reviewing and updating them. In order to effectively design security policy, the organization should begin with

Table 6.5

Factors Affecting the Success of Information Security Policy

Visible commitment from management	(4.60)
A good understanding of security risks	(4.48)
Distribution of guidance on IT security policy to all employees	(4.36)
A good understanding of security requirements	(4.35)
Effective marketing of security to all employees	(4.26)
Providing appropriate employee training and education	(4.26)
Ensuring security policy reflects business objectives	(4.11)
An approach to implementing security that is consistent with the organizational culture	(3.93)
Comprehensive measurement system for evaluating performance in security management	(3.56)
Provision of feedback system for suggesting policy improvements	(3.52)

Source: Adapted from Fulford and Doherty, 2003.

Note: Factors ranked from most to least important to the successful implementation of IT security policy, values indicated in parenthesis on a 5-point scale.

"(1) gathering key materials, (2) defining the framework for the policies, (3) prepare a 'coverage matrix' laying out the topics to be covered in each document, and then create the policies in such a way as to balance the tradeoffs between costs and security, between flexibility and security and ease-of-use and security" (Wood, 1995).

Improving the Effectiveness of Information Security Policy Development

In 2003, Fulford and Doherty identified ten factors that affected the success of information security policy. These are presented in Table 6.5.

The top item, visible commitment from management, is echoed in other recommendations: Kabay (1996) identified five procedures in the establishment of security policy: (1) to assess and persuade top management; (2) to analyze information security requirements; (3) to form and draft a policy; (4) to implement the policy; and (5) to maintain the policy. Kabay likens this method to a security policy life cycle (Kabay, 1996). This same approach is represented in another methodology known as

PFIRES (policy framework for interpreting risk in e-business security) (Rees, Bandyopadhyay, and Spafford, 2003). The PFIRES model was also designed as a framework for designing and implementing information security policy. The model uses a four-phase life cycle to assess, plan, deliver, and operate more as a risk assessment and implementation model, with clear information security policy development and assessment activities.

NetIQ's Adrian Duigan (2003) offers "10 steps to a successful security policy" from an automated policy management vendor's perspective:

1. Identify your risks.
2. Learn from others when developing policy.
3. Make sure the policy conforms to legal requirements.
4. Level of security equals level of risk.
5. Include staff in policy development.
6. Train your employees on the policy.

7. Get it in writing (employees read, signed and understood the policy).
8. Set clear penalties and enforce them.
9. Update your staff on changes in policy.
10. Install the tools you need to enforce information security policies.

Fulford and Doherty (2003) identified several factors determined to affect the success of information security policy, provided in Table 6.5. They concluded that "although security policies appear widely implemented, there is little commonality in terms of the scope of such policies" (Fulford and Doherty, 2003). Hone and Eloff (2002) concur, adding that even renown standards for information security fail to specify the specifics of what should be contained in an effective information security policy.

Lichtenstein and Swatman (1997) in their study of Internet acceptable usage policies found that "inadequacies in guidelines and policies included: highly general subpolicies which are never made specific; ambiguity; the omission of reference to any underlying corporate Internet strategy; and ad hoc, limited identification of the Internet risks faced by the organization." Smith's (1993) examination of policies' effect in meeting expectations with respect to users of personal information found that policy was commonly developed in response to some external threat—that is, negative publicity or legislative scrutiny—and as a result tended to serve as a reaction rather than a proactive strategy. This response was most commonly a senior executive level action, and focused most on immediate protection against negative situations, rather than the long-term protection of information and privacy.

Policy Should Be Tailored to the User

In his work on "Building Effective, Tailored, Information Security Policy," Pescatore (1997) advises: "The goal is to influence behavior; you need to enable, not just to deny behavior as users can route around controls all too easily. Security policy should focus on the business needs by understanding the following questions. What data will be handled? How can that data be accessed? What is your organization's paranoia level? What controls are required on that data?" Pescatore also states, "Security policy needs to match the risk acceptance profile of an organization: for instance, identifying the realistic threats, understanding the level of visibility of the organization, understanding the consequences of an incident and identifying the level of risk sensitivity of the organization to the costs of an incident (both tangible and intangible)" (Pescatore, 1997). When writing security policy, one must match the policy to the organization's culture, use several sources for templates, involve legal, HR, and public affairs, and attempt to issue the policy from as high in the organization as possible. Lindup (1995) found several similarities between the development of policy in organizations and the development of treaties in government, further paralleling the preferred model for developing policies as a decentralized method, similar to that of a federation of states.

Steinke (1997) proposes that "security policy based on user's need to know and need to do should be specified on the basis of a user's tasks." He applies a task modeling approach in defining a group security model, designed to restrict a user's access to information on this "need to know basis" but requires that the selection of the information that the user does need to know must be effectively based on an analysis of the tasks the user is expected to perform in the observance of his or her duties. This type of policy is representative of the configuration rules of a systems-specific security policy, and illustrates the need for policy to guide IT's implementation of security configurations in systems, based on an administrative assessment of the user's tasks.

As mentioned earlier, one of the earliest examples of recommendations for the use of policy to reinforce positive employee behavior and reduce the risks associated with computer fraud and abuse is Hoffer and Straub (1989). In this paper, the authors conclude that "certain actions effectively deter computer abuse . . . [specifically]

- Establishing a data and systems security organization
- Communicating clearly that appropriate penalties will be imposed on abusers
- Defining and communicating to all personnel, using a wide variety of means, what the organization considers improper behavior; and
- Using security software packages and making users aware that these mechanisms are in place."

The authors also recommend formulating a security administrative function including:

- Developing a plan for security and disaster recovery.
- Developing and distributing system guidelines.
- Conducting regular orientation programs that communicate policies and penalties for violations.
- Classifying information, programs and all vital records.
- Designing/selecting and implementation software packages for monitoring and preventing abuses.
- Constantly monitoring the effectiveness of security policies, procedures, software and training. (Hoffer and Straub, 1989)

Security Policy Frameworks

When designing security policy, it is helpful to have established frameworks to provide a blueprint. The outlines provided earlier were based on an analysis of hundreds of security policies of various types as well as the works represented in the NIST SP 800–12 (1995), RFC 2196 (Fraser, 1997) and others, such as Forcht and Ayers (2000) and Whitman (2003).

Baskerville and Siponen (2002) propose an information security meta-policy seeking to provide guidance for emergent organizations. The purpose of their meta-policy is to "control policy making: how policies are created, implemented and enforced." Baskerville and Siponen recommend the use of this meta-policy to "specify processes by which policy makers will determine and specify how policies are to be implemented." While implementation will be organizationally specific, the use of this policy development and implementation guidance can facility the effective implementation of policies. The meta-policy approach includes the following security policy features:

- Policy requirements—Identification and classification of security subjects and objects.
- Design processes—Creation of policy and sub-policy hierarchy, adjusting the levels of abstraction and enforcement needed.
- Implementation specifications.
- Testing requirements (Baskerville and Siponen 2002).

It is the authors' intent that this meta-policy structure serve as a framework for subsequent research, recommending, for example, the empirical evaluation and usability of the framework.
Several studies have indicated that many organizations have implemented information secu-

rity policies (Fulford and Doherty, 2003; Whitman, 2003; DTI, 2002; Andersen, 2001; Ernst & Young, 2001; among others). What these studies do not report is the type of policies involved, the effectiveness in design of these policies, and the degree of compliance with the policies (Moule and Giavara, 1995; Hone and Eloff, 2002; Whitman, 2003). Thus while many organizations may indicate policy implementation, these policies may be ineffective in providing guidance for information security programs. Interestingly, in the Andersen (2001) study, there was a discrepancy between the reported level of policy implementation by business managers (82 percent) and IT managers (66 percent), indicating a lack of communication about policy. The studies cited above do allude to a trend, with a reported increase in the numbers of organizations reporting having security policies, from 65 percent in the Andersen (2001) to 76 percent in Fulford and Doherty (2003). However other studies, like Whitman and Mattord (2004), find the use of security policy consistently reported at approximately 63 percent. The differences in these studies could be attributed to questionnaire wording, subject audience, or respondent bias.

Areas for Future Research in Information Security Policy

There are a host of topics yet to be explored in information security policy design research. The first and foremost is an open examination of the *critical success factors in the design of effective security policy.* The CSF approach was first defined by Rockart (1982), and later redefined by Boynton and Zmud (1984) as involving "those few things that must go well to ensure success for a manager or an organization, and, therefore, they represent those managerial or enterprise areas, that must be given special and continual attention to bring about high performance." This approach, originally developed for an enterprise perspective, can be adapted to assess critical factors for the implementation of the key areas of policy, as described.

The challenges in this type of study begin with the *definition of effective security policy.* The host of possible factors that could define and influence the development of information security policy are also undefined. While societal factors identified in studies described above certainly play a critical role, until the researcher can define the difference between an effective and an ineffective policy, little can be done to delineate the factors that contribute to success. Many experts (e.g., Charles Cresson Wood) are qualified to describe the components and structure of effective policy; however, these are merely architectural factors that need to be adapted and examined in the context of the environment. One can recommend the design of an effective building, yet the same building will require substantial modification to be constructed within severe environmental regions, like California's earthquake regions, or Alaska's severe cold regions, or another "non-standard" region. In fact, all organizations can be defined as non-standard to some extent or other, and as such require modification beyond an original framework or model. Thus research must begin with defining effective policy and then continue to examine what organizations do to adapt these policy frameworks and models to achieve effectiveness within their particular environments. Once this is complete, the identification of factors critical to the success of this policy creation and modification will serve as guidance for other organizations to consider as they tackle similar problems.

Similarly, additional research is needed in the identification of *critical success factors in the implementation of information security.* While this chapter presented five factors that must be present for policy to withstand external, legal scrutiny, these factors alone will not guarantee effective policy. For each of the areas discussed (distributed, read, understood, agreed-to, and uniformly applied), an examination of what factors will directly, and indirectly, contribute to successful completion of the corresponding area is needed. Building on the work of Eloff and

Badenhorst (1990) and others in better understanding these factors, we can begin to improve our ability to implement policy, increasing the awareness of the organization's personnel, and reducing the probability of loss, damage or unauthorized modification to organizational information.

The next area of future research builds on the well-researched theories in ease of use and usefulness and the technology acceptance model (Davis, 1989), extending this research into the realm of policy development and use. A number of related tangents arise, including the *fundamental ease of use and usefulness of the templates for information security policies* presented earlier. While these templates technically are not technology, it would be interesting and helpful to find out if these templates, based on federal standards and other related research, result in documents that are both valuable to the organization in protecting the information and easy to understand and comply with on the part of the users. When considering automated policy management software, one can apply the traditional metrics for ease of use, and so on, to determine if these materials assist not only in the development of information insecurity policies, but also in the implementation and compliance.

Another area for future research in information security policy development is the *effect of a clear champion in the development and implementation of information security policy*. It is a well iterated statement that a champion—or sponsoring senior executive—is necessary to support systems development, but the documentation for the application of this concept to policy development is anecdotal at best.

One of the key areas of interest to information security professionals, especially chief information security officers, is the *degree of policy compliance* within and between organizations. With the increased interest in meeting international standards (see Hone and Eloff, 2002), it is insufficient to demonstrate implementation of policy without the follow-up assessment of degree of compliance. While, as discussed earlier, organizations may claim ownership of policy, until the compliance is assessed at the user level, a "difference gap" between managerial expectation and user performance may exist and may be much larger than organizations want to admit.

Another area of interest for future research is the actual *effect of policy on user behavior*. Does policy deter user behavior? What aspects of the policy most contributes to this deterrence, if any? Is it the presence of penalties, the awareness of expectations of performance, or simply an understanding of the "right and wrong ways of user behavior"? Until both managers and users are interviewed, as was accomplished at the microcomputer level in the 1990s by Bergeron and Bérubé (1990), this difference gap will continue to be unknown.

A further area of interest is a legal assessment of laws and codes of conduct associated with *legal and regulatory issues in policy implementation: compliance, enforcement, and employment impact*. While the areas of legal requirement presented here were based on an assessment of case law and other research, recent legislative and case law may have changed the perceptions of the courts to the implementation of policy. Is current law more or less restrictive on the organization's interpretation of "legally enforceable" policy? What laws at the national or state level directly impact an organization's ability to regulate and censure its employees? How do privacy laws impact an organization's ability, or make it necessary, to craft and enforce policy with its employees? With its customers? An assessment of the legal issues will provide additional answers in this arena.

Finally, an assessment of the *impact of organizational change*—structural, technological, market, or environmental—on the development and implementation of information security policy would provide additional insight into the nature of the policy development life cycle and the challenges associated with maintaining policy in such a dynamic environment.

CONCLUSIONS

As is evident, the development and implementation of effective information security policy is a complex but necessary foundation for any information security program. Only through established design methodologies, like a policy development life cycle, can the organization ensure the policies developed will provide the structure and guidance the organization needs. Only through effective implementation techniques can the organization ensure that the policies will provide more "good than harm" and will withstand both internal and external scrutiny. It is imperative that organizations develop "good policy now, rather than perfect policy never" and work with representative groups of users to implement information security policy that will protect the confidentiality, integrity, and availability of critical information and support a productive and incident-free work environment.

REFERENCES

Abrams, M., and Bailey, D. 1995. Abstraction and refinement of layered security policy. In M. Abrahms, S. Jajodia, and H. Podell (eds.), *Information Security: An Integrated Collection of Essays*. New York: IEEE Computer Society Press, pp. 126–136.

Andersen, I.T. 2001. Sicherheit in Europa. *Status Quo, Trends, Perspektiven*, Studie 2001. Dusseldorf: Andersen.

Backhouse, J., and Dhillon, G. 1995. Managing computer crime: a research outlook. *Computers and Security*, 14, 7, 645–651.

Baskerville, R., and Siponen, M. 2002. An information security meta-policy for emergent organizations. *Logistics Information Management*, 15, 5/6, 337–349.

Bergeron, F., and Bérubé, C. 1990. End users talk computer policy. *Journal of Systems Management*, 41, 12, 14–32.

Bloom, B.S.; Mesia, B.B; and Krathwohl, D.R. 1964. *Taxonomy of Educational Objectives*. New York: David McKay.

Blumstein, A. 1978. Introduction. In A. Blumstein, J. Cohen, and D. Nagin (eds.), *Deterrence and Incapacitation: Estimating the Effects of Criminal Sanctions on Crime Rates*. Washington, D.C.: National Academy of Sciences.

Boynton, A., and Zmud, R. 1984. An assessment of critical success factors. *Sloan Management Review*, 25, 4, 17–27.

CERIAS. n.d. *E-Commerce Information Security Policy Life Cycle*. Purdue Center for Education and Research in Information Assurance and Security (available at www.cerias.purdue.edu/about/history/andersen_consulting/slide3.php, accessed on January 14, 2005).

Confucius. n.d. Chinese proverb, Kung Fu-tse (available at www.geocities.com/Athens/Oracle/6517/learning.htm, accessed on February 4, 2005).

Davis, F. 1989. Perceived usefulness, perceived ease of use, and user acceptance of information technology. *MIS Quarterly*, 13, 3, 319–340.

DTI. 2002. *Information Security Breaches Survey*. UK Department of Trade and Industry Technical Report. London.

Duigan, A. 2003. 10 steps to a successful security policy. *ComputerWorld*, October 8 (available at www.computerworld.com/printthis/2003/0,4814,85583,00.html, accessed on January 8, 2005).

ECSA. 2003. *Definition of Terms to Support the ECSA Standards and Procedures System*. Engineering Council of South Africa Standards and Procedures System, January 8 (available at www.ee.wits.ac.za/~ecsa/gen/g-04.htm#Comprehension, accessed on January 10, 2005).

Eloff, J., and Badenhorst, K. 1990. Managing computer security: methodology and policy. *Information Age*, 12, 4, 213–219.

Ernst & Young. 2001. Information Security Survey. London.

Executive Order 12958. n.d. *Classified National Security Information* (available at www.dss.mil/seclib/eo12958.htm, accessed on September 15, 2003).

FASP. n.d. *Federal Agency Security Practices* (available at fasp.nist.gov, accessed on December 10, 2004).

Forcht, K., and Ayers, W. 2000. Developing computer security policy for organizational use and implementation. *Journal of Computer Information Systems*, 41, 2, 52–57.

Fraser, B. 1997. *Site Security Handbook*—RFC 2196, September (available at www.faqs.org/rfcs/rfc2196.html, accessed on October 15, 2003).

Fulford, H., and Doherty, N.F. 2003. The application of information security policies in large UK-based organizations: an exploratory investigation. *Information Management and Computer Security*, 11, 2/3, 106–114.

Gordon, L.; Loeb, M.; Lucyshyn, W.; and Richardson, R. 2004. *Annual CSI/FBI Computer Crime and Security Survey*. Computer Security Institute (available at www.gocsi.org, accessed on October 15, 2004).

Hansche, S. 2001. Designing a security awareness program: part I. *Information Systems Security*, 9, 6, 14–23.

Higgens, H. 1999. Corporate systems security: towards an integrated management approach. *Information Management and Computer Security*, 7, 5, 217–222.

Hoffer, J., and Straub, D. 1989. The 9 to 5 underground: are you policing computer crimes? *Sloan Management Review*, 30, 4, 35–43.

Hone, K., and Eloff, J. 2002. Information security policy: what do international information security standards say? *Computers and Security*, 21, 5, 402–409.

Kabay, M. 1996. *The NCSA Guide to Enterprise Security*. New York: McGraw-Hill.

Lee, J., and Lee, Y. 2002. A holistic model of computer abuse within organizations. *Information Management and Computer Security*, 10, 2, 57–63.

Lichtenstein, S., and Swatman, P. 1997. Internet acceptable usage policy for organizations. *Information Management and Computer Security*, 5, 5, 182–187.

Lindup, K. 1995. A new model for information security policy. *Computers and Security*, 14, 691–695.

Merriam-Webster. 2002. Policy. *Merriam-Webster Online* (available at www.m-w.com/cgi-bin/dictionary, accessed on June 24, 2002).

Moule, B., and Giavara, L. 1995. Policies, procedures and standards: an approach for implementation. *Information Management and Computer Security*, 3, 3, 7–16.

NetIQ. 2005. *VigilEnt Policy Center: Key Benefits* (available at www.netiq.com/products/vpc/default.asp, accessed on February 10, 2005).

NIST. 1995. *An Introduction to Computer Security: The NIST Handbook*. SP 800–12. National Institute of Standards and Technology, October (available at csrc.nist.gov/publications/nistpubs/800–12/800–12-html/index.html, accessed on December 5, 2004).

NIST. 1996. *Generally Accepted Principles and Practices for Securing Information Technology Systems*. Special Publication 800–14. National Institute of Standards and Technology, September (available at csrc.nist.gov/publications/nistpubs/800–14/800–14.pdf, accessed on December 5, 2004).

Nosworthy, J. 2000. Implementing information security in the 21st century. *Computers and Security*, 19, 4, 337–347.

Pescatore, J. 1997. *Building Effective, Tailored, Information Security Policy*. NISSC presentation (available at csrc.nist.gov/nissc/1997/panels/isptg/pescatore/html, accessed on December 20, 2004).

Plous. S. 2000. Tips on creating and maintaining an educational web site. *Teaching of Psychology*, 27, 63–70.

Rees, J.; Bandyopadhyay, S.; and Spafford, E. 2003. *PFIRES: A Policy Framework for Information Security* (available at www.cba.ufl.edu/dis/papers/021ist_files/0211102.pdf, accessed on January 14, 2005).

Ricks, D.A. 1993. *Blunders in International Business*. Cambridge, MA: Blackwell.

Rockart, J. 1982. The changing role of the information systems executive: a critical success factors perspective. *Sloan Management Review*, 24, 1, 3–13.

Siponen, T. 2000. A conceptual foundation for organizational information security awareness, *Information Management & Computer Security*, 8, 1, 31–41.

Skinner, W., and Fream, A. 1997. A social learning theory analysis of computer abuse among college students. *Journal of Research in Crime and Delinquency*, 34, 4, 495–518.

Smith, H. 1993. Privacy policies and practices: inside the organizational maze. *Communications of the ACM*, 36, 12, 105–122.

Steinke, G. 1997. A task based approach to implementing computer security. *Journal of Computer Information Systems*, 38, 1, 47–54.

Straub, D., and Nance W. 1990. Discovering and disciplining computer abuse in organizations: a field study. *MIS Quarterly*, 14, 1, 45–60.

Straub, D., and Welke, R. 1998. Coping with systems risk: security planning models for management decision making. *MIS Quarterly,* 22, 4, 441–469.

Tursi, S. 2003. *Information Security/User Policies SANS-GIAC Certification-Security Essentials,* November 10 (available atwww.giac.org/practical/GSEC/Steven_Tursi_GSEC.pdf, accessed on February 4, 2005).

Whitman. M. 2003. Enemy at the gate: threats to information security. *Communications of the ACM,* 46, 8, 91–95.

Whitman, M.E., and Mattord, H.J. 2004. *Management of Information Security.* Boston: Course Technology.

Whitman, M., and Mattord, H. 2005. *Principles of Information Security,* 2nd ed. Boston: Course Technology.

Whitman, M.; Townsend, A.; and Aalberts, R. 1999. Considerations for an effective telecommunications-use policy. *Communications of the ACM,* 42, 6, 101–109.

Wilson, M., et al. (eds.). 1998. *Information Technology Security Training Requirements: A Role- and Performance-Based Model.* National Institute of Standards and Technology, April (available at csrc.nist.gov/publications/nistpubs/800–16/800–16.pdf, accessed on June 15, 2005).

Wood, C. 1995. Writing InfoSec policies. *Computers and Security,* 14, 8, 667–674.

Wood, C. 2000. Integrated approach includes information security. *Security,* 37, 2, 43–44.

Wood, C. 2003. *Information Security Policies Made Easy,* 9th ed. Houston: Pentasafe.

Wood, C. 2004. *Key to Policy Success: Centralized Information Security Training* (available at searchsecurity.techtarget.com/tip/1,289483,sid14_gci961081,00.html, accessed on November 15, 2004).

Wood, C. 2005. *Information Security Policies Made Easy,* v. 10. Houston: InformationShield.

WUSTL. n.d. *Information Security Policy.* Washington State University in St. Louis (available at www.wustl.edu/policies/InfoSecurity.html, accessed on April 12, 2003).

Zajac, B. 1988. Personnel: the other half of data security. *Computers and Security,* 7, 2, 131–132.

CHAPTER 7

BUSINESS CONTINUITY PLANNING AND THE PROTECTION OF INFORMATIONAL ASSETS

CARL STUCKE, DETMAR W. STRAUB, AND ROBERT SAINSBURY

Abstract: The terrorist attacks of September 11, 2001, the northeast U.S. power blackout, and Katrina and other natural disasters are driving managers to reconsider organizational risk and the need for business continuity planning. In this new environment, organizations need to see business survivability as a critical imperative that motivates an updated enterprise risk management strategy. This chapter introduces and examines the concepts of business continuity planning and disaster recovery within overall risk and crisis management. Best practices and select models are illustrated. A discussion of future research topics and directions concludes the chapter.

Keywords: Business Continuity Planning, Disaster Recovery, Information Assets, Risk Assessment and Management, Asset Dispersal, Survivability, Information Security

INTRODUCTION

It is tempting to restrict the discussion of information security and information asset protection to the basic need to recover hardware and software after a disaster, whether the disaster is natural or man-made. But there are good reasons why this is too limiting and why we need to always move our thinking up to the level of the entire organization. The literature to date indicates quite clearly that the protection of information assets cannot be achieved in a vacuum. And so this larger scope should be our venue for thought and action.

A poignant example illustrates this key point. On 9/11 a number of businesses physically located in the World Trade Center had plans in place for recovering from disasters (Castillo, 2004). The best of these plans even anticipated the need for remote "hot" sites that would be unaffected by the loss of infrastructure, including electricity, water, and accessibility, in lower Manhattan. But the plans did not include the loss of life and the loss of expertise of employees. Thus the ability to transfer operations to alternative sites was hampered or in some cases rendered impossible by this lack of foresight (Castillo, 2004; Zuckerman and Cowan, 2001; Zuckerman et al., 2001).

Is this being too harsh? Were managers truly so lacking in vision that they did not anticipate the possibility of such a disaster? It is important to remember that previously, in 1993, the World Trade Center had come under attack and had miraculously survived. Prudent managers might have anticipated another attack of some sort since the Twin Towers were such a potent symbol of capitalism in the West and the target of hatred for fanatics and terrorists around the world.

Since the intent of the 1993 attack was to collapse the entire tower, it would have been relatively straightforward to forecast the extent of damage to the businesses in the tower and to the surrounding area. For starters, it is clear that the other tower would have been severely damaged even if it had not also collapsed. It, like the businesses within a large area of lower Manhattan, would have been inaccessible for months or up to a year. The repair of the infrastructure is only a part of it if there were critical records housed in a remaining intact tower but no one could get to them.

What was needed, and what few businesses in the Twin Towers had, were contingency plans that eased a transition of operations to other sites and the rapid restoration of relatively normal business activities. The tragic loss of key employees was compounded by the inability of the business that did survive to recover operations, and, also important, to meet customer needs. Katrina, the northeast blackout, and the Southeast Asia tsunami all heighten the urgency of this kind of planning.

This example illustrates two points. First, protecting information assets alone is inadequate. Information asset recovery must be seen in a larger context: the overall contingency plan that allows for business continuity. Second, business continuity requires back-up strategies for loss of more than just physical and software assets. Strategies for replacement of employee expertise are likewise essential. Knowledge of workflows and business processes needs to be available to sustain business function or, if necessary, for the business to pick itself up and resume service.

KEY DEFINITIONS

BCP and DR

Several essential definitions need to be delineated before any in-depth discussions of business continuity planning (BCP) and disaster recovery (DR)—that is, recovery of informational assets—can take place. Castillo (2004) defines BCP as "the ability to maintain a revenue stream through a crisis (p. 18).[1] This is as reasonable and brief a definition of BCP in the profit-making sector as one finds in the literature.[2] A broader organizational view could speak of maintaining or of restoring mission-critical functionality, and that definition could also be useful. DR has a narrower focus, and is oriented toward information technology (IT) and restoring the IT capabilities of an organization (Herbane et al., 2004). It tends to focus on recovery or "remedies" more than on prevention or deterrence, which are prior stages in the security action cycle, as shown in Figure 7.1. This action cycle is derived from earlier work by Straub and Welke. Here one might deter future abuse by strong enforcement of sanctions for perpetrating abuse. For those who will not be deterred and who attempt abuse, safeguards are erected to halt these attempts. Ideally, the effectiveness of deterrence and prevention is maximized. Detection mechanisms are necessary since deterrence and prevention will not be completely effective. When abuse is detected, remedies are enacted, including sanctions to increase deterrence, stronger safeguards to thwart abuse attempts, better detection mechanisms, and improved prosecution techniques to minimize abusers who go unpunished. This completes the cycle.

Catastrophic events are typically immediately detected, but the broader detection process involves finding out how and why something happened (in case actions could be taken so such a catastrophe either would not happen again or would have a lessened impact). Therefore this security action cycle with its process improvement feedback loop also provides a process improvement feedback loop model for planning and prevention (and recovery) activities within BCP and DR.

Nemzow (1997) provides an enlightening comparison between the two. As seen in Table 7.1, he compares the shorter-term DR mechanisms with the broader, more automatic, longer-term, and less disruptive BCP configurations and techniques. A few parenthetical comments have been added.

Focusing for a moment on replacement of employee expertise highlights this difference. Disaster recovery would tend to plan for a search for a replacement through the job market. But this

Figure 7.1 **The Security Action Cycle**

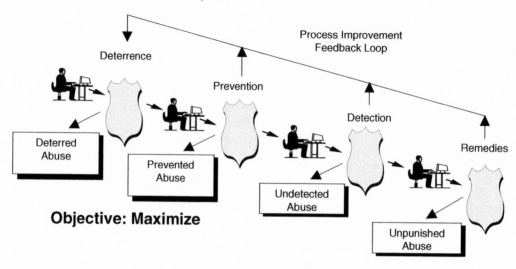

Source: Adapted from Straub and Welke, 1998.

process would take a lot of time and if the employee were instrumental enough and, in effect, a core competency of the organization (Huber, 1993), this loss could lead to severe damage or failure of the firm. Nemzow (1997) argues that cross-trained employees or persons who could backup the lost employee could meet the immediate need and run less of a risk for the organization. This goes beyond the narrower scope of DR, and thus if DR planning were the entire effort of an organization, it could conceivably not be enough in such a case.

Crisis Management

Other commentators remark on similar differences between DR and BCP, but take this further by pointing out that BCP is even part of a larger effort termed "crisis management" (Castillo, 2004; Herbane et al., 2004; Karakasidis, 1997). Crisis management applies to a very wide range of major problems that organizations may suffer, from a public relations disaster to evacuation of employees as a result of a civil war. It can also refer to disasters that strike at the firm's facilities and employees, planning for which we have termed BCP/DR. Crisis management, generally speaking, is a set of measured responses to challenges that could threaten the existence of individuals, organizations, or societies. Crisis management thinking is pervasive in actual disaster management. This leads Herbane et al. (2004) to describe their higher-order view of BCP/DR as managing a crisis, namely as occurring in the three stages of pre-crisis, trans-crisis, and post-crisis.

BC/DR Planning versus Plan Execution

This staged view of how DR and BCP fit into a set of event-response phases leads to an elaborated model in Castillo (2004) that separates planning from execution of plans (see Figure 7.2).

Castillo's model will be discussed in greater detail later. For the moment, it is useful to define what she seems to mean by "preparedness." "Preparedness" of either the DR plans or BCP can

Table 7.1

Comparison of Disaster Recovery and Business Continuity Planning

DR	BCP
Battery backup	Shadowed operations
Soot cleanup (takes time)	Use offsite records; trash everything else (continue functioning)
Advertise, interview, hire a replacement manager (after event)	Move the backup (or cross-trained) person into the new role (ready to go)
Sue for possession of rolodexes	Use alternative sales records and contact lists
Backup tapes	Backup tapes and tape readers; common format CD-ROMs; RAID (redundant array of independent disks)
Phone company forwards phone lines to new numbers (after you get the numbers)	Call-forward lines (already configured)
Build (or rebuild) a new site	Salvage and activate warehouse
Send sales people to a new territory	Expand product line in other territories
Try to read damaged backup media	View records on microfiche or electronic images
Splice damaged lines in conduit	Switchover to alternative delivery (reroute or satellite)

Source: Based on Nemzow, 1997.

be thought of the readiness of the organization to resume operations, at either the technical (IT) level or the business level. Organizations can range widely on how prepared they are by having plans in the first place and, second, how prepared they are in actuality (Castillo, 2004). This same distinction in the literature is often made between the *creation* and the *testing* of plans. It is clear that preparedness is the result of a planning process and that this process may or may not be effective when a disaster occurs. The execution of the plan is a distinct set of activities such as "DR and BC response," "IT recovery" "stabilization of business," "assessment," and "resumption of normal business." These represent the implementation of the plans, and the quality of the BCP can only be measured, in the final analysis, by how well the plans work.

"Hot" Sites versus "Cold" Sites

Another set of definitions is useful for this chapter. Off-site recovery facilities are generally classified as either "hot," "cold," or an in between "warm." Straub (2004) defines and explicates off-site IT recovery facilities as follows:

> You have a contract with a cold site disaster recovery outsourcer that will allow you to begin reorganizing your operations. Necessary network connections are present at this site, as well as backup copies of your software and data, but there is no computer hardware. The plan calls for bringing in rented equipment, including furniture, desks, workstations, and so forth, from a three state area. Contracts with these rental firms and other outsourcing firms specify that the requisite materials will be on-site and installed within 24 hours. Although the burden on the remaining physical distribution center will be severe, the main problem is the Web connection. However, with successful deployment of the plan, the firm

Figure 7.2 **Integrating BCP and DR**

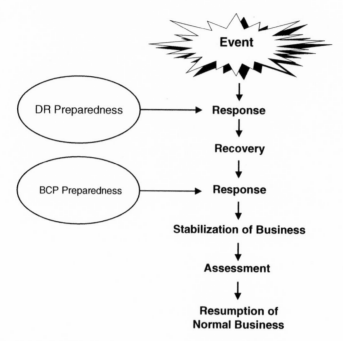

Source: Adapted from Castillo, 2004.

can continue its computing. . . . Your company might have considered a more costly plan called a hot site. Hot sites also have duplicates of the hardware you are running, as well as the network connections. Hot sites (and cold sites) are shared; in the sense that if all clients of the outsourcer were in need of services at the same time, the facilities could not usually accommodate the demand. In other words, there is not a large room ready and waiting for a firm at the hot site, with the name of the firm stenciled on the door.

Additional options include mobile, shared, and mutual backup where two corporations are prepared to be the recovery site for each other (Whitman and Mattord, 2004).

MTBU

MTBU is a term and concept that asks how long an organization can survive without a recovery of essential functionality. The acronym stands for "maximum time for belly up," which in the parlance of standard American English means the period of time before a company goes bankrupt. MTBU gives us insight into how vulnerable a firm is. Just how long can a particular organization survive without information assets and the concomitant personnel to run them? Or how long can it survive without its call centers, which take orders as well as perform other service functions? From the beginning of the information revolution, commentators have been puzzling over these questions.

One of the original discussions of this issue in the IT context was a working paper at the University of Minnesota's MIS Research Center (Aasgard et al., 1978). The concept of MTBU that evolved after that paper emphasized the survivability of organizations, especially profit-making organizations.

Figure 7.3 **MTBU for Two Types of Firms**

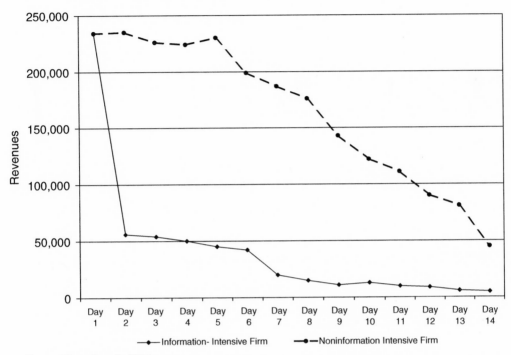

Source: From Straub, 2004.

Straub (2004) argues that there will be a marked difference in firms that are highly information-intensive, such as financial institutions, and those that are not (see Figure 7.3). Nevertheless, without mission-critical resources all modern firms will fail within a relatively short time.

Nemzow (1997) estimated that by 1997 the average time period that any firm, irrespective of information intensity, could survive was four days. Moreover, the literature indicates that 80 percent of firms that have experienced a major disaster do not survive for a year and that over a five-year period, only 10 percent are still in existence (Nemzow, 1997). So it is obvious that knowing the MTBU of one's organization is an important macro-level number for planning for worst-case scenarios.

RISK AND RISK ASSESSMENT

Technically speaking, the risk of an event is the probability of the event times the expected loss. Insurance actuaries and underwriters calculate the risk of an automobile accident for a certain specific driver by examining the past history of drivers in certain categories such as those with DUIs and those within certain age ranges, and so on. The history of average losses is also available to them and so, taking into account numerous other factors, they can determine that the risk today of an individual sustaining an accident that the company would have to pay on is, say, $1,000 per annum. Since the company's risk is $1,000 to insure an individual, the firm must charge more than a $1,000 premium to ensure that the account will be profitable.

Whereas there are many examples of automobile accidents and other areas for insurance are well understood, such as life expectancies, disasters are by their very nature rare events. In that the calculation of risk is a function of both probability of a disaster and the expected losses from a disaster, we would need a reliable assessment of both variables in order to accurately assess risk in this case. One might come close to assessing monetary losses in the case of specific disasters. But the difficulty with rare events is that they do not occur with enough frequency to show a distinct pattern and, therefore, yield a viable probability figure. Without believable quantities (probabilities) to work with, the assessment of risk in BCP/DR tends to be qualitative. While tools are emerging for quantitative risk assessment, their utility is limited to areas where sufficient actuarial information exists to model risk. Such information is scarce, especially in areas where divulging event specifics might endanger the public's trust in the reporting institution.

Risk and the Need for BCP/DR

Most organizations have never had and may never experience a catastrophe. Thus one might think that any and all risk assessments would be necessarily low (Nemzow, 1997) and the typical managerial response might be to cover critical areas allowing a firm whose assets are not too badly damaged to limp along to a recovery, and then to use insurance as a risk mitigation strategy for the remainder of an organization's vulnerabilities. But it is possible to lose the entire business without good recovery planning, and even though the losses might be covered monetarily, and the shareholders reimbursed, the loss of jobs and livelihoods could be daunting for the larger group of stakeholders. Stakeholder theory (Freeman, 1984) has pushed organizations to think beyond the narrow view that profit-making organizations are entirely defined by how much wealth they bring to their owners. Employees, customers, suppliers, governmental agencies, organizational beneficiaries, and the communities in which organizations exist also have a stake in the survival of organizations and their needs are not met by the financial compensations offered by insurance.

Nemzow (1997) also cautions against applying traditional risk assessment approaches to possible organizational disaster: "Because they are so rare, is it right not to plan for them? Even a monetary analysis might show that the expected losses factored by the risk likelihood (the typical actuarial method for insurance and disaster planning) may create the false impression of the insignificance of a disaster. Nonetheless, beware" (p. 130). However, acceptance of risk may be a valid strategy if the cost of proper preparation exceeds the expected loss.

Value of Planning Efforts

Assuming for the moment that there is a case to do something about disasters, in spite of the low risk. But why should organizations plan for disasters? The question is not as frivolous as it might first appear. It might be more cost effective, for example, to wait for an event to occur and then to mobilize a response dynamically.

The difficulty with a response-only strategy is that one cannot predict all the things that can go wrong, and without a plan to handle what can be predicted, the extent of the losses and the delays in recovery will be even longer, sometimes catastrophically so. If a firm's MTBU is seven days, and predictable events recovery takes five days with planning and twelve days without it, the firm will go bankrupt without a plan. But if a firm's MTBU is six days, predictable events recovery only takes three days with a plan and six days without a plan, we might be tempted to think that the firm had escaped in this case. Not necessarily true. Assume that unpredictable events recovery takes another two days. The firm with no plan will go belly-up, but the firm with planning will survive.

These are perhaps fanciful scenarios, but the point of the analysis is straightforward. Planning can shorten the time to recovery and this can mean the difference between life and death for a firm. The determination of how much this planning should cost to be a reasonable investment is not an easy managerial decision. But when the firm's survival is at stake, it could be considered a matter of due diligence to invest to at least a measured extent in BCP/DR.

Are unpredictable events that dangerous? There are numerous anecdotes in the case history that are illuminating in this respect. NASDAQ was dramatically affected two times by squirrels chewing through telecommunications lines that were serving the trading floor (Nemzow, 1997). Whereas rodent damage might have been predicted and prepared for, the NASDAQ managers also suffered a loss of electricity and found out when they tried to refuel by bringing hoses into their buildings that they were in violation of a building code. The combination of events was not predictable and threatened NASDAQ's ability to offer a trading environment.

During the 1993 terrorist bombing of the World Trade Center, many backup systems were in place, but firms did not anticipate that they would not be allowed to retrieve rolodexes, charts of accounts, and so forth (Nemzow, 1997). The need to get at these physical assets was hampered by damage that occurred in the basement not immediately affecting most firms' facilities. The irony was that the tight security that surrounded the area prohibited some firms from carrying out normal business activities.

Hurricane Andrew created similar problems. In some cases, the destruction was total (Nemzow, 1997). Workstations, marketing reports, disk and tape backups, and cabinets were scattered across the Everglades, miles away. Offices were completely devastated. And most recently, Hurricane Katrina brought devastation to the Gulf Coast of the United States. While damage from a hurricane is expected, the extent of the damage in both these cases was a surprise to many.

The Distribution of Disasters

What are the forms of catastrophe that can overtake an organization? Knowing the basics of where threats are coming from is a crucial element for planning. Nemzow (1997) asserts that only 1 percent of disasters are natural. He goes on to say that hot sites cover hardware and even software, but human side impacts, including loss of employees, customer dissatisfaction, and other market effects, are not generally covered in planning.

Other commentators also discuss the issue of man-made acts such as sabotage. Rodetis (1998) does not believe that that terrorism and other man-made disasters are larger occurrences percentage-wise than natural disasters, but that their impact can still be huge. After the Oklahoma City bombing, forty square blocks were cordoned off and 210 of the 4,000 businesses in that area went out of business. This is a 5 percent loss rate.

Defining man-made events as both normal and abnormal crises, Castillo (2004) makes the same point, showing that abnormal and normal business crises account for a larger proportion of loss over the last decade than natural disasters. Normal crises include power outages, strikes, turnover of key personnel, recession, and even events like the Columbia Shuttle loss. Abnormal crises are criminal acts like those at Enron, cyber attacks, and product tampering. The reason this makes a difference is that businesses tend to plan for natural disasters, but depend on risk mitigation and recovery efforts for man-made events. This being the case, many/most BCPs do not anticipate responding to product tampering or a cyber attack, for instance.

Planning versus Adaptability

The 9/11 terrorist attack could be categorized as an abnormal crisis, and if the observation that this kind of event is generally not planned for by organizations, then we would expect more ad hoc solutions to be reported. This seems to be the case.

In their study of BCP, Herbane et al. (2004) say that after 9/11, "over half of Lehman Broth-ers' staff worked from home in the immediate aftermath as result of the previous roll out of an extensive remote access programme. One of its senior managers commented that 'crisis adapt-ability is the key to continuity'" (Herbane et al., 2004, p. 436). Lehman Bros. was fortunate that they were positioned to adapt their telecommuting option to respond to this crisis, but this was, apparently, not actually part of their BCP. This explains why their senior manager uses the term "adaptability" in the quotation above.

In our view, this managerial stance works against the basic underlying concept of BCP: that a thorough (i.e., "good") plan will meet most contingencies. It undermines the belief that an organization can be well prepared for a disaster, whether intentional or unintentional, and that training in best practices can lead to a quick and felicitous recovery. If the major requirement for recovering from disaster is adaptability, then planning is of marginal usefulness. It would be better in such cases to send managers for outward bound training than training in how to rapidly move the organization to temporary but functioning operational readiness. Addressing this point above, under the rubric of predictable and unpredictable events, it is our position that adaptability is certainly indispensable in a crisis, but that, overall and primarily, organizations should depend on their well-tested plans for recovery and not on ingenuity.

After the World Trade center bombing in 1993, it should have been obvious to Lehman man-agement that a catastrophic failure in the vicinity would have wiped out backup facilities as well as the primary operations center. A solid BCP would have anticipated this and moved the backup facilities to another borough of New York City, or, even better, another state or country.

Managerial Commitment to BCP/DR

Few organizations have BC and DR plans in place and even fewer test them (Castillo, 2004; Nemzow, 1997; Pitt and Goyal, 2004). Nemzow (1997) asserts that only 1 percent of organizations have disaster recovery plans. It is clear that, as with many other aspects of information security, managers do not view this form of protection as very mission-critical (Straub and Welke, 1998).[3] But is this a reasonable response, given the enormous challenges that profit-making firms especially face in the current era? How important is it that organizations engage in this type of planning? We have made the argument again and again in this chapter that the risk of not surviving in the event of a disaster where the managers have not planned is too high. Important stakeholders of the firm require due diligence in this area.

Herbane et al. (2004) also make the point that a recovery advantage could be a competitive advantage, which is a subtle and even profound point. Since it is clear that organizations can be harmed or fatally damaged by poor BCP (Zuckerman and Cowan, 2001; Zuckerman et al., 2001), it is a key to survival and, hence, a strategic necessity. Firms viewed it this way in the four cases discussed in Herbane et al. (2004), but is there a theoretical linkage between viewing BC as a strategic goal and its successful implementation? We have only case study data to make the con-nection at this point.

Creating BC/DR Plans

There are standard approaches that have been articulated for how an organization goes about creating a BCP/DR plan (Karakasidis, 1997). Table 7.2 shows a typical set of steps (Karakasidis, 1997). The National Institute of Standards and Technology (NIST) special publication 800–34 also contains an excellent process.

Table 7.2

The BC Planning Process

Step	Action
1	Obtain top management approval and support
2	Establish a business continuity planning (BCP) committee
3	Perform business impact analyses
4	Evaluate critical needs and prioritize business requirements
5	Determine the business continuity strategy and associated recovery process
6	Prepare business continuity strategy and its implementation plan for executive management approval
7	Prepare business recovery plan templates and utilities, organize/develop the business recovery procedures
8	Develop the testing criteria and procedures
9	Test the business recovery process and evaluate test results
10	Develop/review service level agreement(s) (SLAs)
11	Update/revise the business recovery procedures and templates

Source: Karakasidis, 1997.

The steps are intuitive, but a short description of each is not unwarranted. Projects need management sponsorship and BCP is not an exception. Karakasidis (1997) recommends that the key activities in the process be carried out by a relatively high level committee for greater firm buy-in.

Once the process is in motion, it is critical to first see where the business would be impacted by different disasters. This helps to prioritize the responses. For each area that is identified as critical, a recovery procedure must be specified. These can be templated and standardized so that it is simple to maintain them.

Testing is an absolutely essential element in the planning process. Specifications on how to test as well as the testing itself are both components. The final three stages of the process (9–11) are iterated in the sense that tests should be run and rerun, service level agreements should be sculpted and re-sculpted for outsourcers as they assist in the process. SLAs, in fact, are based on the test results to a large extent. Planning updates are also a continuous process and will require the managers to examine the plan on a regular basis.

BEST PRACTICES

Zsidisin et al. (2003) studied four firms that were reputed to have reasonable-to-excellent BCP for their supply chains and determined that the fifteen practices (see Table 7.3) were the means by which firms could recover revenues quickly after a disaster. Many or most if these practices can be generalized to other firm processes.

The first five best practices are related to risk and the identification of where the organization is vulnerable. Organizations that were successful according to Zsidisin et al. (2003) performed risk audits to prioritize the risk the firm was facing in different areas. These tended to be generalized risk assessments that did not necessarily require loss estimates. At least a qualitative assessment of full risk was undertaken in the third best practice, looking closely at extreme cases where the firm would be seriously in danger.

Practices 6 through 13 deal with ensuring that the BCP is accurate and timely and will eventually

Table 7.3

Effective Business Practices according to Zsidisin et al. (2003)

#	Best practices
1	Supply chain risk audits
2	Assessing probability and impact—expected values and extreme values
3	Supplier risk profiling
4	Differentiating between current-state risk and transitional risk
5	Supplier preparedness as a part of regular supplier assessment
6	Supply chain continuity created as part of a larger strategy
7	Supply chain continuity included in IT contingency plans
8	Relationships and business continuity
9	Supply chain mapping[1]
10	Importance of visibility
11	Managing cost and time of disruptions, including multi-source risk monitoring and quality management/risk management
12	Dual sourcing policy
13	Product and process standardization
14	Developing, implementing, and monitoring BCP-specific metrics
15	Developing and monitoring *predictive* BCP metrics[2]

[1]"Supply chain mapping is a technique frequently used by management to lay out the structure of the supply chain" (Zsidisin et al., 2003).

[2]"Predictive metrics are measures that are used to identify potential problems before they occur. In the case of BCP, predictive metrics capture supplier behavior that indicates financial distress, which subsequently affects the continued viability of the supplier" (Zsidisin et al., 2003).

work. Strategic issues head the list. Does the top management consider SCM to be critical to the survival of the firm? If not, education of top management may be required before a viable plan can be turned out. The managers must see the sharing of information (visibility) and the relationships within the supply chain as critical elements in the overall plan. Supply chain mapping should be conducted to gain a complete understanding of the supply process so that when a catastrophe occurs, there is no doubt about the effectiveness of the plans in dealing with it.

Certain practices are just good management practices with respect to supply chain efficiency, such as multisource risk monitoring and a total quality management (continuous improvement) approach. Dual sourcing options lower risk by making supplies more reliable. Finally, standardizing on products and processes not only makes the supply chain smoother, but it also makes it easier to restore it to seamless operation should it be disrupted.

The final two best practices are important if the firm is to learn from where BCP works and where it does not. These deal with metrics that affect operations, those that monitor operations, and those that predict performance. Benchmarks aid in the restoration of full capacity and provide valuable information for a reassessment and adjustment process after a disaster occurs and the firm recovers. This feedback loop will be discussed under BCP/DR models later in the chapter.

GENERIC PRINCIPLES AND SOLUTIONS

Both the best practices just covered and other arguments put forth so far suggest that organizations can use a set of principles to guide their planning. The one dominant principle with respect to protecting a firm's assets is dispersion and partial duplication of the most essential resources (Snow et al., 2005). As stated in Snow et al. (2005), "while individual firms' strategies will vary in the extent and type of decentralization, the overall tendency should be toward further dispersal of people, technology, and physical assets. . . . These future risk mitigation strategies may result in the implementation of dispersal strategies in organizational design and more geographically distributed organizations" (p. 1).

What is the reasoning for this most basic concept? If an organization is spread over five locations that are not geographically contiguous, the loss of any one node is a limited exposure for the organization. In the case of informational resources, it is also possible to duplicate many of them at a relatively low physical cost, and the coordination costs need to be factored in to reach some happy medium. Nemzow (1997) makes essentially the same point when he says: "Ideally, the best planning looks to diversification as a strategy for protecting an organization even with a direct disaster hit" (p. 133).

SPECIALIZED ORGANIZATIONAL STRUCTURES

Computer security incidents can be sufficiently destructive to invoke an organization's BC/DR plan. And computer security incidents can be particularly complicated to handle and to properly collect and preserve evidence that enables prosecution. This motivates the increasing popularity of a specific team-based approach to recovery from security violations. This specialized organizational structure should be considered to be a general principle in the sense that scientific evidence shows that dedicated personnel are correlated with significantly lower computer abuse (Straub, 1990). Without a focused management effort in BCP/DR, the resulting plans are much less likely to be successful.

With respect to incidents that are primarily major breaches of computer security, or where computer security lies at the heart of the disaster, Carnegie Mellon University has pioneered the concept of CSIRT, or "computer security incident response teams" (Killcrece et al., 2003). These are teams of trained experts, spread worldwide at this point (Killcrece et al., 2003), who can rapidly assess damage, plug vulnerabilities, and assist the organization in its recovery efforts. These teams can be either trained and certified within organizations or hired. IBM has a practice in this vein, for example. For additional CSIRT information, see CMU's CERT CSIRT website at www.cert.org/csirts/.

The CSIRT concept has been expanded to include a network of CSIRTs that allow organizations to share their knowledge and tie into assistance, in some cases. The Forum of Incident Response and Security Teams (FIRST) functions as a virtual knowledge management system to help in recovery efforts (Killcrece et al., 2003). As of January 2006, it had over 170 members and a website at: www.first.org.

One of the possible responsibilities for CSIRTs is BCP/DR (Killcrece et al., 2003). Because of the shared experience of other CSIRTs and the FIRST network, it is worthwhile considering the establishment of a CSIRT to handle this critical risk domain for the firm.

MODELS FOR BCP/DR

The set of activities that precede and surround a disaster are fairly well documented and do not differ substantially from one another across commentators. Specific techniques and implementations will differ significantly, however, and this can spawn research that would assess the effectiveness of varying approaches. Before examining one or two such models, we can step our way through

Figure 7.4 **Parallel Model of BCP/DR Activities**

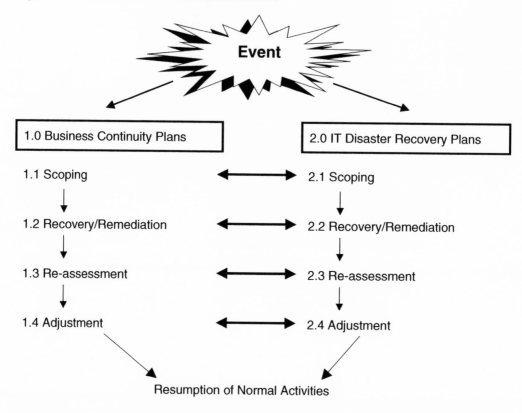

the events and see why the stages of BCP and DR are so similar from author to author and from year to year.

As shown in Figure 7.2, Castillo (2004) has a model that starts with the event then moves to operational recovery (DR activity) then to business stabilization (BC and thereafter) then to damage assessment and then to BCP feedback. There should be two planning stages that lead to the DR recovery and business stabilization. These are termed "preparedness" in Castillo (2004).

Clearly, there are planning processes that lead to the planned-for activities in the IT/DR stages and the BC stages. This goes without saying. But the natural response to an event is to engage in a rapid evaluation of the problem before beginning the recovery. This is true for both the IT recovery as well as the business recovery. Commentators (e.g., Zsidisin et al., 2003) frequently envision a post-recovery evaluation of the success of the processes. This stage aids organizational learning and helps to improve the process of response for the next disaster.

Our own model of BCP and DR recommends carrying out IT and business assessment and recovery phases in parallel, as shown in Figure 7.4. Our model is consistent with Herbane et al. (2004), who make a nice distinction between BCP as a one-off process or as embedded. Their data show a distribution across several dimensions about which functional area leads the project in disaster recovery planning, versus BCP, versus BC management. Their findings are also consistent with Whitman and Mattord (2004).

The parallel model accounts for the fact that many or most disasters disable functions across the full gamut of the firm's processes. The first stage is the planning process (1.0 and 2.0), which specifies in detail how scoping (1.1 and 2.1), recovery/remediation (1.3 and 2.3), and adjustment (1.4 and 2.4) should take place. Phases 1.1–1.4 and 2.1–2.4 are the execution phases.

The first phase in the resumption of normal business activities is to find the plans, 1.0 and 2.0, and read the relevant passages that describe what should happen. The plans should be considered to be guidelines that are generally followed to the letter, but in special cases can be set aside.

The scoping activity in phases 1.1 and 2.1 deals with determining the nature of the problem and the extent of damage. It is an information-gathering, decision-making, and communication activity carried out by personnel are in charge of the execution of the plans. Once the extent of the damage is known, for instance, decisions have to be made about who should be involved in the recovery and how the recovery should proceed. A list of relevant key executives should be informed and a public relations stance outlined.

The differences between the business continuity activities and the IT DR activities in each of the phases is reasonably clear and needs little explication. Personnel assignments will be a primary differentiator, but the underlying principle is that the restoration of systems and the restoration of the business need to be coordinated, as shown in the model.

Once scoping is completed, remediation per se (1.2 and 2.2) can begin. If personnel are involved, there should be procedures for assistance with medical care and informing family members. Employees who are unhurt but unable to use the original facilities need to be informed about what they should do. Arrangements for replacement of facilities and computer hardware would be part of this phase. If a move to a hot or cold site is called for, then this would be carried out during this phase. If this phase is successful, the firm has restored its essential processes before MTBU.

In phases 1.3 and 2.3, a more detailed assessment of the scope of the problem and the damage that has resulted takes place. Organizations frequently skip this learning phase, but it is critical to engage in this assessment in order not to repeat the mistakes that will have undoubtedly occurred in the prior execution phases. Moreover, the adjustment stage (1.4 and 2.4) will only be possible if the organization has learned how to refine the recovery procedures.

Application of the Model to a Hypothetical Example

Consider a situation where a firm adheres to this parallel model in a disaster. Imagine a terrorist act that destroys a firm's main data center facility which also houses a central branch of the online sales order division. Key personnel have been injured or killed. There is widespread physical damage to the facilities themselves.

In this case as in many others, restoration of computer equipment and systems is an activity that must take place in parallel with the restoration of business processes. BCP and the DR plan, up-to-date copies of which are present in numerous site locations, specify how the firm should restore services. The DR plan says that distributed databases are housed in the firm's online division. These are fully recoverable from sites that were not subject to the destruction, and the handling of business transactions can be switched to the new locations. Activities to restore the revenues of the firm need to consider personnel and facilities, as well as systems. Fortunately, personnel in the firm's undamaged facilities in remote locations have been cross-trained to handle customers for both traditional and online orders. Detailed workflow diagrams are also available to assist the temporary personnel until full-time replacements can be found. Activities to replace the facilities and the personnel, who, note, span the IT and sales departments, are likewise specified in the BC plan.

Once the business has stabilized, the firm engages in an analysis of how well its staff did. They learn that the databases were not fully recoverable at the ancillary sites and that some customer orders where lost. They also learn that the back-up facilities did not have complete workflows and that some of the employees who had been cross-trained had forgotten the procedures. Methods for dealing with each of these deficiencies are identified and corrections made so that should another emergency occur, the firm will be even better prepared.

There may be occasions when a disaster at first seems to be restricted to systems, but turns out to be broader than that. In this case, one can conceive of the activities taking place serially, in the manner suggested by Castillo (2004). The first activity when an event involving computer systems or personnel occurs is to respond with a rapid assessment of damage and actions to ensure that no further damage occurs. This response "phase" is followed by a repairing of the damage created by the event. The intention here is to restore normal information processing as soon as possible.

Let us consider a short example that illustrates the various dimensions of the recovery process. Suppose that a hacker has successfully attacked a firm's e-mail system and destroyed current files on the server and planted viruses in others. Employees, suppliers, and customers cannot now connect with each other and the business is suffering losses of new orders as well as good will from current customers expecting information.

IT managers and professionals must first assess which files have been destroyed and why the system has ceased to function. Actions to secure the e-mail system against further abuse are now relevant as are actions to recover the system through loading of backup files and software into the system.

Let us further suppose that the manager of the network responsible for the system has been unable to restore the system after a week of frantic work. The firm's customers are extremely dissatisfied and the firm's executives have terminated the employ of the network manager. The BC plan is activated at this point and an interim manager is appointed who has been cross-trained in network matters. This person is able to restore the system, but not without hiring fairly expensive consultants who had been vetted as part of the BCP. Archives that had been created the week before the system went down were also corrupted, apparently, and the interim manager and the consultants discover this problem and retrieve and restore uncorrupted files and reactivate the system.

Thus what at first seems to be a problem restricted to the IT unit soon involves personnel matters that go beyond what is covered in the DR plan. This is the power of always thinking of recovery as a parallel process.

NEW STUDIES TO INCREASE UNDERSTANDING OF BCP/DR

The overriding problem in the domain of BCP/DR is the lack of scientific effort in this vein. There have been important technical solutions regarding restoration of systems, and the technologies to mirror systems or distribute the computing needs are well understood at this time. Systems development processes incorporating security concerns, including BC and DR, are still fairly rare,[4] and that continues to be a serious technical issue. But the technology to guarantee a full recovery is already present. The primary issues that remain in BCP and DR, are, therefore, managerial.

It is easier to present what we do know rather than what we do not know about the management of BC and DR. As stated earlier, there is some empirical evidence that organizations are ill-prepared for disasters. Even when they have plans, which may be rare, these plans tend not to be thoroughly tested. Organizations have adopted a strategy of deploying scant resources in this area and to make up losses, in the rare event that they do occur, with insurance.

Table 7.4 presents a set of questions, the answers to which could make a huge difference

Table 7.4

Scientific Questions in Need of Further Study

Area	Issue	Impact
1. Overall BCP/DR	1.1 Are organizations that plan for recovery of business and systems and test their plans better able to cope?	Knowing a break-even point in order to gain a comfort level of protection would help organizations manage this activity.
	1.2 What are their relative levels of investment?	
	1.3 Do customers and suppliers of the firm view an integrated effort of the firm for high preparedness to be strategic?	Insights into whether preparedness is only a cost or could be positioned as a strategic advantage would strengthen business cases for BCP/DR.
2. Models of BCP/DR	2.1 What are successful models of the phases of recovery?	Knowing whether there is a standard model would aid firms in the normative development of their own plans.
	2.2 What factors lead to greater awareness and commitment of managers (and other stakeholders) to the concept of BCP/DR?	BCP/DR involves large-scale investments. Gaining executive support is critical, but at the moment, it is unclear how this should be done.
3. Outsourcing of BCP/DR	3.1 What are the risks and benefits to outsourcing the entire effort or selected parts of the effort?	Security planning and execution functions for BCP/DR are different enough from other outsourcing domains that they call for separate research efforts.
4. Deployment of BCP/DR	4.1 What are the differential costs and benefits of cold sites versus hot sites versus distributed processing?	Organizations currently lack guidelines with respect to facilities solutions.

in the creation and implementation of contingency plans. Each of them will be discussed in detail below.

Details on Issues 1.1–1.2

Before a study of the overall effects of BCP/DR can take place, we need to know the relative levels of investment of different industries. There is some evidence (McEachern, 2002) that the larger players in financial services are spending significant funds in this effort, but this is likely a function of the stringent regulatory environment, in the United States at least. Organizations that are not required to invest may not be doing so. Anecdotal evidence suggests that this is the case, but our real knowledge of the state of affairs is lacking at this time.

Risk management expertise would seem to be a natural in applying schools of thought that can pit levels of investment and risk against outcomes like adequacy of response and non-survival. The underlying question is whether BC/DR plans that have been exercised make a real difference or not. One could speculate that there is a U-shaped curve about investments in this area. If one spends too much, there may be no justification for the expenses and the firm becomes uncompetitive. This is the opposite of the argument of Herbane et al. (2004), which is that BCP can be seen unreservedly as a strategic advantage.

Details on Issue 1.3

It is one thing to argue that BCP/DR is cost beneficial. It is another matter to argue that it actually confers a strategic and competitive advantage. Theories of competition could be very relevant in exploring this angle. Is the presence of a well-built set of plans a resource in its own right? If it is perceived that way by suppliers and customers, as well as other stakeholders, then managers would need to market this capability besides just developing it. Knowing the answers to such questions helps to position BCP/DR among the various competing projects that are attempting to get the attention of management.

Details on Issues 2.1

Case studies and even field studies with a limited number of organizations can only take us so far in our ability to generalize and to theorize about models of BCP/DR processes, as in the work of Zsidisin et al. (2003). Do the BC/DR planning and execution models that have been put forth (and discussed above) prove out in practice? Are these models normative, mapping out how a good set of plans can lead to higher-performing organizations? Or are these models descriptive, under the assumption that, overall, organizations already know what is in their own best interest? In any case, larger-scale empirical work would help to address such pressing issues.

Details on Issue 2.2

There is little to no knowledge about why certain executives embrace BCP and others ignore it; thus, desperately needed are intellectual innovations to learn why it is that managers are so woefully underprepared to holistically protect their information assets. Is it cultural factors or lack of a severe incident the problem as in the case of computer abuse (Straub, 1990)? We simply do not know for sure in that scholars have not pursued these issues.

There are a wide variety of other arenas where psycho-sociological theories can and should be applied to BCP/DR. Awareness of the problem of catastrophes is an important first step, according to the case study work of Zsidisin et al. (2003) and other surveys (McEachern, 2002). Building on previous work by Goodhue and Straub (1991), Straub and Welke (1998) offered a theoretical model of the effect of awareness on managerial perceptions of security risk (see Figure 7.5), but while their hypothesis tests were significant, the explained variance was low. Researchers need to rejoin the stream of work and examine this "managerial perceptions" model in new and varying contexts.

Details on Issue 3.1

Most commentators acknowledge that there is a large outsourcing component in BCP/DR efforts. There has been a large-scale scientific push to understand this phenomenon, especially in the IS arena (Dibbern et al., 2004). One might be tempted to believe that outsourcing is not a fruitful arena for further inquiry in BCP/DR. We would argue, however, that BCP/DR pose challenges that go far beyond the work in information systems to date in that the effort crosses functional lines and engages the vital question of what part of the firm should or could not be outsourced.

Figure 7.5 **Model for Managerial Perceptions of Security Risk**

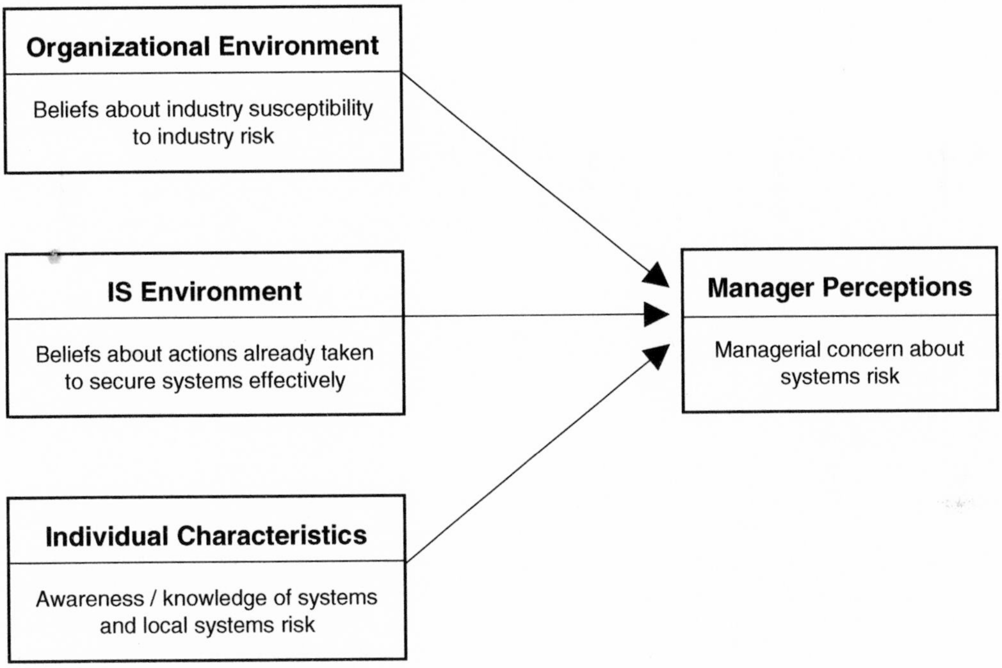

Source: From Straub and Welke, 1998.

In short, the scale of inquiry is much larger than the typical IS outsourcing research project. And the results are exceedingly important.

This is a fallow field at the moment. We are aware of no work that has pursued these critical questions. The theory bases are readily apparent in the literature (Dibbern et al., 2004). What is required is the commitment of a new generation of scholars to address the need.

Details on Issue 4.1

Traditionally the solution to a loss of facilities, either business or data center facilities, has been "cold" or "hot" sites (Straub, 2004). Cold sites are less expensive because they provide access to only the basic infrastructure, such as heated/air-conditioned space, electricity, loading docks, network connections, and so on. In a hot site, office furniture, file cabinets, printers, work stations, large-scale mainframes and servers, and so forth, are added to the basic infrastructure at a price.

What we do not know about these two options is whether one outperforms the other, especially under certain circumstances. Is the extra cost of a hot site worthwhile? One clear disadvantage of a cold site is that it takes time to purchase the furniture and workstations, have them installed, and then, in the case of restoring the computing environment, reloading all the relevant software and data on them. Are the opportunity costs, lost customers, and disgruntled suppliers and employees worth the difference in cost? The answer to these questions is not clear in that there has been no significant scientific work along these lines.

Another viable question is how well the third major solution, distributed computing, works.

As Snow et al. (2005) argue, there would be few occasions where a distributed computing option would not work, and the costs in this case are embedded in the redundancies in h/w, s/w, and personnel required at multiple sites.

CONCLUSION

BCP/DR has been a subject of some interest in the trade press for decades. There has been a smattering of academic interest in the topic, but beyond a few case studies, the scientific effort in the domain has been slight. The current models for how to organize the effort, how to develop good plans, and how to exercise them have been articulated, but remain, for the large part, unexamined from a scientific standpoint.

Researchers who are interested in the intersection between organizations, systems, and management would profit from conducting research in this increasingly indispensable area. Whereas this research is fraught with problems, particularly because organizations are being asked to divulge their internal security arrangements, it is important for society and the academy itself that the initiative be seized and that a commitment be made to the scientific endeavor.

NOTES

1. Herbane and Elliott (1997) define BCP as a process that "seeks to assess and prepare for disruptions in all business activities." This definition stresses what happens in BCP, whereas Castillo's definition (2004) focuses on BCP's primary goal: to maintain revenues.

2. This definition accords well with other definitions and conceptualizations in currency in this domain for a long time. Smith and Sherwood (1995) say that "the objective of the business continuity planning exercise is to ensure the recovery in an acceptable time frame of the business as a whole, following an incident which causes major disruption to business operations" (p. 15).

3. The situation is much better in financial services, as might be expected given the intensive regulatory environment for this industry (McEachern, 2002). Even here, smaller firms were much less prepared for emergencies than larger firms, with their surplus resources.

4. The seminal work on this was carried out by Baskerville (1993). In spite of this earlier identification of the problem, little has been done to rectify the issue since the 1990s.

REFERENCES

Aasgard, D.O.; Cheung, P.R.; Hulbert, B.J.; and Simpson, M.C. 1978. *An Evaluation of Data Processing "Machine Room" Loss and Selected Recovery Strategies.* MISRC-WP-79-04. Minneapolis: University of Minnesota.

Barney, J.B. 1991. Firm resources and sustained competitive advantage. *Journal of Management,* 17, 1, 99–120.

Barney, J.B. 1996. The resource-based theory of the firm. *Organization Science,* 7, 5, 469.

Baskerville, R. 1993. Information systems security design methods: implications for information systems development. *Computing Surveys,* 25, 4, 375–414.

Castillo, C. 2004. Disaster preparedness and business continuity planning at Boeing: an integrated model. *Journal of Facilities Management,* 3, 1 (June), 8–26.

Dibbern, J.; Goles, T.; Hirschheim, R.; and Jayatilaka, B. 2004. Information systems outsourcing: a survey and analysis of the literature. *DATA BASE for Advances in Information Systems,* 35, 4 (December), 6–102.

Eisenhardt, K.M., and Martin, J.A. 2000. Dynamic capabilities: what are they? *Strategic Management Journal,* 21, 1105–1121.

Freeman, R.E. 1984. *Strategic Management: A Stakeholder Approach.* Boston: Pitman.

Goodhue, D.L., and Straub, D.W. 1991. Security concerns of system users: a study of perceptions of the adequacy of security measures. *Information & Management,* 20, 1 (January), 13–27.

Herbane, B., and Elliott, D. 1997. Contingency and continua: achieving excellence through business continuity planning. *Business Horizons,* 40, 6, 19.

Herbane, B.; Elliott, D.; and Swartz, E.M. 2004. Business continuity management: time for a strategic role? *Long Range Planning*, 37, 5 (October), 435–457.

Huber, R.L. 1993. How Continental Bank outsourced its "crown jewels." *Harvard Business Review*, (January–February), 121–129.

Karakasidis, K. 1997. A project planning process for business continuity. *Industrial Management & Data Systems*, 97, 8, 320–326.

Killcrece, G.; Kossakowski, K.-P.; Ruefle, R.; and Zajicek, M. 2003. *State of the Practice of Computer Security Incident Response Teams (CSIRTs)*. Carnegie Mellon University Technical Report CMU/SEI-2003-TR-2001, ESC-TR-2003-2001.

McEachern, C. 2002. BCP survey yields first look at Wall Street's post Sept. 11 preparedness. *Wall Street & Technology Online*, October 31.

Nemzow, M. 1997. Business continuity planning. *International Journal of Network Management*, 7, 127–136.

Pfeffer, J., and Salancik, G.R. 2003. *The External Control of Organizations: A Resource Dependency Perspective*. Stanford, CA: Stanford University Press.

Pitt, M., and Goyal, S. 2004. Business continuity planning as a facilities management tool. *Facilities*, 22, 3/4, 87–99.

Rodetis, S. 1998. Can your business survive the unexpected? *Journal of Accountancy*, (February), 27–32.

Sambamurthy, V.; Bharadwaj, A.; and Grover, V. 2003. Shaping agility through digital options: reconceptualizing the role of information technology in contemporary firms. *MIS Quarterly*, 27, 2 (June), 237.

Smith, M., and Sherwood, J. 1995. Business continuity planning. *Computers & Security*, 14, 1, 14–23.

Snow, A.P.; Straub, D.; Baskerville, R.; and Stucke, C. 2005. The survivability principle: IT-enabled dispersal of organizational capital. Georgia State University working paper.

Straub, D.W. 1990. Effective IS security: an empirical study. *Information Systems Research*, 1, 3, 255–276.

Straub, D.W. 2004. *Foundations of Net-Enhanced Organizations*. Hoboken, NJ: John Wiley & Sons.

Straub, D.W., and Welke, R.J. 1998. Coping with systems risk: security planning models for management decision making. *MIS Quarterly*, 22, 4 (December), 441–469.

Swanson, S.; Wohl, A.; Pope, L.; Grance, T.; Hash, J.; and Thomas, R. 2002. *Contingency Planning Guide for Information Technology Systems*. NIST Special Publication 800–34 (available at http://csrc.nist.gov/publications/nistpubs/800–34/sp800–34.pdf, accessed on February 4, 2006).

Teece, D.J.; Pisano, G.; and Shuen, A. 1997. Dynamic capabilities and strategic management. *Strategic Management Journal*, 18, 7, 509–533.

Wheeler, B.C. 2002. The net-enabled business innovation cycle: a dynamic capabilities theory for assessing net-enablement. *Information Systems Research*, 13, 2 (June), 125–146.

Whitman, M.E., and Mattord, H.J. 2004. *Management of Information Security*. Boston: Thomson.

Zahra, S., and George, G. 2002. Wheeler's net-enabled business innovation cycle and a strategic entrepreneurship perspective on the evolution of dynamic capabilities. *Information Systems Research*, 13, 1 (March).

Zsidisin, G.A.; Ragatz, G.L.; and Melnyk, S.A. 2003. Effective practices in business continuity planning for purchasing and supply management. Michigan State University working paper.

Zuckerman, G., and Cowan, L. 2001. At the top: Cantor Fitzgerald took pride in its position at the World Trade Center. *Wall Street Journal*, September 13, C11.

Zuckerman, G.; Davis, A.; and McGee, S. 2001. In the wake of carnage of terror attacks, the Cantor that was will never be again. *Wall Street Journal Online*, October 27.

PART III

PROCESSES FOR SECURING THE EXTRA-ORGANIZATIONAL SETTING

CHAPTER 8

INFORMATION SECURITY POLICY IN THE U.S. NATIONAL CONTEXT

WILLIAM J. MALIK

Abstract: This chapter addresses the history, current state, and likely future evolution of information security policy in the national context. The first section surveys events over the past forty years that had significant consequences for the development of information security policies. The second section evaluates the current state of information security policy in the United States. The third section examines gaps between what an effective information security program in a national context might require and what is available now, with some suggestions as to future areas requiring attention.

Keywords: Information Security Policy, Information Security National Policy, Information Security Social Impact, Information Security Societal Impact, Information Security Political Impact, Cyberspace Policy

INTRODUCTION

Throughout the history of computing, the people involved have chosen one of four strategies for governance (as defined by Lessig, 1999). These choices were made unconsciously. Now that computing is available to society at large, the mechanisms for governance require enhancement to address the needs and challenges that a larger, untutored population faces.

Information security is primarily a matter of economics, not technology: If the value of the information is greater than the cost of obtaining it, the information is not secure. Information security policy is the second element of an information security program. The primary element is effective governance. The remaining elements are discussed below.

Governance is more than law. Within an enterprise, information security governance consists of those management mechanisms designed to assure the executive leadership team that the employees are (1) aware of the information security policy and (2) in conformance with it. While the primary sanction for violation of any corporate policy may be job loss, enterprises rarely fire individuals. Instead, through effective governance mechanisms, the employees perform their business function while maintaining conformance with policy.

In civic society, governance is again more than law. This chapter explores the possible governance mechanisms available to national leadership to ensure that citizens generally are (1) aware of information security policy and (2) in conformance with it. The primary sanction imposed by government may be legal, but police rarely arrest—and prosecutors rarely prosecute—citizens for information security breaches. It is the intent of this chapter to explore the full range of effective governance mechanisms applicable to civic society.

175

U.S. INFORMATION SECURITY POLICY EVOLUTION

An information security policy should guide people to correct behavior when using information technologies. Effective guidance takes many forms. Lessig (1999) observes that there are four ways to govern behavior:

- Economics
- Social pressure
- Architecture
- Law

He illustrates this by discussing how this might apply in a school where students speed in the parking lot. The use of law would mean posting a speed limit sign, with the implication that speeders when caught might face legal sanctions. Economic pressure might mean assigning a monitor the task of observing traffic: When someone drives too fast, the monitor would note the car and assess a surcharge on the owner's school fees. Social pressure might mean asking the teachers to mention that speeding in the parking lots is dangerous. Finally, an architectural solution might mean installing speed bumps.

For the purposes of this discussion, we will observe how various forms of behavioral governance come into play across the history of information technology use, where they work, and how they fail. The decision to deploy one or another of these techniques is an expression of governance, embodied in policy.

IT Governance through Economics

Social information security governance presents distinct problems compared with governance in corporations. A well-crafted corporate information security policy may have a statement similar to this:

> The information technology resources of this firm are to be used for management-approved purposes only. Any other use may lead to disciplinary action, possibly including termination of employment or legal action.

Corporations exercise effective economic pressure over their employees. Civic society lacks this capability. For that reason, social groups rely on the other forces of governance.

In addition, corporations can exercise economic pressure over trading partners, requiring, for example, adherence to minimum security policies. For example, the rush by both startup and established companies into Internet commerce led to increased concerns about the adequacy of security policies. Businesses were eager to exploit the low-cost channel the Internet provided, but there were concerns that, without a trustworthy platform, consumers would not be willing to purchase goods and services over the Internet. During the late 1990s the rate of fraud for Internet transactions paralleled the rate for card-not-present transactions, such as catalog orders over the telephone. In response, Visa commissioned a structure to govern merchants wanting to use Visa cards on the Internet. Mandated in June 2001, Visa's Cardholder Internet Security Program (CISP) (Visa, 2005) set technical and procedural standards to minimize the risk of financial fraud. Firms wishing to use Visa cards must comply with CISP. Visa audits merchant compliance occasionally. In 2005, a consortium of payment card processors defined the Payment Card Industry (PCI) Data Security Standard (DSS), which mandates security measures that merchants must follow or risk losing their ability to process credit and debit cards (PCI, 2007).

IT Governance through Social Pressure

In 1977, personal computers like the Apple II, the Tandy TRS-80, and Commodore Pet arrived on the retail market, and by 1979 Software Arts was formed to market VisiCalc, soon acknowledged to be the "killer application" for personal computers. By 1981, IBM added substantial recognition of personal computers as serious business tools with the IBM Personal Computer. Eventually, cheap PC modems drove e-mail to overtake spreadsheets as the "killer app." These early personal computers evolved rapidly to offer hobbyists widespread public telecommunications connectivity to bulletin board services and electronic mail. These personal computer hobbyists formed small, self-organizing communities wherein social pressure served to govern behavior.

As local area networking (LAN) for personal computers flourished in the early 1980s, relatively small workgroups already governed by organizational policies and peer pressure suppressed aberrant behavior. Security issues were limited to the accidental introduction of a virus via a floppy disk. Small groups informally set their acceptable use policies by consensus and enforced them with social pressure.

Also in the mid-1980s, Pacific Bell experienced a series of hacks that ultimately were traced to an individual in the Netherlands. Cooperation between U.S. and Dutch authorities eventually located the hacker, a sixteen-year-old boy. The Netherlands had no law criminalizing the acts. The investigators spoke with the boy's mother, who told him to stop hacking Pacific Bell. Where law failed, social pressure actually worked!

In 1986 USENET undertook the "Great Renaming" in response to the concerns of some ARPANET users who were uncomfortable with transmitting unconventional content. Long-time users observed an informal code of conduct that preserved anonymity and privacy—despite the ease with which those characteristics could be violated. However, these same long-time users were disturbed by the behavior of newer users, and the kinds of content these newer users were distributing. The earlier structure of USENET had three high-level qualifiers: net.* for unmoderated groups, mod.* for moderated groups, and fa.* for topics from ARPANET. The specific capability introduced was the "alt.*" qualifier, for content that fell outside the norms. Derived as an abbreviation for "alternative," the alt.* hierarchy became informally known as the acronym for "anarchists, lunatics, and terrorists" (The Great Renaming, 2005). Social pressure as a mechanism for maintaining information integrity eroded.

IT Governance through Architecture

Policies of Physical Access Control

In the 1960s and before, computers were expensive, solitary devices securely locked in guarded facilities. Some organizations, wanting to display their multi-million-dollar investment, built large interior windows opening on to the computer room, giving rise to the name "glass house." Access controls included passing a guard, presenting credentials, and signing in. Work, in the form of a deck of key-punched 80-column cards, was delivered to a scheduler's window. Jobs were processed in batches overnight, with the output listings delivered the next morning. Many of these terms in use today incorporate meanings developed in those early days.

Policies of Logical Access Control

In the late 1960s, commercial computers began to offer non-programmable terminals. These networks were static, with changes controlled centrally. Computer security was entirely provided by restricting physical access to the computer itself and to the terminals. Jobs ran one at a time, with access to data governed by the operator, who mounted tape or DASD volumes in response to requests from the batch job. Storage was expensive, so little information was permanently on-line. Innovations in system design allowed multiprocessing systems, in which multiple jobs could run concurrently. This presented the problem that job A might be able to access data being used by job B. Many vendors took measures to prevent this possibility, and access control requirements became well understood. In October 1981 IBM issued a statement of system integrity (IBM, 1981) committing to fix within twenty-four hours any situation allowing any user to access another user's information.

Policies of Network Perimeters

With the development of the networking, the problem of computer security grew beyond the problem of physical access to the computer. Tensions developed between the problem of data confidentiality versus ease of access for enhanced collaboration. There was no effective model and commercial information security relied on physical isolation and the preservation of a perimeter.

Internet-connected computers by default were open on all ports and responded to all protocols. This openness was ideal for research but inappropriate for commerce, where protection of intellectual property is paramount. Eventually, a portfolio of technology emerged to manage risk from Internet connectivity, for example, firewalls (Cheswick and Bellovin, 1994).

While the opening technologies for the World Wide Web were relatively unsecured, by 1994 Mosaic Communications released Netscape (Mosaic, 1994). Aside from its graphical interface, the product included security features such as encryption and server authentication. Commercial services like online shopping and banking became feasible. It accelerated Internet use and broadened the number and diversity of users. Opportunities to use social pressure to establish mores of behavior declined. The lack of governance of content or use of internet-based materials enabled a wide diversity of expression (sometimes causing concern among various sub-communities of users).

Policies Established on External Standards

In 1984 a series of standards designated ISO 7498 described the seven-layer OSI reference model and mapped core systems management functions against that model. These standards collectively defined basic quality of service requirements. ISO 7498–2 mapped security requirements against the OSI reference model. This standard identified five core information security functions:

- Identification and authentication (user identification)
- Access control (what rights does an identified user have)
- Data confidentiality (usually encryption)
- Data integrity (how to verify that information has not been altered)
- Non-repudiation (a legal concept meaning that the author of a message could not deny authorship)

Note that these functions represent the impact of networking on computing. In a stand-alone mainframe, the only relevant security functions are I&A, and access control. There is little reason to encrypt data on a mainframe (baring hardware or software failures, such as a failure in the access control mechanism); data integrity issues only arise when data move from one location to another; and without transmission of information, non-repudiation is trivial.

The mechanisms to define and maintain these functions gave rise to policies within various organizational contexts—enterprises or governmental agencies, for instance. However, computing had not yet attracted a mass audience, which would have required governmental influence over citizens. Most people who interacted with computers did so through those formal organizational contexts, and the governance and policy mechanisms defined for those organizations were sufficient. Nothing in the ISO standards suggested any systematic approach to the governance of information technology as a whole.

The rainbow series was published from 1983 (the original Orange Book on Trusted Computer System Evaluation Criteria—TCSEC) through February 1994 (the Purple Book, covering contract and procurement guidelines for secure systems). The rainbow series discusses aspects of the software development life cycle for secure systems, although the approach did not actually provide an overall critique of the software development life cycle. TCSEC defined four levels of security with increasing strength, and subordinate graduations:

A1 Verified design
B3 Trusted recovery, security domains
B2 Structured protection
B1 Mandatory access control, labeled protection
C2 Controlled protection
C1 Discretionary access control
D Minimal protection

The U.S. government attempted to use its leverage as a large consumer of information technology to drive vendors to improve information security in their products. The rallying cry was "C2 in '92!" Some vendors followed that lead; IBM released a series of products supporting B1 level security for the mainframe environment in late 1990 (IBM, 1990). In general, however, the commercial uptake was very limited because of the extra cost and complexity. Regardless, there followed a proliferation of national computer security policy initiatives styled after the U.S. rainbow series, such as the British White Book and the German Green Book. Recognizing that multiple national approaches did not resolve the global, borderless nature of computer security, in January 1996 the United States, the United Kingdom, Germany, France, Canada, and the Netherlands jointly published the Common Criteria as agreed joint criteria (NSA, 2005; Common Criteria, 2005). Ultimately this joint criteria statement evolved into ISO/IEC standard 15408.

In 1993 a group of British business people met informally in London to derive a set of baseline information security functions useful for business, where data confidentiality was one, but not the only or most important, concern. This informal group eventually developed BS7799, originally published in 1995, which offered independent security evaluation for these various functions, rather than one rating for an entire environment. This standard became ISO 17799 in December 2000.[1]

At the same time, a group in Europe sought a better way to organize the information security program by making explicit the organizational context in which policy was applied. This group, including the head of security for the SWIFT network (Europe's equivalent to FedWire), developed a standard called COBIT (Control Objectives for Information and related Technology). COBIT required a clear statement of not only what was to be done but who performed the task, where the inputs came from, where the outputs went, and who verified the completion of the task. This standard was sponsored by the Information Systems Audit and Control Association (ISACA). By making the audit function an integral part of the workflow, the standard made regulatory compliance straightforward (ISACA, 2005). The most recent versions of these standards reach past the existing framework for conventional audit to suggest governance and policy approaches for managing information security risk.

IT Governance through Law

In November 1983 Fred Cohen showed a self-replicating software program to a weekly seminar on computer security. Len Adleman, leading the seminar, named the program a virus (Cohen, 1984). His requests for resources to perform further experiments were denied by the university. Their rationale was that any successful security breach weakened the security of the system. This conceptual error resulted from the administration's reliance on the notion of a perimeter—a breech in a physical wall only exists after it has been created by an attack. In fact, Cohen's subsequent work in his doctoral dissertation (Cohen, 1986) showed that systems that perform useful work will be vulnerable. He demonstrated that there is no perimeter. The closing sentences of his 1984 report state:

> The problems with policies that prevent controlled security experiments are clear; denying users the ability to continue their work promotes illicit attacks; and if one user can launch an attack without using system bugs or special knowledge, other users will also be able to. By simply telling users not to launch attacks, little is accomplished; users who can be trusted will not launch attacks; but users who would do damage cannot be trusted, so only legitimate work is blocked. The perspective that every attack allowed to take place reduces security is in the author's opinion a fallacy. The idea of using attacks to learn of problems is even required by government policies for trusted systems. It would be more rational to use open and controlled experiments as a resource to improve security. (Cohen, 1984)

From a policy perspective this position was untenable; policy only covered a closed set of individuals—those with physical or network access to a computer. Others were not covered and so considered trespassers or criminals. From a civic governance perspective, the absence of law for electronic crime was seen as a major impediment. Such prosecutions as did take place were based on other acts—illegal wiretaps, theft, extortion or embezzlement—that followed from the hack, not for hacking itself.

In 1984 the U.S. Senate passed the first version of the Computer Fraud and Abuse Act (18 USC 1030). Initially it intended to define penalties for unauthorized access to classified information on federal government computers, as well as financial records and credit information on federal computers or on computers belonging to financial institutions. The original motivation was to deter hackers from attacking government computers. The law was amended in 1986 to include any protected computer. The Act set jail terms and fines for misusing computers to commit fraud, to violate privacy, or to disrupt legitimate activities. Prosecution required total damages in excess of $5,000, and damages could be aggregated across victims (Computer Crime and Intellectual Property Section, 2003). The governance issue here was limiting the access of private information. No actual transfer of data was required nor was any actual conversion of information for gain required. This law addressed privacy issues for computer-based information. Law began to form the basis for social governance with this act.

During this same period, a scandal known as the "Iran Contra Affair" included attempts to destroy damaging evidence contained in e-mail. Then CIS director Admiral John Poindexter and White House staffer Lt. Col. Oliver North collectively deleted nearly 6,000 messages. Unknown to them, a back-up system was available that retained the evidence, and investigators were able to retrieve copies of the deleted messages for use in court (Walsh, 1994, ch. 3).

The two men had attempted to destroy evidence but were thwarted in that attempt by the existence of backup tapes (Walsh, 1994). This incident underscored the criticality of information integrity, and the need for explicit organizational records retention policies, consistently applied. The lesson would be learned again when organizations attempted to destroy computer-based evidence (along with the massive shredding of documents) in the Enron scandal in 2001.

In October 1988, Robert Morris released his "worm" on the Internet. Soon 10 percent of the 60,000+ hosts on the Internet were infected. Robert Morris was prosecuted under the Computer Fraud and Abuse Act, and was sentenced to three years probation, 400 hours of community service, and fined $10,050 in Federal court. Following this incident, DARPA created its Computer Emergency Response Team (CERT) at Carnegie Mellon University (Longstaff et al., 1997). While CERT did receive incident reports and provide analysis on solutions, it functioned as a clearinghouse for technical information shared among systems administrators. CERT did not address policy issues.

In 1990, the hacker club Masters of Deception cracked into Citibank over a 9,600 baud modem. Eventually a task force under the U.S. Secret Service captured the responsible parties. They served jail terms of ten months and up. One member of that task force, Bob Weaver, started the U.S. Secret Service New York Electronic Crime Task Force a few years later.

As IT security technologies improved, early attempts to regulate IT security itself emerged. The NSA classified strong encryption as regulated under the ITAR (International Traffic in Arms Regulations), and prohibited its export from the United States. This policy was intended to keep strong encryption out of the hands of regimes that might pose a threat to the United States. While perhaps well intentioned, the regulation encompassed both innocent and socially progressive software such as Pretty Good Privacy (PGP), a peer-structured encryption product (Zimmerman, 1995). Phil Zimmerman released PGP driven by his motivation to give secure communications capabilities to individuals working for change in repressive societies. Another unintended consequence of this regulation was that other countries enacted legislation to impede the attempts of foreign (usually, U.S.-based) companies to protect their own proprietary information. Unilateral trade restrictions do not usually resolve global policy concerns.

In response to commercial pressure, the encryption export restrictions were shifted to the U.S. Department of Commerce, where they were dropped in 2000. U.S.-based businesses could not protect their secrets overseas because foreign governments enacted retaliatory regulations. For example, Shell Oil's discovery of oil under the Caspian Sea in 1997 was announced not by Shell but by the government of Azerbaijan, which required that foreign companies provide a copy of any passwords and encryption tools used in its territory. The government knew of the discovery at the same time as Shell's headquarters.

The government of France prohibited the use of encryption (citing pre-WWII misuse of personal information as grounds) without the permission of the president and National Assembly. How did firms cope? One executive from a large manufacturer revealed that he did not encrypt information, since that would violate the law. Instead, his firm used a "simple data-masking algorithm" to preserve the privacy of certain critical information.[2] This indicates a failure of governance—when a rule is overly broad, people will find ways of circumventing it.

In December 1992, Marc Andreesen wrote Mosaic at NCSA over Christmas break. The product was released in February 1993 and quickly became the face of the World Wide Web and thereby of the Internet itself (Anonymous, 2005). Within two years, a hacker on the West Coast of the United States was found not guilty of trespassing on another computer because the home page said "Welcome!"—and it was taken as an invitation. The vagueness of law in this area permitted this interpretation, even though no housebreaker was ever found "not guilty" by noting the presence of a doormat offering a similar invitation. This led to vigorous discussion of policy statements on websites. Following this incident, corporate web home pages read: "This site is the property of XYZ Corp. If you do not have permission to enter, you are trespassing and should go away." The effect of this policy realignment was to transform what had been a social convention, respect for the property of others, into a possible tort of trespass.

In late 1993 and early 1994, David LaMacchia, then a student at MIT, distributed copies of certain copyrighted programs without charge. Since the copyright laws prohibited violation of copyright for gain, this act was not prosecutable under copyright violation. He was indicted under the 1952 wire fraud statute, but the judge dismissed the case because of the bad fit between the activities Mr. LaMacchia undertook and the intent of the statute (Hylton, 1995).

In 1994 the U.S. Secret Service New York field office stood up the Electronic Crime Task Force (NYECTF) under Special Agent Robert Weaver. The unit's initial workload was investigating phone fraud and theft of cable services. Then-Special Agent Weaver recognized that the Secret Service itself could not cope with the pace of technological innovation; his insight was to develop a forum where large companies (typically those that could become victims of electronic crime), law enforcement, prosecutors from various jurisdictions, private investigators, vendors of information security and technology products and services, and industry analysts (but not the press) would meet and discuss topics of common interest to understand, thwart, and help solve criminal acts. The first meeting had eleven people; the last one before SA Weaver's retirement in 2003 had over 400.[3] His activities identified limitations and gaps in the legal system that required a rethinking of the relationship between police agencies and the public. His innovative solution to resolve those incongruities became a model for other initiatives nationally. The NYECTF was cited as a model for public-private partnership in the USA Patriot Act (Thieme, 2001).

In October 1995, the European Union issued EU Directive 95/46/EC, commonly known as the European Data Protection Directive. This directive proposed a model law protecting personal privacy, following a tradition dating back over a century (European Parliament and Council, 2002). In the 1880s the development of portable cameras allowed for photographing individuals without their prior consent. Lawsuits alleging a violation of privacy against newspapers publishing embarrassing photographs followed. In December 1890 Justices Warren and Brandeis published "The Right to Privacy" in the *Harvard Law Review* (Warren and Brandeis, 1890). They defined three fundamental principles that collectively create privacy: first, an individual has the right to know what information is being gathered about him; second, an individual has the right to govern how that information is used; and third, an individual has the right to be left alone. These three principles reappear in the EU directive, in Canada's PIPEDA (GOC, 2000), and in the national legislation in EU member countries enacting national laws to meet the EU directive.

The President's Commission on Critical Infrastructure Protection (1997) identified vulnerabilities of the U.S. economy based on the degree to which information technology was incorporated in business and government. This commission, organized in the face of the growing commercial importance of the Internet and information technology generally, and the vulnerabilities this dependency brought, sought to pair federal departments with representative industry groups to address information security risks. For instance, the finance industry (represented by the Financial Services Roundtable's BITS) was aligned with the Treasury Department (BITS, 2005). Public-private partnerships like this are the current model for governance of information security issues at the national level. However, such partnerships still face limitations and concerns (see below).

Following the recommendations of the PCCIP, Presidential Decision Directive 63, dated May 22, 1998 (PDD 63, 1998), expanded CERT and imbedded CERT functions in each federal agency. PDD 63 identified eight lead agencies addressing 19 critical infrastructures. The document includes:

> 6. *Education and Awareness:* There shall be Vulnerability Awareness and Education Programs within both the government and the private sector to sensitize people regarding the importance of security and to train them in security standards, particularly regarding cyber systems.

Despite this national policy, as of this writing no such programs have begun.

In Cleveland, Ohio, in 1996, the FBI field office founded InfraGard to link the FBI with local businesses, in a model similar to the New York ECTF (InfraGard, 2002). FBI agents, other law enforcement agents, prosecutors, and business owners meet regularly to develop mutual understanding and dialog before a computer crime occurs. The Department of Homeland Security was made a co-partner with the FBI in InfraGard in 2004. Most InfraGard activity now consists of providing information to the FBI and DHS, and distributing alerts from those agencies to the current 8,000 or so InfraGard members across 76 or so chapters nationally. InfraGard might become a regional or local resource for governance or policy, but to date no such initiatives have begun.

In 1999, Elliot Turrini, then USADA for New Jersey, successfully prosecuted David Smith for authoring the Melissa virus. His case included a comprehensive economic analysis of the damage caused by the virus globally (U.S. Department of Justice, 1999). The method he used (the prosecution hired an economist to develop the analysis) has helped other prosecutors assess the economic damage resulting from broad-based computer incidents. The defendant pled guilty, so the economic analysis was never produced in court.

In the mid-1990s organizations began to worry that certain coding practices (specifically encoding years with only the last two digits) could lead to computer failures. This was the Y2K bug. As it happened, little actual damage occurred. (Ghana suffered a national power blackout, two safety systems at nuclear power plants in Japan failed but no critical systems were interrupted, and some firms reported that their printed documents erroneously displayed dates intended to be "2000" as "1980" until the underlying defect was fixed.) The Securities and Exchange Commission enacted a regulation stating that firms had to attest to the magnitude of their exposure to Y2K failures in their annual reports, 10K filings, and quarterly filings, as of calendar year 1998. As a result, some firms took the Y2K or Millennium Bug as an opportunity to restructure their IT infrastructure, move from legacy to contemporary platforms, upgrade or replace key applications, or outsource maintenance of potentially vulnerable systems.

Useful discussions took place over the possibility of product liability lawsuits for Y2K-related failures, but as such failures did not materialize, the discussions did not lead to regulatory or legal proceedings. Concerns over code quality briefly entered public discussion, and some organizations reviewed their application development methods to avoid similar vulnerabilities in the future. The basic concerns that were left unanswered included:

- Should software developers be professionally certified like architects, doctors, or massage therapists?
- Should information security professionals be professionally certified?
- Does the state have the competence to grant such certifications?

- What professional certifications exist now? (CISA/CISM from ISACA, CISSP from ISC2, vendor specific certifications—MSCE, CSNE, etc.)
- How effective are such certifications?
- How often are individuals expelled for noncompliance (as opposed to being dropped for not renewing their license or paying their dues)?

Reacting to the events of September 11, 2001, Congress enacted the USA Patriot Act of 2002. This compendium of measures granted law enforcement additional powers for search and seizure, permitted wiretaps without judicial supervision based on the judgment of law enforcement personnel alone, and promoted greater cooperation between the private sector and the public sector, but with fewer protections for individuals. The Chief Privacy Officer of Sun Microsystems, Michelle Dennedy, referred to it as a "bad law" during a webcast on Privacy, Identity and Information Security in June, 2003.[4] Among other problems, it granted police investigators subpoena powers without judicial oversight, required libraries to divulge the lending history of citizens, and required booksellers to disclose the purchasing habits of buyers, without any specific cause (Patriot Act, 2001).

With the publication of the National Strategy to Secure Cyberspace in February 2003, the federal administration sought to provide guidance to individuals, small businesses, state and local governments, and businesses for information security and risk management (White House, 2005). Richard Clarke, then cybersecurity czar under President George W. Bush, led the development of this document, with the support of a committee of industry representatives (Evers, 2002). Its practical value as a national policy is debatable. It lacks an organizing principle, provides no governance or policy development guidance, and is diffuse—the various sections are unrelated and uncoordinated. While it offers information security hints and tips, it does not provide a coherent statement of policy. While there are suggestions for specific actions, the document provides no mechanism to verify that they are done properly, how one might learn to do them correctly, and whom one might turn to for guidance in case of a suspected problem. In other words there is no effective governance.

In response to increasing identity theft incidents, the U.S. Senate held hearings on identity theft in 2000 and again 2002. The County of Los Angeles reported that identity theft was the most rapidly growing crime in its jurisdiction in 2002, and the FTC reports that it is the most reported problem it received in 2003. Additional U.S. Senate hearings were held on May 10, 2005, in the aftermath of the ChoicePoint incident (Specter, 2005). Further hearings before the U.S. Senate Special Committee on Aging were held on July 18, 2005. Attorney Fred Chris Smith, former AUSA for New Mexico and author of New Mexico's cybercrime bill, spent a year to reverse a family member's identity theft problems (Smith, 2005). Currently individual victims of identity theft must devote their own time and resources to resolve and correct the consequences of their victimhood.

NATIONAL INFORMATION SECURITY POLICY AS OF 2005

While the efforts to develop widespread and effective forms of IT security governance have been extensive, particularly in the area of law, the ultimate impact is questionable. Speaking at the first Gartner Information Security Conference in Chicago in June, 1994, Scott Charney, then Assistant U.S. Attorney for Computer Crimes under Attorney General Janet Reno, announced the Charney Theorem: "At any point in time, a certain number of people are up to no good."[5] Generally 2 to 3 percent of the population will engage in aberrant behavior; as the population of network-connected users increases, the likelihood that a talented and amoral individual will emerge increases. Social pressure fails as a governance mechanism because the population is so large that such individuals can remain anonymous. Architectural design choices made in the 1960s and 1970s prohibit strong security. Technological fixes (for instance, IP version 6 for strong user and platform identification) take extensive amounts of time to deploy effectively.

The alternative governance mechanisms are either legal or economic approaches. Economic motivations require a level of user identification and authentication, and corresponding auditing and logging, which the Internet lacks. Legal sanctions can only be brought into play after a crime has been committed. Aberrant behavior and criminal activity flourish until someone gets caught.

In this section we will assess the status of information security programs outside corporate organizational structures in the United States. There are growing issues that involve consumers of information technology in its various forms. For example, home computer users are facing rising risks of identity theft. The economic and emotional consequences of identity theft are substantial and damaging. To date there has been no information technology product liability lawsuit successfully concluded for the plaintiff. Should such a lawsuit come to light, it seems likely that the civic governance of information technology will evolve toward regulation, including certification and licensing of users and manufacturers. These represent the legal aspect of governance. In the architectural domain, IPv6 will introduce improved authentication, data integrity, and confidentiality capabilities that should curtail classes of information security problems. The IPv6 authentication header will eliminate host spoofing. The encapsulation security header will provide encryption for the packet's contents. This will stop inadvertent disclosure of network traffic.

Governance

At no level of government is there any office offering oversight or recommendations regarding information security nor any office that welcomes the expression of concerns about information security. Sporadic, ad hoc Senate hearings; uncoordinated Department of Justice and FTC prosecutions; anemic funding; and degradation of the Federal cybersecurity leadership mark the current political landscape. Following Richard Clarke's resignation, Amit Youran of Symantec accepted the post. Unlike Clark, he did not report to the National Security Administrator, Condoleezza Rice. Amit was three levels down from the Secretary of the DHS. He left in 2004 (Hulme, 2004).

The federal budget for cyber training for law enforcement in FY 1999 was $20M. The Clinton administration proposed $170M for FY 2000, but the funds were never disbursed. There are about 16,000 city, state, and federal law enforcement agencies needing cybersecurity training. Total disbursed funds average $600 per agency annually. Of the FY 2000 budget, 80 percent went to the FBI. While additional mandates for cybersecurity activities have been passed since then, they have generally not been accompanied with comparable funding, leaving those goals remote. From a governance perspective, the national leadership desires improvements but is neither providing funding nor a model structure to achieve those improvements.

Policy

The current U.S. approach to policy is to address industry specific concerns as opposed to blanket regulation: compare the USA Patriot Act, GLBA, Sarbanes-Oxley, HIPAA, 21 CFR part 11, and COPPA with the European Data Privacy Directive or Canada's Personal Information Protection and Electronic Documents Act (PIPEDA). Industry specific or data specific measures leave gaps and loopholes in the policy. Disjointed policy is generally ineffective even in a rigid corporate structure. In the public policy sphere, disjointed policy is utterly ineffective. "Friends don't let friends drive drunk" is an effective exhortation when backed by laws punishing drivers who are intoxicated. To date there is not even so much as a slogan along the lines of "Nice people don't connect weak computers to the Internet," much less any legal, economic, or architectural structure to enforce the sentiment.

Architecture

The closest national guidance on information security architecture available consists of gleanings from PDD 63, ISO 17799, the National Strategy to Secure Cyberspace, and the Common Criteria. A great deal has to be inferred. None of these standards or documents explicitly defines an information security business architecture. There is no consistent or even nascent mapping of basic security policy directives to commonly understood information security primitives.

IPv6 will eliminate spoofing, but that architectural transformation will also eliminate a cornerstone of anonymity. Lawrence Lessig discusses this problem in his book *Code.* (1999). To date no effective proposal providing a compensating capability for pseudonymity (partial anonymity) has come forward, although there are various initiatives under discussion.

Awareness and Training

Computer training in K–12—inconsistent, no model curriculum for security policy (Alexander and Rackley, 2005). Some schools have computer labs, with volunteers of varying competence providing such guidance as might occur to them.

Undergraduate Curriculum—information security policy and program information is scattered among various computer science programs. Currently there is great variability among educational institutions as to the quality of their own operational information security programs.

Advanced degree curriculum—few universities offer PhD level classes in information security policy in the United States.

The United Kingdom launched 2/23/2005 IT SAFE (Security Awareness for Everyone) (IT Safe, 2005). Compare this to the U.S. government's program (CERT 2005), with its ten top tips for safe computing at home.

There is no consistent understanding of what basic principles users should follow to use the Internet safely. Various information security vendors offer piecemeal guidance, but even a highly skilled information technology professional will be baffled by the complexity and disorganization of the multitude of information protection solutions offered, their competing, unverifiable, and unregulated claims, the absence of any warranty or baseline standard of protection, and the lack of any mechanism to find help should a problem occur.

Technology

Currently no software or systems vendor faces the risk of product liability lawsuits for poor quality. There is no economic motivation to excel in quality; consumers may speak of quality as a fundamental requirement, yet they continue to purchase substandard, although the shift to open source alternatives to Microsoft in some cases may be driven by quality concerns as much as by economic ones. In 1965, Ralph Nader published *Unsafe at Any Speed,* exposing the auto manufacturer's culpability for delivering poor quality products. This book gave rise to a wave of product liability lawsuits, and the car industry sought regulation to shield itself from liability. It is far from clear that the regulations introduced then, and following the oil crisis of the early 1970s (Corporate Average Fuel Economy, CAFÉ), stifled innovation in the automotive industry. In fact, the opposite may be the case.

In 2004, the U.S. Department of Homeland Security proposed including chips in passports containing digitized identifying information to speed a traveler through customs. However the chip's information is not encrypted. Any individual with the right reader could get enough information from a passport to steal the passport holder's identity. On August 14, 2006 the U.S. Department of State issued the first tourist electronic passport. To reduce "skimming" (illegal reading of the information on the passport's RFID chip) the passport has metallic fibers woven into the passport's covers, creating a Faraday cage around the chip, so it can only be read when opened (U.S. Department of State, 2007). Here technologists take architectural constraints for granted, relying on technology to fix a policy problem. The goal of the program was forgotten when the first technical impediment appeared (Zetter, 2005).

Logging, Reporting, and Auditing

Attempts to gather data about security breeches have not gathered much momentum. The public-private partnership still has open issues that impede cooperation and progress. Three concerns are:

1. Some speculate that the Department of Justice may view cooperation among competing industries as a possible antitrust violation. However, the Department of Justice approves of firms working together to combat crime. Even so, corporate consul has done a good job training employees to avoid any forum that might have the appearance of antitrust, so most organizations are reluctant to participate in information sharing.

2. If a firm uncovers evidence of a breech and submits it to a central clearinghouse, will that information be discoverable under a Freedom of Information Act lawsuit, leading to damage to the reputation of the victimized firm? This situation is complex. FOIA lawsuits cannot reveal information pertinent to an ongoing criminal investigation. During a trial, the prosecution can request the courtroom be closed during presentation of evidence that includes corporate secrets. At one moot court competition the judge declined to close the court. The judge ruled that since the individual's freedom was at stake, the defendant's right to a fair and open trial was more important than a corporation's secrets or reputation.[6] Also, organizations fear the possibility that an inadvertent breech could still cause harm. A simple way to minimize this and the previous potential exposures is to provide sufficient information to analyze the technical or procedural defect that opened the breech without providing sufficient information to determine the identity of the firm suffering the attack.

3. If a firm discovers a breech and develops internal mechanisms to react to it, but does not reveal it to outsiders, could it be subject to a 10-B lawsuit from stockholders seeking redress for the firm withholding information that might have a material impact on earnings? Proper handling is mandatory: a report commissioned by an audit firm need not be kept by the commissioning organization. Without the existence of such a report, the firm can legitimately refute such a claim.

It appears that the concerns are generally not valid. By following appropriate procedures, firms can effectively share information about weaknesses and attacks without risking their reputation.

However, as of this writing, there is insufficient case law to establish a precedent codifying these assertions.

Citizens experiencing information security problems have no "help desk" or clearinghouse to which to report such problems nor is there a clearinghouse to investigate a problem. Instead, individual users are responsible for their own environment. They must maintain a growing, diverse portfolio of security products, select and assess competing alternatives with no guidance or method for performing that assessment, train themselves on the user interface, and determine on their own which products they need, what price to pay, when to upgrade, and how to diagnose, report, and fix a security problem. In some cases following a breech people simply abandon their computer and purchase a replacement rather than attempt to fix the older system at all. Who backs up their personal computer at regular intervals?

Revitalization

By reflection on the automobile experience, we can see where we are today and where we might be in fifteen or twenty years. Today, we lack any licensing mechanism for users of the Internet. Individual firms craft their privacy policies and consumers opt in or out, depending on the structure, to make use of the website's features. At some point schools will develop a consistent approach to educate and prepare young users for cyberspace. This element of civic governance will be through law with social pressure to bolster it.

Today we have no inspection or safety criteria for computers that connect to the Internet. There is no baseline requirement for security software or robust hardware—any machine capable of responding to the protocols is allowed. In the future we may see a baseline defined to include virus protection, a properly configured firewall, regular update capability, and indication of recent service for problems. Some networks may deny access to nonconforming computers, directing users instead to sites where they can upgrade their machine to that baseline. This form of governance may be economic but with legal elements as well. The economic motivation will create markets.

Today there is no linkage between a computer on the Internet and that computer's owner or user. It remains difficult to even ascertain the identity of a computer on the Internet. In a decade or less we may have IPv6 or some equally effective capability deployed broadly enough that users will be identifiable—and spoofing, phishing, and spamming will be rendered obsolete just as Windows 95 ended the threat of boot sector viruses a decade ago. This form of governance will be through architecture directed by law.

Vendors, universities, and research organizations may investigate how to provide emergency response capabilities to citizens at large. Safe computing environments will need not only defensive measures but also education and awareness programs. This form of governance will marry architecture with social pressure, and with the discovery of an economic incentive, a market or set of markets will arise.

CURRENT THREATS AND VULNERABILITIES

Today's major information security concerns include phishing, spam (but is this really a security concern or a quality of service concern?), and viruses, worms, and blended threats (collectively called malware). Embezzlement and extortion—usually involving insiders—remain responsible for the majority of financially significant computer crimes.

To regulate or not to regulate remains the hot topic. The current administration is disinclined to introduce regulation, favoring industry self-regulation. The impetus for self-regulation has to be dislike of the alternative, which would be governmental regulation. The threat of governmental regulation must be credible to induce voluntary compliance. If the likelihood of governmental regulation is low, self-regulation will not take hold. For example, in the early years of President George W. Bush's first term, the FCC under Michael Powell sought self-regulation among Internet service providers (ISPs). The ISPs developed guidelines for self-regulation, the FCC accepted them, and then the ISPs ignored them. The FCC took no action. The ISPs doubted that the FCC would issue regulations, and therefore did not feel any need to comply.

At the RSA Security conference in February 2005, the need for regulation was debated between Bruce Schneier, author of numerous books and Cryptogram; Richard Clarke, cybersecurity czar under presidents Clinton and Bush; Harris Miller, president of ITAA; and Rick White, president and CEO of TechNet (RSA, 2005). Bruce's point was that without an economic incentive businesses would not deploy adequate protections—like the installation of sprinkler systems in buildings. Richard Clarke—after disavowing the national strategy—explained that he had shifted his position from being against regulation to being in favor of it because it would be better to deploy sensible regulation now as opposed to waiting for a major problem and having senseless regulation thrust on the industry following a major incident. Harris Miller raised the specter of regulation stifling innovation. Rick White outlined the history of bad federal regulation, and cited automobiles as an example of overregulation. On balance, the pro-regulation argument seemed more convincing.

FUTURE DIRECTIONS FOR NATIONAL INFORMATION SECURITY POLICY

At the Seton Hall conference on Software Quality and Product Liability in November 2002 (Seton Hall, 2002) the panelists weighed in on the pros and cons of using product liability lawsuits as a remedy for defective software products. Historically, the risk of a product liability lawsuit provided manufacturers with the economic incentive to improve product quality. From handguns in the nineteenth century to automobiles in the mid-twentieth century, product liability awards motivated improvements. Industry sectors subject to product liability lawsuits sought governmental standards for performance to shield themselves from liability. To date the information technology industry has been free of these incentives and the quality of the IT infrastructure reflects that reality.

The software development methodology known as the capability maturity model (CMM), devised by Carnegie Mellon University's Software Engineering Institute, can lead to process improvement enhancing code quality by orders of magnitude (Software Engineering Institute, 1995). This technology has been known since the early 1980s. In 1984 IBM Poughkeepsie used a CMM analysis for the processes developing the MVS operating system, yielding a four order of magnitude improvement in the quality of that product.[7] However, the largest software vendors in the world remain disinclined to invest in the procedural changes necessary to effectively implement this decades-old proven remedy. A recent article in the *Wall Street Journal* suggested that Microsoft's organization is facing up to the need for more mature software development processes than the creative anarchy of extreme programming (*Wall Street Journal*, 2005).

If we map national information security programs against the seven-step information security program outline, we see significant missing elements.

Governance

Currently governance is piecemeal. There is no information security authority—central, regional, or local—and no effective governance mechanism. Problem reporting is uncoordinated, software quality is variable, alert notification is haphazard, and participation in security measures is entirely voluntary. Individuals using computers or the Internet are treated today as hobbyists in an experimental and unregulated realm.

Over time certain leading cities may deploy "secure cyber zones" offering baseline protections and a mechanism for seeking help both for education and for resolving problems. Should these succeed and attract wider attention, they might serve as a model for public governance.

Policy

Today there are independent and uncoordinated information security policies covering specific products, applications, and environments. Information security policies apply to users of ISPs, for instance, but there is no commonality across policies. Software end user license agreements make little mention of information security other than to limit or exclude liability on the part of the manufacturer or publisher if the product fails. Policy is ad hoc, with no integration or broadening away from point issues and focus on the fundamental problem of governing the behavior of individuals in a democracy.

National leadership concerning safe computing, with recommendations for baseline security and mores of behavior, and legislative or regulatory sanctions for violations, would be preferable to architectural constraints (Lessig, 1999).

Architecture

There is no awareness of the problems caused by not having a consistent, agreed to, effective set of information security primitives. Such a set would help conversations among implementers using different platforms but facing similar business issues. Lacking an architectural framework, incompatible platforms cannot be managed collectively. Each computing platform has its own intrinsic information security architecture. Making those architectures explicit allows for comparative analysis, common reporting and audit, and aggregated management. At times various software companies have developed information security architectures, but these have never risen above the level of product marketing or branding exercises. There does not seem to be a market for effective information security architectures. There is no benefit to any one firm to develop a general, comprehensive information security architecture, since that investment will only benefit the firm's competition and increase the firm's cost. Today's market offers a few alternative sources for such a work: governmental agencies, universities, or research organizations might develop a baseline. To date no such activity has successfully occurred.

The IPv6 protocol represents an architectural improvement that could reduce the likelihood of certain classes of problems, as discussed above.

Awareness and Training

Some training is happening but it is sporadic, task-focused, and dry. Information security can be taught effectively to elementary school students. The Association for Computing Machinery (ACM) is developing a model curriculum, but it is far from a standard. WGBH in Boston was developing video in late 2004 to support such a curriculum. As was the case with architecture, governmental agencies, universities, and research organizations might provide a curriculum. At this point even the statement "Nice people don't connect weak computers to the Internet"—spoken with authority by a committed civil servant—would be a solid step forward. And yet, by comparison, how effective would the slogan "Friends don't let friends drive drunk" be without the real consequences of DWI/DWAI laws?

Comprehensive education and training for citizens eager to use the net would reduce the incidence of identity theft and slow the spread of certain classes of malware, just as driver's training programs reduce the incidence of accidents among new drivers—and remedial classes improve the performance of experienced drivers, as shown by reduced collision insurance premiums, and removal of "points" on the license, for drivers who take such classes.

Logging, Reporting, and Auditing

Most logging is platform-specific or application-specific. There are no tools providing a comprehensive view of the firm's information security risk portfolio. The problem may be addressed with effective standards for describing information security problems, organizational maturity, and potentially effective countermeasures. There is a market opportunity once such standards are in place.

Reporting is improving under regulatory directives; however, the regulatory regime in the United States remains siloed and piecemeal, providing ample opportunities for exceptions and evasions. Pending successful prosecutions, and the corresponding body of legal precedent, compliance will remain desultory.

Auditing has strengthened considerably since the Enron collapse in 2001. Section 404 of the Sarbanes-Oxley Act of 2002 requires the CEO and CFO of public firms to attest to three separate facts: first, that the algorithms used to derive the financial data in reports from publicly traded firms are correct; second, that only certain designated individuals have access to the source data and the processes creating those reports; and third, that these first two assertions can be verified by independent audit tests. As these executives face individual legal sanctions should their attestations prove false, compliance is proceeding briskly. Resolving these issues requires an identity management infrastructure. However, deploying technology, without a context of policy and governance, merely accelerates dysfunctional processes. Procedural clarity is a prerequisite for effective automation.

Revitalization: maintaining the information security program's relevance and currency should be the chief information security officer's (CISO's) most important function. No CISO at any level of government addresses the needs of civic society, and no regulatory framework exists to make such an individual effective.

On February 2, 2006, Connecticut's attorney general, Richard Blumenthal, announced that his office was initiating an investigation of Myspace.com (Connecticut Attorney General's Office, 2006). His comments pointed to the danger to minors from the site. He advised Connecticut residents that his office was exploring possible criminal persecution. He also stated that "Internet sites have a legal and moral responsibility to protect children" and that parents should monitor their children's Internet activity. He was invoking both the legal and the social dimensions of governance to mitigate the threat posed by Myspace.com.

During January 2006 a series of unsettling announcements arose concerning China's use of legal mechanisms to force major ISPs to disclose individuals whose activities were considered dangerous to the Chinese state. Congressional testimony from a number of individuals including Lucie Morillon of Reporters Without Borders and Tom Malinowski of Human Rights Watch before the Congressional Human Rights Caucus on February 1, 2006, detailed a history of disturbing actions that limit or punish free speech and the free flow of ideas (Congressional Human Rights Caucus, 2006). On February 15, 2006, Michael Callahan, Yahoo's general consul, testified before the House Subcommittee on Africa, Global Human Rights and International Operations, and Asia and the Pacific (Yahoo!, 2006). His remarks underscored Yahoo's values and beliefs but noted that the firm had to comply with the laws of the country in which it operated. As reported in the *Register,* Representative Tom Lantos, Dem-CA, compared the actions of Microsoft, Yahoo, Google, and others as similar to IBM's compliance with laws in Nazi Germany during the 1930s (Haines, 2006). From a governance perspective, the United States has a limited set of capabilities to influence Chinese social policy. Civic information security governance is a proper subset of politics, not technology, not law.

AREAS FOR FURTHER RESEARCH

At this writing there is no operational definition of a civic information security program. One area for research would be what an effective civic information security program might consist of. Another would be what elements of law can bear on awareness and training.

Civic information security programs lag corporate information security programs in every dimension. Military and secret agency information security programs are much simpler: Often all the data and processing associated with an operation (which in corporate terms may be analogous to a line of business, or, in civic terms may be analogous to a jurisdiction) is classified. This dramatically simplifies the information security program: personnel are under very clear regulations and information security efforts are subsumed within physical security and secrecy efforts. These constraints make bridging military approaches to corporate or civic environments problematic.

In corporations, individuals face social and economic constraints, but legal and architectural limitations are difficult to bring to bear. One area for research might be how to extend corporate information security program elements to the civic sphere. Should there be a government-sponsored emergency phone number for computer problems, a 911 for Internet issues? Should there be "driver's licenses" for Internet users? Can schools effectively train safe computing techniques to the population? Will insurance companies grant reduced rates for Internet liability insurance policies to individuals who have successfully completed a certain level of training? Will diverse jurisdictions develop and enact a model code for prosecution of Internet crimes? Which crimes can be so defined and prosecuted? Will local law enforcement agencies adopt a uniform standard of evidence for investigating Internet-related crimes?

Civic information security governance could avail itself of architectural constraints—but a population would require a great degree of knowledge to make informed choices or pursue an effective debate. One area for research would be in the domain of education—for citizens regardless of age or educational attainment—on information security.

At some future time, state and local CIOs will expand their scope of control from the internal workings of their client departments in government to include the public constituency of their locales. As they understand the expectations and limitations facing the citizenry within their domain, they will call for the help of their CISO. At some future time, there will be a call for review and enhancement of the civic information security program. At this writing, we have not yet begun this valuable, necessary, and urgent work.

NOTES

1. The author has subsequently spoken with one of the participants in this seminal meeting. It was recounted that disaster recovery was problematic: some of the participants felt that if the situation had deteriorated to the degree that required invoking the disaster recovery plan, the situation had gone beyond salvaging.

2. The author participated in this conversation.

3. The author participated in the New York Electronic Crime Task Force from 1998 through Special Agent Weaver's retirement.

4. The author was a speaker in this webcast.

5. The author created and chaired the Gartner Group Information Security Conferences from their beginning in Chicago in June 1995 annually through June 2001.

6. The author participated in this moot court competition as an expert witness.

7. The author was a member of the team at IBM in Poughkeepsie that implemented these procedural changes.

REFERENCES

Alexander, T., and Rackley, C. 2005. Integrating information assurance into K–5 curriculum. Paper presented at *Information Security Curriculum Development Conference '05,* Kennesaw, GA, September.
Anonymous. 2005. *Internet Pioneers: Marc Andreesen* (available at www.ibiblio.org/pioneers/andreesen.html, accessed on October 11, 2005).
BITS. 2005. *BITS Financial Services Roundtable* (available at www.bitsinfo.org/index.html, accessed on October 11, 2005).
Carson, Rachel. 1962. *Silent Spring.* New York: Houghton Mifflin.
CERT. 2005. *United States Computer Security Readiness Team Mailing Lists and Feeds* (available at www.us-cert.gov/cas, accessed on October 11, 2005).
Cheswick, W., and Bellovin, S. 1994. *Firewalls and Internet Security: Repelling the Wily Hacker.* Reading, MA: Addison Wesley.
Cohen, F. 1984. *Experiments with Computer Viruses.* Report published by Fred Cohen & Associates (available at www.all.net/books/virus/part5.html, accessed on October 11, 2005).
Cohen, F. 1986. *Computer Viruses.* Ph.D. Dissertation, University of Southern California.
Common Criteria. 2005. See www.commoncriteriaportal.org/ for information on the common criteria (accessed on October 11, 2005).
Computer Crime and Intellectual Property Section. 2003. The National Information Infrastructure Protection Act of 1996: Legislative Analysis. United States Department of Justice, July 31 (available at www.usdoj.gov/criminal/cybercrime/1030_anal.html, accessed on October 11, 2005).
Congressional Human Rights Caucus. 2006. Testimony of Lucie Morillon, Washington Director, Reporters Without Borders, CHRC Members' Briefing: Human Rights and the Internet The People's Republic of China (February 1) (available at http://lantos.house.gov/HoR/CA12/Human+Rights+Caucus/Briefing+Testimonies/02–06–06+Testimony+of+Lucie+Morillon+China+Google+Briefing.htm, accessed on February 19, 2006).
Connecticut Attorney General's Office. 2006. Attorney General Investigating Myspace.Com for Allowing Minors Easy Access to Pornography, Inappropriate Material. Press release, February 2 (available at /www.ct.gov/ag/cwp/view.asp?Q=309712&A=2426, accessed on February 19, 2006).
European Parliament and Council. 2002. *Directive 2002/58/EC of the European Parliament and of the Council Concerning the Processing of Personal Data and the Protection of Privacy in the Electronic Communications Sector (Directive on Privacy and Electronic Communications),* July 12 (available at http://europa.eu.int/eur-lex/pri/en/oj/dat/2002/1_201/1_20120020731en00370047.pdf, accessed on October 11, 2005).
Evers, J. 2002. Feds draft national strategy to secure cyberspace. *PC World* (available at www.pcworld.com/news/article/0,aid,105002,00.asp, accessed on October 11, 2005).
GOC. 2000. Personal Information Protection and Electronic Documents Act of 2000 (available at www.privcom.gc.ca/legislation/02_06_01_01_e.asp, accessed on October 11, 2005).
The Great Renaming. 2005. See http://cse.stanford.edu/class/cs201/projects-98–99/controlling-the-virtual-world/history/rename.html for a detailed discussion of the history of the Great Renaming (accessed on October 11, 2005).
Haines, L. 2006. Google and Yahoo! take a beating. *Register,* February 16 (available at www.theregister.co.uk/2006/02/16/china_committee/, accessed on February 19, 2006).
Hulme, G. 2005. Homeland Security cybersecurity chief abruptly resigns. *Information Week,* Oct. 1 (available at www.informationweek.com/showArticle.jhtml?articleID=49400205, accessed on October 11, 2005).
Hylton, J. 1994. David LaMacchia cleared; case raises civil liberties issues. *The Tech,* 115, 4 (February 7), (available at http://wild-turkey.mit.edu/V115/YIR/lamacchia.00n.html, accessed on October 11, 2005).

IBM Corp. 1981. *Software Announcement P81–174,* October 21 (available at www.os390-mvs.freesurf. fr/mvsinteg.htm, accessed on October 11, 2005).

IBM Corp. 1990. *GC28–1440: MVS/ESA SP V5 Planning: B1 Security.* Armonk, NY.

InfraGard. 2002. *Combating Cybercrime: FBI's InfraGard Program Promotes Security Awareness,* November 4 (available at www.infragard.net/library/combating_cybercrime.htm, accessed on February 8, 2008).

ISACA. 2005. *ISACA: Serving IT Governance Professionals* (available at www.isaca.org, accessed on February 8, 2008).

IT Safe. 2005. *IT Security Warning Service: Sign Up for Free Warnings* (available at www.itsafe.gov.uk, accessed on February 8, 2008).

Lessig, L. 1999. *Code and Other Laws of Cyberspace.* New York: Basic Books.

Longstaff, T.; Ellis, J.; Hernan, S.; Lipson, H.; Mcmillan, R.; Pesante, L.; and Simmel, D. 1997. Security of the Internet. In *Froehlich Kent Encyclopedia of Telecommunications* vol. 15. New York: Marcel Dekker, pp. 231–255 (available at www.cert.org/encyc_article/tocencyc.html, accessed on February 8, 2008).

Mosaic. 1994. *Mosaic Communications Offers New Network Navigator Free on the Internet.* See www.jwz. org/gruntle/newsrelease1.html for the initial Netscape product announcement (accessed on February 8, 2008).

Nader, R. 1991. *Unsafe at Any Speed.* New York: Grossman Publishers, 1965; Knightsbridge Pub. Co. Mass; Rp/25th anniversary edition March 1991.

National Research Council. 1991. *Computers at Risk: Safe Computing in the Information Age.* National Academies Press. See www.nap.edu/openbook/0309043883/html/ for details on the book (accessed on February 8, 2008).

NSA. 2005. *National Information Assurance Partnership.* See http://www.nsa.gov/industry/niap.cfm, for information on the common criteria (accessed on February 8, 2008).

Patriot Act. 2001. Uniting and Strengthening America by Providing Appropriate Tools Required to Intercept and Obstruct Terrorism (USA PATRIOT ACT) Act of 2001 (available at www.epic.org/privacy/terrorism/ hr3162.html, accessed on February 8, 2008).

PCI, 2008. *The PCI Security Standards Council* (available at https://www.pcisecuritystandards.org/index. htm, (accessed on February 8, 2008).

PDD 63. 1998. *The Clinton Administration's Policy on Critical Infrastructure Protection: Presidential Decision Directive 63.* White Paper. May 22 (available at www.fas.org/irp/offdocs/paper598.htm, accessed on February 8, 2008).

RSA. 2005. Security Conference, *Panel Discussion: To Regulate or Not to Regulate—That Is the Question.* San Francisco, February 16.

Seton Hall. 2002. Seton Hall Law School, *Conference on Software Quality and Product Liability,* Newark, NJ, November 15. The author was a panelist at this event. Participants included Barbara Moo, Steve Lipner of Microsoft, Steve Bellovin of Lucent, and Melanie Schneck then of the law firm of Steptoe and Johnson. The event's announcement is at http://law.shu.edu/administration/public_relations/press_releases/2002/ software_security_liability_symposium.htm (accessed on February 8, 2008). The *Newark Star-Ledger* reported the event at www.nj.com/business/ledger/index.ssf?/base/business-3/1039504241203751.xml, but access required a paid subscription when accessed February 8, 2008.

Shimomura, T., and Markoff, J. 1995. *Takedown: The Pursuit and Capture of Kevin Mitnick, America's Most Wanted Computer Outlaw—By the Man Who Did It.* New York: Hyperion.

Sinclair, U. 1992. *The Jungle* (available at http://sunsite.berkeley.edu/Literature/Sinclair/TheJungle/, accessed on February 8, 2008).

Smith, Fred Chris. 2005. Personal communication with the author.

Software Engineering Institute. 1995. *Capability Maturity Model: Guidelines for Improving the Software Process.* Carnegie Mellon University. The Carnegie-Mellon work on the capability-maturity model continues. See www.sei.cmu.edu for a comprehensive discussion of its history and direction (accessed on February 8, 2008).

Spar, D.L. 2001. *Ruling the Waves: From the Compass to the Internet.* New York: Harcourt.

Specter, A. 2005. Senator Arlen Specter, chairman of the Senate Judiciary Committee, Remarks of February 24. as reported in Tech Law Journal, (available at http://www.techlawjournal.com/topstories/2005/20050224. asp, accessed on February 8, 2008).

Stoll, C. 1989. *The Cuckoo's Egg.* New York: Pocket Books.

Thieme, R. 2001. *Bob Weaver and the Electronic Crimes Task Force.* November. Report. TruSecure Corp.: Information Security (available at www.thiemeworks.com/write/archives/electronictaskforce.htm, accessed on February 8, 2008).

U.S. Department of State. 2007. The US Electronic Passport Frequently Asked Questions (available at http://travel.state.gov/passport/eppt/eppt_2788.html#Six, accessed on February 8, 2008).

U.S. Department of Justice. 1999. Creator of "Melissa" Computer Virus Pleads Guilty to State and Federal Charges. Press release, December 9 (available at www.usdoj.gov/criminal/cybercrime/melissa.htm, accessed on February 8, 2008).

Visa. 2005. *Cardholder Information Security Program 2005.* For details of the VISA information security program for merchants, see http://usa.visa.com/business/accepting_visa/ops_risk_management/cisp.html (accessed on February 8, 2008).

Wall Street Journal. 2005. Microsoft changes how it builds software. Sept. 23.

Walsh, L. 1994. *Final Report of the Independent Counsel for Iran-Contra Matters.* June. Darby, PA., DIANE Publishing Co.

Warren, S., and Brandeis, L. 1890. The right to privacy. *Harvard Law Review,* December (available at www.lawrence.edu/fast/boardmaw/Privacy_brand_warr2.html, accessed on February 8, 2008).

White House. 2005. *The National Strategy to Secure Cyberspace* (available at www.whitehouse.gov/pcipb/, accessed on October 11, 2005).

Yahoo! 2006. Testimony of Michael Callahan, Senior Vice President and General Counsel, Yahoo! Inc., Before the Subcommittees on Africa, Global Human Rights and International Operations, and Asia and the Pacific. Press release, February 15 (available at http://yahoo.client.shareholder.com/press/ReleaseDetail.cfm?ReleaseID=187725, accessed on February 19, 2006, since removed).

Zetter, K. 2005. Feds rethinking RFID passport. *Wired Magazine,* April 26; summarizes the tortuous progress of the RFID-enabled passport (available at www.wired.com/news/privacy/0,1848,67333,00.html, accessed on October 11, 2005).

Zimmerman, P. 1995. *The Official PGP User's Guide.* April. Cambridge, MA: MIT Press. See www.mit.edu/prz/ for background on Phil Zimmerman and PGP (accessed on February 8, 2008).

CHAPTER 9

THE INTERNATIONAL LANDSCAPE OF CYBER SECURITY

DELPHINE NAIN, NEAL DONAGHY, AND SEYMOUR GOODMAN

Abstract: This chapter addresses the history, development, effectiveness, and prospects for international cooperation against cybercrime. The first section introduces the question and growing significance of cybercrime. The second provides an overview of international intergovernmental cybercrime organizations at the global level. The effectiveness and potential for different bilateral and multilateral information sharing and cooperative prosecution regimes along with measures for standardizing international conventions on cybercrime are discussed. The third presents the actions of regional intergovernmental organizations such as OPEC, APEC, the EU, OAS, and the SADC. In section four, public-private and purely private-sector actors are also presented. The authors conclude with an assessment of the current and prospective effectiveness and scalability of these efforts.

Keywords: Cyberspace, Cybercrime, CERT, CSIRT, Critical Infrastructure, Internet Security, Private-Public Partnerships, Council of Europe Convention on Cybercrime

AN EMERGING LANDSCAPE

Worldwide open IP-enabled public network infrastructure for communications, commerce, and government—cyberspace—is rapidly expanding. The Internet, the largest of these networks, has taken root in over two hundred countries and is used by almost a billion people. Each country in the world now shares a porous border with every other country, not just those physically adjacent.

By any measure, cyberspace is "critical infrastructure" (DHS, 2003). Individuals, commercial enterprises, and governments are becoming increasingly dependent on this network infrastructure for an extensive and expanding range of needs. Other critical infrastructures, notably electric power, banking and finance, emergency services and other government functions, industrial processes, and transportation, have also become increasingly dependent on such network infrastructure for control, communications, and management. Unfortunately, cyberspace is plagued by a set of poorly understood vulnerabilities that are being exploited extensively by a wide range of malicious actors. The easy access and relative anonymity and openness of the Internet has allowed fast-paced cybercrime and other serious hostile activities to flourish on a global scale with relatively weak capabilities available to law enforcement and organizations concerned with national and international security. Policy makers and senior industry management in the more developed countries have only recently appreciated the scale and transnational dimensions of these problems.

A majority of the countries connected to these critical infrastructures have little experience or capacity for dealing with these problems. The number of users there may soon rise dramatically with the spread of Voice over IP (VoIP—essentially digital telephony via the Internet), bringing a tidal wave of exacerbated security problems. These countries have often been given little attention, or help, from the more advanced countries, but they are part of the problem and need help to become part of the solution.

In the last few years an array of relatively autonomous activities in law and standards-making bodies, the private sector, and government agencies began to unfold in response to the challenges of cybercrime and critical infrastructure protection. At the national and international levels, in governmental and intergovernmental bodies, a trio of communities have begun forming: (1) reinvented legacy telecommunication regulatory agencies, (2) homeland security and critical infrastructure protection agencies, and (3) IT-oriented justice and law enforcement bodies. The instruments being crafted range from treaties and other vehicles for new kinds of global collaboration, to capability requirements instituted by statutory and regulatory provisions, to real-time operational and monitoring arrangements and capabilities.

A fourth category of security-service-providing organizations is emerging at the international level. A few are narrowly focused, for example, on spam control, while others are more broadly chartered, for example, covering such things as training, and providing early warning, information sharing, and other forms of cooperation. Some are private and others are nongovernmental organizations (NGOs). Many are national, others regional, and still others are broadly international.

This chapter is an initial attempt to survey the organizations that are explicitly international and that try to promote international cooperation to deal with these problems. It does not profess to provide exhaustive coverage, but tries to cover the most prominent organizations we could identify as of 2005. We treat them in three categories: international intergovernmental organizations, regional intergovernmental organizations, and private-public partnerships. Together they form a sometimes complementary, sometimes disjointed, set of national, regional, and multilateral initiatives.

We will try to answer the following questions. What kinds of organizations are emerging? What are they trying to do? Are they doing it well? Are they coming up with enforceable, scalable, and readily usable solutions that reduce vulnerabilities? What meaningful metrics can be used to assess their success? Do they collectively amount to a whole that is somehow significantly greater than the simple sum of the separate parts? Can a good case be made that they are making cyberspace more secure, or at least slowing the rate at which things are getting worse?

INTERNATIONAL INTERGOVERNMENTAL ORGANIZATIONS

Policy-Making Bodies

Large international organizations such as the United Nations (UN) and the Organization for Economic Cooperation and Development (OECD) began publicly debating computer crime in the mid-1980s. Their most important impact has been to raise awareness of the dangers of cybercrime among the more developed nations and help shape national and regional policies toward cybercrime.

OECD and the UN: Toward a Policy for Cybercrime

In 1986, the OECD published *Computer-related Crime: Analysis of Legal Policy*, a report that surveyed existing laws and proposals for reform in a number of member states and that also recommended a minimum list of abuses that countries should consider prohibiting under criminal laws (OECD, 1986). In 1990, the Eighth UN Congress on the Prevention of Crime and the Treatment of Offenders adopted a resolution calling upon member states to intensify their efforts to combat computer crime (UNCJIN, 1990). It articulated specific needs such as the modernization of national criminal laws and procedures as the OECD had recommended in 1986. The UN also recommended other mechanisms besides legal policy: improved computer security, the adoption of training measures, and the elaboration of the rules of ethics in the use of computers (UNCJIN, 1990). The UN General Assembly endorsed the recommendations in its resolution 45/121 (December 14, 1990), and since then the topic of cyber security has been on the UN agenda at every session, resulting in many other resolutions.[1] In particular, a United Nations Resolution was adopted by the General Assembly in 2000 (res. 55/63) on combating the criminal misuse of information technologies.

In its successive resolutions, the UN recommended international efforts in the development and dissemination of a comprehensive framework of guidelines and standards for computer-related crime. The first important international effort toward developing such a framework started in 1992 when the OECD issued *Guidelines for the Security of Information Systems,* intended for both government use and the private sector (OECD, 1992). The framework document focuses on nine principles: awareness, risk assessment, responsibility, response, security design and implementation, security management, reassessment, ethics, and democracy. The guidelines were reviewed in 1997 and 2001 by the Working Party on Information Security and Privacy (WPISP) and accelerated in the aftermath of the September 11 tragedy. The most recent guidelines were adopted in July 2002.[2]

Impact of UN and OECD Policies

The UN and OECD issued guidelines and recommendations for a global culture of cyber security but do not enforce any mechanisms for their implementation. Ultimately it is the task of every country to create and maintain its own mechanisms to fight cybercrime. Therefore the main impact of these organizations has been to set the stage for a culture of cyber security, but whether this culture develops and successfully fights cybercrimes depends on the level of commitment and the level of cooperation among nations to implement their own mechanisms.

Some regional organizations such as the Council of Europe (COE), the Asia-Pacific Economic Cooperation (APEC), and the European Union (EU) have taken steps to promote a culture of cooperation among their members at the regional level in the fight against cybercrime and refer to the UN resolution as a motivation (APEC, 2005).

A questionnaire circulated in July 2003 to OECD member countries (COE, 2004b) surveyed the initiatives undertaken since the release of the 2002 guidelines. The survey addresses how the guidelines are disseminated, whether countries have developed a national policy on information security, the types of programs and initiatives set up to raise awareness, foster best practices, educate, and support security research, and the amount of dialogue between the government and businesses and civil society. Overall, twenty-two out of thirty member countries responded. A notable point of the survey is that fifteen of these twenty-two had developed national policies for the security of information systems and networks and the remaining seven were in the process of doing so. All respondents reported using the guidelines as a reference framework. A second notable point is that most responding countries reported having enacted a set of measures to combat cybercrime. The most widely adopted measures were the identification of national cybercrime units (17 countries); initiatives to set up institutions, whether public or private, that exchange threat and vulnerability assessments such as computer security incident response teams (CSIRTs) (17 countries); designation of international high-technology assistance contact points (14 countries); cooperation between governments and business in fighting cybercrime, including between law enforcement organizations and business about the security of information systems and networks (13 countries); and specific measures on the collection of evidence of cybercrime (12 countries, 1 in preparation). Less widely adopted were legislative measures such as preservation of traffic data in order to support law enforcement activities to deal with cybercrime (5 countries, 3 in preparation).

Initiatives to foster international cooperation received less attention. Only three countries mentioned such initiatives: Japan, the United States, and Australia. Japan supports cooperation among CSIRTs in the Asia Pacific region. The United States mentioned support of initiatives at the international level (APEC, OECD, G8), and Australia mentioned supporting initiatives within APEC to assist with the implementation of the security guidelines, for example by helping the development of the APEC cybercrime legislation and enforcement capacity building project. Another weak point revealed by the survey is the sharing of best practices among countries.

Overall, the OECD survey is helpful for assessing the state of implementation of the guidelines, but not for measuring success. The OECD recognizes that the survey failed to address the impact of the initiatives (COE, 2004b). By asking countries to measure the success of initiatives in a consistent way, the OECD would in effect require the members to agree on appropriate metrics. To really assess positive change, meaningful measures are needed and a public debate should exist to come up with such measures. For example, countries could report the number of cyber criminals arrested and prosecuted as a direct result of guideline implementation, and the number of incidents successfully handled by CSIRTs. Such measures might also help countries identify and prioritize successful mechanisms, and help plan and justify budget decisions based on other countries' experience. For example, the survey reveals two interesting initiatives that other countries could follow if their measured impact is positive. Finland has legislation in preparation to make it mandatory for their computer emergency response team (CERT) to inform the government of serious infringements of the security of information systems and networks, and the United States is the only country to have a formal audit system for government agencies to check the implementation of the OECD guidelines.

International Mechanisms to Secure Cyberspace

The OECD survey revealed that in response to the UN and OECD guidelines, most countries initially focused on developing their own cyber security mechanisms. The survey also indicates a two-tiered process when implementing mechanisms to deal with cybercrime. In a first wave, most of the twenty-two countries set up national cybercrime units, early-warning centers such as CERTs or CSIRTs and contact points for high tech crime prosecution. In a second wave, some countries have started modernizing their legislation and crime prosecution procedures to better address cybercrime issues.

Beyond national initiatives, some *regional* mechanisms have been set up as well, particularly in Europe and the Asia Pacific region, which will be surveyed below. However, no single point of governance creates and monitors mechanisms at the *international* level. It is still up to individual countries and coalitions of countries to create their own. This has led to a series of uncoordinated bilateral and multilateral initiatives for information sharing, law enforcement training, and legal mechanisms that we survey in this section.

International Information Sharing and Early Warning Systems

When widespread cyber events occur, it is critical that mechanisms be in place to effectively detect and identify the activity, provide early warning to affected populations and constituencies, notify others within the Internet and security communities of potential problems, effect a coordinated response to the activity, share data and information about the activity and corresponding responses, and track and monitor this information to determine trends and long-term remediation strategies (Killcrece, 2004).

G8: Toward an International 24/7 Point of Contact Network. The G8 is an informal group of eight countries: Canada, France, Germany, Italy, Japan, Russia, the United Kingdom, and the United States of America (G8, 2005). The Lyon Group, established by the G8 in 1995, has worked on forty recommendations to combat transnational organized crime. One recommendation calls on members to "review their laws to ensure that abuses of modern technology are criminalized." Five subgroups were created to implement the Lyon Group recommendations, including the Subgroup on High-Tech Crime in 1997. At its July 2000 summit in Japan, the G8 affirmed its commitment to a common concerted approach to combating cybercrime by publishing the Okinawa Charter on Global Information Society (GIS Charter) calling for "coordinated action to foster a crime-free and secure cyberspace" (G8, 2000b).

The G8 has been active in developing information sharing mechanisms to deal with cyber-crime intended for use at the international level. The Subgroup on High-Tech Crime's mission is to "enhance the abilities of G8 countries to prevent, investigate, and prosecute crimes involving computers, networked communications, and other new technologies" (G8, 2004). Countries are represented in the subgroup by multidisciplinary delegations that include cybercrime investigators and prosecutors, and experts on legal systems, forensic analysis, and international cooperation agreements. For all stakeholders in protection of critical information infrastructures, the subgroup has published various best practices documents, including guides for security of computer networks, international requests for assistance, legislative drafting, and tracing networked communications across borders; conducted training conferences for cybercrime agencies from every continent (save Antarctica); and organized conferences for law enforcement and industry on improved co-operation and tracing criminal and terrorist communications. Recent examples include industry workshops held in 2000 in Paris (G8, 2000a), in 2001 in Berlin and Tokyo (G8, 2001), and in 2003 in Paris (G8, 2003).

The most significant mechanism created by the subgroup is the 24-Hour Contacts for International High-Tech Crime (also known as High-Tech Crime 24/7 Point-of-Contact Network) in 1997. The 24/7 Network requires participating countries to maintain a cybercrime unit and designate a 24-hour, 7-day-per-week point-of-contact for the purposes of providing information and/or responding to requests for assistance on urgent cases involving electronic evidence. The network is open to non-G8 members as well, and all countries are encouraged to join the G8 network. In particular the European Union calls on its members to join the network in a *Council Recommendation of June 25, 2001* (Europa, 2001b), and the APEC in its 2002 recommendations calls on all its member countries to join the network (APEC, 2002c). As of 2002, there were twenty members (USDOJ, 2005) and forty as of 2004 (G8, 2004).

One limitation of the network is that it does not entail the establishment of a high-tech operations center open around the clock, but just the means to reach a high-tech expert at all hours who is knowledgeable in investigations involving computer and electronic evidence. Since the network is just a way to connect already existing infrastructures, it is left to each country to create that infrastructure. This is a concern for countries of low capabilities that do not have the means to set up such infrastructures and train experts in high tech crime investigations.

The G8 has not issued any official document surveying the success of the network. A simple metric would be to count the number of investigations helped by the network. However, in a letter of invitation to countries, a paragraph indicates some of the successes:

> This network has been used successfully in many instances to investigate threats and other crimes in a number of countries. For example, the network has been used to help secure the conviction of a murderer in the United Kingdom by facilitating the preservation and disclosure of Internet records in the United States. The network has also been used on several occasions to avert hacking attacks, including attacks on banks in the United States, Germany and Mexico. Conversely, in the context of the ongoing investigation into the September 11th 2001 terrorist attacks, the lack of a point of contact in a particular country impeded the investigation of a serious threat. (USDOJ, 2005)

It would be very informative if a formal survey of member countries was conducted annually to collect data about the successes of the networks, such as the number of investigations that used the network and the partnering countries. The public release of these data could show the impact of the network by looking at the percentage of international investigations that use it. It would also help indicate which countries are most active in using the network and could share their best practices.

Computer Security Incident Response Teams (CSIRTs). The concept of a public service CSIRT emerged in the United States in 1988 with the creation of the CERT Coordination Center (CERT/CC), located at the Software Engineering Institute, a U.S. federally funded research and development center operated by Carnegie Mellon University (CERT/CC, 2005b). Its charter was to assess and respond to computer security incidents and related activity, becoming the cyber analog to the emergency number 911 in the United States.[3] The CERT/CC was also chartered to serve as a model for the operation of other response teams around the world and to foster the creation of additional teams, each focused on meeting the needs of a particular constituency (Killcrece, 2004). Guidelines for establishing a CSIRT have been formulated and published by the Carnegie Mellon University SEI (Killcrece et al., 2003).

Following the CERT/CC model, since 1988 hundreds of CSIRTs have been created in North America and Europe (Escobar, 2004), dozens in the Asia Pacific region (APCERT, 2005b) and Latin America (Solha, 2002), and a few in the Middle East/Africa region (Anderson, 2004; Balancing Act News, 2004b).[4] These organizations use either CERT or CSIRT as acronyms.[5]

The services of each CSIRT are normally performed for a defined constituency, such as a private, governmental, or education organization, or a region or country. In order to be considered a CSIRT, a team must:

- provide a secure channel for receiving reports about suspected incidents,
- provide assistance to members of its constituency in handling these incidents,
- disseminate incident-related information to its constituency and to other involved parties.

CSIRTs often have the additional responsibilities of providing technical advice, identifying intrusion trends, working with other security experts, disseminating information to the public, publishing technical documents, and offering training (Killcrece, 2004; West-Brown et al., 2003).

International Cooperation among CSIRTs. The structure and level of cooperation among CSIRTs remains voluntary and informal (CERT/CC, 2005a). CSIRTs around the world vary in their specific approaches to incident response based on a variety of factors such as consistency, geographical and technical issues, authority, services provided, and resources. Reporting a cybercrime to a CSIRT is voluntary in most countries. Finland is one of the first to pass legislation that makes it mandatory to report serious cyber infringements to CSIRTs (OECD, 2004).

Most international cooperation initiatives are point-to-point and informal collaborations based on trusted links between national CSIRTs. For example, in December 2004, India's Cyber Emergency Response Team announced plans, including the signing of an e-security protocol, to work with Russian law enforcement to address cybercrime (PTI, 2004). The US-CERT encourages information sharing at the international level by establishing regular international information sharing conference calls with government cyber security policy makers from five key allied countries: the United States, the UK, Australia, Canada, and New Zealand (US-CERT, 2005).

Currently, there is no infrastructure to globally support a coordinated international incident response effort. However, there are efforts underway to develop cooperative relationships that support such a capability at the regional level. The APCERT (Asia Pacific Computer Emergency Response Team), a coalition of fifteen CSIRTs across the Asia Pacific region (APCERT, 2005a) and the European TF-CSIRT Task Force (TERENA, 2006) are examples that will reviewed below.[6]

Prospects for an International/Global Incident Response Team. According to the CERT/CC philosophy, a worldwide CSIRT is not a feasible option:

> The diverse technologies, constituencies, global demographics, and breadth of services needed by these constituencies could not be provided by any single organization. No one team would ever be able to effectively respond to all attacks against computer networks or network connected systems—the problem would become too large, the technical knowledge required too broad, the user constituencies needing help too diverse, and the likelihood of developing universal trust too small. (Killcrece, 2004)

There is indeed no worldwide CSIRT. Rather, the model of cooperation has been to link national CSIRTs at the regional level, therefore building a "network of regional CSIRTs" both in Europe and Asia.

One possibility for the future might be to try to link those networks of regional CSIRTs to form a worldwide network. However, issues of trust and national security might restrict CSIRT cooperation to trusted regional spheres. Issues of national security arise for example when CSIRT employees holding high levels of security clearance are forbidden to travel to or disclose data to other, nontrusted countries.

So far, the only attempt at forming a worldwide network of CSIRTs has been the Forum of Incident Response and Security Teams (FIRST), founded in 1990. FIRST is defined as "a network of individual computer security incident response teams that work together voluntarily to deal with computer security problems and their prevention," and consists of more than 170 teams (FIRST, 2006a). Many of these are CSIRTs, representing government, law enforcement, academia, the private sector, and other organizations from Asia, Oceania, Europe and the Americas. FIRST promotes international cooperation through the sharing of technical information, tools, methodologies, and best practices, as well as holding conferences open to nonmembers and encouraging the development of CSIRTs. Although FIRST is a truly international effort at addressing cyber security, its membership is exclusive. Depending on the level of membership, applicants must be sponsored by either one or two existing Full Members and complete an extensive application, including an on-site visit. FIRST is selective about membership as the organization is predicated upon trust (FIRST, 2006b). This model limits countries with low capabilities from joining.

Gaps in incident response, management, and coordination processes mean that some nations are more at risk than others. One current noteworthy gap is that very few CSIRTs exist in Africa. Consequently, these countries lack adequate staff and resources to effectively monitor such activity, protect critical services and supporting networks, and respond to incidents that affect critical infrastructure services.

International Law Enforcement Cooperation

Given the borderless nature of cybercrime, cooperation among law enforcement agencies is often essential to collect data about crime and help prosecutions. To combat international cybercrime, law enforcement needs the authority to obtain evidence from networks regardless of jurisdiction and more quickly than offenders can move or erase incriminating material. In addition, it is essential for countries to train skilled investigators and attorneys to deal with cybercrime issues.

Interpol is one of the largest international police organizations in existence, and has been combating cybercrime since 1990 (Westby, 2004). Today, it consists of 182 members spread over five continents and provides local police forces with a mechanism for international coordination and information sharing (Interpol, 2005). To rely on existing expertise, Interpol utilizes the mechanism of expert "working parties." The working party consists of the heads or experienced members of national computer crime units. These working parties have been designed to reflect regional expertise and exist in Europe, Asia, the Americas, and Africa. According to Interpol, "the working parties are not Interpol's only effort, but they certainly represent the most noteworthy contribution. Other initiatives include collaborations with the U.S. FBI and Secret Service" (Interpol, 2003).

While the working parties are at different stages of development, the European Working Party is currently the most advanced. It meets three times a year and has had tangible impact, including the compilation of the Information Technology Crime Investigation Manual (ITCIM), a best practice guide for law enforcement investigators, which is continually updated; the holding of numerous training courses; the support of an international 24-hour response system, the National Central Reference Points (NCRP), which lists responsible experts within more than eighty-five countries and is now being expanded and has been endorsed by the High Tech Crime Sub-group of the G8. The Asia-South Working Party meets once a year and follows the European working party model. So far, it has been most active in providing training sessions. The African Working Party also meets once a year, but has yet to set up programs. Its goal for 2005 is to run an awareness program for top management in African countries and regional police organizations, and to start targeting all African countries with information on cybercrime on a regular basis. The Americas Working Party does not provide publicly available information.

To further promote international cooperation, Interpol has proposed the creation and implementation of a fixed international training unit. This unit should consist of a pool of trainers from the Interpol member states. It has been further proposed that the training team, made from the pool of trainers, would visit the different countries and conduct the course locally. Interpol envisions that with the aid of the American, Asian, African, and European working groups a sufficiently large pool of potential lecturers could be created.

The existence of manuals and trained law enforcement officers is already a measure of the success of the Interpol initiatives. To further measure impact, Interpol should publicly provide statistics about the number of cybercrime investigations that have benefited from its manuals and training programs.

Current International Legal Landscape: Little Harmonization

From 1999 to 2002, many countries in Europe updated their legislation for computer crimes according to the recommendations formulated in the 1980s and 1990s by the UN, OECD, and the EU. In North America, similar laws were passed in the United States and Canada, and in the Asia Pacific region, in Australia, Japan, Singapore, India, and Malaysia.[7] Due to heightened attention to terrorist threats after the events of September 11, 2001, the growing economic impact of cybercrimes, and pressure from countries with existing cybercrime laws, an increasing number of countries have been introducing national legislation on all or at least some of the aspects concerning cybercrime or cyber security. Since 2002, European countries have had to harmonize their cybercrime laws under the *Council Framework Decision on Attacks Against Information Systems.*

However, there are still countries without cybercrime laws and in many countries cybercrime laws are not harmonized (Comptroller and Auditor General of India, 2003; McConnell International, 2000; Dunn and Wigert, 2004; Gelbstein and Kamal, 2002; Techlawed, 2005). The lack of harmonization is a problem as soon as nations have to deal with cybercrime on a bilateral basis. Mutual legal agreement treaties (MLATs) have dual criminality requirements, meaning the crime has to be defined in the law similarly in both countries. The situation is much more complex when three or more countries investigate cybercrime on a multilateral basis. A famous incident exacerbated by lack of harmonization involves the "I love you" virus, released on May 4, 2000, and causing an estimated $10 billion in damages (*Washington Post,* 2000).[8] This virus collected Internet passwords from infected computers around the world and sent them to e-mail accounts in the Philippines. The FBI and the Philippines National Bureau of Investigation worked with Internet service providers to trace the program to a telephone line in the apartment of Onel de Guzman, a former college computing student. Since the Philippines had no law against destructive computer activity, investigators charged Mr. de Guzman with traditional crimes like theft and violation of an "access devices" law that normally applies to fraud using credit cards. However, in August 2000 prosecutors were forced to dismiss all charges against Mr. de Guzman because the laws cited did not apply to computer activity and there was insufficient evidence showing intent to gain from the e-mail program. President Joseph Estrada immediately signed a law outlawing most computer-related crimes, but the law could not be applied retroactively to the "Love Bug" author.

The "Love Bug" case shows that if only some countries adopt cybercrime laws and dedicate law enforcement to help other nations, the perpetrators may not be arrested and prosecuted unless all countries involved in the prosecution have harmonized cybercrime laws. To deal effectively with the problem, countries can no longer be allowed to be "safe havens," in which cyber criminals legally launch attacks against computers located elsewhere.

Council of Europe Convention on Cybercrime: Prospects for Harmonization. The only multilateral treaty that addresses harmonization of laws for the global problems of computer-related crime and electronic evidence gathering is the Council of Europe Convention on Cybercrime (COE, 2006a).[9] The COE, distinct from the twenty-five-nation European Union, has forty-six member countries (COE, 2006b).[10] The main objective of the convention is to establish a treaty that requires member states to pursue a common criminal policy aimed at the protection of society against cybercrime, especially by adopting appropriate legislation and investigative procedures and fostering international cooperation. The forty-six COE members and four nonmember states (United States, Canada, Japan, and South Africa) participated in the drafting the convention from 1997 to 2001. As of September 2006, the treaty was signed by forty-two countries, and ratified by sixteen. The full, updated list can be found on the convention website (COE, 2006a). The sixteen ratified countries are: Albania, Bosnia and Herzegovina, Bulgaria, Croatia, Cyprus, Denmark, Estonia, France, Hungary, Lithuania, Norway, Romania, Slovenia, the former Yugoslav Republic of Macedonia, Ukraine and the United States.

Overview of the Convention on Cybercrime. The convention contains forty-eight articles. The main themes are the common definition of offences for harmonization of the national laws, the definition of investigation and prosecution procedures to cope with global networks, and the establishment of an effective system of international cooperation. An explanatory report (ER) accompanies the convention and provides an analysis of the convention as well as the understanding of the parties in drafting convention provisions. The ER is thus accepted as a fundamental basis for interpretation.

Articles 2–13 address substantive criminal law. Parties are required to domestically criminalize cybercrime. The offences are divided into categories: (1) offences against the confidentiality, integrity and availability of computers, data and systems (also known as CIA crimes); (2) computer-related traditional offences (forgery and fraud); (3) content-related offences (including child pornography); (4) offences related to infringement of copyright and related rights (intellectual property); and (5) infringement of privacy (personal data).

Articles 14–22 address procedural law. Electronic evidence relevant to cybercrime cases can be difficult to secure and can be quickly altered, moved, or deleted. To address these issues, the convention requires each party to ensure that competent authorities have certain powers and procedures for use in investigations. These include, but are not limited to: preservation of computer-stored data; preservation and rapid disclosure of data relating to traffic, system search, and seizure; real-time collection of traffic data; and interception of content data.

Articles 23–35 address international cooperation. The convention's provisions for international cooperation are subject to existing international agreements, such as MLATs, and the domestic laws of the parties. The main theme is to provide mechanisms for mutual assistance if existing international agreements are not applicable or to expedite existing agreements. One strategy to expedite international cooperation is the establishment of a 24/7 network, intended to handle requests for mutual assistance quickly and efficiently (Art. 35). Each party is required to designate a point of contact available twenty-four hours a day, seven days per week, to facilitate rapid investigation of cybercrimes, similar to the G8 High-Tech Crime 24/7 Point-of-Contact Network. The 24/7 networks are required to be able to communicate rapidly with their counterparts in other locations, and the parties must ensure that trained and equipped personnel are available to staff the network.

Articles 40–42 deal with declarations and reservations. To encourage widespread acceptance of the treaty, the drafters have allowed for considerable flexibility in interpretation of provisions. This occurs formally through a number of possible declarations (Art. 40) and reservations (Art. 42), and more informally through other suggested interpretations in the treaty's explanatory report (ER). Through "declarations," parties may posit additional elements in their interpretations of offenses and procedural obligations, and through "reservations" parties may limit or qualify those same obligations.

Debates around the Convention on Cybercrime. Much has been written about the convention (Hopkins, 2003; Jones, 2005; COE, 2004b; and Westby, 2004). Certain provisions were controversial during its drafting and negotiation phases. We summarize here the major issues:

- Lack of governance and no support for countries of low capability: Critics argue that the COE should provide for an agency or other concrete mechanism to facilitate international cooperation. Although the convention requires parties to adopt a set of detailed investigative procedures to help catch cyber criminals, it provides no guidance as to how countries of low capability could implement this. The convention obliges parties to "ensure that their competent authorities have the capacity to collect or record traffic data by technical means" (ER, Par. 219, and Art. 20). Securing the cooperation of vulnerable countries—and ensuring that they have the means to cooperate—is critical because such countries are arguably most likely to be "safe havens" for cyber criminals. It is not likely that some of the current ratifying countries are able to fully implement these guidelines and/or provide proper training to the various actors that help enforce the convention.

• Undesirably broad coverage: The convention's broad coverage of offenses has drawn extensive criticism. It is argued that it should limit itself to protecting the information infrastructures by criminalizing "pure" (confidentiality, integrity, access) cybercrimes. There may also be insufficient international consensus on whether and how to criminalize "content-related offenses" like child pornography and copyright infringement. The drafters' general response to these objections is that parties are free to issue reservations and declarations, allowing them to interpret offenses flexibly with due respect for national and cultural differences.

• Insufficient protection of privacy, civil liberties, and human rights: Privacy advocates, civil liberty groups, and industry associations were especially concerned with provisions that appear to intrude on preexisting constitutional and legal rights and place restrictions on privacy, anonymity, and encryption (COE, 2004a; GILC, 2003). In response, the drafters argue that parties differ too radically in their conceptions of civil liberties and privacy to mandate any specific levels of protection, and it is left to individual countries to counterbalance the new powers consistent with their established privacy laws and cultural norms. In addition, under the convention, no party is required to carry out an investigative measure that violates rights protected in domestic law.

• There is too high a burden on industry to assist law enforcement in investigation: Through the World Information Technology and Services Alliance—WITSA (WITSA, 2005), industry has argued that the requirements on service providers to monitor communications and to provide assistance to investigators would be unduly burdensome and expensive. Although it does not require any assistance outside of a provider's "existing technical capability," the convention does not provide for any reimbursement of costs associated with complying with the new procedures, for data interception, storage, and surveillance, should service providers have the technical capability to cooperate.

Impact of the Convention on Cybercrime. One success of the convention is the level of involvement of all countries in the drafting process, including the four nonmember states. For example, during the drafting and negotiation process, the United States sought comments and other input from a variety of groups representing U.S. interests (USDOJ, 2003). As a result of these consultations, the United States obtained several important revisions to the convention's text and Explanatory Report. In addition, the COE made drafts available to the public for comment. The first publicly released draft of the convention was Draft 19, made available for comment in April 2000. Several more drafts were then released, culminating in the final draft, released on June 29, 2001. This process led to an important public debate about cyber security, as indicated by the level of involvement of civil and industrial groups during the drafting process (USDOJ, 2003).

In a survey circulated at a September 2004 conference in Strasbourg, France (Octopus Interface, 2004), signatory states were asked to discuss the level of implementation of the convention. The signatory states that had not ratified the convention could be divided into three categories.

About one-third thought themselves able and willing to ratify within a short time (6–9 months). Legislation against cybercrime has been adopted or is about to be adopted in another third. Finally, states in the last third are about to introduce proposals for relevant legislation or would do so in the near future.

This survey indicates that the major hurdle against ratification is the time needed to review and amend existing laws or propose new laws to the national governments. Out of the two-thirds of countries that have already reviewed their laws, most appear to be adopting a compromise approach by reporting that they intend to update parts of their domestic cybercrime laws to comply with the convention, and use reservations and declarations to comply with existing domestic laws that cannot be changed, or would be too cumbersome to change.

A more thorough survey is needed to fully address the progress of ratification in each member country. The cited survey lacked details. A future survey might include a full review of laws that need to be modified or added by the member countries to comply with the convention and a detailed overview of the mechanisms that each country is putting in place to address expedited collection of data and prosecution and mechanisms for international cooperation. However, the conference already revealed that despite the criticisms of the convention, most countries within the COE are in the process of ratifying it.

In the United States, the Bush administration urged rapid ratification of the convention, and transmitted it to the Senate's Committee on Foreign Relations for review on July 17, 2004. According to the State and Justice Departments, existing U.S. federal law, coupled with six reservations and four declarations, would be adequate to satisfy the convention's requirements (Cybercrime, 2003). On June 29, 2005, a coalition of industry groups and individual companies representing different sectors of the economy issued a letter to the U.S. Senate Foreign Relations Committee, urging ratification (PR Newswire, 2005).[11] In the letter, the coalition argues that ratification would minimize obstacles to international cooperation that currently impede U.S. investigations and prosecutions of computer-related crimes. On July 26, 2005, all nine members of the Foreign Relations Committee who were present said by voice vote that they broadly agreed with the Council of Europe Convention on Cybercrime and the U.S. Senate ratified the convention on August 3, 2006.

An assessment of whether the updated laws and new cooperation mechanisms set in place by the ratifying countries have helped prosecute crimes has not yet been explored by the COE. Inasmuch as five years have passed since the first ratification, it would be timely to find meaningful metrics to assess the impact of the mechanisms put in place by ratifying countries or by those that have signed but not yet ratified, perhaps in collaboration with the OECD. An obvious issue is that the critical mass of ratifying countries might be too low to measure impact, particularly when it comes to the expedited 24/7 network; however, it would be important to measure whether the ratifying countries have even been able to implement mechanisms put forth by the convention.

COC Additional Protocol. In November 2002, the Council of Europe introduced an "Additional Protocol to the Convention on Cybercrime, concerning the criminalization of acts of a racist and xenophobic nature committed through computer systems." This protocol entails an extension of the Convention on Cybercrime's scope, including its substantive, procedural, and international cooperation provisions. The additional protocol contains, for example, a definition of racist or xenophobic material and provides for the criminalization of these acts committed through computer networks, including the offering and the distribution of such material through computer networks. It was opened for signature in January 2003; it has been signed by twenty-three countries and ratified by two, as of February 19, 2005. The United States and other countries have indicated that they will not sign it out of concern that it would violate domestic freedom of speech protections.

REGIONAL INTERGOVERNMENTAL ORGANIZATIONS

In the late 1990s, regional organizations such as the European Union, the APEC forum, and the Organization of American States (OAS) began developing their own policies to combat cyber-crime in a coordinated fashion, following OECD guidelines. These organizations have been trying to supplement policies with mechanisms to encourage cooperation among their member states. These mechanisms fall under the categories of information sharing, collective early warning, law enforcement cooperation, and legal harmonization.

Cybersecurity policies and mechanisms are in different stages and forms of implementation in different parts of the world. Some organizations, such as the EU, take a regulatory approach to enforce legal harmonization and information sharing mechanisms. Others, such as the APEC, are encouraging, but not requiring, information-sharing mechanisms among members, without yet focusing on harmonizing legal mechanisms. The OAS has not yet enacted mechanisms to implement its policies.

Countries in Africa have yet to form a comprehensive cyber security policy, although the four-teen member countries of the Southern Africa Development Community (SADC) have recently agreed to harmonize their cyber laws (Betts, 2005). While recent developments in countries like Nigeria indicate that mechanisms are to be put into place at the national level to address cybercrime (EFCC, 2004; Oyesanya, 2004), no single organization has been forming a regional African policy towards cyber security (Balancing Act News, 2004a).

Europe

Europe has been very active in trying to create a unified cyber security policy and mechanisms. We review the most significant initiatives, both from the EU and other European organizations.

The European Union (EU) Policies: Toward Regional Cooperation

The EU's main decision-making body is the Council of the European Union. Member states are represented in the Council by their ministers. The Commission of the European Union proposes legislation, policies, and programs of action for implementing the decisions. Since 1997, the EU has been surveying its members on cyber security (Europa, 2005). In January 2001, the Commission issued a communication to the Council entitled *Creating a Safer Information Society by Improving the Security of Information Infrastructures and Combating Computer-related Crime* (Europa, 2001a). This surveyed problems that computer-related crimes pose for national law enforcement authorities and reviewed the cybercrime laws of member countries. Council resolutions in January 2002 (Europa, 2002a) and January 2003 (Europa, 2003) stressed the need for a comprehensive European strategy to "strive towards a culture of security taking into account the importance of international cooperation." The resolutions reiterate the need for better education and awareness campaigns, promoting best security practices in small and medium-sized enterprises, and the use of international standards.

EU Mechanisms for Securing Cyberspace

Initial EU initiatives for cyber security remained voluntary for its member states. As a first step, the EU encouraged its members to participate in existing initiatives. On March 19, 1998, the Council invited the member states to join the G8 24-hour information network for combating high-tech crime, a recommendation reiterated in 2001 (Europa, 2001b).

Subsequent initiatives were more formal and binding. Under the *Proposal for a Council Framework Decision on Attacks against Information Systems* issued by the Commission in 2002, member states are required to exchange information about certain cybercrime offences and must establish operational points of contact available twenty four hours a day and seven days a week. In addition, member states will inform the General Secretariat of the Council of their points of contact and of any other measures adopted to comply with the Framework Decision (Europa, 2002b).

Despite these initiatives, the European authorities indicated in 2004 that the "reactions of the Member States have proved disparate and not sufficiently coordinated to ensure an effective response to security problems. Apart from certain administrative networks, there is no systematic cross-border cooperation on this issue between Member States, even though security matters cannot be regarded as an isolated issue for any one country alone" (Europa, 2004).

To address this issue, the EU established in March 2004 a European Network and Information Security Agency (ENISA) (ENISA, 2005a). The aim in creating the ENISA is to "enhance the capability of the Community, the Member States and the business community to address and to respond to network and information security problems." The agency is focused on the tasks of collecting and analyzing data on security incidents in Europe and emerging risks; promoting risk assessment and risk management methods; and promoting awareness-raising and cooperation between different actors, notably by developing public/private partnerships.

The initial goal of the agency is to start work in awareness raising and promotion of best practices. The first study funded by the agency will provide the European Commission and ENISA with an overview of achievements of the EU-25 Member States and the EEA States (European Economic Area) with respect of Council Resolutions (2002/C 43/02 and 2003/C 48/01) to create a culture of network and information security and ensure a common approach amongst the members.

An important milestone will be a 2007 review, when the agency's activities are to be evaluated in order to decide whether it has achieved its objectives and tasks and whether it will continue to function after its initial five years' duration. This has led the agency to set up a clear work plan for 2005, including performance evaluators to monitor its success (ENISA, 2005b).

The overall goal of ENISA is to serve as a center of expertise where member states, EU institutions, and industry can seek advice on network and information security and in particular collect appropriate information to analyze current and emerging risks, and to pay attention to small and medium-sized enterprises. If ENISA fulfills this goal, then it could serve as a model for other regional agencies and perhaps a model for an international information-sharing agency.

European Initiatives for CSIRTs' Cooperation

In Europe, the TF-CSIRT Task Force was established in 1999 (TERENA, 2006). The aim of the task force is to promote the collaboration between CSIRTs in Europe. TF-CSIRT has been active in promoting common standards and procedures for responding to security incidents and assisting in the establishment of new CSIRTs and the training of CSIRT staff. TF-CSIRT is focused on Europe and neighboring countries. Its most important activity is the TI accreditation service that is meant to facilitate trust among CSIRTs by formally accrediting them. The rigorous accreditation scheme requires a minimum set of services and initiatives from CSIRTs (TERENA, 2005a) and is updated every four months. Once accredited, CSIRTs gain access to the restricted information that facilitates information sharing with other accredited CSIRTs (TERENA, 2005b).

Another important European mechanism is TRANSITS (Training of Network Security Incident Teams Staff) (TRANSITS, 2005b). It is a three-year European project to promote the establishment of CSIRTs and the enhancement of existing CSIRTs by addressing the problem of the shortage of skilled CSIRT staff. Since 2002, six training programs have been held, training over one hundred participants (TRANSITS, 2005a).

European Initiatives for Law Enforcement Cooperation

Since July 1999 Europol has been the European Union law enforcement organization that handles criminal intelligence. The Europol Computer System (TECS) scheduled to be deployed in 2005 will facilitate cybercrime investigations (Europol, 2005). The new system is specifically designed to facilitate sharing and analysis of criminal data between EU members and law enforcement organizations in other countries. Each EU member nation has assigned two data protection experts to Europol to closely monitor how personal data are stored and used.

The Centrex National Centre (CPTDA), based in the UK, has developed a model for regional law enforcement training for policing excellence (Centrex, 2003). Centrex has been providing an accredited, modular European training program for all twenty-eight EU and candidate countries as well as Norway, Switzerland, Interpol, and Europol to harmonize cybercrime training across EU borders. The EU AGIS funds the program (POLCYB, 2004).

The program allows for transfer of academic credit from country to country so that investigators are able to communicate effectively during investigations with people who can be identified as having similar knowledge and skills. A register of those who have successfully completed the training and who receive the status of European CyberCrime Investigator (ECCI) is being created in order to enhance the capacity for international operational collaboration. Over sixty officers from across Europe have received training in introductory IT forensics and network investigations. The training material is being made available to all countries. Officers from the UK, Germany, Denmark, Ireland, Hong Kong, Greece, and France have delivered the training. The next stage of the project is to create a network of European cybercrime training. The creation of the proposed network of cybercrime training institutes would be an important mechanism and could be scaled to include countries from outside the EU.

Asia-Pacific Economic Cooperation (APEC)

The APEC forum was established in 1989 to promote economic growth and integration in the Pacific Rim among twenty-one members.[12] On September 21, 2001, the APEC Telecommunications and Information Working Group noted the importance of cooperation in the effort to secure information systems and share information in accordance with the UN General Assembly Resolution 55/63: *Combating the Criminal Misuse of Information.* In China in 2002, at the Fifth APEC Ministerial Meeting on Telecommunications and Information Industry, declarations emphasized both multilateral cooperation and a need for a legal basis to combat cybercrime (APEC, 2002b). APEC members agreed to support the implementation of the measures included in UN Resolution 55/63, taking into account international initiatives in this area such as the work of the Council of Europe and OECD (APEC, 2002a).

APEC's eSecurity Task Group has also been developing a policy on cyber security. Establishment of information sharing institutions and early warning systems such as CSIRTs and 24/7 networks have been aims of this group along with promoting guidelines, public education, and laws. APEC also has an initiative for a regional CSIRT, launched in March 2003, aimed at providing in-country training to enhance capabilities in developing countries in the region and to develop guidelines for computer response teams (APEC, 2003a).

CSIRTs' Cooperation Initiatives in the Asia Pacific Region

APCERT (Asia Pacific Computer Emergency Response Team) is a coalition of fifteen CSIRTs from twelve economies across the Asia Pacific region created in 2002 (APCERT, 2005a). The goal of the coalition is to accelerate active sharing of information about computer threats, vulnerabilities, and incidents among regional CERTs and to provide cross training. In addition, APCERT organizes APSIRC, an annual meeting for information sharing (APCERT, 2005a). APCERT decided to have its own accreditation scheme to certify member teams in order to be able to handle sensitive information within the members with trust.

A 2003 report shows that APCERT has enabled regional cooperation. For example, the Australian government through its AusAID program has provided funding for in-country CSIRT training. As part of this program AusCERT provided training for Thailand, Vietnam, the Philippines, Indonesia, and Papua New Guinea in 2003–4 (APCERT, 2003). AusCERT also sponsored MyCERT's (Malaysia CERT) successful application to FIRST, an international private-public information sharing network. For incident response, the Thai CERT indicated a much faster response to the Blaster virus in 2003 thanks to communication channels with the APCERT than its response to the Slammer worm earlier in the year when cooperation with APCERT was not as active.

APEC explicitly supports APCERT and recognizes the role of CSIRTs and the need to establish teams in member countries to promote information exchange and cooperation. To achieve this, APEC launched an initiative for a regional CSIRT in March 2003, aimed at providing in-country training to enhance capabilities in developing countries in the region and to develop guidelines (APEC, 2003a). The experienced Australian and U.S. organizations have actively led this program by providing training and funding. In addition to the Australian training just described, the United States has funded part of the project to provide CERT training to Russia, Mexico, Peru, and Chile in 2005.

Law Enforcement Cooperation in the Asia Pacific Region

In the Asia Pacific region, APEC has been promoting cooperation among law enforcement agencies. In July 2003, APEC-TEL held a Cybercrime Legislation and Enforcement Capacity Building Conference of Experts and Training Seminar in Bangkok (APEC, 2003b). The seminar had three main goals: to promote the development of comprehensive legal frameworks relating to cybercrime, to provide assistance in the development of law enforcement cybercrime units, and to improve cooperation between industry and law enforcement in combating cybercrimes. As of 2005, assistance events were provided for the Philippines, Indonesia, Vietnam, Chinese Taipei, Peru, and Thailand (Downing, 2003). However, most of these cooperative measures remain voluntary and highly dependent on funding from countries such as the United States (Downing, 2003).

Organization of American States (OAS) Initiatives

Formed in 1948, OAS membership includes thirty-four nations of the Americas (OAS, 2005). The issue of cybercrime was first addressed in the OAS at the Second Meeting of Ministers of Justice in March 1999, when it was recommended that a working group be created in this area (OAS, 1999b). The working group issued a report in 1999 describing significant variance among its members with regard to their perception of the impact of cybercrime. It recommended a policy to "develop, adapt, and harmonize the legislation, procedures, and institutions required to combat cybercrime" (OAS, 1999a). In addition, it recommended that states become members of the G8 24-Hour/7-Day-a-Week point of contact group, or participate in other mechanisms for exchange of information.

At a June 2003 meeting in Washington, the OAS General Assembly approved a resolution "that calls for building an inter-American strategy against threats to computer information systems and networks." The resolution notes that other OAS meetings on the subject have called cyber-security-related crimes an "emerging terrorist threat." Foreign ministers and high-level officials met in Mexico City in October 2003 to review and update the hemisphere's overall security structure and listed cyber security as a new concern. The ministers reasserted the need for cooperation mechanisms, highlighting the Governmental Experts Group on Cybercrime (REMJA) and the Inter-American Telecommunication Commission (CITEL) as forums to discuss issues (REMJA-V, 2004). The OAS has not yet set up concrete mechanisms to enhance cyber security in the American continents.

PRIVATE-PUBLIC ORGANIZATIONS

Since the IP-based network infrastructures are shared and managed by public and private entities, there is an intrinsic interdependency between these sectors. Although a government may not own or control critical networks, it is nonetheless dependent upon the security, reliability, and availability of these infrastructures for national and economic security. Given that the ownership, operation, and supply of networks and critical systems are mostly in the hands of private industry in many countries, private-public cyber security initiatives have become a pillar of cyber security policies. Various types of international partnerships are emerging, led by businesses, NGOs, or governments. Their missions are usually very specific to a private sector, such as banking, or a type of attack, such as spam. As a result, their actions are largely uncoordinated.

Multinational Public-Private International Policy Initiatives

Many international organizations recognize the need for private and public sector cooperation to secure information infrastructures. The EU, G8, COE, APEC, OAS, OECD, and UN have all recognized the need to promote public/private sector cooperation in policy making. These organizations are developing ways to facilitate partnerships that share information and experiences, best practices, management procedures, and technical solutions (Westby, 2004).

One forum for companies and governments to discuss standards and ideas about cyber security is the International Telecommunication Union (ITU), the specialized agency of the UN responsible for telecommunications standards where public/private dialogue takes place (ITU, 2005b). TheITU's membership includes 189 member states and over 650 private companies and other organizations and the ITU is the only intergovernmental organization within the UN system that has had a partnership between governments and industry. It has published over seventy recommendations in the field of security and has organized workshops and symposiums on security during recent years. In 2002, the ITU, following a proposal by the government of Tunisia, resolved to hold a World Summit on the Information Society (WSIS) and place it on the agenda of the United Nations. Subsequently, the UN General Assembly endorsed holding WSIS in two phases (ITU, 2002). The first, held in December 2003, the Geneva Summit, laid the foundation with a declaration of principles and a plan of action. Two major themes were identified: "building confidence, trust and security" and "establishing stable regulatory frameworks (good governance)." The second phase, held in November 2005, the Tunis Summit, reviewed and evaluated progress on the action plan and devised an agenda that will target goals for achievement by 2015. InfoSec emerged as one of the primary areas of concern and attention.

Business-led International Policy Initiatives by the Private Sector

During the 1990s, international organizations representing the private sector became active in promoting cyber security, issuing guidelines to their members, and trying to influence international cyber security policy.

International organizations in the banking sector have been particularly active. The World Bank has issued a series of papers, reports, presentations, and events to address the security of financial transactions (Glaessner et al., 2002). The bank issued recommendations for twelve layers of security in *Electronic Security: Risk Mitigation in Financial Transactions—Public Policy Issues.* These recommendations have been put into operation by the World Bank Treasury, incorporated in the Monetary Authority of Singapore's Risk Management Guidelines, and added to the latest ISO Information Security Banking Standard 13569.[13] In addition, the infoDev Program of the World Bank Group funded the creation of the *Information Technology Security Handbook,* which provides technology-independent best practices and addresses issues relevant specifically to individuals, small and medium sized organizations, government, and technical administrators (Sadowsky et al., 2003). The handbook's focus is international: the authors report that they have attempted to provide practical guidance applicable anywhere and to include examples from developing countries.

Another international banking organization addressing cybersecurity issues is the Bank for International Settlements (BIS), which fosters international monetary and financial cooperation and serves as a bank for fifty-five central banks (BIS, 2005). In 2003, the Basel Committee on Banking Supervision of BIS issued the *Risk Management Principles for Electronic Banking* (BIS, 2003). The committee called on banks to review their risk management programs, policies, and procedures for electronic banking activities and listed fourteen risk management principles. These include principles pertaining to board and management oversight, security controls, and legal and reputation risk management.

The International Chamber of Commerce (ICC) has been representing the interests of international businesses and associations worldwide and provides recommendations to the UN, the EU, and the G8 (Westby, 2004). The ICC addresses cybersecurity issues in its *Global Action Plan for Electronic Business* in coalition with the Business and Industry Advisory Committee (BIAC) to the OECD, the Global Information Infrastructure Commission (GIIC), the International Telecommunication Users Group (INTUG), and the World Information Technology and Services Alliance (WITSA) (ICCWBO, 2002). The action plan recognizes the need to protect critical information infrastructure to ensure economic security. In particular it recommends cooperation between business and law enforcement.

The ICC addresses cybersecurity issues in its Commission on E-Business, IT and Telecoms (EBITT). Its Task Force on Cybercrime/Cybersecurity "articulated business interests in international and regional policy initiatives related to cybercrimes, aiming to ensure the reliability and trustworthiness in electronic communications systems while safeguarding the interests of providers and users in initiatives to counter cybercrime" (EBITT, 2003). The task force provided input on the Council of Europe (COE) Convention on Cybercrime and obtained major amendments, including the prevention of "routine data retention," in the final text of the convention. The ICC also provided comments to national governments of signatory countries regarding key considerations for legislation to implement the COE Convention on Cybercrime and its First Additional Protocol (EBITT, 2003).

In 2003, the ICC also teamed with the BIAC to the OECD to publish a booklet, *Information*

Security Assurance for Executives, that describes how the OECD Security Guidelines can be used to promote a culture of security both inside and outside of a corporation (ICCWBO, 2004).

International Public-Private Partnerships that Target Specific Attacks

Interesting partnerships are emerging to treat specific types of cybercrimes, such as phishing, pharming, spoofing and spamming.[14] The Anti-Phishing Working Group (APWG) is a "global pan-industrial and law enforcement association focused on eliminating the fraud and identity theft that result from phishing, pharming and email spoofing of all types" (APWG, 2005). Although the 1,200 members are confidential, they include eight of the top ten U.S. banks and four of the five top U.S. ISPs. The APWG offers resources to industry and law enforcement that allow them to stay current with phishing techniques and attack scenarios, and offers technical advice. The APWG also serves as a reporting and trend analysis center for scams.

Other organizations, such as Spamhaus, are composed of volunteers. According to its website, Spamhaus "tracks the Internet's Spammers, Spam Gangs and Spam Services, provides dependable real-time anti-spam protection for Internet networks, and works with law enforcement to identify and pursue spammers worldwide"(Spamhaus, 2005a). Based in the UK, it is run by eighteen volunteers located around the world. They maintain a real-time database of IP addresses of verified spam (SBL advisory) and provide it as a free service to help email administrators better manage incoming email streams (Spamhaus, 2005b). As of August 2005, Spamhaus claims on their website to be protecting the mailboxes of 485,456,881 Internet users. It also maintains a real-time database of IP addresses of illegal third party exploits (XBL) and a Register of Known Spam Operations (ROKSO) database on known professional spam operations (Spamhaus, 2005a; 2005b). Spamhaus has also taken an active role in lobbying governmental and intergovernmental agencies to effect strong anti-spam law at the UN World Summit on the Information Society (WSIS).

Some individual companies are helping the legal system directly. Microsoft has been active in that area due to its expertise in the software industry. On November 2003, Microsoft announced the creation of the Anti-Virus Reward Program, initially funded with $5 million, to "help law enforcement agencies identify and bring to justice those who illegally release damaging worms, viruses and other types of malicious code on the Internet" (Microsoft, 2003). Since then, the software company has placed quarter-million-dollar bounties on those responsible for the Sasser worm, MSBlast worm, the Sobig virus, and the MyDoom virus. It is stated that residents of any country are eligible for the reward, according to the laws of the country in which they reside, because Internet viruses affect the Internet community worldwide. This program led to the arrest of the Sasser worm author in Germany (Blau, 2004; Lemos, 2004; Sophos, 2004).

Private companies provide training to law enforcement agencies as well as information and technical assistance to such agencies in specific cases. For example, Microsoft provided technical information and investigative assistance to FBI agents in August 2003 in the case against Jeffrey Lee Parson, author of the Blaster worm (Sophos, 2003). Despite those efforts, a main issue limiting public-private cooperation for law enforcement is underreporting. CERT/CC recently stated that many companies still seem unwilling to report e-crime for fear of damaging their reputation (CERT/CC, 2004). It has been estimated that 98 percent of incidents committed against financial institutions are not reported to law enforcement (Workshop, 2005), the reasons being that the institutions are able to handle the incidents themselves or that the damage does not warrant involving law enforcement. Regardless, this trend is troubling, as the smaller incidents could be part of a larger effort and with events unreported, it is harder for law enforcement to correlate attacks and identify patterns.

MAKING GLOBAL CYBERSPACE MORE SECURE . . . ?

The information gathered on the organizations and initiatives that have been described in this chapter comes from websites and other documents and from international meetings where representatives spoke publicly and then privately with the authors. There is a great deal of public information on mission statements and charters, organizational structure, and what they are trying to do.

Are they doing it well? Are they coming up with enforceable, scalable, and readily usable solutions that reduce vulnerabilities, deter malicious activity, and make cyberspace a safer and more secure infrastructure globally, or at least slow the rate at which things are getting worse? So far, there is little public information that would help us to provide convincing positive answers to these questions.

One issue is that many of the organizations are still in the realm of nascent formation and discovery. Many are recently created (most significant surveyed initiatives are ten years old or less), becoming aware of each other, adapting, and seeking means of collaboration. Almost all proclaim a desire to harmonize laws and improve international cooperation, a necessity given the scale of attacks and a multitude of jurisdictional problems where attackers in one set of countries can launch through a second set against targets in a third.

A second issue is that surveyed organizations do not provide much in the way of metrics, statistics, or examples on how many companies they saved from cyber catastrophe, how many serious cyber criminals they helped eliminate in one way or another, how much spam or phishing or other forms of unwanted and fraudulent onslaughts they deterred or intercepted before it could reach its intended targets, and so on.[15] In the following section, we discuss how InfoSec researchers can identify (or help define) effective operational models and success metrics for several types of these organizations that would help the research community assess their impact and help the organizations become more effective.

A third issue is scalability. Unfortunately, transnational cybercrime seems to scale very well in every way cyberspace is expanding. This is partly the result of easy and inexpensive technical feasibility, international reach via connectivity, and the lack of other constraints (e.g., controlled physical borders, well-established laws) that help keep some kind of cap on other forms of crime. Accordingly, it would seem desirable that the effectiveness of the international and regional organizations and initiatives surveyed in this chapter should also be expected to scale with the problems. We discuss this issue in the remainder of this section.

Cyber laws may or may not scale well. A good case can be made that having laws that explicitly identify, forbid, and punish certain behavior is a necessity. People and organizations are subject to national laws. Given the transnational technical structure of these networked infrastructures, it is desirable that all nations have a common core of cyber laws in order to preclude safe havens and the like. In theory, a nearly universal multilateral convention, with participating states having a common set of laws as national laws, would scale well, as it has in the civil aviation and maritime domains. In contrast, the use of bilaterals, for example, MLATs, to cover crimes involving multiple jurisdictions does not scale well due to the non-transitive nature of MLATs.

The COE Convention is the most advanced initiative in this regard. Not only is it trying to bring the forty-six COE members under its umbrella, but also many others. For example, officials from the COE invited all of the countries present at the June 28–July 1, 2005 ITU Geneva meeting on cyber security to consider joining, although many of these countries are among the less developed and could not currently meet the obligations under the convention. An argument can be made that it is desirable to get as many countries as possible to officially acknowledge the importance and legitimacy of concerns over cybercrime and then help them develop capacity to enforce the convention. In this sense the convention might scale well, but the COE at this time has no clear program to help develop and strengthen the capacities of the countries that ratify.

Cyber law enforcement does not scale well. Identification, apprehension, prosecution, and punishment are all often technically difficult, time consuming, and costly, especially internationally; so much so that it is relatively safe to be a cyber criminal. Many of the organizations and programs surveyed in this chapter are concerned with one or more of these aspects of international cyber law enforcement, and any improvement over what little there is now should be welcomed. Realistically, one cannot expect law enforcement to succeed in this realm as much as it has (rather unevenly) in some other criminal areas. Perhaps all that can be expected is success in the most serious cases. Dealing with cybercrime is very intelligence intensive. It is not easy, especially in early stages, to clearly identify a serious attack as criminal vs. one that should be of national security concern. The common assumption in many places is that it is to be considered the former until there are indications otherwise. As a result, international cooperation gets much trickier when national security agencies need to share intelligence information. At this time, cooperative training programs and the establishment of international contacts are the most prominent mechanisms that could help promote cooperation. However, statistics on whether these mechanisms are helping international apprehensions and prosecutions on a large scale are not readily available.

How well does deterrence scale? One would hope that a combination of laws and education and a stronger ethical culture in cyberspace would serve as a de facto deterrent to a larger volume of malicious activity. We can always hope that most people are basically law abiding and, once they appreciate what is against the law, they would be inclined not to violate those laws. However, given what we have seen so far, and how unlikely it is that cyber offenders will be identified or punished, we should have the expectation that a lot of malicious activity will not be deterred. Education at a minimal level, for instance, to promote awareness, caution, and better behavior, may scale fairly well, and most of the organizations surveyed here may contribute to that. Education to produce highly skilled defenders will not scale well against the less demanding learning curve that needs to be traversed by many kinds of attackers.

How well does prevention scale? In this realm, it may be argued that the most important form of scalable prevention is technology and procedures that eliminate vulnerabilities. For example, many attacks would have been precluded if buffer overflow vulnerabilities had not existed or had been removed from widely used software systems. But once less vulnerable software exists, it is necessary that it be widely adopted, something that often does not happen as quickly or extensively as necessary. A similar statement can be made with regard to best management practices and procedures. There would seem to be a potential role for a number of the organizations surveyed here in this regard, but as yet we do not detect that it has been strongly and effectively pursued.

Another prevention possibility is early warning and information sharing, which seems very consistent with the missions of a fair number of these organizations. This is a very complex subject (e.g., the "who" and "how" of warning, consequences of false alarms, etc.) that is further complicated by the extraordinary speed at which attacks can propagate. Many mechanisms for information sharing have been created, including point of contact networks and CSIRTs. These efforts are often uncoordinated, informal, and rely on a point-to-point model of communication, which does not scale well. For CSIRTs, one more scalable model would be a "network of regional networks" of CSIRTs to emerge, where individual CSIRTs first connect with others in their geographic vicinity forming a regional network, such as the APCERT, and ultimately each would start cooperating with other regional networks. Another might be to have a network of regional information sharing agencies. In this realm, the EU has taken the lead by creating the European Network and Information Security Agency (ENISA).

Private sector initiatives are currently numerous, often uncoordinated, and narrowly focused on either a particular private sector or particular attacks. This model of partnerships is not readily scalable. Given the experience of the private sector in dealing with cybercrime, a centralized collection and analysis of private sector data through a trusted third party might be created. The FIRST initiative is a step in this direction; however its exclusive membership restricts countries with low capabilities from accessing valuable information.

In general, the lack of national policies and mechanisms in some regions of the world, most notably Africa, presents a major challenge to global cyber security. Industrialized nations must offer technical assistance to these nations to help them build mechanisms such as CSIRTs and to create and update cybercrime laws. However, so far most of the surveyed organizations have made little or no significant political and/or technical-economic effort to help countries with little in the form of cyber security policies and mechanisms.

SUGGESTED INTERNATIONAL CYBERSECURITY RESEARCH TOPICS

As we have seen in this chapter, numerous international organizations/partnerships/initiatives have been created in the past two decades to encourage and address international cooperation against cybercrime. The chapter has provided a broad overview of the current landscape, from analysis of websites and other documents, and from international meetings where representatives spoke publicly and then privately with the authors.

However, further in-depth studies of these organizations are needed to analyze their impact, both individually and collectively, on information security. In particular, InfoSec researchers can identify (or help define) effective operational models for several types of these organizations that would help the research community assess their impact and help the organizations become more effective. In particular, Table 9.1 presents a set of important questions that need to be investigated. Each of them will be discussed in detail below.

Details on Issue 1

Many organizations/initiatives have been created in the past two decades to address cybercrime. These amount to substantial financial, organizational, and human investments. Have money and time been used effectively to help fight cybercrime? This question is critical for shareholders and governments (and ultimately tax-payers and potential victims of cybercrime) to keep investing in such initiatives and to ensure that the human and financial investments have an impact. In particular, if the efforts have not been focused on the right issues or have not been successful, how can these organizations do better?

In order to answer these questions, metrics are needed to assess the impact of organizations targeting cybercrime at the international level. Researchers need to identify standard international metrics to measure the success of existing and new initiatives. For example, countries could collect statistics on the number of cyber criminals arrested and prosecuted as a direct result of OECD guideline implementation, and the number of incidents successfully handled by CSIRTs. Public and private initiatives need to report how many companies they saved from cyber catastrophe, how many serious cyber criminals they helped eliminate in one way or another, how much spam or phishing or other forms of unwanted and fraudulent onslaughts they deterred or intercepted before it could reach its intended target. Such measures will help countries and the private sector identify and prioritize successful mechanisms and help plan and justify budget decisions. Additionally, it will reveal which issues are not being addressed properly by current organizations.

Table 9.1

Problems in Need of Further Study

Area	Issue	Impact
1. Overall assessment/metrics of success	1.1 No organization provides much in terms of metrics, statistics or numerous examples on it success in fighting cybercrime at the international level	Researchers need to identify meaningful metrics that can be used to assess the success of organizations/initiatives
2. Identification of operational models	2.1 Our analysis indicates regional coordination is currently the most popular model (e.g., "network of regional networks" of CSIRTs such as APCERTs, regional information sharing mechanisms, such as European ENISA agency, numerous regional cyber security initiatives, such as EU, APEC, OAS initiatives)	Is the regional model a viable, scalable operational model to fight cybercrime at the international level? If so, how can communication between these regional entities be effective? Can developing regions such as Africa follow this model without the help of other entities?
	2.2 Most collaborations of the surveyed organizations/initiatives are uncoordinated, informal, point to point	Is this informal, point-to-point communication model a viable and scalable operational model to fight cybercrime? In particular, does this model increase or decrease the speed and effectiveness at which organizations can adapt to the ever-changing landscape of cybercrime?
3. Analysis of underdeveloped areas of focus	3.1 Few surveyed organizations/initiatives focus on research and development (R&D) for cybercrime prevention using technology and procedures that eliminate vulnerabilities	What are the barriers limiting organizations from focusing on/funding international R&D initiatives? How can those barriers be overcome?
	3.2 Few surveyed organizations/initiatives focus on political and/or technical-economic effort to help countries that lack cybersecurity policies and mechanisms, especially developing economies in the Middle East/Africa	What are the barriers limiting organizations from helping developing economies? How can those barriers be overcome?
	3.3 Private sector initiatives are currently numerous, often uncoordinated and narrowly focused on either a particular private sector or particular attacks. A key issue limiting public-private cooperation for law enforcement is under-reporting of cybercrimes.	How can public-private cooperation be more effective, without affecting the private sector protection of IP and shareholder value?

Details on Issues 2.1–2.2

Regional and *informal* initiatives have been the most popular forms of cooperation to tackle cybercrime at the international level, particularly in Europe and the Asia Pacific region. Why is this model currently the most popular? Is it possible for countries/regions to forego geopolitical barriers and cooperate when it comes to cybercrime issues? Given the current geopolitical reality, is this regional and informal model a viable one?

No single formal point of governance creates and monitors mechanisms at the *international* level. Would an international agency in charge of cyber security be a viable model? How would such an agency be funded? What would be its scope? Would it be a branch of the United Nations or a standalone entity? Should such an agency punish criminal cybercrime activities?

Details on Issue 3.1

InfoSec specialists need to understand what the barriers are limiting organizations from focusing more on international R&D initiatives and how those barriers can be overcome. Additionally, how can the findings of the InfoSec community, epistemic in nature, successfully transform into a set of norms?[16] If a new technological advance is discovered, how can we ensure that it is *rapidly* adopted by governments and the private sector, especially in developing economies that often lack funds to access all relevant technologies? Can the private sector help in this rapid adoption, given its interest in curbing cybercrime? (See Microsoft anti-virus and anti-piracy actions, [Microsoft, 2003].)

Details on Issue 3.2

Few surveyed organizations/initiatives focus on political and/or technical-economic effort to help countries that lack cyber security policies and mechanisms, especially *developing economies* in the Middle East/Africa. Some efforts stand out, such as:

The Telecommunication Development Bureau (BDT), a branch of the International Telecommunication Union (ITU), whose mission statement is to "assist developing countries in the field of information and communication technologies (ICTs), in facilitating the mobilization of technical, human and financial resources needed for their implementation, as well as in promoting access to ICTs" (ITU, 2005a). From its 2005 report (ITU, 2005c), it seems that its efforts for cyber security are concentrated on seminars and workshops (one for CEE/CIS/Baltic States, two for the Americas, one for Syria) and one ongoing project entitled "development of tools for addressing security and trust issues for e-applications and e-transactions and guidelines for implementation of e-application projects."

APEC provides in-country training to enhance capabilities in developing countries in the region and to develop guidelines (APEC, 2003a).

The infoDev Program of the World Bank Group funded the creation of the *Information Technology Security Handbook,* which provides technology-independent best practices and addresses issues relevant specifically to individuals, small and medium sized organizations, government, and technical administrators (Sadowsky et al., 2003). The handbook's focus is international; the authors report that they have attempted to provide practical guidance applicable anywhere and to include examples from developing countries.

Based on these observations, three important lines of research emerge:

1. Further analysis by Information Security researchers to evaluate whether the BDT workshops, the APEC training, infoDev guidelines, and the couple of CSIRTS in the Middle East/Africa region are successful in impacting cybercrime in developing nations (also tied to issue 1.1, identifying metrics).

2. Understanding what the barriers are that limit organizations from helping developing economies. How can those barriers be overcome? What are effective incentives for both the public and private sector?

3. Based on the previous point, information security researchers need to develop an effective operational model for current organizations (or a new organization) to successfully help developing economies.

Details on Issue 3.3

As discussed earlier in the chapter, a major issue limiting public-private cooperation for law enforcement is underreporting. Additionally, existing private or public-private initiatives are often uncoordinated and narrowly focused on either a particular private sector or particular attacks.

Information security researchers need to develop effective alternatives to increase the amount of trust among public-private sector actors and encourage cybercrime reporting. The reasons for underreporting need to be further analyzed and the impact needs to be clearly stated to the private sector and law enforcement to start a dialogue between the entities and find a solution to the underreporting issue.

Additionally, is there a need to create a venue or mechanism for exchange of R&D information between multinational industries, governments, and academia at the international level, with recommendations raised during these exchanges, such as the U.S. NSTAC model (NSTAC, 2005)? Or is there a more effective model to rapidly exchange and, especially, to implement R&D breakthroughs?

CONCLUSIONS

Cybercrime is becoming an increasingly significant feature in the landscape of worldwide information processing. In surveying the many regional and global organizations and initiatives, it is clear that organizations like the UN, OECD, the Council of Europe, the Asia-Pacific Economic Cooperation Forum and the Organization of American States are performing their role as policy-making bodies in the creation of international mechanisms to help protect cyberspace against crime. These mechanisms include most prominently a consistency in law making, information sharing, and law enforcement cooperation. Over the past two decades, these initiatives created a common charter element to improve international cooperation. At this time, it is not possible to quantitatively conclude whether these organizations have been successful in making cyberspace more secure due to the lack of pertinent metrics and publicly available statistics to assess positive impact. Qualitatively however, five types of cooperation surveyed in this chapter stand out for their potential to shape cyber security due to their large geographic footprint and ambitious charters. These are (1) the Council of Europe Convention on Cybercrime, (2) regional Computer Security Incident Response Teams initiatives in Asia Pacific and Europe, (3) cooperative training programs such as the Interpol international training units, (4) regional information sharing agencies such as the European Network and Information Security Agency, (5) public-private partnerships that target specific attacks. Many of these initiatives are still in their early stages and future analysis will need to assess whether they collectively amount to a whole that is significantly greater than the simple sum of the separate parts. Most of these initiatives, however, are at the regional level. International enforcement and prosecution of cybercrime will prove difficult without a sincere global political, economic, and technical commitment from wealthy nations to assist not only each other but especially less-wealthy nations in combating cybercrime of all types.

ACKNOWLEDGMENTS

The authors are very grateful to Michael Murphree, research assistant at the Georgia Institute of Technology Sam Nunn School of International Affairs, for his help with this chapter. This work has been funded in part by the John D. and Catherine T. MacArthur Foundation for the Georgia Institute of Technology Sam Nunn Security Program.

NOTES

1. Since 1994, the UN passed various resolutions on cyber security. Its resolutions fall under three main topics:

(1) Creation of a global culture of cyber security (resolution 57/239 of 20 Dec. 2002 and resolution 58/199 on 23 Dec. 2003).
(2) Establishing the legal basis for combating the criminal misuse of information technologies (resolution 55/63 of 4 Dec. 2000 and 56/121 of 19 Dec. 2001).
(3) Developments in the field of information and telecommunications in the context of international security (53/70 of 4 Dec. 1998, 54/49 of 1 Dec. 1999, 55/28 of 20 Nov. 2000, 56/19 of 29 Nov. 2001, 57/53 of 22 Nov. 2002, 59/61 on 3 Dec. 2004). The item "developments in the field of information and telecommunications in the context of international security" will again be on the provisional agenda of its sixtieth session.

2. The WPISP brings together representatives from the thirty OECD member country governments, the private sector, and civil society to foster the emergence of solutions to build trust online.

3. An incident is an adverse event, or the threat of such an event, in an information system.

4. To this date, the authors have found two CSIRTs in the Middle East/Africa region: the Algeria CERIST, created with the help of USAID, and the Etisalat Corporation in the United Arab Emirates, which joined FIRST in 2004 (Balancing Act News, 2004b).

5. "CERT" is a CMU trademark and its use by an organization requires CMU approval.

6. TERENA—Trans-European Research and Education Networking Association—was formed in October 1994 by the merger of RARE (Réseaux Associés pour la Recherche Européenne) and EARN (European Academic and Research Network). Within this organization, the TF-CSIRT task force encourages collaboration and cooperation among European CSIRTS.

7. For more information on national or regional laws concerning cybercrime visit:

Australia	Cybercrime Act 2001, available at http://parlinfoweb.aph.gov.au/piweb//view_document.aspx?TABLE=OLDBILLS&ID=910, accessed on September 1, 2005
Britain	Computer Misuse Act 1990, available at www.bailii.org/uk/legis/num_act/cma1990204/, accessed on September 1, 2005
Canada	Canadian Criminal Code: Unauthorized Use of Computer & Mischief (342.1 and 430[1.1]), available at www.hackcanada.com/canadian/freedom/canadacode.html, accessed on September 1, 2005
EU	The Techlawed Project, available at www.techlawed.org/page.php?v=24&c=2&page=crime, accessed on September 1, 2005
Germany	Telecommunications Act (in translation), available at www.netlaw.de/gesetz/tkg.htm, accessed on September 1, 2005
India	The Information Technology Act—2000, available at http://cag.nic.in/cyber_laws/india.htm, accessed on September 1, 2005
Japan	Unauthorized Computer Access Law (Law No. 128 of 1999), available at www.meti.go.jp/english/report/data/gMI1102e.htm, accessed on September 1, 2005
Malaysia	Laws of Malaysia, Act 563, Computer Crimes Act 1997, available at http://cag.nic.in/cyber_laws/malaysia.htm, accessed on September 1, 2005
Singapore	Salient features of Electronic Transactions Act 1998, available at /www.ida.gov.sg/idaweb/pnr/infopage.jsp?infopagecategory=regulation:pnr&infopageid=I1965&versionid=1, accessed on September 1, 2005

United States   Fraud and Related Activity in Connection with Computers (18 U.S.C 1030), available at www.usdoj.gov/criminal/cybercrime/1030_new.html, accessed on September 1, 2005

8. Since true economic damage is impossible to accurately measure and is often based on self-reporting by the private sector, such figures should only serve as an indicator.

9. The COE webpage contains the text of the Convention on Cybercrime, the explanatory report, and charts of signatures and ratifications.

10. The members of the Council of Europe are: Albania, Andorra, Armenia, Austria, Azerbaijan, Belgium, Bosnia and Herzegovina, Bulgaria, Croatia, Cyprus, Czech Republic, Denmark, Estonia, Finland, France, Georgia, Germany, Greece, Hungary, Iceland, Ireland, Italy, Latvia, Liechtenstein, Lithuania, Luxembourg, Malta, Moldova, Monaco, Netherlands, Norway, Poland, Portugal, Romania, Russian Federation, San Marino, Serbia, Slovakia, Slovenia, Spain, Sweden, Switzerland, Macedonia, Turkey, Ukraine, and the United Kingdom.

11. The coalition includes the Cyber Security Industry Alliance (CSIA), the Business Software Alliance (BSA), the American Bankers Association (ABA), the American Chemistry Council (ACC), ASIS International, the Association for Competitive Technology (ACT), the Bankers' Association for Finance and Trade (BAFT), the Business Roundtable, the Dow Chemical Company, the Financial Services/Information Sharing and Analysis Center (FSISAC), the Financial Services Roundtable, the Information Technology Association of America (ITAA), InfraGard, the Internet Commerce Coalition, and Verisign, Inc.

12. APEC members are: Australia; Brunei Darussalam; Canada; Chile; People's Republic of China; Hong Kong, China; Indonesia; Japan; Korea; Malaysia; Mexico; New Zealand; Papua New Guinea; Peru; Philippines; Russia; Singapore; Chinese Taipei; Thailand; United States of America; Vietnam.

13. An updated version of ISO/TR 13569 that incorporates the twelve layers of security was released in summer 2004 and is available for purchase at: www.iso.org/iso/en/CombinedQueryResult.CombinedQueryResult?queryString=13569.

14. The following definitions are available from the Department of Information Technology, at the State of Michigan website, www.michigan.gov/cybersecurity/0,1607,7-217-34415—-,00.html, accessed on September 1, 2005.

- *Pharming* involves Trojans programs, worms, or other virus technologies that attack the Internet browser address bar and is much more sophisticated than phishing. When users type in a valid URL they are redirected to the criminals' websites instead of the intended valid website.
- *Phishing* is the act of tricking someone into giving . . . confidential information or tricking them into doing something that they normally wouldn't do or shouldn't do. For example: sending an e-mail to a user falsely claiming to be an established legitimate enterprise in an attempt to scam the user into surrendering private information that will be used for identity theft.
- *Spoofing* is an attempt to gain access to a system by posing as an authorized user. Synonymous with impersonating, masquerading or mimicking.

The following definition is available from the Spamhaus Project website, www.spamhaus.org/definition. html, accessed on September 1, 2005: "*Spam* as applied to email means *Unsolicited Bulk Email* ("UBE"). Unsolicited means that the Recipient has not granted verifiable permission for the message to be sent. Bulk means that the message is sent as part of a larger collection of messages, all having substantively identical content."

15. Spamhaus is one of the exceptions in this regard, but it should be recalled that it is essentially a small NGO with no authority and relies on the good will of ISPs and other organizations to actually do something with the information Spamhaus provides.

16. Epistemic: a network of experts with an authoritative claim about an issue (knowledge-society). Norms: an expected standard of behavior and belief established and enforced by a group.

REFERENCES

Anderson, C. 2004. *Etisalat Joins the "First" Global Alliance for Computer and Internet Security.* AME Info, Dubai (available at www.ameinfo.com/39573.html, accessed on November 26, 2006).

APCERT. 2003. *APCERT Annual Report.* Asia Pacific Computer Emergency Response Team (available at www.apcert.org/documents/pdf/annualreport2003.pdf, accessed on September 1, 2005).

APCERT. 2005a. *Asia-Pacific Emergency Response Team* (available at www.apcert.org/, accessed on September 1, 2005).

APCERT. 2005b. *Full Member List.* APCERT Secretariat (available at www.apcert.org/member.html, accessed on September 1, 2005).

APEC. 2002a. *APEC Telecommunications and Information Working Group (TEL) Program of Action.* Fifth APEC Ministerial Meeting on Telecommunications and Information Industry. Shanghai, May 29–30 (available at www.apec.org/apec/ministerial_statements/sectoral_ministerial/telecommunications/2002/annex_a.html, accessed on September 1, 2005).

APEC. 2002b. *Shanghai Declaration.* Fifth APEC Ministerial Meeting on Telecommunications and Information Industry. Shanghai, May 29–30 (available at www.apec.org/apec/ministerial_statements/sectoral_ministerial/telecommunications/2002.html, accessed on September 1, 2005).

APEC. 2002c. *Recommendation by the APEC TELWG to SOM for an APEC Cybersecurity Strategy.* APEC 14th Annual Ministerial Meeting, Los Cabos, Mexico, October 23–24, p. 4 (available at www.apec.org/apec/documents_reports/annual_ministerial_meetings/2002.html, accessed on September 1, 2005).

APEC. 2003a. Protecting Developing Economies from Cyber Attack—Assistance to Build Regional Cyber Security Preparedness. APEC media release, March 18 (available at www.apec.org/apec/news___media/2003_media_releases/180303_sin_protecting_developing_economies.html, accessed on September 1, 2005).

APEC. 2003b. *Joint Statement.* Fifteenth APEC Ministerial Meeting, Bangkok, October 17–18 (available at www.mofa.go.jp/policy/economy/apec/2003/joint.html, accessed on November 26, 2006).

APEC. 2005. *Telecommunications and Information Working Group—APEC Cybersecurity Strategy* (available at www.apec.org/apec/apec_groups/working_groups/telecommunications_and_information.html, accessed on September 1, 2005).

APWG. 2005. *What is Phishing and Pharming?* Anti-Phishing Working Group (available at www.antiphishing.org/index.html, accessed on September 1, 2005).

Balancing Act News. 2004a. CSIRT: a route to combating Africa's position as one of the world's cyber-badlands. *Balancing Act News,* 216 (available at www.balancingact-africa.com/news/back/balancing-act_216.html, accessed on September 1, 2005).

Balancing Act News. 2004b. USAID helps to set up first CSIRT in Algeria. *Balancing Act News Update,* 223 (available at www.balancingact-africa.com/news/back/balancing-act_223.html, accessed on November 26, 2006).

Betts, M. 2005. Global dispatches: 14 African countries agree to standardize cyberlaws. *Computer World,* May 16 (available at www.computerworld.com/databasetopics/businessintelligence/story/0,10801,101755,00.html, accessed on September 1, 2005).

BIS. 2003. *Risk Management Principles for Electronic Banking.* Basel Committee on Banking Supervision—Bank of International Settlements. Basel, July (available at www.bis.org/publ/bcbs98.pdf, accessed on September 1, 2005).

BIS. 2005. BIS home page. Bank for International Settlements. Basel (available at www.bis.org, accessed on September 1, 2005).

Blau, J. 2004. German teenager indicted over Sasser worm. IDG News Service on *Computer World,* September 9 (available at www.computerworld.com/securitytopics/security/story/0,10801,95787,00.html, accessed on September 1, 2005).

Centrex. 2003. *Central Police Training and Development Authority* (available at www.centrex.police.uk/cps/rde/xchg/SID-3E8082DF-A3DD3A16/centrex/root.xsl/home.html, accessed on November 28, 2006).

CERT/CC. 2004. *E-Crime Watch Survey Shows Significant Increase in Electronic Crimes.* Carnegie Mellon University Software Engineering Institute CERT Coordination Center (available at www.csoonline.com/releases/ecrimewatch04.pdf, accessed on October 25, 2005).

CERT/CC. 2005a. *The CERT FAQ.* Carnegie Mellon Software Engineering Institute CERT Coordination Center, Pittsburgh (available at www.cert.org/faq/cert_faq.html, accessed on November 28, 2006).

CERT/CC. 2005b. *CERT Coordination Center.* Carnegie Mellon Software Engineering Institute, Pittsburgh (available at www.cert.org/, accessed on September 1, 2005).

COE. 2004a. *Big Brother or Free-for-All—How Can the Law Strike a Balance?* Council of Europe (available at www.coe.int/T/E/Com/Files/Themes/Cybercrime/e_bigbrother.asp, accessed on September 1, 2005).

COE. 2004b. *Summary of the Organized Crime Situation Report 2004—Focus on the Threat of Cybercrime.* Council of Europe Octopus Programme. Strasbourg, December 23 (available at www.coe.int/T/E/Legal_

Affairs/Legal_co-operation/Combating_economic_crime/8_Organised_crime/Documents/Organised%20 Crime%20Situation%20Report%202004.pdf, accessed on November 28, 2006).

COE. 2006a. *Convention on Cybercrime.* CETS No. 185. Council of Europe (available at www.conventions. coe.int/Treaty/Commun/QueVoulezVous.asp?NT=185&CM=12&DF=17/04/05&CL=ENG, accessed on November, 26 2006).

COE. 2006b. *The Council of Europe's Member States* (available at www.coe.int/T/E/Com/About_Coe/ Member_states/default.asp, accessed on November 26, 2006).

Comptroller and Auditor General of India. 2003. *Compilation of Cyber Laws: Summary Analysis of Responses to Cyber Law Questionnaire.* Supreme Audit Institution of India (available at http://cag.nic. in/html/inter_projects_cyber.htm, accessed on November 28, 2006).

Cybercrime. 2003. Message from the President of the United States—Transmitting. U.S. Senate, 108th Congress. 1st Session, Washington, D.C., November 17 (available at www.cybercrime.gov/senateCoe. pdf, accessed on September 1, 2005).

DHS. 2003. *National Strategy to Secure Cyberspace.* Department of Homeland Security, U.S., February (available at /www.dhs.gov/xprevprot/programs/editorial_0329.shtm, accessed on November 28, 2006).

Downing, R.W. 2003. Cybercrime legislation and enforcement capacity building project. *APEC Telecommunications and Information Working Group.* Bangkok, April 3–8 (available at www.apectelwg. org/document/download.jsp?fname=Cybercrime%20Project%20Update%2020050401.pdf&all_ cd=010306&d_seq=2766, accessed on September 1, 2005).

Dunn, M., and Wigert, I. 2004. *CIIP Handbook 2004: An Inventory and Analysis of Protection Policies in Fourteen Countries.* Columbia International Affairs Online (available at www.ciaonet.org/book/dum01/ index.html, accessed on September 1, 2005).

EBITT. 2003. *Former Task Force on Cybercrime/Cybersecurity.* ICC Commission on E-Business, IT and Telecoms (EBITT) (available at www.iccwbo.org/home/e_business/Cybercrime%20Cybersecurity.asp, accessed on September 1, 2005).

EFCC. 2004. Nigerian Cyber-crime Working Group (NCWG). Economic and Financial Crime Commissions (EFCC). Abuja, Nigeria (available at www.efccnigeria.org/, accessed on September 1, 2004).

ENISA. 2005a. European Network and Information Security Agency. EUROPA (available at europa.eu.int/ agencies/enisa/index_en.htm, accessed on September 1, 2005).

ENISA. 2005b. *Work Programme 2005—"Information Sharing Is Protecting."* Brussels: European Network and Information Security Agency, February 25 (available at www.enisa.eu.int/doc/pdf/management_board/ decisions/work_programme_2005.pdf, accessed on September 1, 2005).

Escobar, M. 2004. Framework for establishing an inter-American CSIRT watch and warning network. *Third Plenary Session of the OAS Committee on Hemispheric Security of the OAS.* Montevideo, Uruguay, January 29.

Europa. 2001a. *Communication from the Commission to the Council, the European Parliament, the Economic and Social Committee and the Committee of the Regions: Creating a Safer Information Society by Improving the Security of Information Infrastructures and Combating Computer-related Crime.* Brussels, January 26 (available at http://europa.eu.int/ISPO/eif/InternetPoliciesSite/Crime/CrimeComEN.pdf, accessed on September 1, 2005).

Europa. 2001b. *Organized Crime: Contact Points to Combat High-tech Crime.* European Union Documents, June 25 (available at http://europa.eu.int/scadplus/leg/en/lvb/l33157.htm, accessed on September 1, 2005).

Europa. 2002a. Council resolution of 28 January 2002 on a common approach and specific actions in the area of network and information security. *Official Journal of the European Communities,* C 043 (2002), 0002 (available at http://europa.eu.int/eur-lex/pri/en/oj/dat/2002/c_043/c_04320020216en00020004.pdf, accessed on October 25, 2005).

Europa. 2002b. Proposal for a Council Framework Decision on Attacks against Information Systems. Commission of the European Communities. Brussels, April 19 (available at europa.eu.int/eur-lex/en/ com/pdf/2002/com2002_0173en01.pdf, accessed on September 1, 2005).

Europa. 2003. Council resolution of 18 February 2003 on a European approach towards a culture of network and information security. *Official Journal of the European Communities,* C 048 (2003), 0001–0002 (available at http://europa.eu.int/eur-lex/lex/LexUriServ/LexUriServ.do?uri=CELEX:32003G0228(01): EN:HTML, accessed on October 25, 2005).

Europa. 2004. *Establishment of a European Network and Information Security Agency (ENISA)* (available at http://europa.eu.int/scadplus/leg/en/lvb/l24153.htm, accessed on September 1, 2005).

Europa. 2005. *Activities of the EU: Fight against Cybercrime* (available at http://europa.eu.int/scadplus/leg/en/lvb/133193b.htm, accessed on September 1, 2005).

Europol. 2005. *Fact Sheet on Europol 2005.* The Hague (available at www.europol.eu.int/index.asp?page=facts, accessed on September 1, 2005).

FIRST. 2006a. *FIRST Operational Framework.* Forum of Incident Response and Security Teams. Mountain View, CA (available at www.first.org/about/policies/op-framework/index.html, accessed on November 26, 2006).

FIRST. 2006b. *Member Process at a Glance.* Forum of Incident Response and Security Teams. Mountain View, CA (available at www.first.org/membership/, accessed on November 26, 2006).

G8. 2000a. G8 Conference on Dialogue between the Public Authorities and Private Sector on Security and Trust in Cyberspace. Final press release, Paris, May 15–17 (available at www.g8.utoronto.ca/crime/paris2000.htm, accessed on September 1, 2005).

G8. 2000b. *Okinawa Charter on Global Information Society.* Kyushu-Okinawa Summit 2000. Okinawa: Government of Japan, July 22 (available at www.g7.utoronto.ca/g7/summit/20000kinawa/gis.htm, accessed on September 1, 2005).

G8. 2001. *Report of Workshop IV: Protection of E-commerce and User Authentication.* G-8 Government-Industry Workshop. Tokyo, Ministry of Foreign Affairs of Japan, May (available at www.mofa.go.jp/policy/i_crime/high_tec/conf0105–7.html, accessed on September 1, 2005).

G8. 2003. *Meeting of G8 Ministers of Justice and Home Affairs.* Paris, June 9 (available at www.g8.utoronto.ca/justice/justice030505.htm, accessed on September 1, 2005).

G8. 2004. *Background on the G8.* Meeting of G8 Justice and Home Affairs Ministers. Washington, D.C., May 11 (available at www.usdoj.gov/criminal/cybercrime/g82004/g8_background.html, accessed on September 1, 2005).

G8. 2005. *How the G8 Works* (available at www.g8.gc.ca/work-en.asp, accessed on September 1, 2005).

Gelbstein, E., and Kamal, A. 2002. *Information Insecurity: A Survival Guide to the Uncharted Territories of Cyber-threats and Cyber-security.* United Nations ICT Task Force, November.

GILC. 2003. Global Internet liberty campaign: latest news. *Global Internet Liberty Campaign,* May 5 (available at www.gilc.org, accessed on September 1, 2005).

Glaessner, T.; Kellermann, T.; and McNevin, V. 2002. *Electronic Security: Risk Mitigation in Financial Transactions—Public Policy Issues.* World Bank, July (available at www-wds.worldbank.org/servlet/WDSContentServer/WDSP/IB/2002/08/23/000094946_02081004010495/Rendered/PDF/multi0page.pdf, accessed on September 1, 2005).

Hopkins, S.L. 2003. Cybercrime convention: a positive beginning to a long road ahead. *Journal of High Technology and Law,* 2, 1 (available at www.jhtl.org/docs/pdf/SHOPKINSV2N1N.pdf, accessed on September 1, 2005).

ICCWBO. 2002. *A Global Action Plan for Electronic Commerce, Prepared by Business with Recommendations for Governments,* 3rd ed. Alliance for Global Business, July (available at www.iccwbo.org/home/e_business/word_documents/3rd%20Edition%20Global%20Action%20Plan.pdf, accessed on September 1, 2005).

ICCWBO. 2004. *Securing Your Business: A Companion for Small or Entrepreneurial Companies to the 2002 OECD Guidelines for the Security of Network and Information Systems: Towards a Culture of Security.* International Chamber of Commerce (available at www.iccwbo.org/home/e_business/RESOURCES-rev4.pdf, accessed on September 1, 2005).

Interpol. 2003. Interpol Joins Microsoft in Fight against Cybercrime: Agrees to Assist in Global Anti-virus Reward Program. Interpol media release, November 5 (available at www.interpol.int/Public/ICPO/PressReleases/PR2003/PR200331.asp, accessed on September 1, 2005).

Interpol. 2005. *Introduction to Interpol.* Lyon (available at www.interpol.int/Public/Icpo/introduction.asp, accessed on September 1, 2005).

ITU. 2002. *Resolution Adopted by the General Assembly—World Summit on the Information Society.* UN Resolution 56/183, January 31 (available at www.itu.int/wsis/docs/background/resolutions/56_183_unga_2002.pdf, accessed on Oct 25, 2005).

ITU. 2005a. *About Telecommunication Development Bureau (BDT).* International Telecommunications Union (available at www.itu.int/ITU-D/aboutbdt.html, accessed on March 15, 2006).

ITU. 2005b. International Telecommunications Union website (available at www.itu.org, accessed on September 1, 2005).

ITU. 2005c. *Status Report on the Implementation of ITU-D Activities 2005.* ITU-D, November 1 (available at www.itu.int/ITU-D/pdf/imple-stat-rep05.pdf, accessed on March 15, 2006).

Jones, C.W. 2005. *Council of Europe Convention on Cybercrime: Themes and Critiques.* Berkeley: University of California at Berkeley, April 5 (available at www.sims.berkeley.edu/~cjones/Full%20Text%20Papers/Council%200f%20Europe%20Convention%200n%20Cybercrime%20-%20Themes%20and%20Critiques.pdf, accessed on September 1, 2005).

Killcrece, G. et al. 2003. *Handbook and Organizational Models for CSIRTs.* CMU/SEI-2003-HB-001. Pittsburgh: Carnegie Mellon Software Engineering Institute (available at www.cert.org/archive/pdf/03tr001.pdf, accessed on September 1, 2005).

Killcrece, G. 2004. *Steps for Creating National CSIRTs.* Pittsburgh: Carnegie Mellon Software Engineering Institute (available at www.cert.org/archive/pdf/NationalCSIRTs.pdf, accessed on September 1, 2005).

Lemos, R. 2004. Sasser bounty hangs on conviction, says Microsoft. *CNET News.com,* September 13 (available at http://news.zdnet.co.uk/internet/security/0,39020375,39166398,00.htm, accessed on September 1, 2005).

McConnell International. 2000. *Cybercrime . . . and Punishment? Archaic Laws Threaten Global Information.* December (available at www.mcconnellinternational.com/services/CyberCrime.pdf, accessed on November 28, 2006).

Microsoft. 2003. *Microsoft Announces Anti-virus Reward Program.* Washington, D.C., November 5 (available at www.microsoft.com/presspass/press/2003/nov03/11–05AntiVirusRewardsPR.asp, accessed on September 1, 2005).

NSTAC. 2005. *R&D Exchange.* President's National Security Telecommunications Advisory Committee (available at www.ncs.gov/nstac/rd/nstac_rd_about.html, accessed on March 15, 2006).

OAS. 1999a. *Final Report of the Second Meeting of Government Experts on Cybercrime.* Organization of American States, Washington, D.C., October 14–15 (available at www.oas.org/juridico/english/cybGE_rec.doc, accessed September 1, 2005).

OAS. 1999b. *Final Report of the Second Meeting of Ministers of Justice or of Ministers or Attorneys General of the Americas.* Lima, March 1–3 (available at www.oas.org/juridico/english/Minjusti.htm, accessed September 1, 2005).

OAS. 2005. *The Organization of American States.* Washington, D.C. (available at www.oas.org/, accessed on September 1, 2005).

Octopus Interface. 2004. *The Challenge of Cybercrime.* Octopus Interface Conference, Strasbourg, France (available at www.coe.int/T/E/Legal_affairs/Legal_co-operation/Combating_economic_crime/Cybercrime/International_conference/Octopus-Interface-2004.asp, accessed on September 1, 2005).

OECD. 1986. *Computer-related Crime: Analysis of Legal Policy.* Paris.

OECD. 1992. *Recommendation of the Council Concerning Guidelines for the Security of Information Systems.* OECD/GD(92)10. Paris.

OECD. 2004. *Summary of Responses to the Survey on the Implementation of the OECD Guidelines for the Security of Information Systems and Networks: Towards a Culture of Security.* Paris: Working Party on Information Security and Privacy-OECD, September 24 (available at www.olis.oecd.org/olis/2003doc.nsf/43bb6130e5e86e5fc12569fa005d004c/81dd07040a1c0e43c1256eb6005423d4/$FILE/JT00169904.DOC, accessed on September 1, 2005).

Oyesanya, F. 2004. A performance review of EFCC and the Nigerian cyber-crime working group. *Nigerian Village Square,* December 22 (available at www.nigeriavillagesquare1.com/Articles/oyesanya/2004/12/performance-review-of-efcc-and.html, accessed on November 26, 2006).

POLCYB. 2004. *Cybercrime Investigation—Developing an International Training Programme for the Future.* National Centre for Policing Excellence (available at www.polcyb.org/Events/ILECA/04_ILECA_Other.htm, accessed on September 1, 2005).

PR Newswire. 2005. Multiple industry groups join together to urge Senate ratification of the cybercrime treaty. PR Newswire Association LLC, June 29 (available at www.prnewswire.com/cgi-bin/stories.pl?ACCT=104&STORY=/www/story/06–29–2005/0003988022&EDATE=, accessed on September 1, 2005).

PTI. 2004. India to work jointly with Russia to tackle cybercrime. *Press Trust of India, Nationwide International News,* December 4 (available through LexusNexus at: web.lexis-nexis.com.gtel.gatech.edu:2048/universe/document?_m=174547b04acd7eb6ebe3a9b84d8f25e8&_docnum=1&wchp=dGLbVlb-zSkVA&_md5=37342b61a2088a83ec289d09d2587c65, accessed on November 26, 2006).

REMJA-V. 2004. *Conclusions and Recommendations of REMJA-V.* Fifth Meeting of Ministers of Justice or of Ministers or Attorneys General of the Americas, Washington, D.C., April 28–30 (available at www.oas.org/juridico/english/cybV_CR.pdf, accessed on September 1, 2005).

Sadowsky, G. et al. 2003. *Information Technology Security Handbook*. Washington, D.C.: International Bank for Reconstruction and Development—The World Bank (available at http://infodev-security.net/handbook/, accessed on September 1, 2005).

Solha, L.E.V. 2002. *CSIRTs in Latin America.* 14th FIRST Conference. Hawaii (available at http://72.14.203.104/search?q=cache:GY6RAFtjUlMJ:www.first.org/events/progconf/2002/d5–08-teamupd-csirts-latin-america.pdf+CSIRTS+in+Latin+America,+FIRST+Conference+2002&hl=en, accessed on September 1, 2005).

Sophos. 2003. *FBI Set to Arrest Blaster Worm Suspect, Sophos Anti-Virus Comments.* August 29 (available at www.sophos.com/virusinfo/articles/blasterarrest.html, accessed on September 1, 2005).

Sophos. 2005. *Sasser Computer Worm Trial Delayed, Sophos Reports.* October 25 (available at www.sophos.com/virusinfo/articles/sasserdelay.html, accessed on September 1, 2005).

Spamhaus. 2005a. *Rokso: The Register of Known Spam Operations* (available at www.spamhaus.org/rokso/index.lasso, accessed on September 1, 2005).

Spamhaus. 2005b. *SBL Advisory: Spamhaus Block List* (available at www.spamhaus.org/sbl/index.lasso, accessed on September 1, 2005).

Spamhaus. 2005c. *XBL Advisory: Exploits Block List* (available at www.spamhaus.org/xbl/, accessed on November 28, 2006).

Spamhaus Project. 2005. *The Spamhaus Project* (available at www.spamhaus.org/, accessed on September 1, 2005).

Techlawed. 2005. *The Techlawed Project.* University of Ottawa (available at www.techlawed.org/page.php?v=1&c=1&page=home, accessed on November 28, 2006).

TERENA. 2005a. *Invitation Package for TI "Accredited" Status. Trusted Introducer for CSIRTs in Europe* (available at www.ti.terena.nl/ti_process/invitation.pdf, accessed on September 1, 2005).

TERENA. 2005b. *Trusted Introducer for CSIRTs in Europe.* Amsterdam, January 4 (available at www.ti.terena.nl/, accessed on September 1, 2005).

TERENA. 2006. TF-CSIRT. TERENA, Amsterdam (available at www.terena.nl/activities/tf-csirt/, accessed on November 26, 2006).

TRANSITS. 2005a. *Report on the Sixth Training Workshop: Training of Network Security Incident Teams Staff.* Amsterdam, March 18 (available at www.ist-transits.org/d10_transits.pdf, accessed on September 1, 2005).

TRANSITS. 2005b. *Training of Network Security Incident Teams Staff* (available at www.ist-transits.org/, accessed on September 1, 2005).

UNCJIN. 1990. *International Review of Criminal Policy—United Nations Manual on the Prevention and Control of Computer-related Crime.* Eighth UN Congress on the Prevention of Crime and the Treatment of Offenders. Havana, August 26–September 7 (available at www.uncjin.org/Documents/EighthCongress.html, accessed on September 1, 2005).

US-CERT. 2005. *Fact Sheet: Protecting America's Critical Infrastructure—Cyber Security.* United States Computer Emergency Readiness Team. Arlington, VA (available at www.us-cert.gov/press_room/050215cybersec.html, accessed on October 25, 2005).

USDOJ. 2003. *Frequently Asked Questions and Answers—Council of Europe Convention on Cybercrime.* Department of Justice, November 10 (available at www.usdoj.gov/criminal/cybercrime/COEFAQs.htm#QA2, accessed on September 1, 2005).

USDOJ. 2005. *G8 24/7 High Tech Contact Points Invitation.* U.S. Department of Justice. Washington, D.C. (available at www.cybersecuritycooperation.org/moredocuments/24%20Hour%20Network/24%207%20invitation.pdf, accessed on September 1, 2005).

Washington Post. 2000. I LoveYou, don't prosecute me, August 24, p. A24.

West-Brown, M.J. et al. 2003. *Handbook for Computer Security Incident Response Teams (CSIRTs),* 2nd ed. Pittsburgh: Carnegie Mellon Software Engineering Institute, April (available at www.cert.org/archive/pdf/csirt-handbook.pdf, accessed on October 25, 2005).

Westby, J.R. (ed.) 2004. International guide to cyber security. *ABA Section of Science and Technology Law,* 95.

WITSA. 2005. WITSA Press Center. Press releases. World Information Technology and Services Alliance. Arlington, VA (available at www.witsa.org/press/, accessed on September 1, 2005).

Workshop on the International Dimensions of Cyber Security. 2005. Georgia Institute of Technology and Carnegie Mellon University, Atlanta, GA, April 6–7.

PART IV

FORCES AND RESEARCH
LEADING TO FUTURE
INFORMATION SECURITY PROCESSES

CHAPTER 10

EMERGING UBIQUITOUS COMPUTING TECHNOLOGIES AND SECURITY MANAGEMENT STRATEGY

GIOVANNI IACHELLO AND GREGORY D. ABOWD

Abstract: *Emerging IT applications are increasingly embedded in environments of everyday life and run autonomously and without supervision from the user. These technologies introduce several new security concerns, both technical and organizational, including problems related to public knowledge and education, legality, privacy and acceptance. In this chapter, we define the salient features of these technologies and provide a framework for analyzing data exchanges within these systems. We then discuss security issues related to management, administration, oversight, legality, liability, acceptance, and security strategy design. We employ two research ubicomp applications to show how these issues manifest themselves.*

Keywords: *Ubiquitous Computing, Security Management, Capture and Access, Advanced IT Applications*

INTRODUCTION

Over the past twenty years, a new generation of computing applications has been silently entering our daily lives. RFID technology (Radio Frequency Identification) is used to track items within supply chains, computer-controlled actuator systems such as ABS (Anti-Blocking Systems) control the brakes of our cars, meetings and lectures are automatically recorded, most people carry integrated location and communication systems in the form of cell phones, and the list could continue. Computing technology is increasingly embedded in environments of human action, such as homes, transportation infrastructure, and consumer artifacts. In fact, without realizing it, we interact with hundreds if not thousands of computing devices throughout our daily activities. Moreover, these applications are increasingly networked through wired and wireless connections. Collectively referred to as *ubiquitous computing* (or *ubicomp*), these applications run continuously, unattended, and unsupervised (Weiser, 1993).

Ubicomp applications have been enabled by the converging developments of several strands of information technology (IT), including networking, the miniaturization of computing devices, reduction in power consumption, and novel sensing, data processing, and storage techniques. These applications are characterized by advanced computing capabilities and complex operating behaviors, and by the collection and use of large amounts of information sensed from physical environments (e.g., video in conjunction with image recognition, biometrics, or environmental data).

Researchers have long recognized that the automatic collection and use of extensive and detailed information from physical environments can cause security and safety risks and upset current social practices and norms (Langheinrich, 2001; Lessig, 1999; Palen and Dourish, 2003; Patton, 2000). For this reason, privacy and security have come to the forefront of the ubicomp research agenda. Past efforts in this area focused on *design,* suggesting principles, methods, and techniques to increase application security or to protect user privacy. These include both general efforts (e.g., reinterpreting privacy-enhancing *principles* such as information minimization) (Langheinrich, 2001), as well as more focused analyses involving specific applications such as office video awareness systems and employee locator applications (Bellotti and Sellen, 1993; Harter and Hopper, 1994).

In practice, most research on ubicomp security has hitherto concentrated on technical issues, be it the specifics of a particular technology or architectural solutions. However, the kind of information handled by ubicomp applications, and their social setting of use, suggest that the management of these technologies will present significant challenges. This is because security management typically rests on assumptions that are not necessarily true for ubicomp systems. These assumptions include:

- sufficient resources and competent personnel to implement and overview security controls;
- user interfaces to inspect and audit system performance and operation;
- effective regulation and policy enforcement.

Therefore, managing ubicomp applications with current data protection and security strategies (used, for example, for managing financial or health data) may prove difficult. Research has not yet tackled the management issues related to ubicomp applications, due in part to the lack of experience in using these applications in real-world settings. Acknowledging the urgency and scale of issues, in this chapter we concentrate on the security management issues for ubicomp systems. The purpose of this discussion is to point out the fundamental management challenges for ubicomp systems and to suggest some instruments for achieving more secure ubicomp environments.

In the following section, we provide an overview of some representative ubicomp applications and a description of the technological evolution that has made these applications possible. We also introduce a characterization of information based on semantic density, richness, and sensitivity, which can be used in the security analysis of these applications. We then describe the two case studies that will lead the discussion throughout the remainder of the chapter. These two applications (the *Personal Audio Loop* and *CareLog*) are research platforms developed at our institution and are representative of some of the security management issues discussed here. Using the two case studies as backdrops to the discussion, we catalog the main security management challenges brought on by ubiquitous computing applications. Finally, we briefly discuss future research directions.

APPLICATIONS AND TECHNOLOGY

In this section, we provide a sample of some applications in general terms. We describe ubicomp systems as abstract flows of information (see below, Figure 10.1). We describe the types of information collected by and used in ubicomp systems, and propose three attributes (semantic density, richness, sensitivity) useful for security and risk analysis. Information flows and the characterization of information are used as guides for the discussion of security management strategies in the remainder of this chapter.

Early ubicomp applications included automated meeting recording in workplaces. These applications collected audio and video of meetings that can be used for future reference; examples of this are the Tivoli system developed at PARC (Pedersen et al., 1993) and the Teamspace system (Geyer et al., 2001). The efficiency of search within the multimedia data can be increased by recording additional information, such as the identity of the speaker, salient events (e.g., slide changes like in the ADEPT system developed at Stanford, people entering and exiting the room, etc.) or student notes (e.g., in the eClass developed at Georgia Tech) (Brusilovsky, 2000).

Other early ubicomp applications were "awareness" tools for office environments, through which remote coworkers could "see and hear" each other on audiovisual links, to foster collaboration and ease communication (Gaver et al., 1992). Other systems made use of localization technology to find people within an office complex for call routing purposes (Harter and Hopper, 1994). In these environments, designers were aware of social dynamics that might resist these applications, for example, out of fear of potential misuse for monitoring workers' performance (Bellotti and Sellen, 1993).

The capture and retrieval of video recordings is typically used in public space for security and access control, and increasingly for leisure and commercial activities. The use of surveillance cameras in cities started in the United States during the late 1960s (Columbia Human Rights Law Review, 1973). Video capture has been proposed in distributed office environments to provide a background, continuous communication channel among remote workers (Bellotti and Sellen, 1993). Recently, simple webcams have been used for leisure and marketing activities, for instance, to broadcast the interior of nightclubs and bars or beaches (British Institute of International and Comparative Law, 2003).

In the home, ubicomp technology has been proposed to help people finding lost objects (Orr et al., 1999): in that application concept, video cameras track the location of the inhabitants and statistical algorithms are used to suggest possible locations of misplaced objects. Alternatively, RFID tags applied on the objects can be used for tracking their movement. Automatic monitoring systems deployed in the homes of elderly people can be used by caregivers and relatives to maintain an eye on the person's well-being and have been proposed as a way of prolonging the permanence of people in their own home by increasing their sense of security (Mynatt et al., 2001).

In health care, ubicomp technology can also be used for monitoring, such as patient observation, anomaly detection, and telemedicine. Implantable sensors are used to monitor the health of patients for several weeks after surgery (Maheu et al., 2001) and information sensed from the body is automatically transmitted to a processing center, analyzed for anomalies, and forwarded to the medical personnel in charge.

Transportation systems have used these types of technologies for several years. The distributed nature of these systems and high usage volume are raising the costs of direct, continuous, human surveillance, thus prompting the development of automated technologies. Automatic payment systems based on RFID technology, associated with automatic video capture and license plate recognition, for fraud prevention have been used on motorways in several countries from the early 1990s (Foresti et al., 2000). More sophisticated systems are currently being developed to use location technologies for automating toll collection on entire highway networks (*The Economist*, 2004).

Flows of Environmental Information

The ubicomp applications mentioned above collect information from environments of human action and translate it into operational resources for later use. These applications share the same general information flows structure. Figure 10.1 depicts this structure. We employ the term *capture and access,* proposed by Truong et al. (2001), to characterize a specific set of ubicomp applications, as a general label for these technologies.

Figure 10.1   **Flow of Environmental Information**

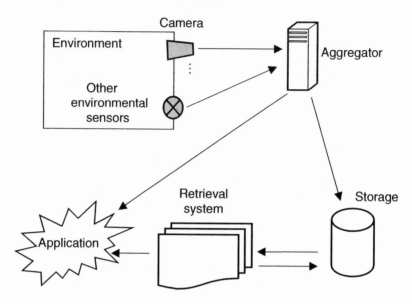

Sensors collect environmental information in digital form, which is delivered via telecommunication channels to an aggregator. According to military terminology, the term "sensor" can refer to any device, person, or system that is able to collect and forward information from the environment, from disposable vibration detectors to satellite-based reconnaissance systems (Libicki, 2000). In this context, we will use the term *sensor* to indicate devices at the simpler end of the spectrum. An important security characteristic of sensors is that low reliability must be taken into account as a normal operating mode. This is in contrast with the basic assumption underpinning digital information systems, which are generally considered highly reliable.

The aggregator correlates and translates the data in formats appropriate for storage or immediate delivery to applications. Information originating from different sensors can be integrated in a coherent whole (sensor *fusion*). Stored information may be collected and analyzed by a retrieval system, and possibly stored again, or delivered to the final consumer of information. The connections between components are not necessarily permanent. For example, applications can be placed on mobile devices and communicate over wireless networks with whatever sensors are present in the environment to collect data. Other components can be mobile as well; for example, the storage system could be located in a "personal server" (i.e., a personal, wearable, networked, UI-less storage device) (Want et al., 2002).

The collected information can be retrieved, played back, and searched, both for direct consumption by a user and for supporting human-machine interaction (e.g., by providing the system with a description of the environment and the activities in which the user is engaged—such a description is referred by the ubicomp literature as *context*). Retrieval systems typically provide facilities for relating, cataloging, and accessing information at a level of abstraction that is higher than that normally afforded by typical databases, using criteria based, among others, on temporal range, geographic position, and on the identities of the individuals to which the captured information pertains.

Table 10.1 synthesizes the current state and pace at which various components of this infrastructure are developing.[1] The table suggests that over the next few years, sensor technology will

Table 10.1

Technologies Used in Ubiquitous Computing

Type of technology	Cost	Forecast
Video	Decreasing 10–20 percent/year (Global Information Inc., 2003)	Cost is related to image quality. In the medium term, the capture and perceptual qualities of these devices will not improve drastically.
Audio	Stationary	High-quality microphones are still relatively large and expensive devices, and have not improved much over the recent past.
Presence, motion, contact	Stationary	These sensing devices are relatively reliable and inexpensive, and little innovation has occurred in the recent past.
Location technologies	Stationary	The introduction of the Global Positioning System (GPS) has enabled a host of applications, notwithstanding its poor performance in densely built areas and indoors. Other emerging location technologies are based on an infrastructure of RF beacons (e.g., cell phones towers, radio stations, 802.11 base stations).
Identification technologies	Slowly decreasing	ID technologies for people and objects have undergone dramatic changes over the past few years, with the introduction of RFID tagging. Other kinds of identification technologies, based on video or audio and pattern matching algorithms, are still resource-intensive and too unreliable to be used effectively. These technologies might become relatively viable in the near future.
Telecommunications and networking	Decreasing 40 percent/year	The evolution of these technologies is typically incremental, although from a customer endpoint different technologies (e.g., POTS, DSL) are introduced in steps, enabling different categories of applications. The cost/bandwidth ratio has steadily decreased over the past decade, roughly averaging 40 percent/year over the 1990s (Australian Information Economy Advisory Council, 2004).
Storage	Decreasing 45 percent/year	Magnetic storage cost per byte has decreased an average of 45 percent/year between 1992 and 2004, and this trend is likely to continue. While this allows to store increasing amounts of multimedia information on a random-access device, access speeds and throughput have evolved more slowly, due to limits to the mechanical properties of disks (dimensions and rotation speed). Thus the transfer speed/capacity ratio has worsened (Berghell Associates LLC, 2004; Grochowski and Halem, 2003).
Multimedia data mining	Stationary	Has been gaining speed over the past years (Elmagarmid et al., 1997; Foresti et al., 2000). Currently, retrieval methods rely on meta-data associated with multimedia information and gathered at the point of capture or created during archival, or on statistical algorithms.[1] Once data is stored, exhaustive search bears high costs due to the amount of the stored information. While performance will increase with faster algorithms and more processing power, data mining cost will not decrease radically in the near term.

[1]Such as commercially available systems like Autonomy. See www.autonomy.com/.

not provide groundbreaking improvements in performance, but its cost/capability ratio will slowly decrease. Stored data access speed will grow slowly. Unless novel storage technologies are introduced, the relative performance of exhaustive analysis and retrieval will not increase at the same rate as storage capacity, as the amount of stored information overgrows access speed.

Semantic Density, Richness, Sensitivity

We point out three ways of characterizing information that we found useful for our analysis: semantic density, richness, and sensitivity. Although the three properties are defined loosely, and correlated with one another, distinguishing among these qualities can help high-level security and risk analysis. Table 10.2 shows an overview of the three properties of sensed data, and of the risks associated with high and low levels of semantic density, richness, and sensitivity. The rightmost column includes some security goals to counter the listed risks.

Semantic density, measured in relation to a specific coding, indicates the relationship between the information storage size and the interest of its informational content with regard to a specific metric. For example, in an application that tracks people entering and exiting a building, a video recording of the entrance might provide low semantic density (i.e., much data must be analyzed to obtain specific desired information), while the log of all accesses based on an electronic badge lock will provide the same information in a very compact fashion (high density). Sensor fusion may increase semantic density, as data from different sources can be used to cross-reference and facilitate access to sensed information.

The semantic density of information and its relationship with search cost is an important parameter during design and affects both system and user security and privacy, because it influences the cost-risk tradeoff intrinsic to countering security and privacy threats.

Data with high semantic density can be processed efficiently, and searched for items matching specific search criteria. It is thus easier to use or misuse after the fact (i.e., after a database has been created). This increased malleability highlights the risks associated with database repurposing, and exposes the relevance of unforeseen attacks or misuse. Since high-density data are particularly prone to misuse through after-the-fact analysis (e.g., through data mining), technical and organizational safeguards should focus on access control, both to the information itself and to the processing tools (e.g., management, data mining tools). Low-density data, instead, are difficult to search to pinpoint information items of interest, if the search criterion is not among the "natural" criteria of how the data are organized.[2]

Low-density data can be protected from undesired access by reducing the access rate. That is, it may not be necessary to implement access control on the tools used to access the data, but it may be sufficient to make access expensive enough to discourage exhaustive searches. In the case of a database of individual video recordings, for example, access control to the data may allow checking out from storage only one video recording at a time. The data are not technically confidential, but the cost of obtaining enough information for systematic abuse may be made excessive. Similar misuse-prevention techniques protect information in many organizations today.

Richness refers to the quality of data providing a large amount of interrelated details. The richness of a video feed is much higher than that of an access control log. While more costly to analyze, richer information constitutes good evidence because it is more difficult to fabricate. This fact is acknowledged by courts: for example, in the United States a database record printout does not have any value as evidence per se unless a person can be brought to testify about its accuracy and reliability (United States Department of Justice, 2002), whereas a video recording or audio interception, if obtained legally, does not need any further validation. Low sensor reliability may affect the richness of collected information and its relative strength as evidence.

Table 10.2

Properties of Sensed Data at a Glance
Risks and Security Goals for the Management of Stored Data

	Characteristics	Risks	Security management goals
Semantic density			
High	Efficient search	Unforeseen analysis and use of data	Prevent unauthorized disclosure of data
	High value		Prevent unauthorized access to processing/mining tools
Low	Costly to search	Mismanagement of data	Limit the rate of access to the information
		Inability to comply with challenges on personal data (e.g., external audit/access requests)	Implement access and challenge procedures
		Incorrect fusion	
Richness			
High	Trustworthy	Misuse of personal information	Prevent unauthorized disclosure of data
	Accurate	Inability to comply with requests for amendment or deletion	Control replication
	Difficult to make up		
Low	Easy to fabricate	Unauthorized modification	Integrity safeguards
		Forging of data	Detect tampering
			Ability to assess data trustworthiness
Sensitivity			
High	Special legal status	Claims caused by mismanagement (breaches of regulatory requirements)	Integrity safeguards
	High social value	Loss/corruption	Prevent unauthorized disclosure of data
		Two-tier leaks	Prevent unauthorized uses of data
			Implement secure handling procedures
Low	Lower social value	Management costs higher than value of preserving information	Cost-effective security controls

Protecting rich information highlights aspects related to integrity and trustworthiness. Rich information such as an audio recording is much more trustworthy than a transcript, and its disclosure can present higher risks of misuse. This is likely to affect the use of data in legal proceedings. Storage modalities should be taken into consideration when designing systems that require strong levels of accountability or unaccountability. For example, the Sarbanes-Oxley Act of 2002 imposes specific security requirements on information related to the financial performance of publicly traded companies.[3] Such requirements may be harder to satisfy with rich data such as video recordings of meetings as opposed to more traditional databases.

Finally, *sensitivity* is a concept introduced by data protection legislation. It is used to describe the social characteristics of information. Sensitive information typically includes health-related, financial, political, religious, and other types of information that could be used to affect adversely an individual.

In general, personal information must be protected by appropriate security safeguards. However, regulation often mandates specific additional security controls for sensitive information. For example, in the United States, health service providers must protect health-related personal information according to specific security requirements, detailed in the Health Insurance Portability and Accountability Act (HIPAA) Security Rule (U.S. Department of Health and Human Services, 2003). In the EU, privacy legislation provides for specific requirements on sensitive information, including stronger informed consent requirements, and additional security provisions when disclosing the data to third parties (European Union, 1995).

In order to contain security-related costs, a two-tiered system with different security policies for different types of data (sensitive and not sensitive) can be employed. However, such a setup presents the risk of sensitive information leaking to the nonsensitive partition of the system. This is a classic security problem in the military domain, typically solved using mandatory access control. However, solutions from that domain may be difficult to transfer to commercial organizations and rapidly evolving technology.

CASE STUDIES

Having introduced some background concepts used throughout our analysis, we now discuss two case studies. These applications will be used as a conceptual test bed of the security management options discussed in the next section. These case studies are relevant because they both display technical security issues and are used in a complex social environment: in the first case our analysis of the security strategy focuses on the application's developers and on its users; in the second case, our analysis focuses on the broad organization surrounding the application. It should be noted that we are not providing a comprehensive security management solution for either of these applications, which are, in reality, much more complex than what emerges from this discussion. The case studies are only used to provide concrete examples for some of the challenges and solutions that we suggest.

The Personal Audio Loop

The Personal Audio Loop (or PAL) is a portable, near-term audio reminder service, implemented on a consumer market mobile phone (Hayes et al., 2004a). PAL was motivated by the everyday experience of conversational breakdowns, as people try to remember something that was said recently, such as the topic of a conversation before being interrupted, or a name or number briefly heard in situations of high cognitive load. The device allows the user to replay, at any moment in time, any sound that was heard by the user in the recent past, up to a defined maximum time span, or *buffer length* (for example, up to one hour in the past). Audio older than the buffer length is automatically overwritten and cannot be replayed.[4]

PAL is integrated in a cell phone, but the device only records sound from the environment, and not phone conversations. Since PAL uses the speakerphone microphone of the device, the range of the recording might be of up to a few meters from the person carrying the phone. The user can replay the recording, rewind and fast forward through it or jump to bookmarked positions ("earmarks"). The stored audio can be heard either through the loudspeaker on the phone or through the external speaker/mike.

This application presents obvious concerns related to the communication partner's privacy, unrelated third parties' privacy (e.g., passersby), and risks related to the loss or theft of the device. Several security measures can be employed to control these risks, including using trusted implementations, monitoring the co-evolution of social norms of its use, and influencing the social acceptance of the device.

This application highlights the role of the user in conforming to social expectations that protect others' privacy. Our analysis, discussed further below, suggests that manufacturers should "package" part of the security management functions of the device it its design, in order to drive the user toward appropriate behaviors and reduce risks associated with the application.

CareLog

The second application we consider is a system that supports diagnosis and evidence-based care of children with learning or behavioral disabilities. The care of these children involves several groups of people, including parents, teachers, caregivers, and professional therapists. Caregivers administer specific programs, such as engaging the child in one-to-one tasks. Teachers and parents sometimes act as caregivers. Professional therapists plan diagnostic and intervention strategies and supervise other caregivers, but may not always administer one-to-one intervention.

Measurement of performance and of other therapy-related data is an integral part of such diagnostic and intervention strategies. Detailed notes are often taken both for quantitative measurement of the child's performance with regards to the therapy, and for qualitatively assessing the causes and consequences of particular episodes (e.g., a temper tantrum, or when the child runs away from the classroom). It should be noted that the broad term "care" includes not only specific therapies but may also include preventive and follow-up monitoring.

These data can greatly benefit the effectiveness of the child's care, by allowing specialists to subsequently review and understand the causes and triggers of a particular behavior and action. Over the past ten to fifteen years, researchers have proposed to install cameras in the classrooms and homes where these interventions take place. These cameras automatically collect qualitative information about specific events, to augment the notes that teachers and caregivers take on paper. Early experimentation employed analog camera technology (Guidry and van den Pol, 1996). Recently Hayes et al. have proposed the use of an integrated digital capture and access system called CareLog (Hayes et al., 2004b). CareLog's purpose is to relieve caregivers of the burden of taking extensive notes, both qualitative and quantitative, on the child's behavior and performance, by capturing, among other things, video footage of his or her activity.

The cameras keep record of salient children activity, and the therapist can mark up the recording to indicate relevant events (e.g., critical events that cannot be foreseen, or are very infrequent) for subsequent review and archival purposes. Video recordings have also been employed, with good results, to train caregivers (Beck et al., 2002). Furthermore, videos can be very useful as a communication tool between teachers and parents, who might not be able to be present during daily school activities or therapy.

In general, the automatic or even semiautomatic capture of such rich and sensitive data in classrooms (or in homes) raises concerns regarding information control, safety, and privacy (European Commission Article 29 Working Party, 2004). These risks may include obvious security risks such as the disclosure of personal information to unauthorized parties (which may cause legal liability), but also more subtle risks such as the misinterpretation of video sequences out-of-context by parties who were not present at the time of capture.

This application highlights the role of the system operators in securing the collected information, as well as the social and organizational aspects of the technology, which requires a broad consensus on its merits and risks in order to be effectively deployed.

ELEMENTS OF A SECURITY MANAGEMENT STRATEGY FOR UBICOMP APPLICATIONS

The social consequences of environmental data capture have been recognized since the beginnings in the ubicomp community: for example, surveillance technologies have long been the topic of critics, law researchers, and civil liberties unions (Bennet and Grant, 1999; Columbia Human Rights Law Review, 1973; Patton, 2000; Zarski, 2002). Researchers have long acknowledged that users may reject ubicomp applications due to concerns with the collection of massive amounts of information (Walmsley and Nielsen, 1991).

Most efforts on ubicomp security and privacy have concentrated on the technical aspects of these systems. Both general guidelines and solutions for specific applications have been published. Among the former are proposals to use the appropriately tailored versions of the FIPS (Fair Information Practices) (OECD, 1980) for ubicomp applications (Garfinkel, 2002; Langheinrich, 2001). Other researchers have used economic theories of information flows to formulate design guidelines for these applications (Jiang et al., 2002). Risk evaluation models have been also proposed for addressing privacy concerns (Hong et al., 2004). Some research groups have proposed solutions for specific applications as well; for example, for "awareness" applications (Bellotti and Sellen, 1993).

The data protection community in Europe has published management guidelines for video, telephone, and email surveillance in workplaces (e.g., Swiss Federal Data Protection Commissioner, 2000; UK Information Commissioner, 2003) and for CCTV systems (e.g., UK Information Commissioner, 2000). European Data Protection Authorities (or DPAs) have also published opinions that provide guidelines on the management of automated sensing technology, for example, video surveillance on commercial premises and private dwellings (European Commission Article 29 Working Party, 2004). The British Institute of International and Comparative Law compiled a summary of DPA rulings on video surveillance across the EU (British Institute of International and Comparative Law, 2003). A very interesting account of how CCTV systems are operated and managed on a day-to-day basis is provided by Norris and Armstrong (1999). Graham frames the development of CCTV systems as a fifth *utility*, and this conceptual approach is very similar to ours (Graham, 2004).

Except for these publications, there are very few practical management recommendations in the light of real-world experience and existing legislation. There are even fewer published resources on how integrated environmental information systems employing advanced technology such as pattern matching are managed. Traditional IT security management resources such as the publications of the National Institute of Standards and Technology (NIST, 1995) and the International Organization for Standardization (ISO, 2000) standards may provide some guidance, especially in relation to physical security management and the related controls. However, these standard guidelines were designed for traditional information systems and thus lack fundamental elements needed in the management of ubicomp technologies.

Based on experience gained in investigating and developing some of these technologies (both directly and through exchanges with our colleagues), we have identified a number of challenges to the effective security management in ubicomp systems:

- a thrust toward *decentralization of management functions,* which empowers individual users with new abilities and responsibilities;
- a dramatic change in the role of *administration and oversight* functions;
- an *widening gap between legislation's regulatory power and new technology's capabilities,* which impacts both policy makers and industry and engenders liability risks;
- disruptive development patterns with consequences for the capability of people to understand the tools they are using and the ensuing *acceptance* problems.

In this section, we discuss these challenges and suggest guidelines for the management of security of ubicomp systems. The discussion will draw upon the case studies introduced above and will highlight the different roles of manufacturers, users, and organizations in security management. The management suggestions provided below are not intended to be complete: traditional security management practices are still necessary in addition to these proposals (e.g., allowing access on a need-to-know basis, personnel management, etc.). We will also point out when traditional management approaches might not work well for ubicomp applications.

Management Decentralization

Ubicomp systems collect large amounts of data, which must be secured either because of regulatory requirements or because of its commercial or social value. As ubicomp systems increasingly pervade society, the ratio between the number of computers and the number of individuals responsible for their management decreases.

IT systems' governance is a complex problem, as highlighted in Chapter 3. However, these developments challenge even tested security management techniques, which rest on the assumption that responsibilities can be identified and allocated within an organized structure in order to deliver security policy implementation and enforcement.

As specialized personnel, able to tend to the system, become less available, information security management responsibilities must in part transition to the individuals who operate daily with the data. However, these individuals may not be motivated to enact strong security practices, due to several reasons, including that enacting security policies is not part of their mission within the organization or of their personal goals. Furthermore, users may lack necessary training and knowledge.

Exploiting Social Norms in Design

In personal applications such as PAL, security management responsibilities are assigned to the end user. However, security policies can be influenced up front by the manufacturer, by appropriately designing the system.

In order to avoid a PAL user knowingly and surreptitiously recording conversation partners, appropriate design could induce the user to refrain from using the application in certain situations, for instance, when it could cause security risks to himself/herself or to bystanders. Research in the social sciences has highlighted that the use of privacy-invasive technologies fits within a boundary negotiation process between individuals (Altman, 1975; Palen and Dourish, 2003). This process could be exploited to achieve specific security goals. For example, if all individuals are aware of and knowledgeable about the device, awareness cues about its presence could be made available to the people standing within its microphone range.

This case is similar to that of camera phones, which have recently enjoyed strong press coverage, including numerous news stories of abuse. Eventually, specific legislation, such as the U.S. Video

Voyeurism Prevention Act of 2004, has been enacted prohibiting inappropriate uses. Furthermore, some countries (e.g., South Korea) have mandated that picture-taking devices produce a "click" sound to inform the individuals present when a picture is being taken (Sung-jin, 2003).

With time, users may become accustomed to PAL's operation mode and develop an etiquette regarding the use of the device. PAL users may disable the device voluntarily while in situations that demand trust and confidentiality. For example, some participants of the PAL user studies told us that they would turn off PAL when they entered what they thought would be sensitive or confidential conversations.[5]

Not all management functions can be taken on by technology that imposes desired security management practices. In the CareLog system described above, for example, a video recording taken in a classroom may be provided to an external entity (e.g., a consultant) for examination. Designers might not be able to enforce security policies preventing misuse of those data. Clearly, organizational controls and oversight are still necessary for some applications.

Use of Licensing Schemes

A second option for reducing the potential negative implications of applications such as PAL is that of limiting their use to certain categories of users (thus, centralizing control back to regulatory authorities). Granted that PAL may be mostly useful for people with memory disabilities, a certification of such disability might be required for acquiring and using this application.

While this is common practice with numerous other technologies (e.g., motor vehicles), it should be considered that often the administrative costs imposed by a licensing scheme would be excessive in relation to the potential harm that the application may cause and to its expected profit.

Administration

The explosive growth of the number of ubicomp applications and devices makes system administration increasingly problematic, because competent IT personnel are being outnumbered by a plethora of small and widely dispersed computing systems.

Training

A typical approach for increasing the quality of IT administration has included training, which is often based on standardized management guidelines. These guidelines provide not only reference to sample applications, but also baseline guidance on matters relating to security, affordances and perceptual properties, retention times, and usage policies. Some of these guidelines, such as ISO 17799 (ISO, 2000), could be extended to ubicomp systems. Increasing, training efforts may be feasible only in structured settings, such as the schools in which CareLog is deployed. However, that application may be used in unconstrained settings, such as homes, and here formal training might not be easily implemented.

Self-Managing Software

Human administration can be expected only for computing systems of a certain minimum size. As ubicomp is characterized by automatic and unattended operation of large numbers of computing devices, it may be necessary that many everyday system administration tasks related to security become automatic, as suggested by the proponents of *autonomic computing* (Kephart and Chess, 2003).

To address the challenges brought on by the decentralization of systems management, researchers have been working on self-maintaining systems. For example, automatic patch installation is now commonplace on desktop operating systems. More sophisticated solutions, such as autonomic computing, foresee systems able to manage and repair themselves without user intervention, based on high-level human defined operational guidelines. Designers of ubicomp applications should include provisions for automatic administration early on in their designs.

Ubicomp Applications as Services

An alternative way to provide administration functions through technology is that of implementing ubicomp applications not as stand-alone, locally operated devices, but as services, provided for a fee by centralized organizations. For example, the CareLog application could be provided as a service to schools, externally managed by specialized entities, and not as a product under local control. In such a situation, management functions such as backups, software updates, and access control would be centralized. Further, by employing this kind of service provision, consultants and other stakeholders could be allowed to access recorded data while being prevented from further distributing the information, thus better ensuring confidentiality.

However, a third-party service provider may introduce additional confidentiality risks to pupils' personal information. These concerns could be addressed by contractual means, further increasing organizational complexity. Given these considerations, in practice, a service provision model may not be appropriate to schools in the United States because of the tight confidentiality requirements imposed by federal regulation such as FERPA, state, and local policies, and existing education professionals' practice.

Integrated Management Structure

In systems like CareLog, security management controls (such as maintaining proper backups, removing unnecessary data, etc.) can only be implemented to a limited degree by the primary users of the system (i.e., the caregivers and consultants). The reason is that this application needs to be used within preexisting educational and care practices, and therefore any management control that gets into the way of these practices is likely to be worked around or ignored, as prior experience in security management suggests. In addition, the deployment environment is not a high-security environment, and the personnel responsible for the day-to-day operation of the system are not ICT professionals.

Nevertheless, legislation as well as social and organizational expectations need to be complied with. In the CareLog case, in order to simplify security management, a straightforward option is to enact security management controls similar to those currently in place for other school records. The advantage of leveraging existing practices within the school organization reduces the need for training. However, the introduction of CareLog in schools may extend the knowledge about the information system to individuals who might have been previously unaware of the internals of school organization, such as parents. And parents' involvement (especially the parents of the children who are not benefiting directly from the system) is essential for acceptance.

Data Retention Management

Multimedia information collected within ubicomp systems may need to be stored for long periods of time. Long-term management of data presents very different technical and organizational requirements than short-term retention. While short-term storage can be accomplished within a framework of day-to-day activity (i.e., tapes or digital recordings of video can be overwritten systematically, media are in constant use in the recording cycle, etc.), permanent storage requires implementing physical and logic storage procedures and responsibilities. This implies resource accounting and tracking, responsibility allocation and transfer (if the person in charge changes), backup and data transfer procedures, and data destruction criteria and procedures. These are typical *data protection* concerns, which require comprehensive planning and oversight.

Oversight

A fundamental difference between the two case studies discussed in this chapter is the role and structure of oversight functions. As mentioned above, the responsibility for avoiding abuse of personal applications such as PAL largely rests on the individuals using them, and oversight is enacted through the day-to-day social interaction among users (Hayes et al., 2004a). For example, the fear of causing contentious reactions might discourage the user of PAL from activating the application in certain social settings or while talking with certain people.

Systems that are operated within organizations might be more amenable to formal oversight (e.g., CareLog deployed in a school). This kind of structured oversight is already required by some data protection legislation: organizations that manage personal data identify an individual responsible for the compliance of the organization's data processing practices with regulation and the data subject's rights (EU Directive 95/46, 1995 §18).

Oversight of Proliferating Applications

While, at the organizational level, local oversight as described above may be possible, the proliferation of ubicomp applications might require policy makers to rethink the role and functions of oversight authorities (e.g., DPAs), thus impacting security management practices.

Oversight authorities today are limited in their ability to regulate new applications. Apart from publishing sector-specific guidelines, their interventions are typically limited to providing opinions, granting permits for select applications, and responding to a few specific complaints. Extensive oversight of a booming ecosystem of applications that gather personal information, such as capture and access applications described here, would be impractical and costly.

From the security management standpoint, this requires planners and designers to become more aware of the opinions and guidelines published by oversight authorities and develop communication mechanisms with these entities. This is not always easy, since communication overhead with authorities like DPAs (in the United States, various government agencies such as the FCC and FTC are attributed similar functions) may be quite high. Manufacturers of mass-market technologies might be in a better position to interact with these entities than individual system integrators.

Oversight of Customizable Technology

The sheer number of installations is not the only reason why oversight systems might not be able to provide detailed guidance. Current trends in ubiquitous computing research are heading toward providing *tools* that end users can tailor to their needs rather than self-contained applications (Truong et al., 2004). The increasing relevance of interoperable tools will shift much responsibility from designers to system operators and end users. The ability to mix and match capture devices, analysis tools, and storage systems will enable many more individuals to create tailored applications, which will defy systematic oversight.

Oversight functions will require new tools for effectively monitoring and preventing abuse, both at the organizational and policy levels. This requires designers and security managers to perform, when making certain tools available, an analysis of the capabilities that users may acquire by combining different pieces of available information technology (and how likely it is that this might happen, based on skills required and associated cost).

Legality

In this section, we discuss the impact of legislation on various aspects of ubicomp system design and management, including data retention, informed consent, and the area affected by environmental sensing.

In both case studies, we performed a legislative analysis that provided valuable guidance.[6] The interpretation of legislation can be problematic for applications that do not fit the categorizations that the lawmakers had in mind when drafting existing legislation. This is especially true for legislation that is technology-dependent (e.g., the Electronic Communications Privacy Act or ECPA), and for implementation guidelines that accompany legislation, for instance, HIPAA rules (U.S. Department of Health and Human Services, 2002 and 2003), which often are a response to existing information management needs and consequently lack foresight.

Our experience has also shown that current regulation of IT security and privacy in certain domains (e.g., health care or financial applications) is not well fit for regulating ubicomp applications. There are few management or design guidelines that can be proposed for these problems, and we offer the following observations as warnings of where legal analysis may be cumbersome and produce uncertain results.

While it is not in the scope of this chapter to indicate how it might be enacted, policy or legislation change should not be discounted as a security management strategy, especially for very large systems—like has happened for CCTV surveillance or mandatory retention of telecommunication records (European Commission, 2004) or applications that might become very widespread (e.g., PAL).

Characterization of Data and Applications

In certain situations, legislation may curtail useful applications based on blunt rules instead of a realistic risk-benefit analysis. From the management standpoint, this causes uncertainty in both the requirements-definition process and in the identification of an optimal liability structure. For example, while the Personal Audio Loop does not keep a persistent record of the captured conversations, laws often fail to account for this nuance. ECPA does not contemplate transitory recordings, and regulates PAL just as it regulates the use of any ordinary audio recorder.[7] However, the risks engendered by PAL are arguably inferior to those that arise from an audio recorder because the recording is automatically deleted after a short time.

European legislation, touted as technology-neutral, attempts to address this issue by stating flexible requirements and by creating specific bodies in charge of interpreting the law for specific applications (national DPAs and the so-called Article 29 Working Party). These entities are responsible for issuing opinions on specific technologies or applications. In fact, DPAs have a large leeway in their decisions, as long as a plausible proportionality assessment shows that the benefits and the risks of the application are commensurable.

In the United States, regulation is more specific and the interpretation role of DPAs is assigned to the FTC, FCC, and in most cases to courts, which have, however, considerably less freedom in deciding what may be acceptable or not.

Differences across Jurisdictions

Often, subtle differences in legislation across jurisdictions can have complex technological consequences. For example, in the United States, the ECPA provides for the so-called one-party-consent rule, in which informed consent (to recording a conversation) by all conversation partners is not necessary as long as one party to the conversation is aware of the recording (i.e., the user of PAL). ECPA acts only as a baseline, however, and some states have introduced additional regulations that require *two-party consent*. This means that all conversations partners must agree. Further, some local legislation also introduces stronger safeguards such as notification cues such as "recorder beeps" or an indicator light, and privacy expectations vary across cultures (Altman, 1977).

It may not be sufficient for manufacturers to enforce these requirements by limiting the sale of devices and applications in different markets (which also has an economic impact), because users may carry (mobile) devices across national or state boundaries, thus making sale control ineffective. Different security policies or operating modes could be applied automatically in different jurisdictions, based on the location of the device. For example, PAL could easily calculate its location based on the identification number of the cell phone tower to which the phone is connected, and use this information to disable itself where using the application might pose a legal risk.

Leeway and Imprecise Legislation

Often, legislation does not provide clear guidance, and this can impact the security management of the technology. As example, consider informed consent requirements in the case of the PAL application.

In general, the user of PAL is supposed to request informed consent for recording from the other conversation partners. However, this is impractical due to the operating mode of the application. EU Directive 95/46/EC (European Union, 1995) exempts data collected for personal use (e.g., a personal diary or notebook) from informed consent requirements.[8] PAL is arguably a personal application, and users in our pilot study agreed with this characterization. Yet, a DPA might disagree, and in that case, users of very similar environmental recordings have been required to seek informed consent by all present individuals.

ECPA explicitly prohibits capturing a third party's conversation when the owner of the device is not part of that conversation and the conversation takes place with expectation that it is not being intercepted. In the case of PAL, this raises the concern of inadvertently recording passersby if they have an expectation of privacy. The problem is that this "expectation" is very difficult to translate into operational terms: the perceptual properties of sound might not grant constitutional basis in the United States for a reasonable expectation of privacy in public space. However, this has not yet been tested in court, so it would be risky to base a security strategy on this assumption.

Security management planners should identify these weak spots and devise their security strategy accordingly, allowing for alternative compliance methods, depending on what conclusion a court or DPA might reach on the acceptability of the application.

Balancing Application Purpose with Its Burden

A sound security strategy should not only consider the type of information captured, but also the *purpose* for capture. For example, in the CareLog system, videos of classrooms are stored and made available to a small group of individuals for enhancing the care of the observed children. Conceptually, this is a very similar setup to surveillance cameras installed for security purposes. The designer should however not be misled by the similarity, because the different purposes may tip the balance of acceptance against a certain application that may not be perceived as providing sufficient benefits in the face of the burden imposed on its stakeholders.

Legislation and courts often resort to *proportionality assessments* when judging the legality of novel technologies. Such proportionality assessments balance the potential burden imposed on individuals' privacy, security, or safety and the benefits provided by the application. These assessments, made by courts and DPAs, could be applied also to application design (Iachello and Abowd, 2005). However, for security managers or developers, it is often difficult to predict what conclusion a court or DPA would reach.

Impact of Sensor Design on Legality

Design and management choices can have a fundamental impact on the legality of ubicomp applications. In cases involving video surveillance units at home entrances, for example, DPAs have indicated that the area covered by the camera is one of the main factors of a proportionality determination that balances burden on privacy with usefulness (British Institute of International and Comparative Law, 2003). More generally, sensor reach and precision might need to be finely modulated to achieve a proportionality balance as indicated by published DPA opinions. This is not always possible. For example, sound propagates around obstructions. Therefore, while it is relatively simple to limit the view cone of a surveillance camera, limiting the radius of a microphone might be much more complex.

What Constitutes a Technology in Common Use?

Over the past several decades, many cases have centered upon the contrasting requirements of privacy and utility related to recording applications, and especially upon the definition of *reasonable expectation of privacy*. In *Katz v. United States* (1967), the U.S. Supreme Court extended the right of privacy to what the individual seeks to protect from the public—in this case, his phone communication. In the *Kyllo v. United States* (2001) case, the Supreme Court indicated that the subjects of surveillance have a reasonable expectation of privacy if the surveillance technology employed is not *in common use.*[9]

Clearly, this measure varies with time and technological development: the Personal Audio Loop is not in common use, and people do not associate a cell phone with environmental recording. On the other hand, one might argue that portable audio recorders are a readily available technology, and that PAL does not present any further risks than those posed by portable recorders. This requires designers of ubicomp applications and of security management plans to consider technological evolution and knowledge about technology at the social level as components of a comprehensive security strategy.

Contrasting Legislative Requirements

Some times, different applicable laws can produce contrasting requirements for a system design or its administration. For example, Table 10.3 summarizes a subset of U.S. legislation relevant to the CareLog application.

Table 10.3

Privacy Regulation Impacting CareLog

Regulation	Effect
Federal Educational Rights and Privacy Act (FERPA)	Regulates access to and confidentiality of records of students attending any federally funded educational institution
Health Insurance Portability and Accountability Act (HIPAA) (United States Health Insurance Portability and Accountability Act of 1996)	Regulates personal information held by health care service providers (insurances, hospitals, individuals, etc.)
Individuals with Disabilities Education Act (IDEA)	Guarantees children with disabilities a "free appropriate public education" in the least restrictive environment
Local regulation	Use of cameras in schools and related policies
Worker's statutes	Workers rights in workplaces, for example (ILO, 1993)

Consider informed consent requirements for environmental data collection. If personal information about children is collected in classrooms (such as a video recording of them in the classroom), the Federal Educational Rights and Privacy Act requires explicit informed consent by all data subjects involved in the recording in order to disclose such data outside the educational institution (e.g., to provide it to a caregiver external to the school). Normally, such consent would be provided by the parents of the children.

However, FERPA also requires schools to grant access to information collected about students to their guardians. In the case of video recordings, this may represent a significant burden on school authorities, because when disclosing information to one child's family, the privacy of the other children in the video should be preserved. It would thus be necessary to single out the parts of records pertaining to one specific child. Given the low semantic density of this information, searching through extensive video records is a time-consuming task that cannot be undertaken automatically, and is thus extremely expensive. This may in part explain why many schools have adopted the practice of deleting rich data after it has been analyzed.

While schools must comply with this requirement only if it entails a reasonable expense,[10] the letter of the law suggests the risk that such requests could be upheld in court. From a security strategy standpoint there may be various workarounds for avoiding liability, both technical and organizational. For example, in the case of video recordings in classrooms when many children are present, these workarounds may include:

- Asking all parents to partially forgo their rights in accessing these records. This might not be possible under some jurisdictions.
- Deleting nonessential recorded material.
- Limiting recording time and affected physical areas.
- Reducing the field of view of the camera to zoom into the subject and avoid recording other children.

Not all of the above solutions may be appropriate to the work practices of the caregivers, however. For example, reducing the field of view of the camera may exclude from the recording information essential for understanding a specific event (e.g., if something outside of the field of view of the camera has attracted a child's attention).

Another concern where incompatible legislative requirements may arise relates to the area and temporal span of the recording. As mentioned above, the area affected by environmental data capture can be a fundamental discriminator for application acceptance. A possible solution to the concerns of the other children in the classroom could be that of limiting automatic capture activity to special times or places (e.g., in separate rooms). However, current trends in educational and therapeutic communities endorse the inclusion of children with special needs in regular education classroom settings, a trend that is also encoded in legislation such as the Individuals with Disabilities Education Act (IDEA) in the United States.[11]

Adjudication

CareLog provides a compelling case study on how security management is influenced by adjudication issues between the beneficiaries and the secondary stakeholders of the application. In most cases, a security manager would have to heed the opposition of just one parent in the entire class to the use of CareLog.

This is a major issue in CareLog's security management strategy: gaining informed consent by all parents of the children who might be captured by the recordings may be possible, because of the closed environment represented by the school. However, it might be very impractical (that is, costly) to do so, and some parents might not assent, which leads to the issue of how to determine adjudication if some parents refuse to consent.

Parents of other children might perceive no benefit from this kind of capture, because their children do not need the records for their education and care, so they might be less likely to consent to recording. All these concerns cast doubt on whether such technology could be agreed on by all involved parties, notwithstanding its benefits.

Achieving unanimity in the modes and policies involved in the introduction of advanced technology is often impossible. Many successful systems, such as surveillance, have been deployed along different paths, engaging in a comprehensive adjudication process among competing concerns, preceded by lengthy and often acrimonious debate.

In developing a security strategy for these applications it might be more cost effective to bring a majority of stakeholders to buy into a technology or overall information policy rather than requesting informed consent from all of them. In applications such as CareLog, for example, instead of seeking assent from all involved parents on a case-by-case basis, it might be more effective to engage in a public information campaign and to make certain applications an integral part of organizational policy, with sufficient safeguards to gain a majority assent.

Liability

Manufacturers of ubicomp applications are concerned with reducing the liability they may be exposed to. Following industry best practices may help to reduce liability. Ubicomp technologies, from this perspective, are not different from other ICT, except that their interface with the physical world is much more complex, and best practice is not readily available. In many ubicomp applications, there are no set guidelines on what the application should do or what its functional or nonfunctional requirements should be. In this context, risk analysis and threat analysis have been proposed as tools to provide guidance on how the application should be developed, but there is still little experience to evaluate whether these tools are appropriate to the application domain and the development models (Hong et al., 2004).

Manufacturers can take a number of steps to reduce legal liability risks, as mentioned above, such as imposing security and usage policies through design and architectural choices and by limiting the market for certain applications. Finally, manufacturers may opt not to deploy certain applications at all in an effort to reduce liability risks. In the case of PAL this might seem exceedingly cautious, given that audio recording devices are readily available that are much more invasive than PAL. However, for different applications, this option should not be excluded.

Acceptance

The impact of rapidly evolving technology on society has been addressed compellingly elsewhere (Arnold, 2003; Latour, 1991; Lessig, 1999). Acceptance models have been developed in the MIS community (Venkatesh et al., 2003). Here, we do not intend to provide a comprehensive account but want to point out two characteristics of ubiquitous computing that make acceptance problematic: the invisibility of the technology and its automatic operation.

Ubicomp systems are intended to meld into everyday life to such a degree as to become *invisible* to the user. That is, they are intended to provide benefit to their users without being in the way of their goals and tasks and without the need for the users' attention, supervision, or management.

For example, PAL could not be effective if the user had to consciously and preventively activate the recording before speaking or hearing something that he or she might find useful later. An ordinary audio recorder would fit this purpose much better. Moreover, it is difficult to provide noticeable cues of its operation, because the cues could distract the people present. Invisibility is the fundamental reason why it is not compatible with legislation and people's expectations.

In CareLog, the technology is not necessarily invisible to its users, although in permanent installations cameras and microphones might be placed in locations that are somewhat recessed. In schools, it might be possible to place warning signs at the facility entrance, informing visitors of the presence and purpose of the cameras. However, in general, the purpose of the capture technology and its governing policies may not be apparent and understandable at first sight.

The *automatic operation* of ubicomp system presents similar challenges. The usefulness of both case studies hinges upon the ability to collect information automatically without prior explicit intervention.

In PAL, the bystanders' privacy can be achieved by certain technical means (i.e., by reducing the length of buffer storage and retention time, by impeding storage). However, this technical solution is contemplated neither by regulation nor by security best practices. Assessing risks and acting upon security and privacy controls requires knowledge of the status of the system (this is implied in most privacy and security principles, such as informed consent and audit). In fact, most security management best practices are based on the assumption of intentional interaction. This assumption breaks down in ubicomp systems such as those discussed in this chapter.

The acceptance of ubicomp technologies is related to perceptions of usefulness, safety, and security. Reflection on the CareLog case study suggests that evaluating acceptance is a fundamental component of a sound security management strategy.

Understanding and influencing acceptance patterns is a general problem in IT design and forms a research field in its own right. Facilitating acceptance requires a comprehensive strategy that ideally should involve all aspects of design, from conception, to requirements gathering, to development and deployment. Several tools are available to facilitate acceptance, including the use of specific design techniques, user training and education, and sound management planning. Acceptance facilitation is not a one-way process, but should involve a dialogue between designers and stakeholders, with the objective of reaching mutually acceptable compromises.

Participatory Design

It is important to consider that *impressions and opinions* about technology influence the acceptance of technology perhaps even more than legal and technical constrains. Participatory design can provide insight into the peculiarities of the organizational environment where the technology will be deployed.

While the CareLog project is still at the early stages of development, the long-term involvement of interested stakeholders, especially school officials, teachers, and parents has already provided compelling benefits. By building relationships with the involved stakeholders, the researchers involved in the CareLog development have gained understanding of the deployment environment. Interviews with professionals and parents have highlighted a set of concerns that are not necessarily codified in legislation but which affect deployment (for example, concerning informed consent for recording videos by children's parents).

Stakeholders' involvement may also increases acceptance of IT: proponents of participatory design work under the assumption that as people find themselves involved in the design of an application, they appropriate it as their own, and become directly interested in its success (Kensing and Blomberg, 1998). Experience in traditional IT development suggests that participatory design may uncover potential usage problems early on during the design of a system, with a positive impact on security management as well. Clearly, the benefits of participatory design are only felt if systems are developed on a case-by-case basis for each organization and not in mass-market applications.

Education and Training

In some cases, participatory design is not feasible with all the users of an application (e.g., an application like PAL that could be deployed on a large scale as add-on software for a mobile phone). In these cases, other ways of informing the users and the public at large should be employed. "Camera-phones" present a good example of this: initially, people were unaccustomed to their function. Market penetration of these devices has been extremely rapid, and the public has been informed, mainly through the news and advertisement outlets, about functions and potential misuse patterns.

However, the massive effort in the media to make customers knowledgeable of this technology and develop appropriate strategies for coping with privacy concerns has not been considered sufficient to prevent misuse. The concern brought on by that technology was so overwhelming that it prompted specific legislation (for instance, the Voyeurism Prevention Act of 2004 in the United States). Public knowledge of how technology works might also lower liability risks, as it allocates responsibility for misuse and prevention to the users and other stakeholders.

Lobbying Stakeholders

Public campaigning constitutes a valuable tool for facilitating acceptance, especially when the target audience is relatively small and shares common concerns and benefits from the technology being introduced. Below we discuss the analogies and differences between the use of CareLog and video surveillance in schools, and argue that video surveillance technology has been made acceptable to or imposed on a majority of interested parties, in many cases through persistent and concerted efforts of school and law enforcement officials.

Table 10.4

Attributes of Information Collected by PAL

Attribute		Notes
Semantic density	Low	Most of the time and for most users, the audio recorded by PAL may be little interest to attackers (e.g., thieves, or the person carrying of the device). In fact, most of the time, the device may be recording silent surroundings, especially in non-work environments.
Richness	High	Spoken voice is a rich medium because it allows for nuanced communication and for the identification of the speaker.
Sensitivity	Low— occasionally high	In most situations and for most users, everyday conversations do not include sensitive information. However, in some instances the recorded conversations can be sensitive.

In many cases, the question is not whether stakeholders can be convinced to "buy into" this specific technology, but *how much effort* is required to achieve this goal. This problem is not limited to the applications discussed here, but is a typical trait of emerging technologies' acceptance dynamics (Venkatesh et al., 2003). These considerations have a fundamental impact on designers and on the socio-technological balance intrinsic to the development of novel applications, as the cost of technical measures intended to comply with stakeholders' claims should not exceed the cost of convincing stakeholders to forgo such claims.

SECURITY STRATEGY DESIGN AND MANAGEMENT DESIGN

A number of tools are available to designers for designing applications and their management structures while reducing security and privacy concerns. In this book, several chapters provide details on security management methods, such as Chapter 4. In this section, we focus on developing security management strategies specifically for ubicomp applications. Moreover, we briefly discuss how security management can be designed into applications.

Information Characterization and Application Design

Above, we provided a characterization of environmental information that can be useful for the analysis of the security and in the design of ubicomp applications. Table 10.4 shows the attributes of the environmental data captured by the PAL application. By comparing Table 10.4 with Table 10.2, some data management security requirements that are particularly important emerge for PAL, including:

1. preventing the disclosure of information;
2. implementing safeguards to reduce the rate of access to recorded information (and thus, potentially, increase the cost of misuse); and
3. control unauthorized replication of data.

In order to reduce the likelihood of PAL being misused, one of several user interface features or information policies could be manipulated, including the visual appearance of the device (e.g., adding a blinking red light to signal that the device is recording), the range of the microphone, and the tools available for searching and navigating the recorded audio.

Table 10.5

Attributes of Information Collected by CareLog

Attribute		Notes
Semantic density	Low	Most of the time and for most users, video recordings are of little interest; only specific events, of short temporal duration, are of interest to any stakeholder.
Richness	High	Video is a rich medium.
Sensitivity	High	Relates to minors and for the subjects of therapy; also includes health-related data and educational data subject to specific regulatory requirements.

In order to meet security goal 1 above (preventing disclosure of information), various design variables can be manipulated. Retention time should be kept as low as possible and permanent storage should be disallowed by the device. In order to meet security requirement 2 (safeguards to reduce rate of access), the device should have a balanced cost of accessing stored information. In order to meet requirement 3 (avoiding replication), PAL should not allow storing conversations nor should it be easy to transfer the recorded audio to a permanent recording device.

As the flexibility and power of mobile phones increases, it is becoming increasingly easy to develop applications such as PAL without control or consent by the operator or manufacturers. While most manufacturers include an audible "click" when a picture is taken with a camera phone, it is just a matter of time until independent software developers come up with applications that do not incorporate precautions such as the click or limits on the design variables discussed above. For example, in PAL it would be relatively simple to reverse-engineer the software on the phone and increase the retention time—after all, memory is virtually limitless on modern phones. This leaves a number of alternatives to manufacturers for limiting undesired changes to software applications like PAL.

One possibility is that of implementing certification programs for add-on software on what are supposed to be trusted platforms. Nokia has adopted this approach with Java software, which must carry a certificate in order to access some of the more sophisticated phone features. Many manufacturers, however, in the effort to create large markets for their devices, have adopted open development models. Thus, controlling software development may only be a stopgap measure.

Blocking certain hardware functions might be more effective than controlling software development: after all, these highly integrated systems are difficult to modify without large investments in manufacturing facilities. Finally, there have been proposals to use radio transmitters to automatically inform the phone of the allowed activities in a certain environment (Perry, 2005). This would, however, require industry standardization, consensus by manufacturers, and, again, the availability of trusted platforms.

Table 10.5 shows the characteristics of the video data collected by CareLog. The users of the data have interest in two kinds of events:

- exceptional circumstances that need to be investigated (as mentioned above), and that may happen occasionally; and
- activities such as planned therapeutic interventions and specific tasks the child is engaged in.

Both events may span a small fraction of a recording covering the entire day at school. This causes the semantic density of the information to be low. The richness of the information is, again, high, for reasons similar to the PAL case: video is an expressive, rich medium that is difficult to manipulate. Finally, the information contained in these recordings is sensitive, unlike the audio recorded by PAL in most instances. Much of this information relates to minors with special needs; even if this does not cause the information to increase in sensitivity per se, social if not legal convention requires specific controls to avoid disclosures that could affect individuals who are not able to consent to the collection of data about them. Moreover, in the case of the subjects of the interventions, the collected data may be considered health-related and thus subject to relevant requirements.

Cross-comparison with Table 10.2 suggests that relevant security goals for the kinds of information collected and stored in this system include:

- Prevent unauthorized disclosure
- Control access rate
- Prevent replication
- Guarantee integrity
- Control usage of data
- Control data handling

These security goals can be achieved by leveraging appropriate design options. The prevention of unauthorized disclosure and unauthorized replication of the data can be achieved in various ways, including implementing access control and gathering access logs to the information. The deployment environment of this application already has security management policies for personal information in place, and CareLog's implementation could leverage, where appropriate, the organizational knowledge and practice embedded in these policies. The reduction of the access rate to the information can be achieved by manipulating the effectiveness of access and browsing facilities provided with the application. Since this manipulation may have a crucial impact on system usability, this requirement must be balanced among these competing needs.

The control of data handling, use, and integrity may be achieved by a mix of technical (e.g., backup procedures) and organizational (e.g., training of people responsible for handling the data) measures. Typical data protection management techniques may be employed for this purpose (Iachello, 2003), although the type of collected data might make redress compliance onerous for school officials. A solution that has been proposed by the designers of CareLog is to keep video recordings only as long as is necessary for compiling written syntheses of the information of interest and discarding them immediately thereafter. This reflects existing practice in many schools.

Design by Analogy

Traditional IT applications such as those used in marketing, financial services, healthcare, or e-commerce, are, by now, quite well understood, and a wide range of solutions is provided by regulation and industry best practice (British Institute for International and Comparative Law, 2003; UK Information Commissioner, 2003). Conversely, given the limited prior knowledge and experience in designing ubicomp applications, guidelines and best practices are still lacking. Academic research has started only recently to uncover these issues and proposing design guidelines, but much more work is necessary to achieve reliable design techniques.

One approach to the problem is that of *designing by analogy,* that is, analyzing existing applications that are technically and organizationally similar to the one being designed, with con-

Table 10.6

Comparison of Video Surveillance and CareLog

	Security video surveillance	CareLog
Purpose	Security, although deviant student behavior is also being tracked (Paige, 2005)	Behavioral therapy
Beneficiary	School administration, students, teachers	Individual student, parents, teachers
Burdened parties	Students, teachers, school staff	Students, teachers
Oversight	School officials, police	School administration, caregivers
Access	School officials, police	Caregivers, teachers, parents, professional therapists
Deployment areas	Public areas, hallways, entrances, external premises	Classrooms, homes, other places of daily activity

sideration of how differences between the two applications might affect the security management requirements of the new application. Applications that are already deployed incorporate a wealth of knowledge on social practices and economic compromises that might be difficult to assess from scratch with a new system. Given the usefulness of this technique for developing security strategies for ubicomp applications, we will provide below an example of how this technique could be applied by comparing CareLog with security surveillance.

This process provides two advantages: First, it grounds design and policy choices on experience with existing systems, thus lending reliability and credibility to the security analysis. Second, it allows defining expectations on the security management, and defining what security policies will be reasonable to enforce in the new systems.

The knowledge present in the existing benchmark applications might not be available explicitly, but can be recovered by analyzing the application and the related social practices. How the analysis is to be performed depends on the type of application. We propose to focus on five types of differences:

- Purpose of the application
- Stakeholders (both beneficiaries and burdened parties)
- Oversight functions
- Access policies
- Deployment scope

Here, we compare CareLog with video surveillance. While the introduction of surveillance cameras in schools (Paige, 2005) is greeted in some cases by protests, it is nevertheless making its way inside these institutions. Often cameras are installed in the communal areas (entrances hallways, lunch rooms, and so on), but in some cases, also in classrooms. Often, surveillance is deployed after a record of violent or deviant behaviors or acts of vandalism.[12] The use of video recording within classrooms for the purpose of conducting diagnostic, therapeutic, and other activities is, however, different from surveillance functions in various respects, as summarized in Table 10.6. The table shows an overview comparing security surveillance with CareLog in terms of purpose, beneficiaries, burdened parties, and access and oversight functions.

The stated purposes for using video cameras are different for the two applications. Using video recording for security purposes is becoming an increasingly accepted practice, thanks to a great effort expended by school and local authorities to convince the public of its merits. In fact, surveillance cameras are becoming an accepted part of the technological infrastructure of schools and protests about the potential negative impact of these systems have been subdued in the face of the perceived increase of safety and security brought on by the technology. Repurposing existing infrastructure or deploying new cameras for interventions on children with special needs may require spending an additional effort to convince all stakeholders of their appropriateness and utility. Although compelling claims could be made about society's gains from better treatment and integration of individuals with disabilities, the individuals likely to benefit directly from such technology constitute a much smaller group than those gaining from security cameras.

Strict organizational measures are usually in place to ensure the use, confidentiality, and retention of the video data captured by surveillance cameras. Only a few individuals, in key management positions, ordinarily have access to the camera feeds and stored recordings. These policies are regulated at the EU and national levels in Europe, and DPAs have been particularly active in this domain during the past commission (1999–2004), publishing several reports and guidelines documents (European Commission Article 29 Working Party, 2004). Several countries have published similar guidelines—for example, Canada (Information and Privacy Commissioner of Ontario, 2001) and Switzerland. In the United States, regulation of surveillance cameras in public places, including public schools, is performed at the local level, for example, Washington, D.C. (Washington D.C., n.d.) and New York City (New York City, 2004). Often these policies include the following elements:

- Limitations on retention time (e.g., 10–30 days)
- Measures to prevent unauthorized access (need court order to retain recordings, access control)
- Identification and allocation of management and oversight responsibilities
- Limitations on where cameras can be installed
- Limitations on the use of the technology and of the collected data
- Limitations on acceptable objects of observations

Such a strong regulatory framework makes schools' case for installing surveillance cameras relatively acceptable.

The deployment of the CareLog system differs from surveillance. First, the collected video is available to many more individuals than surveillance cameras recordings, which, according to many local and national guidelines, are supposed to be never accessed under normal circumstances (European Commission Article 29 Working Party, 2004). Regulatory contexts change considerably across jurisdictions, however; local policies may give school officials considerable leeway in the security management of video collected through security cameras (New York City, 2004). The openness required by the effective use of the data within an application like CareLog presents a heightened risk of confidentiality breaches. In both types of applications, there is a risk that responsibilities in data management may not be spelled out clearly and allocated among the various individuals having access to the recorded data.

In addition to differences in the stakeholders, oversight responsibilities, and access, intrinsic to the application is that the collected data (video footage) is both personally identifiable and generally considered sensitive because it refers to minors with special needs and may be health related. The collection of video in classrooms is also qualitatively different from video recorded in public spaces such as hallways, because classrooms are occupied for much longer periods and more complex activities take place in them.

Summarizing, this example of design by analogy has suggested three primary elements of a security strategy for the CareLog applications:

- A strong information management policy, that can effectively enforce maximum retention times for data, and limited data capture
- A targeted campaigning effort aimed at convincing secondary stakeholders of the application's usefulness and benefits for the greater community
- A flexible access control policy that encourages all users of the collected data to prevent or minimize inappropriate uses

An important caveat that applies to design by analogy is that, in many organizations, actual practice diverges from written policies. This relates to the classic "dusty shelf" problem of policy and procedures documents: organizational standards are left to gather dust on a shelf and are not really followed—a concern often raised in connection with certification programs like ISO9001. This can happen for a variety of reasons, and it is not in the scope of this chapter to address the problems related to architecture recovery. However, designers should be especially aware of the gap between official policy and actual practice, especially with regard to security requirements, when analyzing existing security management models. Security models, which were initially developed for military applications, are especially vulnerable to this problem because they are often inadequate for the needs of commercial organizations and individuals (Povey, 2003). Therefore, designers should be careful to gain an understanding of how a reference IT application really is used, and not how it was *intended to* be used.

FUTURE RESEARCH DIRECTIONS

Security management for ubicomp is a field that has not been yet considered in depth due to the lack of real-world experience with the technology. However, ubicomp applications are reaching the market, and security management will become increasingly relevant because recent experience with traditional computing systems has shown that it is one of the weakest links in information security.

This chapter has indicated some techniques and options for planning and enforcing particular security policies available to managers and designers. These tools include design by analogy, the analysis of existing legislation, ways to accelerate acceptance, and techniques to reduce industrial liability; we offered two case studies that demonstrate how these tools were used in practice to achieve a security strategy that is both credible and defensible. These tools provide some elements of a comprehensive security management strategy.

However, many issues must still be addressed. Relevant future research themes include:

- how to reconcile traditional information security management, which rests on clear roles definition and on the visibility of the information system, with applications that run unattended and unnoticed;
- how to facilitate acceptance by all involved stakeholders (specifically relating to security, safety and privacy concerns);
- ways of increasing the exchanges between legislative and regulatory bodies and manufacturers and service providers in order to reduce development risks and liability;

- novel design techniques that can incorporate experience from past applications to this novel class of technologies.

We hope that by pointing out some of the relevant issues in this chapter, we will be able to motivate researchers and practitioners to devote more attention to these issues.

ACKNOWLEDGMENTS

This work was funded in part by the National Science Foundation through the GRFP, by the MacArthur Foundation, and Georgia Institute of Technology. We thank for their collaboration on projects related to this work and thoughtful comments: Joseph Benin, Kris Nagel, Shwetak Patel, and Khai Truong. Shwetak Patel and Khai Truong wrote the PAL application. In particular, we would like to thank Gillian Hayes for providing access to her research experience and knowledge of the CareLog project and for greatly improving drafts of this chapter with her sharp and to-the-point comments. This work would not have been possible without her collaboration. We also thank Sy Goodman and Merrill Warkentin for revising drafts of the chapter.

NOTES

1. We are excluding from this table biometrics technologies. Despite current with imminent impact on society (e.g., personal authentication [International Civil Aviation Organization, 2004]), our assessment suggests that biometrics may not be yet reliable and efficient enough for ubicomp applications (e.g., recognition of people in unconstrained, unattended environments) (Balint, 2003).

2. For example, a natural criterion of video recording organization is time, and given a certain moment in time, it is almost immediate to retrieve data relating to it. However, it would be very expensive to find all green objects that appear in a video database; this would entail performing an exhaustive video analysis of the entire recording.

3. "[It is] a crime for any person to corruptly alter, destroy, mutilate, or conceal any document with the intent to impair the object's integrity or availability for use in an official proceeding" (United States Sarbanes-Oxley Act of 2002).

4. This system is conceptually similar to Northrop Grumman's TRIMARC traffic monitoring system (Northrop Grumman Corp., 2002).

5. Caution is due in generalizing this assessment, because we do not know how such behaviors would manifest themselves in large social groups.

6. It should be stressed that *we are not legal scholars*—the analysis of legislation affecting PAL and CareLog is not intended to provide legal opinion on these applications. The purpose of our analysis is only that of extracting initial guidelines and requirements.

7. ECPA (the U.S. Electronic Communications Privacy Act of 1986) applies to any electronic recording device and to any conversation ("oral communication") between two persons "exhibiting an expectation that such communication is not subject to interception," even if the conversations are not transmitted through a telecommunications network—this includes the PAL application.

8. Directive 95/46/EC (European Union, 1995) applies to any personally identifiable information. Historically, the directive regulated the collection of personal data by organizations in large text-oriented databases. Recently, however, Data Protection Authorities (DPA) (European Commission Article 29 Working Party, 2004) have pointed out that audio recordings of voice conversations are covered by the directive. EU Directive 2002/58/EC (European Union, 2002) regulates the provision of telecommunication services (both voice and data), and mandates their confidentiality.

9. Further information on the details of these and other U.S. Supreme Court decisions can be found at www.findlaw.com/casecode/supreme.html. A comprehensive historical account (limited to 1972) can be found in a book published by the Columbia Human Rights Law Review (1973).

10. Historically, this regulation was intended for an information environment based on paper documents and structured database records, which are relatively easy to search and "clean" from other students' data.

11. IDEA guarantees children with disabilities a "free appropriate public education" in the least restrictive

environment (U.S. Individuals with Disabilities Education Act of 1977), often regular education classroom settings.

12. While these kinds of technologies may be installed for a specific purpose, once in place they might be repurposed. So, surveillance cameras installed in schools for preventing or documenting serious crimes could then be used for prosecuting minor offences, such as students smoking.

REFERENCES

Altman, I. 1975. *The Environment and Social Behavior—Privacy, Personal Space, Territory, Crowding.* Monterey, CA: Brooks/Cole.

Altman, I. 1977. Privacy regulation: culturally universal or culturally specific? *Journal of Social Issues*, 33, 3, 66–84.

Arnold, M. 2003. On the phenomenology of technology: the "Janus-faces" of mobile phones. *Information & Organization*, 13, 231–256.

Australian Information Economy Advisory Council. 2004. *National Bandwidth Inquiry: Bandwidth 2000–2004* (available at www.dcita.gov.au, accessed on April 4, 2004).

Balint, K. 2003. No "Snooper Bowl" for San Diego; police won't be using face-scanning technology that sparked ire in Tampa. *San Diego Union-Tribune*, January 20.

Beck, R.J.; King, A.; Marshall, S.K. 2002. Effects of videocase construction on preservice teachers' observations of teaching. *Journal of Experimental Education*, 70, 4, 345–361.

Bellotti, V., and Sellen, A. 1993. Design for privacy in ubiquitous computing environments. Proceedings of ECSCW '93. Dordrecht: Kluwer Academic Publishers, pp. 77–92.

Bennet, C., and Grant, R. (eds.). 1999. *Visions of Privacy: Policy Choices for the Digital Age.* Toronto: University of Toronto.

Berghell Associates LLC. 2004. *Projecting the Cost of Magnetic Storage over the Next 10 Years* (available at www.berghell.com/whitepapers.htm, accessed on April 4, 2004).

British Institute of International and Comparative Law. 2003. *The Implementation of Directive 95/46/EC to the Processing of Sound and Image Data* (available at www.europa.eu.int).

Brusilovsky, P. 2000. Web lectures: electronic presentations in web-based instruction. *Syllabus*, 13, 5, 18–23.

Columbia Human Rights Law Review. 1973. *Surveillance, Dataveillance and Personal Freedoms: Use and Abuse of Information Technology.* Fair Lawn, NJ: Burdick.

The Economist. 2004. Trucking hell. February 19.

Elmagarmid, A. et al. 1997. *Video Database Systems: Issues, Products, and Applications.* Boston: Kluwer Academic Publishers.

European Commission. 2004. *DG INFSO—DG JAI Consultation Document on Traffic Data Retention*, July 30 (available at http://europa.eu.int/information_society/topics/ecomm/doc/useful_information/library/public_consult/data_retention/consultation_data_retention_30_7_04.pdf).

European Commission Article 29 Working Party. 2003. *Working Document on Biometrics.* 12168/02/EN WP80 (available at http://europa.eu.int).

European Commission Article 29 Working Party. 2004. *Opinion 4/2004 on the Processing of Personal Data by Means of Video Surveillance.* 11750/02/EN WP 89 (available at www.europa.eu.int).

European Union. 1995. Directive 95/46/EC of the European Parliament and of the Council of 24 October 1995 on the protection of individuals with regard to the processing of personal data and on the free movement of such data. *European Union Official Journal*, L281, 31–50.

European Union. 2002. Directive 2002/58/EC of the European Parliament and of the Council of 12 July 2002 concerning the processing of personal data and the protection of privacy in the electronic communications sector (Directive on privacy and electronic communications). *European Union Official Journal*, L201, 37–47.

Foresti, G.; Mähönen, P.; and Regazzoni, C. 2000. *Multimedia Video-based Surveillance Systems: Requirements, Issues and Solutions.* Norwell, MA: Kluwer Academic Publishers.

Garfinkel S. 2002. *Adopting fair information practices to low cost RFID systems.* Ubiquitous Computing 2002 Privacy Workshop (available at www.teco.edu/~philip/ubicomp2002ws/, accessed on: January 10, 2005).

Gaver, W.; Moran, T.; MacLean, A.; Lovstrand, L.; Dourish, P.; Carter, K.; and Buxton, W. 1992. *Realizing a video environment: EuroPARC's RAVE system.* Proceedings of the Conference on Human Factors in Computing Systems CHI '92. Monterey, CA: ACM Press, pp. 27–35.

Geyer, W.; Richter, H.; Fuchs, L.; Frauenhofer, T.; Daijavad, S.; Poltrock, S. 2001. *TeamSpace: A Collaborative Workspace System Supporting Virtual Meetings.* IBM Research Report, RC21961.

Global Information Inc. 2003. Press release, October 8 (available at www.the-infoshop.com/press/cg15968_en.shtml, last accessed on January 17, 2005).

Graham, S. 2004. CCTV: the stealthy emergence of a fifth utility? *Planning Theory and Practice*, 3, 2, 237–241.

Grochowski, E., and Halem, R.D. 2003. Technological impact of magnetic hard disk drives on storage systems. *IBM Systems Journal*, 42, 2, 338–346.

Guidry, J., and van den Pol, R. 1996. Augmenting traditional assessment and information: the videoshare model. *Topics in Early Childhood Special Education*, 16, 1 (March 1).

Harter, A., and Hopper, A. 1994. A distributed location system for the active office. *IEEE Network*, 8, 1, 62–70.

Hayes G.R.; Patel, S.N.; Truong, K.N.; Iachello, G.; Kientz, J.A.; Farmer R.; and Abowd, G.D. 2004a. *The personal audio loop: designing a ubiquitous audio-based memory aid.* Proceedings of Mobile HCI 2004, LNCS 3160. Berlin: Springer Verlag, pp. 168–179.

Hayes, G.R.; Kientz, J.; Truong, K.N.; White, D.; Abowd, G.D.; and Pering, T. 2004b. *Designing capture applications to support the education of children with autism.* Proceedings of 6th International Conference on Ubiquitous Computing Ubicomp 2004, LNCS 3205. Berlin: Springer Verlag, pp. 161–178.

Hong, J.I.; Ng, J.D.; Lederer, S.; and Landay, J.A. 2004. *Privacy risk models for designing privacy-sensitive ubiquitous computing systems.* Proceedings of the 2004 Conference on Designing interactive Systems DIS '04. New York: ACM Press, pp. 91–100.

Iachello, G. 2003. *Protecting personal data: can IT security management standards help?* Proceedings of 19th Annual Computer Security Applications Conference ACSAC 2003. Las Vegas, NV: IEEE Press, pp. 266–275.

Iachello, G., and Abowd, G.D. 2005. *Privacy and proportionality: adapting legal evaluation techniques to inform design in ubiquitous computing.* Proceedings of the Conference on Human Factors in Computing Systems CHI 2005. New York: ACM Press, pp. 91–100.

International Civil Aviation Organization. 2004. *Biometrics Deployment of Machine Readable Travel Documents Technical Report.* ICAO TAG MRTD/NTWG, Version 1.9 (available at www.icao.int/mrtd).

Information and Privacy Commissioner of Ontario. 2001. *Guidelines for Using Video Surveillance Cameras in Public Places*, October (available at www.ipc.on.ca/docs/video-e.pdf, accessed on March 7, 2005).

ILO. 1993. Special series on workers privacy Part II: monitoring and surveillance in the workplace. *Conditions of Work Digest*, 12, 1. International Labor Organization.

ISO. 2000. ISO/IEC 17799:2000 *Information Technology—Code of Practice for Information Security Management.* ISO, 2000. International Organization for Standardization/International Electrotechnical Commission.

Jiang, X.; Hong, J.I.; and Landay, J.A. 2002. *Approximate information flows: socially-based modeling of privacy in ubiquitous computing.* Proceedings of 4th International Conference on Ubiquitous Computing Ubicomp 2002, LNCS 2498. Berlin: Springer Verlag, pp. 176–193.

Katz v. United States, 389 U.S. 347; 88 S. Ct. 507 (1967).

Kensing, F., and Blomberg, J., 1998. Participatory design: issues and concerns. *Computer Supported Cooperative Work*, 7, 167–185.

Kephart J., and Chess, D. 2003. The vision of autonomic computing. *IEEE Computer*, 36, 1, 41–50.

Kyllo v. United States, 121 S. Ct. 2038; 150 L. Ed. 2d 94; 2001 U.S. LEXIS 4487 (2001).

Langheinrich, M. 2001. *Privacy by design—principles of privacy-aware ubiquitous systems.* Proceedings of the 3rd International Conference on Ubiquitous Computing Ubicomp 2001, LNCS 2201. Berlin: Springer Verlag, pp. 273–291.

Latour, B. 1991. *We've Never Been Modern.* Translated by Catherine Porter. Cambridge, MA: Harvard University Press.

Lessig, L. 1999. The architecture of privacy. *Vanderbilt Journal of Entertainment Law & Practice*, 1, 1, 56.

Libicki, M. 2000. *Who Runs What in the Global Information Grid.* Santa Monica, CA: RAND.

Maheu, M.M.; Whitten, P.; and Allen, A. 2001. *E-Health, Telehealth, and Telemedicine: A Guide to Start-up and Success.* Jossey-Bass Health Series. San Francisco: Jossey Bass.

Mynatt, E.D.; Rowan, J.; Craighill, S.; and Jacobs, A. 2001. *Digital family portraits: providing peace of mind for extended family members.* Proceedings of the Conference on Human Factors in Computing Systems (CHI 2001). New York: ACM Press, pp. 333–340.

NIST. 1995. *An Introduction to Computer Security: The NIST Handbook.* Special Publication 800–12. National Institute of Standards and Technology (available at http://csrc.nist.gov/publications/nistpubs/index.html, accessed on April 10, 2005).

New York City. 2004. *Introduction No. 150-A 2004, A Local law to amend the New York City charter, in relation to requiring the Department of Education, in consultation with the New York City Police Department, to install security cameras at New York City public schools* (available at www.nyccouncil.info, last accessed on November 28, 2005).

Norris, C., and Armstrong, G. 1999. *The Maximum Surveillance Society: The Rise of CCTV.* Oxford, England: Berg.

Northrop Grumman Corp. 2002. *TRIMARC—Automatic Incident Recording System* (available at www.trimarc.org/perl/about_trimarc.pl and www.nascio.org/scoring/files/2002Kentucky7.doc, accessed on April 2, 2004).

OECD. 1980. *Guidelines on the Protection of Privacy and Transborder Flows of Personal Data.* Organization for Economic Cooperation and Development (available at www.oecd.org).

Orr, R.; Raymond, R.; Berman, J.; and Seay, A.F. 1999. *A System for Finding Frequently Lost Objects in the Home.* GVU Technical Report GIT-GVU-99–24, Georgia Institute of Technology.

Paige, C. 2005. Security cameras in schools debated. *Boston Globe*, February 24.

Palen, L., and Dourish, P. 2003. *Unpacking "privacy" for a networked world.* Proceedings of the Conference on Human Factors in Computing Systems CHI 2003. New York: ACM Press, pp. 129–136.

Patton, J.W. 2000. Protecting privacy in public? Surveillance technologies and the value of public places. *Ethics and Information Technology*, 2, 181–187.

Pedersen, E.R.; McCall, K.; Moran, T.P.; and Halasz, F.G. 1993. *Tivoli: an electronic whiteboard for informal workgroup meetings.* Proceedings of the SIGCHI Conference on Human Factors in Computing Systems CHI 1993. New York: ACM Press, pp. 391–398.

Perry, S. 2005. *HP Blur Photos with Camera Privacy Patent.* January (available at www.digital-lifestyles.info/display_page.asp?section=business&id=1888, accessed on March 7, 2005).

Povey, D. 2003. *Optimistic security: a new access control paradigm.* Proceedings of the New Security Paradigms Workshop NSPW 1999. Ontario, Canada: ACM Press, pp. 40–45.

Sung-jin, K. 2003. Camera phone to require shutter sound from next yr. *Korea Times*, November 11.

Swiss Federal Data Protection Commissioner 2000. 7. Tätigkeitsbericht 1999 / 2000 (7th Annual Report 1999/2000) (available at www.edsb.ch/).

Truong, K.N.; Abowd G.D.; and Brotherton, J.A. 2001. *Who, what, when, where, how: design issues of capture & access applications.* Proceedings 3rd International Conference on Ubiquitous Computing Ubicomp 2001, LNCS 2201. Berlin: Springer Verlag, pp. 209–224.

Truong, K.N.; Huang, E.M.; and Abowd G.D. 2004. *CAMP: a magnetic poetry interface for end-user programming of capture applications for the home.* Proceedings of 6th International Conference on Ubiquitous Computing Ubicomp, LNCS 3205. Berlin: Springer Verlag, pp. 143–160.

UK Information Commissioner. 2000. *CCTV Code of Practice* (available at: http://www.informationcommissioner.gov.uk/).

UK Information Commissioner. 2003. *The Employment Practices Data Protection Code: Part 3: Monitoring at Work* (available at www.informationcommissioner.gov.uk/).

United States Department of Justice—Computer Crime and Intellectual Property Section—Criminal Division. 2002. *Searching and Seizing Computers and Obtaining Electronic Evidence in Criminal Investigations* (available at www.cybercrime.gov).

United States Electronic Communications Privacy Act of 1986. 18 USC § 2510 et seq.

United States Family Educational Rights and Privacy Act of 1974. 20 USC § 1232g et seq.

United States Health Insurance Accountability and Portability Act of 1996. 42 USC § 1320 et seq.

United States Individuals with Disabilities Education Act of 1997. 20 USC § 1400 et seq.

United States Sarbanes-Oxley Act of 2002. 15 USC § 7201 et seq.

United States Video Voyeurism Prevention Act of 2004. 18 USC § 1801 et seq.

U.S. Department of Health and Human Services. 2002. Standards for Privacy of Individually Identifiable Health Information; Final Rule. 45 CFR Parts 160 and 164, August.

U.S. Department of Health and Human Services. 2003. Health Insurance Reform: Security Standards; Final Rule. 45 CFR Parts 160, 162, and 164, February.

Venkatesh, V.; Morris, M.G.; Davis, G.B.; and Davis, F.D. 2003. User acceptance of information technology: toward a unified view. *MIS Quarterly*, 27, 3, 425–478.

Walmsley, T., and Nielsen, S. 1991. *The Videoshare Project. Instruction and Classroom Videotaping Guide,* Education Resources Information Center (ERIC), Publication ED376653 (available at www.eric.ed.gov).

Want, R.; Pering, T.; Danneel, G.; Kumar, M.; Sundar, M.; and Light, J. 2002. *The personal server: changing the way we think about ubiquitous computing.* Proceedings 4th International Conference on Ubiquitous Computing Ubicomp 2002, LNCS 2498. Berlin: Springer Verlag, pp. 194–209.

Washington, D.C. n.d. *Metropolitan Regulations Title 24, Chapter 25.* Metropolitan Police Department Use of Closed Circuit Television.

Weiser, M. 1993. Some computer science problems in ubiquitous computing. *Communications of the ACM,* 36, 7, 75–84.

Zarski, T.Z. 2002. "Mine your own business!": making the case for the implications of the data mining of personal information in the forum of public opinion. *Yale Journal of Law & Technology,* 5 (2002/2003), 1–54.

CHAPTER 11

PROMISING FUTURE RESEARCH IN INFOSEC

DETMAR W. STRAUB, SEYMOUR GOODMAN,
AND RICHARD L. BASKERVILLE

Abstract: This chapter provides an analysis and summary of the key research questions raised in the preceding chapters of the book. It also organizes the needs for future managerial research in the area of InfoSec. Most research being carried out today (and being heavily funded) is technical in nature. It focuses on developing new software and new physical artifacts for securing systems. We are not arguing that this work is not important. However, we are concerned that much of the technology is not being utilized due to problems that are endemic to the human dimension. Buying new technology alone will not solve serious security issues. Questions about why it is not being effectively implemented are critical to make sure that the best technology is meeting its intended purpose. Future management research will provide the answers to these questions.

Keywords: Information Security Processes, Policies, Practices, Guidelines, Technical Versus Managerial InfoSec Research, Key Research Questions, Future Research Directions, National and International Landscape of Information Security

INTRODUCTION

We conclude this book by providing an analysis of the important questions raised in the preceding chapters. This analysis was created by a review of the issues raised by the authors and classifying these issues into categories. The criteria for the categories emerged in this process and delineated the general areas of scholarly contribution for information security. This developed a "wedding cake" model of future work in the management of information security. This wedding cake model is shown in Figure 11.1.

The future research implied by the issues raised by each of the preceding chapters projects these five categories, each building upon the foundation laid by others. At the most fundamental level are issues dealing with the obligations of management to provide information security. These obligations vary in nature, and include the ethical, legal, and economic motives imposed on managers by their stakeholders. These obligations bring a need for the development of concepts and conceptual frameworks in order to understand the responsibilities, constraints, processes, and metrics with which information security managers must operate. The framing of these concepts raises awareness of the myriad contingencies that define and constrain the actions that managers may be able to take in the face of information security demands. Within the constraints defined by these contingencies, managers must create the organizational processes and methods that will effectively and efficiently implement and operate the security technologies and organizational behavior. Once the processes are developed, ways must be found to measure the success of the

Figure 11.1   **Wedding Cake Model of Future Research Needs in Information Security Management**

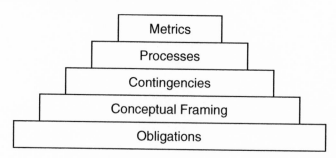

processes. These metrics provide the fundamental and objective means by which managers can plan and control organizational information security.

We will discuss each chapter in order, stressing how the issues the authors have discussed fit in the wedding cake model. This analytical review of these suggestions for future research serves two purposes. It will remind the readers in one place what these issues were. Second, it will allow us to argue once again that the key problems with information security are not technical. The major failings are in what is known about the proper management of information assets. Even with unlimited sources of funds, an organization (and nations) could easily waste them without knowing where to apply them for maximum effect.

FUTURE RESEARCH

Information Systems Security Strategy: A Process View (Chapter 2)

Chapter 2 begins our thinking about organizational needs by discussing security strategy as both a process and a product. It frames the concepts by raising the issue of precedence among these two concepts. In either case, strategy making is complex and managers cannot always be certain that their strategy is working and how it can be adjusted to make it more successful. Policies are one element of an overall strategy, and the authors raise the interesting question of whether strategy drives policy or policy drives strategy. There are likely circumstances when each is called for, and future research needs to sort this out (ideally through theory development) for managers.

This chapter goes on to explore the issues proceeding from this conceptual precedence in terms of methods, processes, and metrics. When the organizational strategy-making setting is too rigid, the result can be catastrophic, and the authors caution that scientific findings would help resolve this issue. Another unresolved issue looms large and that that is which strategies work and which do not? It is unfortunately the case that research to date is woefully inadequate in being able to answer this question. In one sense this is the most vital question of all since we know that managers will persist in their failing courses of action unless the countervailing evidence is very strong (Brockner, 1992; Keil and Robey, 1999). Methods and measures to evaluate how successful a strategy or policy (policies) is are also lacking, and desperately needed.

In the final analysis, the best strategy is probably one that is formulated through the best process, and, once again, we know little about the comparative strengths of various processes. The current book provides some ways of thinking about processes, but science is needed to assure managers that this process has advantages over a variety of situations. At the moment, such innovations as those brought forward in this chapter are obvious. But the proof that they will work better than others has not yet come forth.

IT Governance and Organizational Design for Security Management (Chapter 3)

Chapter 3 brings a focus on those contingencies surrounding information security with which managers must contend. In the face of these contingencies, it deals with how organizations should organize themselves to maximize their security efforts. One side of the equation is the distribution of decision-making rights, which is the usual definition of governance. Questions surrounding governance inevitably revolve around where the decisions should reside, for example in a centralized, federalized, or decentralized structure.

The first issue the authors raise is whether the structuring of the IT/InfoSec governance should parallel the overall structure of the organization. If a firm, for example, is organized around domestic and international divisions, would it be best to have separate security organizations for each of these divisions or would it be best to have global security procedures and practices?

Related to this point, the authors next ask whether a centralized IT security management strategy provides the most assurance. Bringing security closer to those who will be securing their own workstations and local area networks would imply a more decentralized mode. Much more research is needed to try to understand the contingencies that are present whenever such decisions are made.

Firms clearly have strategy alternatives in terms of allocating decision rights. The authors raise the question of whether there are differences in industry when considering such centralization-decentralization governance matters. Finally, they query which variations can occur in individual decisions from one action to another. These are good questions that can only be answered if researchers study security effectiveness and then relate it to these conditions. Governance issues should be high on the agendas of security researchers for this reason.

Information System Risk Assessment and Documentation (Chapter 4)

Chapter 4 raises many issues about the obligations of management to provide information security. These issues proceed as the subject of risk assessment at a tactical level is explored. The procedures for assessing risk are covered as are a set of relevant questions for making an accurate assessment. With regard to future research, the authors of Chapter 4 ask whether risk assessment and reports on security and security violations have an impact on training and educational programs, and whether these in turn reduce computer abuse and crime. They believe this is a crucial area for future research, one that extends and updates prior work and surveys. Further questions include whether formalized reports and procedures work better. Later in the chapter, the authors query whether individuals' and employees' knowledge of abuse affects their receptivity to educational programs. Initial work exploring aspects of this vital issue has been set forth by Goodhue and Straub (1991) and Straub and Welke (1998), but much more research needs to be carried out, assuredly.

There is little doubt that these are crucial questions for both managers and scholars. Insider threats are real, and enlightened training and education could inform perpetrators that there are options to computer abuse and crime, but do these work? We need to have real empirical evidence one way or the other.

Another set of questions raised by the authors asks how organizations should report incidents to law enforcement in order to avoid adverse publicity. We know that organizations typically avoid official reporting, even when they are violating the law in so doing (Straub and Nance, 1988), so finding ways that would encourage greater compliance is an extremely important managerial problem.

Finally, the authors raise the essential question of justification. Does knowledge of risk lead to a stronger justification for increased security measures? One would think that knowing one's risk would inevitably lead to rational decisions about a reasonable investment in security. Unfortunately, rationality does not always hold, especially in InfoSec cases. That is why it is such important research.

Strategic Information Security Risk Management (Chapter 5)

While Chapter 4 develops issues arising from tactical risk assessment, Chapter 5 advances questions about the processes and metrics that information security managers must have in order to set policies about risk management. Certainly, organizations need to devise policies to deal with specific security risks. Yet, there is a larger conceptual framework in which these policies take place, the overall security strategy. The author asks how organizations allow these two different levels to interact and create a viable strategy-policy set. He goes on to question what should happen when there are no preset policies that can help to scope out that overall security strategy. Additional research can shed light on this by probing firms, governments, and nonprofits to see what works well. Both best practices and theoretical approaches might be utilized to address the domain.

Creating strategy is not a trivial exercise, whether it is for goals at level of the entire organization or at the level of information security. Beyond the issue of how to create strategy is how should it be evaluated. The author argues that we know so little about how to measure an effective security strategy that we are trapped in the land of consult-speak and do not have any in-depth understanding of truly "best" practices. It is likely that effective strategy is intimately connected with a setting, such as type of organization or type of industry, size of the organization, manufacturing versus service, and so on. But lacking scientific studies of whether security is seen as a process or as a product, and whether certain strategy development procedures are effective or not, we are unable to answer a whole realm of serious managerial questions.

Security Policy: From Design to Maintenance (Chapter 6)

This chapter represents a return to our focus on contingencies that will inhabit future information security policy setting. It introduces a set of research questions related to the principles that are offered to create effective design-to-maintenance policies. The first area of concern is identification of critical success factors (CSFs) in the implementation of information security. The author presents five factors that must be present for policy to withstand external, legal scrutiny: (1) dissemination (distribution), (2) review (reading), (3) comprehension (understanding), (4) compliance (agreement), and (5) uniform enforcement. Are these all major critical success factors? Are there others that need to be included?

Research should begin in the general area by studying the features or characteristics of effective security policies. These features will no doubt have to be qualified for varying settings, but there are research issues related to this endeavor as well. How do organizations adapt their generic principles for the formulation of policy to fit their needs better?

The author believes there is interesting work to be done in applying the technology acceptance model (TAM) with its constructs of perceived usefulness and perceived ease-of-use to the acceptance of security policies. This requires a broadening of the concept of technology, but this is not a large stretch given that this model has already been applied to such a breadth of artifacts.

The application of TAM to automated policy management software and other software products like intrusion detection software would be perfectly in line with this line of work, and should be carried out, no doubt.

There are specific research questions that the author elicits regarding champions or sponsoring senior executives, the extent to which policies are complied with, and whether policies actually affect user behavior. At a more micro level, he asks whether policies have an organizational impact and can actually improve the overall security environment. How this organizational level might interact with the legal environment is the last framing type of question he raises.

Business Continuity Planning and the Protection of Informational Assets (Chapter 7)

Chapter 7 raises new issues in the obligations of organizations to provide secure information. It explains the types of disasters that can befall an organization and how organizations can organize to minimize the damage. This is typically called business continuity planning (BCP) in the literature. BCP has a number of clear macro-level issues with regard to future research. InfoSec researchers should raise a simple but basic question first: Does BCP work? Of course, knowing the contingencies under which it is more or less effective would be the best designed research. Part of the problem is that top managers are not convinced that suppliers and customers appreciate a firm that has high preparedness, so InfoSec and BCP appear to these managers to be costs rather than a competitive positioning.

We know very little scientifically about phases of recovery. Knowing whether there is a standard model would aid firms in the normative development of their own plans. Are the phases articulated in this chapter the best possible? Sometimes received wisdom is not wisdom at all. We need to know if the standard approaches are as effective as they could be.

Can a firm outsource BCP? The authors ask whether a strategic selection of areas to outsource can be performed. This is a deployment issue, and merges into the general issue of cold sites versus hot sites versus distributed processing. Again, not much is known about which of these works well and when.

Information Security Policy in the U.S. National Context (Chapter 8)

Chapter 8 takes a historical approach to describing how U.S. national security policy has evolved (or not evolved as it should). As we might expect from such a broad chapter, it raises issues of conceptual framing that must always follow historical viewpoints. But this chapter also raises issues of a process in terms of what our learning from the past may be suggesting for us to do in the future. This learning also suggests future work in the obligations of managers and the metrics that are needed to measure the success of managers in meeting those obligations.

In conceptual framing, much of the chapter is organized around Lessig's principles for social governance as described in his book *Code and Other Laws of Cyberspace*. Lessig (1999) argues that there are four ways to govern behavior: (1) law, (2) economics, (3) social pressure, and (4) architecture. Law relates clearly to policy making by various governmental levels, and the author concludes that these governance processes are piecemeal at best. This suggests research questions that would address why this piecemeal situation has developed and what, if anything, can be done to coordinate these national and state policies in the future. Studies in what essential InfoSec domains of products, applications, and environments have been excluded as well as those that have been unnecessarily included in policy making should proceed.

This problem is dwarfed in many ways by architectural problems, namely the lack of an effective set of information security primitives. Common definitions of essential security elements means that incompatible platforms will continue to be created, and these problems transferred to future generations. How can these primitives be developed and a common body of knowledge put forth? Sensible government policies could at least encourage movement in this direction, but none has come forth. The research questions in this area abound. What are the primitives? What process can be used to certify a widely accepted body of knowledge along these lines?

National efforts in educational programs and certification would also be helpful, according to the author. If there is agreement that standards in InfoSec curriculum and certification are desirable, what should these look like? Once promulgated, additional questions arise about their effectiveness, of course. One measure of effectiveness would be whether the certification has teeth. If no one is ever expelled for noncompliance, then the cache of the certificate is weakened.

The chapter also provides directions for future processes, arguing that training and education of the general population could be helpful. Again, the research questions around what literacy curriculum would be best are good ones, as is the question of downstream effects. If there is a heightened level of information security literacy, does the incidence of computer abuse and crime go down? If not, why not?

The lack of tools to provide a comprehensive view of a firm's information security risk portfolio means that it is not possible to have much meaningful government regulation of organizational security. Here we find issues of corporate obligation in the metrics necessary to measure the success in meeting these obligations. What standards could be held up to firms? Irrespective of Enron and Sarbanes-Oxley, a clearer and cleaner set of information security guidelines is needed. This could be carried out by the private sector, as could certification, but government regulatory requirements could speed its development. There are fascinating research questions surrounding how government agencies and the private sector could work together to make this happen. Moving this kind of reporting to a public audience could stabilize many areas of security that are now exceedingly volatile. Studying the long-term effects of sensible national or state level regulation would offer interesting research possibilities.

The chapter concludes by raising the possibility that federal and state CIOs take on the challenge of being responsible for their constituency's security. What form this would take and whether this would really help is a viable research question. At the moment, the research community is virtually silent on this important issue.

The International Landscape of Cyber Security (Chapter 9)

This chapter also raises issues of future processes and the metrics needed in the future to plan and control those processes. Discussing international aspects of cyber security, Chapter 9 first raises the question of how success at fighting computer abuse and crime at the international level should be measured. The issue is serious with highly industrialized countries, so the global metrics are even more elusive. What can be done is for researchers to specify (and validate) the proper metrics. If these are reasonable, and especially if there are provisions for protecting the identity of the responding organizations, it may be possible to create an internationally relevant database of statistics. These would be enormously useful not only for purposes of research, but for benchmarking by organizations of every type and size.

The second major research question articulated by the authors is how scaleable are regional operational models for InfoSec initiatives such as APEC? Regional models seem to be the only game going in the international arena, and if regional models can include sharing amongst themselves, then they may be scaleable. This configuration may break down in certain areas currently under-served, such as Africa. But this remains to be seen. Researchers can surely investigate and report on the various possibilities.

Drilling downward on this question, the same issue can be brought forward about the coordination, or lack thereof, between organizations across national boundaries. Is this feasible? Would it help if there were greater coordination? To this time, the answers to such questions are not known.

Many parts of the world have little in the way of preventive mechanisms. There are barriers to funding such efforts internationally as well. Can anything be done to improve this situation? This is another viable, and understudied, issue, especially for the developing world.

There are also issues here dealing with the obligations of information security. Globally, the problems with underreporting of cyber crime are legion. Can international public-private cooperation assist in dealing with this perennial problem? Can this be done without threatening IP and shareholder value issues? There is a lot of research that can be done in this final area.

Emerging Ubiquitous Computing Technologies and Security Management Strategy (Chapter 10)

Because it is so relatively new, ubicomp brings up a host of good research questions for InfoSec researchers. It brings us a focus on future processes that must be in place to manage new security threats and technologies. Which of these new products is just a gadget and which is truly useful is only one aspect of how well they can be secured. Ubicomp both heightens security problems and addresses them at the same time. Well-designed systems can solve many of their own security problems, but can designers break outside of their traditional molds and truly wrestle with security while they are building such novel technologies? Careful implementation can make a big difference in how well it can be controlled, but we do not know if this is a possible new step for designers.

Security managers are going to have to think outside the box to exercise the requisite control. Can they carry this off? Can they enlist the attention of legislators to help in a legal framework to make the technology safe and secure for users? These are excellent questions that are completely unanswered at the present time.

CONCLUSION

Overall, the issues raised by the authors of the chapters above range broadly across our wedding cake model of future research needs for information security management. There are opportunities for important new work in the obligations, conceptual framing, contingencies, processes, and metrics that must inhabit the daily work lives of effective, future information security managers. The general focus of the issues raised in each chapter is detailed in Figure 11.2.

The current volume clearly does not address all possible issues about policy and practice in InfoSec. We hope that it has served to move to the forefront the essential point that management of information security has not received the attention it needs to secure the world's computer systems. There is available in the world today a great deal of technology that addresses organizational and national-level security concerns. But we lack clear and concise policies at all these levels to make certain that this technology is applied where and when it should be applied. There is much wheel spinning that is not productive and not meeting global needs, especially post-9/11.

Finally, the agenda for future research that has been set forth in this volume is by no means complete. It represents the thinking of this distinguished pool of authors, but a different pool would

Figure 11.2 **Major Areas of Future Research Issues Developed in the Chapters in this Book**

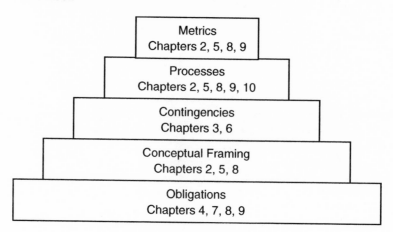

likely have come up with a set that looked somewhat different. We hope and trust that there would be significant overlap in other such lists, but we make no claims to be definitive.

Readers are invited to challenge the assumptions we have made and the lines of thinking that we have pursued, both individually and collectively. More needs to be learned about InfoSec as both a behavioral and organizational issue. We leave the reader with hope that twenty-five years from now many or most of the problems that we have brought to the surface in this book will be addressed and perhaps even solved and that InfoSec takes its rightful place among the important functions that organizations and nations have grown to understand and effectively utilize.

REFERENCES

Brockner, J. 1992. The escalation of commitment to a failing course of action: toward theoretical progress. *Academy of Management Journal,* 17, 1, 39–61.

Goodhue, D.L., and Straub, D.W. 1991. Security concerns of system users: a study of perceptions of the adequacy of security measures. *Information & Management,* 20, 1 (January), 13–27.

Keil, M., and Robey, D. 1999. Turning around troubled software projects: an exploratory study of the deescalation of commitment to failing courses of action. *Journal of Management Information Systems,* 15, 4 (March), 63–87.

Lessig, L., 1999. *Code and Other Laws of Cyberspace.* New York: Basic Books.

Straub, D.W., and Nance, W.D. 1988. Uncovering and disciplining computer abuse: managerial responses and options. *Information Age,* 10, 3 (July), 151–156.

Straub, D.W., and Welke, R.J. 1998. Coping with systems risk: security planning models for management decision making. *MIS Quarterly,* 22, 4 (December 12), 441–469.

EDITORS AND CONTRIBUTORS

Gregory D. Abowd is a Professor in the School of Interactive Computing and GVU Center at the Georgia Institute of Technology. He currently serves as Co-director for the Aware Home Research Initiative and Associate Director for the Health Systems Institute. His research is in the area of human–computer interaction, with particular focus on the engineering and evaluation of mobile and ubiquitous computing applications. Dr. Abowd received a BS in Mathematics from the University of Notre Dame in 1986 and the degrees of M.Sc. (1987) and D.Phil. (1991) in Computation from the University of Oxford, where he attended as a Rhodes Scholar. He is a member of the ACM and of the IEEE Computer Society.

Richard L. Baskerville is a Professor of Information Systems in the Department of Computer Information Systems, Robinson College of Business, Georgia State University. His research specializes in security of information systems, methods of information systems design and development, and the interaction of information systems and organizations. His interest in methods extends to qualitative research methods. Dr. Baskerville is the author of *Designing Information Systems Security* (J. Wiley) and more than one hundred articles in scholarly journals, professional magazines, and edited books. He is an editor for the *European Journal of Information Systems* and serves on the editorial boards of the *Information Systems Journal, Journal of Information Systems Security*, and the *International Journal of E-Collaboration*. Baskerville holds degrees from the University of Maryland (B.S. *summa cum laude*, Management), and the London School of Economics, University of London (M.Sc., Analysis, Design and Management of Information Systems, Ph.D., Systems Analysis).

Gurpreet Dhillon is Professor of Information Systems in the School of Business, Virginia Commonwealth University, Richmond, USA. He holds a Ph.D. from the London School of Economics and Political Science, UK. His research interests include management of information security, and ethical and legal implications of information technology. His research has been published in several journals including *Information Systems Research, Information & Management, Communications of the ACM, Computers & Security, European Journal of Information Systems, Information Systems Journal*, and *International Journal of Information Management*.

Dr. Dhillon has authored six books including *Principles of Information Systems Security: Text and Cases* (John Wiley, 2007). He is also the Editor-in-Chief of the *Journal of Information System Security*, is the North American Regional Editor of the *International Journal of Information Management,* and sits on the editorial board of *MISQ Executive*. He consults regularly with industry and government and has completed assignments for various organizations in India, Portugal, the UK, and the United States.

Neal M. Donaghy holds a Bachelor of Science (1997) from the University of Toronto and a Masters of Science in International Affairs (2005) from the Georgia Institute of Technology. He specializes in global risk oversight for a Fortune 15 company. While attending Georgia Tech, Neal served as a Graduate Research Assistant for the MacArthur Foundation–funded Sam Nunn Security Program and was named the Sam Nunn School of International Affairs 2005 Outstanding Graduate Student of the Year. Neal has seven years' experience working in information technology in the United States, Europe, and Asia.

Seymour (Sy) Goodman is Professor of International Affairs and Computing jointly at the Sam Nunn School of International Affairs and the College of Computing at Georgia Tech, co-Director of the Georgia Tech Information Security Center, and Principal Investigator for the MacArthur Foundation grant supporting the Sam Nunn Security Program. He studies science and technology and international affairs, particularly international developments in information technology and related public policy issues. He recently served as co-chair of the policy group for the study of the vulnerabilities of the U.S. telecommunication infrastructure for the Assistant Secretary of Defense (NII) and NSA, as co-chair of the risks and exposures subcommittee for the Association for Computing Machinery (ACM) study of the impact of offshoring, and on the National Research Council committee concerned with a national R&D strategy for information security. Professor Goodman has been the International Perspectives editor for the *Communications of the ACM* since 1990, and has conducted research on IT in more than eighty countries. He was an undergraduate at Columbia University and obtained his Ph.D. from the California Institute of Technology, where he worked on problems of applied mathematics and mathematical physics.

Giovanni Iachello is a consultant at McKinsey & Co.'s Atlanta office, where he serves High Tech and Media clients on corporate strategy issues. He received a Ph.D. from the Georgia Institute of Technology (2006). His research focuses on security and privacy in mobile and ubiquitous computing applications. Dr. Iachello received a Laurea in Informatics Engineering from Padua University, Italy (1999), with a thesis on IT security evaluation criteria. He worked for Altoprofilo SPA, providing corporate consulting services related to security management and personal data protection, and at Intel Research, developing mobile location-based services. He was a fellow of the NSF Graduate Research Fellowship Program and the Sam Nunn Security Program at Georgia Tech. He is member of the ACM, the IEEE Computer Society, and of IFIP WG 9.6/11.7 "IT Mis-Use and The Law."

Allen C. Johnston is an Assistant Professor of Information Systems at the University of Alabama at Birmingham. He holds a B.S. from Louisiana State University in Electrical Engineering as well as an MSIS and Ph.D. from Mississippi State University. His works can be found in such outlets as *Communications of the ACM*, *Journal of Global Information Management*, *Journal of Information Privacy and Security*, *International Journal of Information Security and Privacy*, and the *Journal of Internet Commerce*, among others. The primary focus of his research has been in the area of information assurance and security, with a specific concentration on the behavioral aspects of information security and privacy.

William J. Malik is an independent consultant with thirty-four years of experience in information technology. He was a programmer at John Hancock in Boston from 1974 through 1978, a programmer, tester, planner, and strategist at IBM through 1990, and a researcher at Gartner through 2001, where he managed the information security research team. He worked at KPMG as an IT auditor, then became CTO of Waveset, a start-up in identity management. On Waveset's acquisition by Sun, he became Sun's Director of Marketing for Security. He established his own firm in February 2005. He developed the material on Information Security Policy in the US National Context for Georgia Tech's graduate level information security policy class taught in spring 2005.

Herbert Mattord completed twenty-four years of IT industry experience before becoming a full-time academic. His experiences as an application developer, database administrator, project manager, and information security practitioner are a valuable background to his role a tenure-track Instructor at Kennesaw State University in Kennesaw, Georgia. During his career as an IT practitioner, he has been an Adjunct Professor at Kennesaw State University; Southern Polytechnic State University in Marietta, Georgia; Austin Community College in Austin, Texas; and Texas State University–San Marcos. He currently teaches undergraduate courses in information systems, and information security and assurance. He was formerly the Manager of Corporate Information Technology Security at Georgia-Pacific Corporation, where his practical knowledge of information security implementation and management was acquired. He is the coauthor of *Principles of Information Security*, *Management of Information Security*, *Incident Response and Disaster Recover Planning*, the *Hands-on Information Security Lab Manual*, and *Readings and Cases in the Management of Information Security* with Dr. Michael Whitman. Their latest title, *Guide to Firewalls and Network Security*, will be available in June of 2008.

Delphine Nain is a consultant for a global management consulting firm, providing strategy consulting services for High Tech and Healthcare Fortune 500 companies. She holds a Bachelor of Science and Masters of Engineering (2002) from the Massachusetts Institute of Technology and a Ph.D in Computer Science (2006) from the Georgia Institute of Technology. Her research has been applied to topics in multi-agent systems, computer networks and computer vision. She was a fellow for Georgia Tech Sam Nunn Security Program (2004-2005) when she researched the international landscape of cyber security and co-authored the chapter included in this book.

Robert H. Sainsbury is a Ph.D. candidate in the Computer Information Systems Department of the J. Mack Robinson College of business at Georgia State University. Sainsbury conducts research in areas including information security, digital supply networks, IT risk management and information warfare.

Detmar Straub is the J. Mack Robinson Distinguished Professor of IS at Georgia State University and conducts research in the areas of information security, e-commerce, technological innovation, and international IT. He holds a DBA (M.I.S.; Indiana) and a Ph.D. (English; Penn State). He has more than 145 publications in journals such as *MIS Quarterly*, *Journal of Management Information Systems*, *Management Science*, *Information Systems Research*, *Journal of the AIS*, *Journal of Global Information Management*, and a variety of other journals. He has served as a Senior Editor for journals such as *Information Systems Research*, *Journal of AIS*, and *DATA BASE*, and Associate Editor for these journals as well as *MIS Quarterly* and others. Former VP of Publications for AIS, he has been the co-program chair for both AMCIS and ICIS. He is an AIS Fellow.

Carl Stucke is Associate Chair of the Computer Information Systems department within the Robinson College of Business at Georgia State University and serves as coordinator of the security SIG. Dr. Stucke teaches security and privacy courses and is an active researcher in information security and risk management. In addition to twelve years of academic experience, he has twenty years' commercial world experience in, among others, senior technical and management positions at Equifax, including Chief Scientist (VP R&D). He is an active member of the Georgia Electronic Commerce Association's Information Privacy Working Group.

Merrill Warkentin is Professor of MIS at Mississippi State University. He has published more than 125 research manuscripts, primarily in computer security management, e-commerce, and virtual collaborative teams, which have appeared in books, proceedings, and journals such as *MIS Quarterly, Decision Sciences, Decision Support Systems, Communications of the ACM, Communications of the AIS, Information Systems Journal, Journal of End User Computing, Journal of Global Information Management, Journal of Computer Information Systems*, and others. Professor Warkentin is the coauthor or editor of four books, and is currently an Associate Editor of *Information Resources Management Journal* and *Journal of Information Systems Security*. Dr. Warkentin has served as a consultant to numerous organizations and has served as National Distinguished Lecturer for the Association for Computing Machinery (ACM). Professor Warkentin holds B.A., M.A., and Ph.D. degrees from the University of Nebraska-Lincoln.

Michael E. Whitman, Ph.D., CISM, CISSP, is a Professor of Information Systems in the Computer Science and Information Systems Department at Kennesaw State University, Kennesaw, Georgia. Dr. Whitman is also the Director of the KSU Center for Information Security Education and the architect of KSU's recognition as a National Center of Academic Excellence in Information Assurance Education by the National Security Agency and the Department of Homeland Security. Dr. Whitman is an active researcher in information security, fair and responsible use policies, ethical computing and information systems research methods. He has published articles in *Information Systems Research*, the *Communications of the ACM, Information and Management*, the *Journal of International Business Studies*, and the *Journal of Computer Information Systems*. Dr. Whitman has six textbooks in the area of information security including *Principles of Information Security*, 3rd ed., *Management of Information Security*, 2nd ed., *Principles of Incident Response and Disaster Recovery, and The Guide to Firewalls and Network Security*, 2nd ed., all from Course Technology. He is an active member of the Computer Security Institute, the Information Systems Security Association, Georgia Electronic Commerce Association's Information Security Working Group, the Association for Computing Machinery, and the Association for Information Systems.

Terry L. Wiant was an Assistant Professor of Management Information Systems at Marshall University for several years following a twenty-two-year career in the military. In May 2005, Dr. Wiant joined the faculty at Kennesaw State University as an Assistant Professor of Information Systems. Dr. Wiant's research and teaching interests were in information security, information security policy, and the development of information security capability models. Dr. Wiant passed away prematurely in July 2005.

SERIES EDITOR

Vladimir Zwass is the University Distinguished Professor of Computer Science and Management Information Systems at Fairleigh Dickinson University. He holds a Ph.D. in Computer Science from Columbia University. Professor Zwass is the Founding Editor-in-Chief of the *Journal of Management Information Systems,* one of the three top-ranked journals in the field of information systems. He is also the Founding Editor-in-Chief of the *International Journal of Electronic Commerce,* ranked as the top journal in its field. More recently, Dr. Zwass has been the Founding Editor-in-Chief of the monograph series *Advances in Management Information Systems,* whose objective is to codify the knowledge and research methods in the field. Dr. Zwass is the author of six books and several book chapters, including entries in the *Encyclopaedia Britannica,* as well as of a number of papers in various journals and conference proceedings. Vladimir Zwass has received several grants, consulted for a number of major corporations, and is a frequent speaker to national and international audiences. He is a former member of the Professional Staff of the International Atomic Energy Agency in Vienna, Austria.

INDEX

Page numbers in italic refer to figures and tables.